A DICTIONARY OF ADMINISTRATIVE AND LEGISLATIVE TERMS

A Dictionary of Administrative and Legislative Terms

(Containing Comprehensive Appendices of Important Terms and Sentences Used in Administration)

ENGLISH-HINDI

Edited and Compiled by

J. L. GUPTA

GYAN PUBLISHING HOUSE

New Delhi - 110002

A DICTIONARY OF ADMINISTRATIVE AND LEGISLATIVE TERMS

ISBN :9788121201032

Published in 2015 in India by
Gyan Publishing House
23, Ansari Road, Daryaganj,
New Delhi - 110002
Phones : 23261060, 23282060 Fax : 23285914
e-mail : books@gyanbooks.com
website : gyanbooks.com

Laser Typesetting at : Vinayak Printers, Delhi
Printed at : Salasar Imaging System, Delhi

PREFACE

Hindi is the official language of Indian Union and quite a few states. It is, therefore, natural that more and more use of this language for all official purpose is being emphasized on. The purpose of this dictionary is to provide with a ready reference book of all technical terms and usages that are necessary for the administrative and legislative wings of the governments. Though the dictionary has been compiled and edited keeping in view the immediate need of the administrative and legislative personnel, it may also prove of immense benefit to the students appearing for the different competitive tests for recruitment in the offices of the government of India.

The dictionary is comprised of nearly four thousand administrative and legislative terms and usages which significantly occur in day-to-day official life and these terms have further been provided with their derivatives and compounds with related phrases. In addition to these terms and phrases the dictionary also contains three important appendices: Appendix I presents some comments, expressions and phrases commonly used in administration. In Appendix II there are some sentences which are generally used in administrative and legislative official practices and Appendix III enlists certain degrees, diplomas and certificates. All efforts have been made to make the dictionary useful and comprehensive.

1987

J. L. GUPTA

CONTENTS

A

Abalienate—अन्यसंक्रामण करना

Abandonment परित्याग **Abandonment of claim** दावे का परित्याग, दावा छोड़ देना

Abate 1. उपशमन करना/उपशमन होना 2. कमी होना **Abatement** 1. कमी, छूट 2. समाप्ति, अन्त **Abatement of rent** भाड़े/कर में कमी/छूट

Abbreviated address संक्षिप्त पता **Abbreviation** संक्षेप/संक्षेपण

Abdicate one's responsibility अपनी जिम्मेदारी छोड़ देना

Abeyance, held in रोक रखी गई, स्थगित रखी गई

Abide by the decision निर्णय/फैसले का पालन

Ability योग्यता **Ability to read and write** पढ़ने-लिखने की योग्यता

Ab initio नए सिरे से, आरम्भ से, शुरू से, आदित:

Able-bodied समर्थांग **Able Seaman (A.B.)** योग्य नाविक/एबल सीमैन (ए०बी०)

Abnormal अपसामान्य **Abnormal situation** अपसामान्य परिस्थिति

Abolition उत्सादन/उन्मूलन/अन्त **Abolition of post** पद तोड़ना/समाप्त करना **—of untouchability** अस्पृश्यता का अन्त/निवारण **—of zamindari** जमींदारी-उन्मूलन

Aboriginal आदिवासी **Aboriginal tribes** आदिम जातियाँ, आदिवासी **—Welfare Officer** आदिवासी कल्याण अधिकारी

Abortive efforts निष्फल प्रयास

Above average औसत से ऊपर, औसत से ऊंचा, औसत से अधिक **Above-cited** उपर्युक्त, ऊपर दिया हुआ, उपर उद्धृत **—given** ऊपर दिया हुआ, लिखित **—mentioned** उपर्युक्त, उपरिऊपर लिखा हुआ, ऊपर अंकित **—noted** उपर्युक्त, ऊपर अंकित, ऊपर लिखा हुआ **—par** अधिक मूल्य पर, प्रत्यक्ष मूल्य से ऊपर **—quoted** ऊपर उद्धृत, ऊपर दिया हुआ **—quoted**

reference उपर्युक्त हवाला/संदर्भ —said उपर्युक्त, ऊपर कहा हुआ

Abridge 1. संक्षेप करना 2. न्यून करना **Abridgement** संक्षेप/संक्षेपण

Abrogate निराकरण करना

Abrupt fall in prices मूल्य में एकदम गिरावट

Absconding offender फरार अपराधी

Absence अनुपस्थिति/गैरहाजिरी **Absence of information, in the** सूचना के अभाव में **Absence without permission** बिना अनुमति/अनुज्ञा के गैरहाजिरी/अनुपस्थिति **Absentee** अनुपस्थित/गैरहाजिर **Absentee landlord** दूरवासी जमींदार, दूरस्थ जमींदार **—statement** अनुपस्थित व्यक्ति विवरण, अनुपस्थिति विवरण **—voting** अनुपस्थित-मतदान **Absent-minded** अन्यमनस्क, विमनस्क **Absent without leeav** बिना छुट्टी लिए अनुपस्थित

Absolute acceptance निरपेक्ष स्वीकृति, पूर्ण स्वीकृति **Absolute and unconditional** सम्पूर्ण और बिना शर्त **Absolute authority** परम प्राधिकारी, परम सत्ता **—discretion** पूर्ण विवेक **—order** पक्का आदेश **Absolutely correct** बिल्कुल सही **—necessary** परमावश्यक, नितांत आवश्यक

Absolve विमुक्त करना **Absolved of the responsibility** जिम्मेदारी/उत्तरदायित्व से विमुक्त

Absorb 1. अवशोषण करना 2. समाहृत करना

Abstract 1. सार 2. संक्षिप्ति (विधि) **Abstract book** सार-पुस्तिका **Abstract of account** लेखा-सार **Abstract budget** सार-बजट, बजट-सार, संक्षिप्त बजट **Abstract of tender** टेंडर का सार, निविदा का सार **Abstract statement** संक्षिप्त ब्यौरा **Abstract statement of disposed of cases** निबटाए हुए मामलों का विवरण **Abstractor** संक्षेपकार

Absurd अर्थहीन/बेतुका **Absurd act** अयुक्त कार्य, बेतुका कार्य **—statement** बेतुका/अर्थहीन कथन **Absurdity** अर्थहीनता/बेतुकापन

Abundant प्रचुर

Abuse दुरुपयोग **Abuse of flag** ध्वज का दुरुपयोग **—of official position** सरकारी पद का दुरुपयोग **—of power** अधिकार का दुरपयोग **Abusive language** गाली, अपशब्द

Academic शैक्षणिक/विद्या-सम्बन्धी

Academic Council विद्या-परिषद **—discussion** बौद्धिक चर्चा **—experience and attainments** शैक्षिक अनुभव तथा निष्पत्तियाँ **—qualification** शैक्षणिक योग्यता **—year** शैक्षणिक वर्ष **Academy** अकादमी **Academy of arts** कला अकादमी

Accede 1. मान लेना 2. **(n.)** अधिमिलन **(vb.)** शामिल होना/सम्मिलित होना **Accede to one's request** किसी की प्रार्थना मान लेना

Accelerated Promotion त्वरित पदोन्नति, तुरन्त तरक्की

Accept स्वीकार करना/मानना **Accept a bill** बिल स्वीकार करना **Acceptability** स्वीकार्यता **Acceptance** 1. स्वीकार/स्वीकृति 2. प्रतिग्रहण **Acceptance, conditional** सशर्त स्वीकृति, सशर्त मानना **Acceptance in principle** सिद्धान्त रूप से स्वीकृति **Acceptance, implied** निहित/ध्वनित स्वीकृति **—of office** पद की स्वीकृति **—of tender** निविदा की स्वीकृति/टेंडर की स्वीकृति

Access प्रवेश/पहुँच **Access, easy** आसानी से पहुँच/प्रवेश **Access, to have** पहुँच होना **Accession** 1. राज्यारोहण 2. पदारोहण 3. अधिमिलन **Accession number** अवाप्ति नम्बर

Accessory 1. **(adj.)** उपसाधक **(n.)** उपसाधन 2. अतिरिक्त/ सहायक **—license** अतिरिक्त लाइसेन्स

Accident 1. दुर्घटना 2. संयोग **Accident, by** संयोग से **Accident, serious** गम्भीर/भारी दुर्घटना **Accidents Investigation Officer** दुर्घटना अन्वेषण अधिकारी

Accommodate स्थान देना, जगह देना, निबाहना **Accommodating terms** सुविधाजनक शर्तें/निबन्धन **Accommodation** 1. वास 2. निर्वाह **Accommodation charges** जगह का किराया, बास प्रभार **Accommodation, class of** वास श्रेणी **Accommodation, leased** पट्टे की जगह **Accommodation of highest class** उच्चतम श्रेणी का स्थान **—of lowest class** निम्नतम श्रेणी का स्थान **Accommodation, office** कार्यालय के लिए स्थान/जगह/वास **—Officer** वास अधिकारी

Accompanied by के साथ, सहित **Accompanying letter** सह-पत्र, साथ का पत्र

Accomplished fact पूरी हुई बात

Accord (**n.**) अनुकूलता **(vb.)** 1. प्रदान करना/देना 2. मेल खाना,

अनुकूल होना **Accord priority, to** प्राथमिकता देना **Accord sanction, to** मंजूरी देना **Accord, to reach an** एक मत होना **Accordance with, in** के अनुसार **According to** के अनुसार **According to merit** योग्यतानुसार, गुणानुसार, क्रमानुसार, आदेशानुसार **—rule** नियमानुसार **—seniority** प्रवरतानुसार **Accordingly** तदनुसार **Accordingly it has been decided** तदनुसार यह निश्चय किया गया है **Account** लेखा/खाता, हिसाब **Account, Advance** अग्रिम राशि लेखा **Account. authorised major headsand minor heads of** लेखों के अधिकृत बड़े और छोटे शीर्ष **Account book** लेखा वही **Account, capital and revenue** पूंजीगत और राजस्व लेखा **Account, commercial** वाणिज्य/लेखा **Account, debt** ऋण-लेखा **Account, deposit** जमा-लेखा **Account, head of** लेखा शीर्ष **Account for** उत्तरदायी होना, लेखा देना **Account, individual** व्यक्तिगत लेखा **Account, initial** आरंभिक लेखा **—,Joint** संयुक्त लेखा/संयुक्त खाता **Account, maintenance of** लेखा करना **—,nomenclature of head** खाता शीर्षकों के नाम **Account, public** सरकारी लेखा, सार्वजनिक लेखा **Account, reconciliation of** लेखा-समाधान **Account, reconciliation of departments** विभागीय लेखों का समाधान **Account, remittance** प्रेषण-लेखा **—,rupee** रुपया लेखा **—,suspense** निलम्बित लेखा, उचंती खाता **—,sterling** स्टर्लिंग-लेखा **Account stock** माल-लेखा **Account subsidiary** गौण-लेखा **Accountable** उत्तरदायी **Accountable for** के लिए उत्तरदायी **Accountant** लेखापाल/लेखाकार **—(Cash-purpose)** लेखापाल (नकदी)/ लेखाकार (नकदी) **Accountant General** महालेखाकार **Accounting rule** लेखा-नियम **—unit** लेखा एकक **Accounts, annual** वार्षिक-लेखा **Accounts Clerk** लेखा-लिपिक, लेखा क्लर्क **Accounts, closing of** लेखा बन्द करना **Accounts department** लेखा विभाग **—office** लेखा कार्यालय **—officer** लेखा अधिकारी

Accoutrement साज-सज्जा

Accreditation प्रत्यायन **Accredited (Correspondent)** प्रत्यायित

(संवाददाता) **Accredited press correspondent** प्रत्यायित प्रेस संवाददाता **Accredited diplomat** प्रत्यायित राजनयज्ञ

Accretion 1. उपचय/जमा होना 2. अनुवृद्धि

Accrue 1. उपचित होना/जमा होना 2. प्रोद्भूत होना **Accrued** 1. उपचित 2. प्रोद्भूत **Accruing from** से प्रोद्भूत, उत्पन्न, से उपचित **Accruing property** प्रोद्भूत सम्पत्ति

Accuracy यथार्थता **Accuracy of statement** कथन की यथार्थता **Accurate** यथार्थ **Accurately** यथार्थतः/यथार्थ रूप से **Accurately done** ठीक-ठीक किया गया

Accusation अभियोग **Accuse** अभियोग लगाना

Acknowledge (fact etc.) अभिस्वीकार करना/मानना/कबूल करना **—(receipt of)** प्राप्ति स्वीकार करना/प्राप्ति सूचना देना/पावती देना **Acknowledgement** पावती/प्राप्ति सूचना/अभिस्वीकृति **Acknowledgement card** अभिस्वीकृति-पत्र पावती प्राप्ति पत्र **—due** रसीदी/पावती-सहित **Acknowledgement of source** सूत्र का उल्लेख

Acquire अर्जन करना **Acquisition** अर्जन **Acquisition of citizenship** नागरिकता प्राप्त करना **—of land** भूमि-अर्जन

Acquittance register पगार-पंजी **Acquittance roll** पगार-चिट्ठा, वेतन का चिट्ठा **Acqiutted, honourably** ससम्मान बरी

Across, have not come से वास्ता नहीं पड़ा, नहीं मिला/देखा **Across the road** सड़क पार

Act (n.) 1. कार्य 2. अधिनियम **Act, Anti-corruption** भ्रष्टाचार निरोध अधिनियम **Act of God** दैवी घटना **Act of indecency** अभद्र कार्य **—of misconduct** कदाचार **—of trespass** अनधिकार प्रवेश-क्रिया, अतिचार कार्य **Acting (as in Acting Director)** कार्यकारी **Acting allowance** कार्यकारी भत्ता **--appointment** कार्यवाहक नियुक्ति **Acting as** के रूप में कार्य करने वाला **Acting as agent** अभिकर्त्ता (एजेंट) के रूप में कार्य करते हुए **Acting incumbent** कार्यवाहक पदधारी **Acting in good faith** सद्भाव से कार्य करते हुए **--in his discretion** स्वविवेक से कार्य करते हुए **—in official capacity** आधिकारिक हैसियत/रूप से कार्य करते हुए **—Lance Daffadar**

(A.L.D.) ऐक्टिंग लांस दफ़ादार (ए० एल० डी०) **Acting Superintendent** कार्यकारी अधीक्षक

Action क्रिया, कार्यवाही/कार्रवाई, कार्यकलाप **Action as at 'A' above** ऊपर 'क' पर बताई कार्यवाई कीजिए **Action, line of** कार्य-दिशा **Actionproposed to be taken** प्रस्तावित कार्यवाई **Action : Ministry of...**कार्रवाई :...मंत्रालय **Action taken thereon** उस पर की गई कार्यवाई **Actionable** कार्य योग्य; व्यवहार्य

Active सक्रिय/क्रियाशील **Active consideration** तत्परता से विचार, सक्रिय रूप से विचार **—list service** सामरिक सूची सेवा **—partner** सक्रिय भागी, क्रियाशील साझीदार **—service** सामरिक सेवा **Activities** क्रियाकलाप **Activities, last year's** गतवर्ष का कार्य-कलाप **Activity, political** राजनीतिक सक्रियता/राजनीतिक क्रियाकलाप

Acts of commission and omission कृताकृत

Actual वास्तविक **Actual cost** वास्तविक मूल्य, असली लागत **Actual cost of haulage** ढोने का असली खर्च **—cost of travelling** यात्रा का असली खर्च **—turnover** वास्तविक कार्य **—wages** असल मजदूरी **Actually employed** वस्तुत: नियुक्त, वास्तव में नियुक्त **Actuals** वास्तविक आंकड़े **Actuals and targets** वास्तविक आँकड़े और लक्ष्य

Actuary बीमांकक **Actuary valuation** बीमांकिक द्वारा मूल्यांकन

Acute shortage अत्यधिक कमी

A.D.C. (Aide-de Camp) ए०डी० सी० **—to the President** राष्ट्रपति के ए०डी०सी०

Adapted to our needs अपनी आवश्यकता के अनुसार अनुकूलित

Adaptation रूपांतर/रूपांतरण, अनुकूलन **Adaptation, radio** रेडियो रूपान्तर/रूपान्तरण

Addendum अनुशेष/संयोजनी

Adding परिवर्धन

Additional (as in Additional Director) अपर **(as in additional expenditure)** अतिरिक्त **Additional amount** अतिरिक्त राशि **—asset** अतिरिक्त कर-निर्धारण **—grant** अतिरिक्त अनुदान **—pay** अतिरिक्त वेतन **—profit** अतिरिक्त लाभ **—remark** अतिरिक्त कैफियत **—remuneration** अतिरिक्त पारिश्रमिक **—Secretary** अपर सचिव **Additions and**

alterations जोड़बदल, परिवर्धन-परिवर्तन

Address (n) पता, अभिभाषण, संबोधन, मानपत्र, संबोधित करना **Address of welcome** अभिनन्दन-पत्र, स्वागत भाषण **Address, postal** डाक का पता, डाक पता **Address,, Presidential** राष्ट्रपति का अभिभाषण **Addressed to** के नाम, को सम्बोधित **Addressee** पाने वाला **Addressee not found** प्रेष्य/पाने वाला नहीं मिला

Addressograph machine पता-लेखी मशीन

Adduced, the reasons which have so far been जो कारण अब तक दिए/बताए गए हैं

Adequate consideration, after समुचित विचार के पश्चात्/बाद **Adequate data** पर्याप्त सामग्री/आंकड़े **Adequate reason** पर्याप्त कारण

Adhere 1. दृढ रहना 2. अनुवर्तन करना **Adhere to earlier decision** पिछले निर्णय पर दृढ़ रहना **Adherence** संसक्ति

Adhesive आसंजक/आसंजनशील/चिपकने वाला — **stamp** चिपकने वाला स्टांप/चिपकने वाला टिकट

Ad hoc तदर्थ **Ad hoc committee** तदर्थ समिति —**payment indent** तदर्थ मांगपत्र/तदर्थ इन्डेन्ट

Ad infinitum निरवधि

Ad interim अन्तकालीन, अन्तरिम

Adjacent पार्श्वस्थ **Adjacent land** साथ की/बराबर की/समीपवर्ती भूमि

Adjourn स्थगित करना/काम रोकना **Adjourned sine die** अनिश्चित काल के लिए स्थगित **Adjournment** स्थगन **Adjournment motion** स्थगन/काम रोको प्रस्ताव

Abjudication of dispute विवाद का न्याय निर्णय

Adjusted provisionally अनन्तिम रूप से समंजित **Adjuster** समायोजक **Adjustment** समायोजन **Adjustment on a liability basis** दायिता के आधार पर समंजन **Adjustment of account** लेखा-समायोजन **Adjutant General** ऐड्जुटेंट जनरल

Administer 1. प्रशासन करना 2. देना/दिलाना —**oath** शपथ दिलाना **Administrate** प्रशासन करना **Administration** प्रशासन —**and Publicity** प्रशासन और प्रचार प्रभाग **Administration branch** प्रशासन-शाखा **Administration, letter of** प्रबंध-पत्र — **of Justice** न्याय-करण **Administrative**

ability प्रशासन-योग्यता **Administrative approval** प्रशासकीय अनुमोदन **—arrangement** प्रशासनिक प्रबंध **—control** प्रशासकीय नियन्त्रण, प्रशासनिक नियन्त्रण **—department** प्रशासकीय विभाग **—directory** प्रशासन निदेशिकी **—division** प्रशासन-प्रभाग **—effectiveness** प्रशासनिक प्रभावशालिता **—expenses** प्रशासन-व्यय **—function** प्रशासनकार्य/प्रशासकीय कार्य **—Head** प्रशासी प्रधान **—instruction** प्रशासनिक अनुदेश **—law** प्रशासनिक-विधि **—machinery** प्रशासन तन्त्र **—Ministry** प्रशासी मंत्रालय **—Officer** प्रशासन अधिकारी **—organisation** प्रशासनिक संघटन **—power** प्रशासन-शक्ति **—Reforms Commission** प्रशासनि सुधार आयोग **—Sanction** प्रशासनिक मंजूरी **—Section** प्रशासन अनुभाग **—Service** प्रशासनिक सेवा **—set-up** प्रशासनिक ढांचा, प्रशासनिक व्यवस्था **—staff** प्रशासनिक अमला, प्रशासनिक कर्मचारी-वर्ग **—standing order** प्रशासनिक स्थायी आदेश **—System** प्रशासनिक पद्धति **Administrative unit, local school** स्थानीय विद्यालय का प्रशासनिक एकक **General Administrator** महाप्रशासक

Admissible ग्राह्य/स्वीकार्य **Admissible evidence** ग्राह्य साक्ष्य **Admissible under rules** नियमानुसार स्वीकार्य **Admissibility** अभिस्वीकृति, प्रवेश/दाखिला **Admissibility of claim** दावे की ग्राह्यता/स्वीकार्यता

Admission अंदर आना **Admission fee** प्रवेश-शुल्क **Admission form** प्रवेश-पत्र **Admission, no** प्रवेश निषिद्ध/वर्जित/अन्दर आना मना है **Admission Pass** प्रवेश-पास, प्रवेश-पत्र **Admission with permission** आज्ञा लेकर भीतर आइए **Admission of claim** दावा मान लेना, दावा स्वीकार करना

Admit प्रवेश करने देना/अंदर आने देना, स्वीकार करना, प्रविष्ट करना/दाखिल करना **Admit one** एक को अन्दर आने दें **Admit one's mistake** अपनी गलती मान लेना **Admit to bail** जमानत मंजूर होना **Admittance** प्रवेशित **Admitted** प्रविष्ट/दाखिल, स्वीकृत

Admonition भर्त्सना **Admonition**

for negligence लापरवाही/उपेक्षा के लिए भर्त्सना

Adopt अंगीकार करना/अपनाना **Adopted son** दत्तक पुत्र, गोद लिया बेटा **Adoption** 1. अंगीकरण 2. दत्तक-ग्रहण

Adrema Operator एड्रेमा प्रचालक

Adult प्रौढ़/वयस्क **Adult education** वयस्क/प्रौढ़-शिक्षा **—Education Officer** प्रौढ़-शिक्षा-अधिकारी **—franchise** वयस्क / बालिग मताधिकार **— Messenger** वयस्क-संदेशवाहक **—School Teacher** प्रौढ़ विद्यालय शिक्षक **-- Suffrage** वयस्क मताधिकार

Adulterated drugs अपमिश्रित औषधियां, मिलावटी दवाएँ

Advalorem यथामूल्य

Advance अग्रिम/पेशगी **Advance acceptance of tender** टेंडर की अग्रिम स्वीकृति, निविदा की अग्रिम स्वीकृति **Advance, adjustable** समंजनीय अग्रिम, समंजनीय पेशगी **Advance copy** अग्रिम प्रति **Advance, emergent petty** आपाती फुटकर पेशगी, आपाती फुटकर अग्रिम **Advance, festival** त्योहार पेशगी **Advance for house building** गृह निर्माण के लिए अग्रिम (राशि) **—from provident fund** निर्वाह निधि में से अग्रिम पेशगी **Advance, in** पहले से, पहले ही, अगाऊ **Advance, increment** अग्रिम वेतन-वृद्धि **Advance, interest bearing** ब्याज पर पेशगी **—,interest free** विना ब्याज पेशगी, विना ब्याज अग्रिम **—,irrecoverable** डूबी हुई पेशगी **Advance of pay** वेतन का अग्रिम/अग्रिम वेतन **—of T.A. (travelling allowance)** पेशगी यात्रा भत्ता, अग्रिम यात्रा भत्ता **—payment** पेशगी/अग्रिम अदायगी **Advance, permanent** स्थायी पेशगी **—,repayable** प्रतिदेय अग्रिम, **—,temporary** अस्थायी पेशगी **—sample** अग्रिम नमूना/अग्रिम प्रतिदर्श **—,special** विशेष पेशगी **Advanced arguments** प्रस्तुत तर्क, पेश की गई दलीलें/युक्तियाँ **— countries** उन्नत देश **—course** उच्च प्रशिक्षण **Advancement** उन्नति

Advantage लाभ/फायदा/भलाई **Advantage, to take** लाभ उठाना **Advantages obtained** प्राप्त किए गए लाभ

Adverse प्रतिकूल **Adverse comment** प्रतिकूल टिप्पणी **—entry** प्रतिकूल इन्दराज **—finding** प्रतिकूल जांच-परिणाम **—party**

प्रतिपक्षी —**remark/report** प्रतिकूल अभ्युक्ति/रिपोर्ट

Advertise विज्ञापन देना/विज्ञापित करना **Advertised post** विज्ञापित पद/जगह —**sale** विज्ञापित विक्री —**tender** विज्ञापित निविदा/विज्ञापित टेंडर **Advertisement** विज्ञापन **Manager, Advertising** विज्ञापन-प्रबंधक **Advertising Assistant** विज्ञापन-सहायक

Advice परामर्श/सलाह सूचना/संज्ञापन **Advice, correct** ठीक सलाह/परामर्श **Advice note** संज्ञापन-पत्र —**of despatch** प्रेषण की सूचना —**of payment** भुगतान संज्ञापन/सूचना—**or concurrence** सलाह या सहमति **Advice, to take** मंत्रणा लेना, परामर्श लेना, सलाह लेना **Adviser (Advisor)** सलाहकार —**in Homoeopathy, Honorary** अवैतनिक होमियोपैथी सलाहकार —**of Factories** कारखाना-सलाहकार/फैक्टरी सलाहकार —,**Soil Conservation** भूमिसंरक्षण सलाहकार **Advisory** सलाहकारी **Advisory and coordinating** सलाह और समन्वय विषयक कार्य **Advisory Board** सलाहकार बोर्ड, सलाहकार मंडल, मंत्रणा-मंडल, मंत्रणाबोर्ड —**Committee** सलाहकार समिति —**Council** सलाहकार परिषद् —**opinion** सलाह सम्मति

Advocacy वकालत/पक्ष-समर्थन **Advocate** अधिवक्ता/एडवोकेट — **General** महाधिवक्ता

Aerated Water Factory Manager वातित जल कारखाना प्रबंधक

Aerial survey हवाई/वैमानिक सर्वेक्षण

Aerodrome हवाई अड्डा/विमान-क्षेत्र सर्वेक्षण **Aerodrome, civil Aeronautical Department** विमान-विभाग

Affairs कार्य/मामले **Affair, Settlement of an** मामले का निपटारा **Affairs of the Union or the State** संघ या राज्य के मामले **Affairs, Parliamentary** संसद-कार्य, संसदीय कार्य/मामले

Affect प्रभाव पड़ना **Affected, prejudicially** प्रतिकूल रूप से प्रभावित

Affection अनुराग

Affidavit शपथ-पत्र / हलफनामा **Affidavit, to file an** शपथ-पत्र प्रस्तुत करना, हलफनामा दाखिल करना

Affiliate संबद्ध करना **Affiliated College** संबद्ध महाविद्यालय/संबद्ध कालेज **Affiliated with** से सम्बद्ध **Affiliation** संबंधन

Affirm पुष्टि करना/प्रतिज्ञान करना (विधि) **Affirm the decision** निर्णय की पुष्टि **Affirmation** पुष्टि/प्रतिज्ञान (विधि) **Affirmation, solemn** गंभीर अभिवचन

Affirmative स्वीकारात्मक **Affirmative act** सकारात्मक अधिनियम **—reply** स्वीकारात्मक उत्तर, हाँ करना

Affix जोड़ना/लगाना **Affix a copy** प्रतिलिपि चिपकाना **—a seal** मोहर लगाना **—one's signature** अपने हस्ताक्षर करना

Afford opportunities/facilities to को अवसर/सुविधा देना **Afforded** दिया जाना

Afforestation वन-रोपण **-- Officer** वन-रोपण अधिकारी

Affranchise मताधिकार देना

Aforesaid पूर्वोक्त/पहले कहा **Aforesaid rule** पूर्वोक्त नियम **—terms** पूर्वोक्त शर्तें

After पश्चात् **After-care Home** उत्तर-रक्षा-गृह **—adequate consideration** समुचित विचार के बाद **—consultation with** से परामर्श करने के बाद/पश्चात् **After-thought** पश्च विचार **Afterwards** उसके बाद

Against के विरुद्ध, के खिलाफ **Against, as** की अपेक्षा **Against, paid** के मद्दे भुगतान किया **Against public interest** लोकहित के विरुद्ध **—the name** नाम के सामने **—the rules** नियमों के विरुद्ध

Age आयु/वय/उम्र **Age and health certificate** आयु और स्वास्थ्य प्रमाणपत्र **Age-entry** वय-प्रविष्टि, उम्र का इन्दराज **Age exemption** वयोविषयक छूट; आयु-विषयक छूट **—for suffrage** मतायु **—limit** वयसीमा **Age of compulsory retirement** अनिवार्य निवृत्ति वय **—of consent** सम्मति-वय **—of discretion** विवेक-वय **—of majority** वयस्कता की आयु **— of retirement** कार्य-निवृत्ति-वय/सेवा-निवृत्ति की उम्र **—of superannuation** वार्धक्यवय

Agency अभिकरण/एजेंसी **Agency commission** अभिकरण/एजेंसी कमीशन

Agenda कार्य-सूची/कार्यक्रम **Agenda Committee** कार्य-सूची समिति **Agenda, item of** कार्य-सूची की मद

Agent अभिकर्ता/एजेंट **Agent, commission** कमीशन एजेंट/आढ़तिया **Agent-General** महाभिकर्त्ता, एजेंट जनरल **Agent, Polling** मतांकन एजेंट **—Selling**

बिक्री एजेंट/बिक्री अभिकर्ता
Aggravate the situation स्थिति संगीन करना/बिगाड़ना **Aggravation** 1. अपवृद्धि 2. गुरुतर होना
Aggregate कुल/समाहार/पूर्णयोग **Aggregate votes** कुल मत **—value** कुल/समस्त मूल्य
Aggrieved व्यथित/आर्त्त/असंतुष्ट **Aggrieved party** व्यथित/असंतुष्ट पक्ष
Agitation आंदोलन **Agitation, peaceful** शान्तिपूर्ण आन्दोलन
Agrarian भूमि-संबंधी **Agrarian law** भूमि सम्बन्धी विधि/कानून **—policy** भूमि-संबंधी नीति
Agree करार करना / अनुबंध करना, सहमत होना / राजी होना **Agree, I** मैं सहमत हूँ **Agreeable proposal** मानने योग्य प्रस्ताव **Agreement** करार/अनुबंध सहमति, **Agreement form** अनुबंध पत्र, करारनामा **Agreement, oral** जबानी करार, मौखिक सहमति/रजामन्दी
Agricultural assistant कृषि-सहायक **—Credit Advisor** कृषि साख सलाहकार **—forecasting** खेती/कृषि सम्बन्धी पूर्वानुमान **—income** कृषि-आय **—land** कृषि-भूमि **Agriculture** कृषि **—, Department of** कृषि-विभाग **—holding** जोत-क्षेत्र **—Officer** कृषि-अधिकारी
Agronomist शस्य-विज्ञानी
Agrostologist घास-विज्ञानी
Aid सहायता/मदद **Aid and advice** सहायता और सलाह **Aid, financial** वित्तीय सहायता, धन की मदद **—, first** प्रथमोपचार, प्राथमिक उपचार **—, grant in** सहायता-अनुदान **Aided school** सहायता प्राप्त स्कूल **Aid-de-camp (A.D.C.)** ए०डी० सी०
Aim लक्ष्य/उद्देश्य
Air Adviser हवाई सलाहकार **—Chief Marshal** एयर चीफ मार्शल **—Commodore** एयर कमोडोर **—Controller** हवाई नियंत्रक/एयर कंट्रोलर **—Co-ordinator** हवाई समन्वयी/एयर कोऑर्डिनेटर **—Crew** हवाई कर्मीदल/एयर क्रू **—Defence Commander** हवाई रक्षा कमांडर **—Despatcher** हवाई प्रेषक **—Field Safety Operator** हवाई मैदान संरक्षा प्रचालक/एयर फील्ड सेफ्टी ऑपरेटर
Air force वायु सेना **—freight** विमान वस्तु-भाड़ा **—Gunner** हवाई तोपंची **—mail** हवाई डाक **—Inspector** हवाई डाक निरीक्षक **—Marshal** एयर मार्शल **—Officer Commanding** एयर अफसर

कमांडिग —**In-charge** एयर अफसर इंचार्ज – **on Special Duty** विशेष ड्यूटी वायु अफसर —**port** हवाई पत्तन **Air route** वायु/हवाई मार्ग —**traffic** हवाई यातायात —**Transport Liaison Officer** हवाईप रिवहन-संपर्क-अधिकारी —**Vice-Marshal** एयर वाइस-मार्शल —**Examiner** वायु-यान परीक्षक **Airconditioning** वातानुकूलन —**Supervisor** वातानुकूलन पर्यवेक्षक **A.C. Mechanic** वातानुकूल डिब्बा मेकैनिक, वातानुकूलन मेकैनिक **Air conditioned room** वातानुकूलित कमरा **Air-conditioning division** वातानुकूलन-प्रभाग **Air craft** वायुयान **Aircraftman** ऐयर क्राफ्टमैन **Air liaison officer** हवाई सम्पर्क (अफसर) अधिकारी **Airline** हवाई कम्पनी **Airline Companies** हवाई कम्पनियाँ **Airman** वायु सैनिक/एयरमैन **Air transport** हवाई परिवहन, विमान परिवहन **Air Transport Licensing Board** हवाई परिवहन लाइसैंस बोर्ड **Airways (airroute)** हवाई मार्ग, वायु मार्ग, वायु पथ

Alderman पौरमुख्य

Alert, to keep सतर्क रहना

Alien resident विदेशी **Alienation** अन्य-संक्रामण, परकीकरण

Alike, proposals are प्रस्ताव समान हैं, प्रस्ताव एक जैसे है **Alike, treated** एकसा समझा/माना गया

All concerned to note सभी सम्बन्धित व्यक्ति ध्यान रखें/नोट **All inclusive price** समग्र/सर्व-समावेशी/सर्वग्राही मूल्य **All India Institute of Medical Sciences** अखिल भारतीय आयुर्विज्ञान संस्थान —**Radio** आकाशवाणी **All India Service** अखिल भारतीय सेवा **All rights reserved** सर्वाधिकार सुरक्षित

Allegation आरोप/अभिकथन **Allegation, serious** गम्भीर आरोप

Alleged कथित/अभिकथित **Alleged statement** कथित/अभिकथित/आरोपित बयान

Allegiance निष्ठा **Allegiance, oath of** निष्ठा की शपथ

Alliance मैत्री

Allocate बाँटना/विभाजन करना **Allocation** बंटवारा/विभाजन **Allocation of time** समय का विभाजन/बंटवारा

Along with के साथ

Allot आवंटन करना **Allotment** आवंटन/बाँट —**letter** आवंटन पत्र —**Officer** आवंटन अधि-

कारी **—of fund** निधि आवंटन **Allotment order** आवंटन-आदेश, अलाटमेंट आदेश **—Supervisor** आवंटन पर्यवेक्षक

Allow अनुज्ञा देना/मंजूर करना **Allow to enter** प्रवेश करने देना, घुसने देना

Allowance भत्ता **Allowance, absentee** अनुपस्थिति भत्ता **Allowance, all India liability** अखिल भारतीय दायित्व भत्ता **Allowance, arrears of** बकाया भत्ता **Allowance, bad climate** खराब आबोहवा भत्ता **Allowance, —band** वाद्य भत्ता **—,camp equipage** शिविर सामग्री भत्ता **—,camp equipment** शिविर उपस्कर भत्ता **—,camp kit**शिविर किट भत्ता **—,capital** राजधानी भत्ता **—,charge** कार्यभार भत्ता **—,charpoy** चारपाई भत्ता **—children** संतान भत्ता **—,children education** संतान शिक्षण भत्ता **—,clothing** वस्त्र भत्ता **—,City** नगर भत्ता **—,compassionate** अनुकम्पा भत्ता **—, compensatory** पूरक भत्ता **—,condiment** जन भत्ता **—Conveyance** सवारी भत्ता/ वाहन भत्ता **—,conservancy water carrier** सफाई और भिश्ती भत्ता **—,constant attendant** सार्वकालिक परिचर भत्ता **—,construction** निर्माण भत्ता **—,contract** संविदा भत्ता **—,controlling officer** नियंत्रक अधिकारी भत्ता **—,cycle** साइकिल भत्ता **—,daily** दैनिकभत्ता **—,dearness** मँहगाई भत्ता **—,disturbance** अशान्ति-क्षेत्र-भत्ता **—,education** शिक्षण-भत्ता **—,entertainment** सत्कार-भत्ता **—,equipment** उपस्कर-भत्ता **—,exchange compensation** विनिमय-प्रतिकर भत्ता **—,expatriation** परदेश-भत्ता **—Extra Duty** अतिरिक्त ड्यूटी भत्ता **—, family** कुटुम्ब भत्ता **—,famine duty** दुर्भिक्ष ड्यूटी भत्ता**—,fixed conveyance** नियम सवारी भत्ता **—,fixed travelling** नियम सफर भत्ता **—,foreign** विदेश भत्ता **—,mess maintenance** रसोई अनुरक्षण भत्ता, मेस अनुरक्षण भत्ता **—,mileage** दूरी भत्ता, मील भत्ता **—,motorcycle** मोटर साईकिल भत्ता **—,mufti clothing** असैनिक वस्त्र भत्ता **—Out station** वहि:स्थान भत्ता **—Overtime** समयोपरि भत्ता/ अतिरिक्त समय भत्ता **—,special**

disturbance अशान्ति क्षेत्र का विशेष भत्ता **—, Travelling** यात्रा भत्ता

Allowed, this cannot be ऐसा करने की मंजूरी/अनुज्ञा नहीं दी

Alone केवल/अकेला

Alphabetical list of names नामों की वर्णक्रम सूची, वर्णक्रम नामावली

Alphabetical order, in वर्णक्रम से, अकारादि क्रम से

Already done किया जा चुका (पहले ही)

Alter परिवर्तन करना **Alteration** परिवर्तन/हेर-फेर **Alteration in draft** प्रारूप/मसौदे में परिवर्तन/अदल-बदल/फेर

Alternate 1. एकांतर 2. विकल्प **Alternative** विकल्प/वैकल्पिक **Alternative method** वैकल्पिक रीति, दूसरा तरीका

Although it is known यद्यपि यह विदित है

Altogether false पूर्णतः/सर्वथा झूठ

Amalgamated, the papers have कागज मिला लिए हैं, कागज एक कर दिए हैं **Amalgamation** समामेलन/एकीकरण **Amalgamation of offices** कार्यालयों का समामेलन/एकीकरण

Ambassador राजदूत

Ambiguous संदिग्धार्थी **Ambiguous suggestion** अस्पष्ट/संदिग्ध सुझाव

Ambulance corps अस्पताली दल **Ambulance Driver** रोगी गाड़ी चालक/ऐम्बुलेंस ड्राइवर **—service** ऐम्बुलैंस व्यवस्था

Amended draft संशोधित मसौदा/प्रारूप **Amendment** संशोधन

Amenity सुख-सुविधा **—Clerk** सुख-सुविधा-लिपिक **Amenities fund** सुख-सुविधा निधि

Amount 1. राशि/रकम 2. मात्रा/परिमाण 3. मिश्रधन **Amount due** देय राशि/रकम **Amount of work** काम की मात्रा, काम का परिमाण

Analogous case सदृश/सजातीय/एक-सा मामला **Analogy of, on the** से सादृश्य पर

Analysis, correct सही विश्लेषण **Analyst** विश्लेषक **Analyst, chief** मुख्य विश्लेषक **Analytical Assistant** विश्लेषण सहायक

Ancestral property पैतृक सम्पत्ति

Anchorage 1. लंगरगाह 2. लंगर शुल्क

Ancient document प्राचीन प्रलेख/कागज

Ancillary आनुषंगिक **Ancillary administration** गौण प्रशासन **—service** अनुषंगी / सहायक सेवाएं

Animal Husbandry पशुपालन

Annex 1. अनुबद्ध करना/जोड़ना/नत्थी करना 2. राज्य में मिला देना **Annexe** उपभवन **Annexure** अनुबंधन **—papers** अनुबंध के कागज़ **Annexure to this letter** इस पत्र के अनुलग्न

Announce आख्यापन करना/ऐलान करना **Announcement** आख्यापन/ऐलान **Announcement, public** सार्वजनिक एलान/आख्यान **Announcer** 1. आख्यापक 2. वाचक

Annual Account वार्षिक रेखा **—administrative report** वार्षिक प्रशासन रिपोर्ट/वार्षिक प्रशासन विवरण **—charge** वार्षिक प्रभार **—financial statement** वार्षिक वित्तीय विवरण **—review** वार्षिक समीक्षा **Annually** प्रतिवर्ष **Annuity** वार्षिकी

Annul बातिल करना/रद्द करना **Annulment** रद्द करना

Anomalous position असंगत स्थिति **Anomaly** असंगति **Anonymous complaint** नाम रहित/गुमनाम शिकायत **Antagonistic attitude** विरोधी रवैया

Antecedents पूर्ववृत्त **Antecedents, verification of** पूर्ववृत्त की पड़ताल/जांच **Ante-dated cheque** पूर्व-तारीखी चैक/पूर्व-दिनांकित चैक

Anthropological Survey of India भारतीय मानवविज्ञान सर्वेक्षण **Anthropologist** मानव-विज्ञानी, नृविज्ञानी

Anticipated expenditure प्रत्याशित व्यय **—revenue** प्रत्याशित राजस्व **Anticipation** 1. प्रत्याशा 2. पूर्वानुमान **Anti-corruption department** भ्रष्टाचार निरोधी विभाग **—Officer** भ्रष्टाचार-निरोध अधिकार **—Police Inspector** भ्रष्टाचार-निरोध पुलिस निरीक्षक **Anti-Inflationary measure** मुद्रास्फीति निवारक उपाय **Anti-Malaria Officer** मलेरिया निरोध अधिकारी **Antiquarian** पुरातनिक/पौरातनिक

Answerable to को उत्तरदायी

Any cases, in किसी भी अवस्था में, बहरहाल **Any other subject** अन्य कोई विषय

Apiarist मधुमक्षिकापाल

Apologise क्षमा मांगना, खेद प्रकट करना **Apology** खेद प्रकाश, क्षमा याचना

Apparatus साधित्र

Apparent on the face of the record अभिलेख से ही स्पष्ट/प्रकट **Apparent reason** प्रत्यक्षक कारण

Appeal (n) अपील **(vb.)** अपील करना **—,Admit an** अपील ग्रहण

करना —,**Allow an** अपील मंजूर करना **Appeal allowed/dismissed** अपील मंजूर/खारिज —**Clerk** अपील लिपिक **Appeals Division** अपील प्रभाग **Appeal, File an** अपील फाइल करना —,**Leave to** अपील के लिए इजाजत

Appear in person स्वयं उपस्थित होना **Appear not to have been received, paper** कागज आए नहीं मालूम होते

Appellate Authority अपील-प्राधिकारी —**Controller of Estate duty** संपदाशुल्क-अपील-नियंत्रक **Appellate powers** अपीलीय अधिकार **Appellation** अभिधान/पदवी

Appendage संलग्नक **Appended** संलग्न **Appended to** से संलग्न **Appendix** परिशिष्ट **Appendix 'A'** परिशिष्ट 'क'

Appliance साधन/उपकरण/साधित्र **Appliances, accounting** लेखा-साधन **Appliance, copying and duplicating** नकल और अनुलिपि साधन/नकल और अनुलिपि साधित्र **Appliance, Instructional** अनुदेश साधन **Appliance, office** कार्यालय उपकरण —,**sorting** छंटाई साधित्र

Applicable to को/पर लागू **Applicability** प्रयोज्यता / लागू होना **Applicable** प्रयोज्य/लागू **Applicant** आवेदक **Application** 1. आवेदन/आवेदन-पत्र/अर्जी 2. प्रयोज्यता/लागू होना **Application of rules** नियमों की प्रयुक्ति, नियम लागू करना/होना **Application rejected** आवेदन पत्र अस्वीकार, अर्जी नामंजूर

Appoint नियुक्त करना **Appointee** नियुक्त व्यक्ति **Appointing Authority** नियुक्ति प्राधिकारी **Appointment** नियुक्ति **Appointment, Clerk** नियुक्ति लिपिक —,**officiating** स्थानापन्न / अस्थायी / स्थायी नियुक्ति —,**Permanent** स्थायी नियुक्ति **Temporary** अस्थायी नियुक्ति **Appointed time** नियत/ निश्चित / निर्धारित समय **Appointing authority** नियुक्ति प्राधिकारी

Apportion प्रभाजन **Apportionment of resonsibility** उत्तरदायित्व/जिम्मेदारी का प्रभाजन, जिम्मेदारी बांटना

Appraisal कूतना, आंकना, मूल्य निर्धारण **Appraiser** मूल्यनिरूपक

Appreciate, you will आप इस बात को मानेंगे **Appreciated,**

his work was उसके काम की सराहना की गई **Appreciation** सराहना, वृद्धि (**as of price**) **Appreciation in price** मूल्य में वृद्धि **Appreciation, letter of** सराहना का पत्र

Apprentice शिक्षु/अप्रेंटिस **Mechanic** शिक्षु यांत्रिक/अप्रेंटिस मेकैनिक **Apprenticeship** शिक्षुता, शिशिक्षुता, **Apprenticeship, period of** शिक्षुता काल, अपरेंटिसी की अवधि

Approach, constructive रचनात्मक दृष्टिकोण **Approached, he can be** उस तक पहुंच हो सकती है

Appropriate (adj.) उपयुक्त/उचित (**vb.**) विनियोजन करना **Appropriate authority** उचित प्राधिकारी, उचित सरकार **—head** उचित शीर्ष **Appropriated** विनियुक्त **Appropriation** विनियोजन **Appropriation account** विनियोग विनियोजन लेखा **—act** विनियोजन-अधिनियम **Appropriate action** उचित/उपयुक्त कार्यवाई

Approval अनुमोदन **Approval, financial** वित्तीय अनुमोदन **Approve** अनुमोदन करना **Approved as per remarks in the margin** हाशिए की टिप्पणी के अनुसार अनुमोदित **Approved as proposed** यथाप्रस्तावित अनुमोदित **Approved Contractor** अनुमोदित ठेकेदार/अनुमोदित संविदाकार **—service** अनुमोदित सेवा **—subject to** इस शर्त (ऐसा होने) पर अनुमोदित **—superannuation fund** अनुमोदित अधिवर्ष-निधि

Approximate cost लगभग लागत

Appurtenance अनुलग्नक/उपाबंध

Aquarium keeper जलजीवपाल

Arable land कृषि योग्य भूमि

Arbitral tribunal विवाचन-अधिकरण

Arbitrary action मनमानी कार्यवाई **Arbitration** माध्यस्थ्य, विवाचन **Arbitrator** मध्यस्थ, विवाचक **Arbitrator's award** मध्यस्थ का अधिनिर्णय

Arboriculture Officer वृक्ष-संवर्धन अधिकारी **Arboriculturist** वृक्ष-संवर्धन-विज्ञानी

Archaeological Officer पुरातत्व-अधिकारी **—Survey of India** भारतीय पुरातत्व सर्वेक्षण **Archaeologist** पुरातत्वज्ञ **Archaeology** पुरातत्व, पुरातत्व विज्ञान

Architect 1. वास्तुक/वास्तुविद् 2. स्थापति **Architectural Assistant** वास्तु-सहायक / स्थापत्य-सहायक **Architecture** वास्तुकला/स्थापत्य-कला

Archives (शासकीय) अभिलेखागार **Archives, National**—राष्ट्रीय अभिलेखागार **Archivist** (शासकीय) अभिलेखपाल

Arduous— श्रम साध्य, दुष्कर

Area क्षेत्र —**Chaser** क्षेत्र चेजर —**Commander** एरिया कमांडर —**Installation Engineer** क्षेत्रीय संस्थापन इंजीनियर **Area, plinth** कुर्सी क्षेत्रफल **Area Rationing Authority** क्षेत्र राशन प्राधिकारी **Superintendent** क्षेत्र अधीक्षक **Area Supervisor** क्षेत्र पर्यवेक्षक

Argue —बहस करना

Argument तर्क **Argument, untenable** असमर्थनीय तर्क

Arising—उद्भूत, पैदा हुए **Arising out of** से उद्भूत/उत्पन्न

Armament Officer आयुध अफसर/आर्मामेंट अफसर —,**Directorate of** आयुध निदेशालय —**Officers Mess** सशस्त्र-सेना-अफसर मेस —**Police Constable** सशस्त्र पुलिस सिपाही **Armature Winder** आर्मेचर वलयक **Armed Forces Medical Corps** सशस्त्र-सेना-चिकित्सा-कोर—**Services** सशस्त्र-सेना-चिकित्सा सेवाएं **Armed police** सशस्त्र पुलिस **Armistice** युद्ध-विराम **Armourer** शस्त्र-साज/आर्मरर **Armoury Officer** शस्त्रागार अफसर—**Sentry** शस्त्रागार संतरी **Arms** बाजु, आयुध, **Arms Clerk** शस्त्रलिपिक/शस्त्र क्लर्क **Army Commander** आर्मी कमांडर —**Reserve Officer** आर्मी रिजर्व अफसर

Arrangement 1. प्रबंध/व्यवस्था 2. विन्यास **Arrangement of files** फाइलों/मिसिलों की तरतीब, मिसिल-विन्यास **Arrangement may be made** प्रबन्ध किया जाय, व्यवस्था की जाय

Arrears बकाया **Arrears of pay** बकाया वेतन —**of files** मिसिल-विन्यास **Arrears statement** बकाया विवरण

Arrival and departure आगमन और प्रस्थान, पहुँच और रवानगी

Art Executive कला-प्रबंधक

Article अनुच्छेद नियम, वस्तु **Article of...Regulations...** विनियम का अनुच्छेद 4 **Articles** नियमावली **Articles of association** संगम की नियमावली —**of impeachment** महाभियोग-लेख —**of the navy** नौसेना-नियम —**of stationery** लेखन सामग्री की वस्तुएँ

Artificer परिशिल्पी

Artificial Insemination Officer कृत्रिम वीर्य-सेचन अधिकारी **Arti-**

ficial silk कृत्रिम/बनावटी/नकली रेशम

Artisan कारीगर

Artist कलाकार **Artistic** कलात्मक

As above जैसा ऊपर दिया गया है, ऊपर जैसा **As against** की अपेक्षा, की तुलना में **As amended** यथा संशोधित **As before** यथापूर्व, पूर्ववत्, पहले जैसा **As compared to** की तुलना में **As defined** यथा परिभाषित, यथोक्त **As desired by** की इच्छानुसार **As directed** यथा निर्दिष्ट, निदेशानुसार, यथा निदेशित **As follows** निम्नलिखित **As modified** यथापरिवर्तित, यथा-परिष्कृत **As proposed** यथा-प्रस्तावित **As regards** के बारे/सम्बन्ध/विषय में **As required** आवश्यकतानुसार, यथा अपेक्षित, जैसा जरूरी हो **As revised** यथा पुनरीक्षित/परिशोधित/संशोधित **As soon as** यथाशीघ्र **As soon as may be** यथासम्भव शीघ्र **As stood on** जैसा···(तारीख) को था **As to** के बारे में, के लिए, विषयक **As usual** सदा की भांति, हमेशा की तरह **As a last resort** अन्तिम उपाय के रूप में, आखिर **As a matter of fact** यथार्थतः, वस्तुतः **As a result of** के परिणाम स्वरूप, के फलस्वरूप **As a whole** समग्र, समस्त, सारा का सारा **As and when** जब और जैसे, जब कभी, जब भी **As early as possible** यथाशीघ्र, जितनी जल्दी हो सके **As far as practicable** जहाँ तक व्यवहार्य हो **As far as possible** यथासम्भव, जहाँ तक सम्भव हो सके **As he thinks fit** जैसा वह उचित समझे **As hereinafter provided** जैसा नीचे लिखा है, आगे उपबन्धित जैसा, इसके आगे दिए अनुसार **As if** मानो **As in force for the time being** जैसा फिलहाल चालू/लागू हो **As is where is** जैसा है जहां है **As it stands** जैसा है **As may be necessary** जैसा/जो आवश्यक हो, यथावश्यक **As nearly as possible** यथासम्भव निकट **As of right** अधिकार रूप में **As per details below** नीचे दिए ब्यौरे के अनुसार **As per need** आवश्यकतानुसार **As per opinion of** के मतानुसार **As per standard distribution list** मानक वितरण सूची के अनुसार **As the circumstances of the case** जैसा परिस्थिति विशेष में जरूरी हो **As the case may be** यथास्थिति, यथा अवस्था, यथा-

प्रसंग, जैसी बात हो **As you are no doubt aware** जैसा आपको निस्सन्देह विदित है

Aspects, from various विभिन्न पहलुओं/दृष्टि से

Assault हमला/प्रहार/धावा

Assay Master अधिपारखी **Assayer** पारखी

Assemble 1. जुड़ना/एकत्र होना/इकट्ठा होना 2. जोड़ना/सम्मिलित करना/एकत्र करना/इकट्ठा करना/समवेत करना **Assembly** सभा, जमाव/सम्मेलन

Assent अनुमति **Assent, President's** राष्ट्रपति की अनुमति

Assess परिगणित करना, निर्धारित करना **Assessed value** निर्धारित मूल्य **Assessment** करनिर्धारण, निर्धारण **Assessment of disability** निशक्तता निर्धारण **Assessment order passed** निर्धारण आदेश दिया गया **Assessment Officer** कर-निर्धारण-अधिकारी **Assessor** असेसर

Assets आस्तियाँ/परिसंपत्ति **Assets and liabilities** परिसम्पत्ति/आस्तियां तथा देयता

Assign 1. समनुदेशित करना/सौंपना 2. नियत करना **Assignee** अधिन्यासी **Assignment** समनुदेशन/नियत कार्य/सुपुर्द काम **Assignment, new** नया नियत/सुपुर्द काम **Assignment Officer** कार्यनियोजन अधिकारी/सुपुर्दी-अधिकारी **—of loss** हानि-निर्धारण **Assignor** अधिन्यासक समनुदेशक

Assistance, financial वित्तीय/आर्थिक सहायता **Assistant** सहायक **Assistant Accounts Officer** सहायक लेखा अधिकारी **—(Administration and Commercial)** सहायक लेखा अधिकारी (प्रशासन एवं वाणिज्य) **—(Books)** सहायक लेखा अधिकारी (लेखाबही) **—(Coaching)** सहायक लेखा अधिकारी (कोचिंग) **—Compensation)** सहायक लेखा अधिकारी (प्रतिपूर्ति) **—(Compensation claim)** सहायक लेखा अधिकारी (प्रतिकर दावा) **—(Construction)** सहायक अधिकारी (निर्माण) **—(Expenditure, Fuel and Inspection)** सहायक लेखा अधिकारी (व्यय, ईंधन और निरीक्षण) **—(Finance)** सहायक लेखा अधिकारी (वित्त) **—(Finance Budget)** सहायक लेखा अधिकारी (वित्त बजट) **—(Goods)** सहायक लेखा अधिकारी (माल) **—(Simplification)** सहायक

लेखा अधिकारी (सरलीकरण) —**(Stores)** सहायक लेखा अधिकारी (भंडार) —**Audit Officer** सहायक लेखा परीक्षा अधिकारी **Assistant Auditor** सहायक लेखा परीक्षक —**Bacteriologist** सहायक जीवाणुविज्ञानी —**Barco Machine Operator** सहायक बारको मशीन प्रचालक —**Block Inspector** सहायक खंड निरीक्षक —**Bridge Engineer** सहायक पुल इंजीनियर —**(Development)** सहायक पुल इंजीनियर (विकास) —**Inspector** सहायक पुल निरीक्षक—**Bromide Printer** सहायक ब्रोमाइड मुद्रक —**Cabin Master** सहायक केबिन मास्टर —**Carpenter Mistry** सहायक काष्ठ मिस्त्री —**Car Refreshment Room Manager** सहायक यान उपाहार कक्ष प्रबंधक —**Carriage Cleaning Inspector** सहायक डिब्बा सफाई निरीक्षक —**Cashier** सहायक खजांची —**Cashier and Pay Master** सहायक खजांची और वेतनपाल —**Catering Inspector** सहायक खान-पान निरीक्षक —**Store Keeper** सहायक खान-पान भंडारी —**Supervisor** सहायक खान-पान पर्यवेक्षक —**Chargeman** सहायक चार्जमैन / सहायक कार्यवेक्षक —**Chemist** सहायक रसायन-विज्ञानी – **Chief Auditor (Central)** सहायक मुख्य लेखा-परीक्षक (केन्द्रीय) —**Claims Inspector** सहायक दावा निरीक्षक —**Prevention Inspector** सहायक दावा निवारण निरीक्षक – **Clerk** सहायक लिपिक/सहायक क्लर्क —**Coal Conveyor Attendant** सहायक कोयला वाहक परिचर —**Commercial Inspector** सहायक वाणिज्य निरीक्षक —**Commercial Inspector (Budget)** सहायक वाणिज्य निरीक्षक (बजट) —**(Job Analysis)** सहायक वाणिज्य निरीक्षक (कार्य विश्लेषण) —**Officer (Claims)** सहायक वाणिज्य अधिकारी (दावा) —**(Claims Disposal)** सहायक वाणिज्य अधिकारी (दावा निपटाना) —**(Complaints)** सहायक वाणिज्य अधिकारी (शिकायत) —**(General)** सहायक वाणिज्य अधिकारी (सामान्य)—**(Outstanding)** सहायक वाणिज्य अधिकारी (बकाया) —**(Railway Freight)** सहायक वाणिज्य अधिकारी (रेल भाड़ा) —**(Reservation)** सहायक वाणिज्य अधिकारी (आरक्षण) —**(Tickets)** सहायक वाणिज्य

अधिकारी (टिकट) **—Publicity Officer** सहायक वाणिज्य प्रचार अधिकारी **—Superintendent** सहायक वाणिज्य अधीक्षक **Assistant Commissioner** सहायक आयुक्त / सहायक कमिश्नर **— Complaints Inspector** सहायक शिकायत निरीक्षक **— Controller of Stores** सहायक भंडार नियंत्रक **—(Construction)** सहायक भंडारनियंत्रक (निर्माण) **—Food Supply Inspector** सहायक खाद्य पूर्ति निरीक्षक **— Foreman** सहायक फोरमैन **—(Maintenance)** सहायक फोरमैन (अनुरक्षण) **—(Mechanical)** सहायक फोरमैन (यांत्रिक) **Assistant Controller of Stores** सहायक भंडार नियंत्रक **(Inspection)** (निरीक्षण) **—(Liaison)** सहायक भंडार नियंत्रक (संपर्क) **—(Metric System)** सहायक भंडार नियंत्रक (मीटर प्रणाली) **—(Out Depot)** सहायक भंडार नियंत्रक (बाहरी डिपो) **—(works)** सहायक भंडार नियंत्रक (संकर्म) **— Dental Surgeon** सहायक दंत सर्जन **Assistant Depot Store Keeper** सहायक डिपो भंडारी **—Deputy General Manager** सहायक उप-महाप्रबंधक **—Director** सहायक निदेशक **—Director/Secretary** सहायक निदेशक/सचिव **Divisional Commercial Inspector** सहायक मंडल वाणिज्य निरीक्षक **—Draftsman** सहायक प्रारूपकार **—Driver** सहायक चालक/ सहायक ड्राइवर **—(Electric)** सहायक चालकबिजली सहायक ड्राइवर (बिजली) **— Efficiency Officer** सहायक दक्षता अधिकारी **— Engineer** सहायक इंजीनियर **— (Bridges)** सहायक इंजीनियर (पुल) **—(Headquartes)** सहायक इंजीनियर (मुख्यालय) **—(Planning)** सहायक इंजीनियर (योजना) **—(Planning & Development)** सहायक इंजीनियर (योजना और विकास) **—(Ring Railway)** सहायक इंजीनियर (रिंग रेलवे) **— Estimator** सहायक प्राक्कलक **—Filter Plant Operator** सहायक निस्यंदक संयंत्र प्रचालक, सहायक फिल्टर प्लांट ऑपरेटर **—Fitter** सहायक फिटर **Foreman (Mechanical and Maintenance)** सहायक फोरमन (यांत्रिक और अनुरक्षण) **— (Plant)** सहायक फोरमैन (संयंत्र) **—G. C. Notekeeper** सहायक सरकारी मुद्रा नोट रक्षक **— Godown Manager** सहायक

गोदाम प्रबंधक **—Goods Clerk (Travelling)** सहायक माल क्लर्क (यात्रा) **—Grade-A Lecturer** ग्रेड-ए० प्राध्यापक **—Grade-B Lecturer** सहायक ग्रेड-बी० प्राध्यापक **—Gunner** सहायक गनर **—Head master** सहायक मुख्याध्यापक **—Head Signaller** 1. सहायक प्रधान सिगनलर/सहायक प्रधान संकेतक 2. सहायक प्रधान तार बाबू **Assistant Hospital Steward** सहायक चिकित्सालय स्टूवर्ड/सहायक अस्पताल स्टूवर्ड **—Store Keeper** सहायक चिकित्सालय भंडारी **—Hostel Warden** सहायक छात्रावासपाल/सहायक वार्डन **—Incharge, Temple and Ferro** सहायक प्रभारी, टेम्प्लेट और फेरो **Assistant Inspector of Works** 1. सहायक संकर्म निरीक्षक 2. सहायक कर्मशाला निरीक्षक 3. सहायक निर्माण निरीक्षक **—Instructor** सहायक शिक्षक **—Janitor** सहायक द्वाररक्षक **Labour Supervisor** सहायक श्रमिक पर्यवेक्षक **—Landing Supervisor** सहायक अवतरण पर्यवेक्षक **— Linen Keeper** सहायक वस्त्र रक्षक **— Supervisor** सहायक वस्त्र पर्यवेक्षक **—Litho Machineman** सहायक लीथो मशीनमैन **—Loco Foreman** सहायक लोको फोरमैन **—Maintenance Inspector** सहायक अनुरक्षण निरीक्षक **—Matron** सहायक मैट्रन **— Mechanical Engineer** सहायक यांत्रिक अभियंता/सहायक यांत्रिक इंजीनियर **—Medical Officer** सहायक चिकित्सा अधिकारी **—Medical Officer (Administration & general)** सहायक चिकित्सा अधिकारी (प्रशासन और सामान्य) **—(Pathology)** सहायक चिकित्सा अधिकारी (विकृतिविज्ञान) **—(Physiology)** सहायक चिकित्सा अधिकारी (शरीरक्रिया विज्ञान) **— (Radiology)** सहायक चिकित्सा अधिकारी (विकिरण चिकित्सा) **—(Surgery)** सहायक चिकित्सा अधिकारी (शल्यक्रिया) **Assistant Mistress** सहायक अध्यापिका **— Monotype Caster** सहायक मोनोटाइप ढलाईकार **—Movement Inspector** सहायक संचलन निरीक्षक **—Operator** सहायक प्रचालक **—Operator (Sub-station)** सहायक प्रचालक (उपस्टेशन) **—Permanent Way Inspector** सहायक रेल-पथ निरीक्षक

—Personnel Inspector सहायक कार्मिक निरीक्षक **—Personnel Officer** सहायक कार्मिक अधिकारी **—(Construction)** सहायक कार्मिक अधिकारी (निर्माण) **—(Publication)** सहायक कार्मिक अधिकारी (प्रकाशन) **Assistant Plant Inspector** सहायक संयत्र निरीक्षक **Progress Inspector** सहायक प्रगति निरीक्षक **—Progress Supervisor** सहायक प्रगति पर्यवेक्षक **—Public Relation Officer** सहायक जन संपर्क अधिकारी **—Radiologist** सहायक विकिरण-चिकित्सक **—Railway Hotel Manager** सहायक रेलहोटल प्रबन्धक **—Rates Inspector** सहायक दर निरीक्षक **—Rates Officer** सहायक दर अधिकारी **—(Coaching)** सहायक दर अधिकारी (कोचिंग) **—(goods)** सहायक दर अधिकारी (माल) **Assistant Research and Development Inspector** सहायक अनुसंधान और विकास निरीक्षक **—Road Van Inspector** सहायक सड़क वाहन निरीक्षक **—Running Shed Supervison** सहायक इंजन शैड पर्यवेक्षक **—Scherzer Bridge Opetator** सहायक शेर्त्सर सेतु प्रचालक **—School Teacher** सहायक विद्यालय शिक्षक **Assistant's Secretary** सहायक सचिव **—to General Manager** महाप्रबंधक के सहायक सचिव **—Operating Superintendent** सहायक परिचालन अधीक्षक **—Security Officer (Crime)** सहायक सुरक्षा अधिकारी (अपराध) **—(Special Intelligence)** सहायक सुरक्षा अधिकारी (विशेष आसूचना) **—(Training)** सहायक सुरक्षा अधिकारी (प्रशिक्षण) **—Shipping Inspector** सहायक पोत-परिवहन निरीक्षक **—Shop Superintendent** सहायक कर्मशाला अधीक्षक **—Signal and Telecommunication Engineer (Power Signal)** सहायक सिगनल और दूरसंचार इंजीनियर (बिजली सिगनल) **—(Wireless)** सहायक सिगनल और दूरसंचार इंजीनियर (बेतार) **Assistant Signal Engineer** सहायक संकेत अभियंता/सहायक सिगनल इंजीनियर **—Inspector** सहायक संकेत निरीक्षक/सहायक सिगनल निरीक्षक **—Signaller** सहायक सिगनलर/सहायक तारबाबू **—Special Inspector** सहायक विशेष निरीक्षक **—Stationery Superintendent** सहायक लेखन-सामग्री अधीक्षक **—Station**

Master सहायक स्टेशन मास्टर —**Storeman** सहायक भंडारकर्मी —**Sub-Inspector** सहायक नायब निरीक्षक —**Superintendent of Police** सहायक पुलिस अधीक्षक —**(Power)** सहायक अधीक्षक (बिजली) —**Supervisor (Mechanical)** सहायक पर्यवेक्षक (यांत्रिक) —**Supply Officer** सहायक पूर्ति अधिकारी —**Surgeon** सहायक शल्यचिकित्सक/सहायक सर्जन —**(Out Patient-Department)** सहायक सर्जन (बहिरंग रोगी विभाग) —**Surveyer** सहायक सर्वेक्षक —**Telecommunication Inspector** सहायक दूरसंचार निरीक्षक —**Telegraph Inspector** सहायक तार निरीक्षक —**Track Supply Superintendent** सहायक रेलपथ पूर्ति अधीक्षक —**Traction Power Controller** सहायक कर्षण शक्ति नियंत्रक —**Traffic Officer (Coaching)** सहायक यातायात अधिकारी (कोचिंग) —**(General)** सहायक यातायात अधिकारी (सामान्य) —**(Movement)** सहायक यातायात अधिकारी (संचलन) —**(Transit)** सहायक यातायात अधिकारी (परिवहन) —**Train Inspector** सहायक गाड़ी निरीक्षक —**Transhipment Inspector** सहायक यानांतरण निरीक्षक —**Transit Inspector** सहायक परिवहन निरीक्षक —**Transportation Superintendent** सहायक परिवहन अधीक्षक—**Vigilance Inspector** सहायक सतर्कता निरीक्षक —**Vigilance Officer** सहायक सतर्कता अधिकारी —**Wagon Inspector** सहायक माल डिब्बा निरीक्षक —**Ward Keeper** सहायक वार्ड-रक्षक —**Water and Drainage Inspector** सहायक जल और जलनिकासी निरीक्षक —**Softening Inspector** सहायक जल-मृदूकरण निरीक्षक —**Welfare Inspector** सहायक कल्याण निरीक्षक —**Movement Inspector** सहायक माल डिब्बा संचलन निरीक्षक —**Work Order Clerk** सहायक कार्य आदेश क्लर्क —**Workshop Foreman** सहायक कर्मशाला फोरमैन —**Works Manager** सहायक कर्मशाला प्रबंधक —**Yard Foreman** सहायक यार्ड फोरमैन —**Yard Master** सहायक यार्ड मास्टर —**Supervisor** सहायक यार्ड पर्यवेक्षक

Associate (vb.) सह, सम्मिलित करना **Association (n.)**

1. संघ/समाज/संगम 2. संबंध/साहचर्य

Assume ग्रहण करना, कल्पना करना **Assumption** ग्रहण, कल्पना **Assumption of charge** भार-ग्रहण, पद संभालना

Assurance आश्वासन, बीमा हस्तांतरण-पत्र **Assurance, given** आश्वासन दिया **Assure** आश्वस्त करना **Assured** आश्वासित, बीमाकृत, बीमा किया हुआ

At all पूर्णतया, बिल्कुल **At an early date** जल्दी **At any rate** किसी भी दशा में, किसी भी तरह **At least** कम से कम **At once** तत्काल, तुरन्त, फौरन **At par** सम मूल्य पर **At public expense** सार्वजनिक व्यय से **At random** यदृच्छया **At the close of** की समाप्ति पर, के बन्द होने पर **At the instance of** की प्रेरणा से, के अनुरोध से, के कहने पर **At this stage** इस अवस्था में, इस हालत में **At your earliest** जल्दी से जल्दी **At your earliest convenience** सुविधानुसार जितनी जल्दी हो सके **At your end apso** आपकी ओर से भी, अपनी ओर से भी

Atlas Branch एटलस-शाखा

Atomic Energy, Department of परमाणु-ऊर्जा विभाग **—Commission** परमाणु-ऊर्जा आयोग **—Minerals Division** परमाणु-खनिज प्रभाग **—Power** परमाणु शक्ति

Attache सहचारी/अताशे

Attachment कुर्की **Attachment order** कुर्की आदेश **Attached office** संलग्न कार्यालय **Attached to** से संलग्न, के साथ लगा हुआ

Attendance register उपस्थिति/हाजिरी रजिस्टर **Attended to, will be** पर ध्यान दिया जाएगा

Attention is invited to की ओर ध्यान आकर्षित किया जाता है **Attention : Shri...** ध्यान दें : श्री···

Attested, true copy अनुप्रमाणित, सही प्रतिलिपि **Attesting officer** साक्ष्यांकन / तसदीक अधिकारी **Attesting witness** साक्ष्यंकन करने वाला, साक्षी, तस्दीकी गवाह

Attributable मिले हुए माने जाने वाले

Auction नीलाम **Auction notice** नीलाम की सूचना

Audiovisual aid दृश्य-श्रव्य साधन/उपकरण

Audit instruction लेखापरीक्षा अनुदेश **Audit objections** लेखा-

परीक्षा आपत्तियां, आडिट आपत्तियां **Audit report** लेखा-परीक्षा रिपोर्ट, आडिट रिपोर्ट **Audited account** परीक्षित लेखा

Austerity scale मितव्ययिता का मान

Authentic अधिप्रमाणित **Authentic translation** अधिप्रमाणित अनुवाद **Authenticate** अधिप्रमाणित करना **Authentication** अधिप्रमाणन **Authenticity of the orders** आदेशों की अधिप्रमाणिकता

Author of a frud न्यास-प्रवर्त्तक

Authorisation अधिकार देना, प्राधिकार देना **Authorise** प्राधिकृत करना **Authorised agents** अधिकृत एजेंन्ट, अधिकृत अभिकर्ता **Authorised expenditure** प्राधिकृत व्यय **Authorities** प्राधिकारी **Authority** प्राधिकारी, प्राधिकार, प्राधिकरण **Authority, competent** सक्षम प्राधिकारी **Authority letter** प्राधिकार-पत्र **Authorize** प्राधिकार देना, अधिकार देना

Auto Exchange Assistant आटो-केन्द्र सहायक **—Lathe Setter** आटो खरादिया **Autograph** स्वाक्षर **Automatic feeding** स्वयं भरण **—mechanical messengers** स्वचल संदेशवाहित्र **—machine** स्वचालित मशीन **—numerator** स्वचालित नंबर-मशीन **Autonomous** स्वायत्त **Autonomous institutions** स्वायत्त संस्थाएं

Auxiliary 1. सहायक/सहकारी 2. अतिरिक्त **— Plant Attendant** सहायक संयंत्र परिचर **—Plant Operator** सहायक संयंत्र प्रचालक

Auxiliary service सहायक/सहकारी सेवा

Available प्राप्य/उपलब्ध **Available capital** उपलब्ध/प्राप्त पूंजी

Average औसत **Average on an** औसतन

Aviation विमानन **—Adviser** विमानन-सलाहकार **Aviation, Civil** सिविल विमानन **—Construction Circle** विमानन निर्माण अंचल **Aviation Directorate** विमानन-निदेशालय

Avoid वर्जन करना/परिहार करना/बचना **Avoided, such delays should be** इस प्रकार की देरी न होने दें

Avow प्रकट करना

Await further report और रिपोर्ट की प्रतीक्षा कीजिए/की जाए **Award reply** उत्तर की प्रतीक्षा कीजिए/की जाए

Award पंचाट/अधिनिर्णय **Award,**

compulsory अनिवार्य पंचाट —judicial न्यायिक/अदालती अधिनिर्णय — of compensation क्षतिपूर्ति-पंचाट — punishment दण्ड देना —,summary तुरंत पंचाट —Voluntary ऐच्छिक पंचाट **Awarding Authority** अधिनिर्णय प्राधिकारी/पंचाट प्राधिकारी

Axiom स्वयंसिद्धि

Axis अक्ष, धुरी **Axis of the attack** हमले का अक्ष, आक्रमण-अक्ष

Background पृष्ठभूमि **Background of the case** मामले की पृष्ठभूमि/पृष्ठाधार **Back out** मुकर/नट जाना, पीछे हट जाना **Back up** पृष्ठपोषण, समर्थन **Backward classes** पिछड़े वर्ग **Bakward Classes Commission** पिछड़े वर्गों का आयोग —tribes पिछड़ी जनजातियां/पिछड़ी आदिम जातियां

Bad behaviour दुर्व्यवहार/बुरा चलन —blood कटुता —books, in नजर में बुरा —character 1. दुश्चरित्रता/बुरा शील 2. दुःशील —conduct दुराचरण — debt बट्टाखाता, अशोध्य ऋण, डूबी रकम —in law विधि अमान्य

Badge बैज/बिल्ला **Badge, shoulder** कंधे का बैज/बिल्ला

Baggage Inspector सामान निरीक्षक

Bail, released on जमानत पर छोड़ना **Bailiff** बेलिफ

Baker बेकर **Bakery Instructor** बेकरी शिक्षक

Balance 1. शेष/अतिशेष/बाकी 2. तुला/तराजू 3. संतुलन **Balance, closing** अथ शेष, रोकड़ बाकी **Balance in hand** अपने पास बाकी, हस्तगत शेष — Keeper शेष (राशि) रक्षक **Balance, opening** अथ शेष, रोकड़ जमा **Balance sheet** तुलन-पत्र **Balanced development** संतुलित विकास

Ballast Checker गिट्टी पड़ताल कर्ता — Inspector गिट्टी निरीक्षक

Ballot 1. मतपत्र/मतपर्ची/बैलट शलाका 2 मतदान **Ballot box** मतपेटी —Officer मतपत्र-अधिकारी **Ballot paper** मत पत्र, मत पर्ची, शलाका — Secret गुप्त-मतदान

Ban प्रतिबंध/रोक/पाबंदी **Ban on further recruitment** आगे भर्ती पर रोक/प्रतिबन्ध/पाबन्दी

Band Boy बैंड बाय —Instructor बैंड शिक्षक - Master बैंड मास्टर **Bandsman** बैंड्समैन

Bank बैंक **Bank draft** बैंक-ड्राफ्ट **Bank guarantee** बैंक-गारंटी **Banker** बैंकर/महाजन **Banking** बैंकिंग/महाजनी **—Company** बैंकिंग कंपनी **—transaction** बैंक कार्य संचालन, महाजनी सौदा

Banquet प्रीतिभोज

Bar रोध/रुकावट **Bar of limitation** परिसीमा वारित **Bar of public opinion, at the** जनता के न्याय पर **Bar, there ir no** कोई रुकावट नहीं है

Barco Machine operator बारको मशीन प्रचालक

Barge Driver बजरा चालक, बजरा ड्राइवर **—Serang** बजरा सेरांग

Barman बारमैन

Barrack Officer बैरक अफसर

Barrier Clerk शुल्कद्वार-लिपिक/नाका-मुन्शी

Barrister बैरिस्टर

Base Engineer Officer बेस इंजीनियर अफसर **—Victualling Officer** बेस विटलिंग अफसर **Base year** आधार वर्ष **Based on** पर आधारित

Basic आधारी / मूल / बुनियादी **Basic education** बुनियादी शिक्षा **—Officer** बुनियादी-शिक्षा अधिकारी **Basic pay** मूल वेतन **—Period** मूल अवधि **—scale of pay** मूल वेतन-मान

Battalian Commander बटालियन कमांडर

Battery Attendant बैटरी-परिचर **—Charging Technician** बैटरी-चार्जकारी तकनीकविद्/बैटरीचार्जकारी प्रविधिज्ञ **—Gunner** बैटरी तोपची/बैटरी गनर **Batteryman** बैटरीमैन/बैटरीवाला

Baudot Supervisor बोदो पर्यवेक्षक

Bazar Inspector बाज़ार निरीक्षक **—Sarkar** बाजार सरकार **Beach Master** पुलिनपाल/बीच मास्टर

Bear out, to समर्थन करना **Bearer** 1. वाहक 2. बैरा 3. परिचर **Bearer, per** वाहक/पत्र-वाहक द्वारा **Bearing Recorder Operator** बेयरिंग रिकार्डर ऑपरेटर

Beat Guard टप्पा चौकीदार **Beat of drum, by** ढिंढोरा/डोंढी पीटकर **—Postman** गश्ती डाकिया **Beatman** गश्तवाला **Beaterman** गैंतीवाला

Because of के कारण

Bee Keeper मधुमक्षिका-पाल

Before cited पूर्व कथित **Before hand** पहले से **Before the expiry of** की समाप्ति के पूर्व/पहले

Beg to be excused क्षमा कीजिए,

क्षमा प्रार्थी हूँ **Beg to state** निवेदन है, निवेदन करता हूँ

Behalf, in that उसके लिए, उस सम्बन्ध में **Behalf of,. on** की ओर से, के निमित्त

Bell-Hop सूचक, संदेशी

Belonging to का, की, के

Below par अवमूल्य पर **Beltman** पट्टेवाला

Bench न्यायपीठ **-- Clerk** न्यायपीठ लिपिक **—Fitter** बेंच-फिटर

Bend (n) (vb.) मोड़, झुकना/मुड़ना/मोड़ना

Beneficial लाभप्रद / फायदाप्रद **Benefit** हित/फायदा/सुविधा **Benefit of doubt** सन्देह लाभ **Benefit period** सुविधा/फायदे की अवधि

Benevolent fund हितकारी निधि

Best of knowledge and belief, to the अधिकतम जानकारी और विश्वास के अनुसार **Best price obtainable** अधिकतम प्राप्य मूल्य **Best terms** सर्वोत्तम शर्तें

Besides this इसके अलावा/सिवाय/अतिरिक्त

Betterment tax समुन्नति कर

Beyond reasonable doubt युक्त सन्देह से परे, युक्त संदेहातीत **Beyond the said period** उक्त अवधि के परे/बाद **Beyond the scope of** की परिधि के बाहर **Beyond the seas** समुद्रपार

Biased opinion पक्षपातपूर्ण मत

Bibliographer संदर्भ-सूचीकार **Bibliography** संदर्भ ग्रन्थ-सूची

Bicameral द्विसदन/द्विसदनी

Bid बोली लगाना **Bidding sheet** बोली-पत्र

Biennial द्विवार्षिक, अर्धवार्षिक **Biennial report** द्विवार्षिक रिपोर्ट **Biennial Session** द्विवार्षिक सत्र

Bilateral-agreement द्विपक्षीय करार

Bill 1. विपत्र/बिल 2. विधेयक **Bill, after date** अग्रतिथि हुण्डी **Bill cashed on** (तारीख) को बिल भुनाया **Bill, clean** निरी हुण्डी **— Clerk** बिल क्लर्क **—Counter** बिल पटल/बिल काउंटर **Bill, medical** चिकित्सा बिल **—of entry** आगम पत्र **Bill of echange** हुंडी विनिमय-पत्र **Bill of indemnity** परिहार-विधियक क्षतिपूर्त्ति-बिल **Bill of lading** लदान-पत्र **Bill of Parcels** बीजक **—(of payment)** बीजक/बिल **Bill, pay** वेतन बिल **—Sircar** बिल-सरकार **Bill, to introduce** विधेयक पेश/प्रस्तुत करना **Bill, overtime** समयोपरि बिल

Bind बाधना; आवद्ध करना **Binder** जिल्दसाज **Binding** बाध्यक/बंधनकारी **—Book** जिल्दसाजी **—Boy (Binder Boy)** सहायक जिल्दसाज **Binding agreement** बाध्यक/बन्धनकारी करार

Biologist जीव-विज्ञानी

Bipartite द्विदलीय/उभयपक्षी **Bipartite agreement** द्विदलीय/उभयपक्षी करार

Birth, place of जन्म स्थान **Birth date** जन्म-तिथि/जन्म की तारीख **—mark** जन्म-चिह्न **—place rate** जन्म-दर

Biweekly पाक्षिक, अर्धसाप्ताहिक **Bi-weekly statement** अर्द्ध साप्ताहिक विवरण, पाक्षिक विवरण

Black list कालो सूची **—listing** कालीसूची में नाम लिखना **Black-market** चोर बाजार/काला बाजार **Blacksmith** लोहकार/लुहार

Blank cheque/form कोरा चैक/फार्म

Block खंड/ब्लॉक/प्रखंड **—and Signal Maintainer** ब्लॉक और सिगनल अनुरक्षक **—Development Officer** खंड-विकास-अधिकारी **—Inspector** ब्लॉक निरीक्षक **—Instrument Mistry** गुटका उपकरण मिस्त्री **—Maker** ब्लॉक-निर्माता **—paragraph** चोकोरपैरा/ब्लॉक पैरा **Block Signaller** ब्लॉक तारबाबू, ब्लॉक सिगनलर **—Signalman** ब्लाक सिगनलवाला **—Tester** ब्लॉक परीक्षक

Blood Transfusion Officer रुधिर-आधान अधिकारी

Blue print रूपरेखा, नीला नक्शा **—Printer** नील मुद्रक

Board बोर्ड/परिषद्/मंडल **Board of...** बोर्ड/मंडल **—of Extra-Mural Studies** बहि:शाल अध्ययन परिषद् **—of Khadi and Village Industries** खादी-ग्रामोद्योग-मंडल **—of Studies** पाठ्य-समिति **Boarding Officer** नौ-आरोहण अधिकारी

Boatsman केवट **Boatswain Store Keeper** बोसुन भंडारी

Body निकाय **Bodily injury** शारीरिक क्षति/चोट **Body corporate** निकाय **—Guard** अंगरक्षक **Body, in a** इकट्ठा, सामूहिक रूप से **Body of a letter** पत्र का प्रधानांग

Bogus voucher फर्जी वाउचर

Boiler Assistant बॉयलर-सहायक **—house** बॉयलर घर **—operator** बॉयलर घर प्रचालक **—Maker** बॉयलर मेकर

—**Chargeman** बॉयलर मेकर चार्जमैन —**Foreman** बॉयलर मेकर फोरमैन —**Supervisor** बॉयलर पर्यवेक्षक

Bonafide सद्भाव से, निष्कपट, नेक-नीयत, वास्तविक असली **Bonafide mistake** सद्भ्रांति **Bonafide Passenger** वास्तविक यात्री **Bonafides** सद्भाव **Bonafides, to suspect** सहायता/नेकनीयत पर सन्देह

Bond बंध-पत्र/बॉण्ड **Bond, Indemnity** क्षतिपूर्ति बन्ध-पत्र/बाण्ड —**Tester** बंध-परीक्षक **Bonded warehouse** करदेय वस्तुगृह/भण्डार/बॉण्ड

Bone of contention विवाद-विषय/विवादास्पद विषय

Bonus बोनस

Book adjustment पुस्तक समायोजन **Book Binder** जिल्दसाज —**Keeper** हिसाब-रक्षक/मुनीम —**Keeping Machine Operator** बही-खाता मशीन-प्रचालक —**of reference** संदर्भ पुस्तक —**post** पुस्तक डाक, बुक पोस्ट —**rate** निर्धारित दर —**value** अंकित मूल्य

Booking Clerk टिकट बाबू/बुकिंग क्लर्क —**Assistant Head** सहायक प्रधान टिकट बाबू/सहायक प्रधान बुकिंग क्लर्क —**Chief** मुख्य टिकट बाबू/मुख्य बुकिंग क्लर्क **Supervisor** बुकिंग पर्यवेक्षक

Boom-man बूम-मैन

Booth कोष्ठ/बूथ **Booth, polling** मतदान कोष्ठ/बूथ

Boot Maker मोची **Border Police Inspector** सीमा-पुलिस-निरीक्षक —**Roads Development Board** सीमा-सड़क-विकास-मण्डल

Borer वेधक/बारक **Boring Mechanic** बोरिंग-मेकैनिक —**Mistry** वेधन मिस्त्री —**Operator** बोरिंग-ऑपरेटर

Borne on the books पुस्तकस्थ, बहीखातों में दर्ज

Botanist वनस्पतिज्ञ **Botanical Assistant** वनस्पति सहायक

Bottleneck मार्गाविरोध, अड़चन, बाधा

Bound for को जाने वाला **Bound to accept** स्वीकार करने के लिए बाध्य

Boundary—सीमा; हद; सीमांत **Boundary dispute** सीमा-विवाद

Bowman बोमैन

Boxing Instructor मुक्केबाजी-शिक्षक

Boy बाल/बॉय **Boy Service** किशोर-सेवा

Bracket—कोष्ठक

Brakesman ब्रेक मैन

Branch शाखा

Brand छाप

Breach of Confidence विश्वास-भंग —**of contract** संविदा-भंग/समझौता तोड़ना —**of discipline** अनुशासन भंग —**of law** विधि-भंग/कानून तोड़ना —**of peace** शांति भंग —**of privilege** विशेषाधिकार-भंग **Breach of trust** विश्वास-भंग, न्यास-भंग, अमानत में खयानत

Break clause विच्छेद-खण्ड **Break down** भंग, टूट-फूट, खराबी, विभंग **Break in service** सेवा-भंग, सेवा विच्छेद **Break up** ब्यौरा, विसर्जन, तितर-बितर करना **Breakage** टूटफूट **Breaking point** सहन सीमा, टूटने की स्थिति

Breeder अभिजनक

Brevity संक्षेप

Bribe उत्कोच/घूस/रिश्वत **Bribery** घूसखोरी/रिश्वतखोरी/उत्कोच-ग्रहण

Bridge Engineer सेतु-अभियन्ता/ब्रिज इंजीनियर/पुल इंजीनियर —**Foreman** पुल फोरमैन —**Inspector** पुल निरीक्षक —**Mistry** पुल मिस्त्री —**Officer** सेतु-अधिकारी / ब्रिजअफसर / पुल अधिकारी

Brief पक्षपत्र, पक्ष कथन/ब्रीफ **Brief check-up** सरसरी जांच **Brief for the meeting** बैठक के लिए पक्ष-कथन/ब्रीफ

Brigadier ब्रिगेडियर

Bring forward, to प्रस्तुत/पेश करना **Bring to book, to** दण्ड/सजा देना **Bring round, to** मना लेना

Broadcast प्रसारण **Broadcast, radio** रेडियो-प्रसारण **Broadcasting Station** प्रसारण-केन्द्र

Broadly classified मोटे तौर से वर्गीकृत **Broadly speaking** मोटे तौर से, मोटे रूप से

Broad outline मोटी रूपरेखा —**outlook** विशाल दृष्टिकोण

Brochure विवरणिका **Brochure, informative** सूचनाप्रद विवरणिका

Broker दलाल **Brokerage** दलाली

Bromide Printer ब्रोमाइड मुद्रक

Brought forward पीछे से लाया गया, पिछला जोड़ **Brought over** आगे ले आया गया

Budget बजट/आय-व्ययक **Balanced** संतुलित बजट/संतुलित आय-व्ययक **Budget, capital** पूंजी बजट —**Deficit** घाटे का बजट —**emergency** आपाती बजट

Budget estimate बजट प्राक्कलन/अनुमान —**grant** बजट अनुदान

—**Officer** आय-व्ययक अधिकारी/बजट-अधिकारी —**provision** बजट व्यवस्था —**Reappropriation** विनियोगांतर बजट/पुनर्विनियोग बजट —**Revised** परिशोधित बजट —**Sanctioned** संस्वीकृत बजट —**Section** बजट अनुभाग **Budget speech** बजट भाषण —**Supplementary** पूरकबजट —**Surplus** बचत का बजट

Bugler बिगुलर

Building Clerk निर्माण-क्लर्क/निर्माण लिपिक —**Division** निर्माण-प्रभाग **Building material** इमारती सामान, वस्तु-सामग्री —**Supervisor** निर्माण पर्यवेक्षक

Bulk indent थोक मांग-पत्र **Bulk inspection** सामूहिक निरीक्षण **Bulk of expenditure** व्यय का अधिकांश **Bulk purchase** थोक खरीद

Bulldozer Operator बुलडोजर ऑपरेटर

Bulletin बुलेटिन **Bulletin, daily** दैनिक बुलेटिन

Bullion market सर्राफा बाजार

Bunglow, Inspection निरीक्षण बंगला

Burden of proof सिद्धि भार, सिद्ध करने की जिम्मेदारी, सबूत का जिम्मा

Bureau ब्यरो/कार्यालय/केन्द्र **Bureau, labour** कामगार कार्यालय, मजदूर कार्यालय —**of Document** प्रलेख-ब्यूरो —**of Higher Education** उच्चतर शिक्षा ब्यूरो **Bureau of Information** सूचना ब्यूरो/केन्द्र/कार्यालय —**of Scholarships & Scientific Research** छात्र वृत्ति और वैज्ञानिक अनुसंधान ब्यूरो —**of School Education** स्कूल शिक्षा ब्यूरो

Bureaucracy अधिकारी तंत्र/नौकरशाही **Bureaucratic approach** नौकरशाही रवैया

Burial ground कब्रिस्तान, शवभूमि

Burser बर्सर/कोषाधीक्षक

Bus Driver बस ड्राइवर/बस चालक **Bus stand** बस का अड्डा, बसस्टैण्ड

Business कार्य / काम / कारोबार/व्यवसाय **Business, conduct of** कामकाज/कार्य का संचालन, काम चलाना **Business hours** कार्य-समय के घण्टे —**Manager** व्यवसाय-प्रबन्धक/कारबार प्रबन्धक —**of Government** शासन कार्य, सरकारी काम —**premises** कारबार/व्यापार परिसर/घर —**reply card/envelope** कारबारी जवाबी कार्ड/लिफाफा —**,rules of**

कार्य संचालन नियम

But not exceeding in any case किन्तु किसी भी अवस्था में, से अनधिक

Butler बटलर

By a certain date किसी नियत तारीख तक **By air mail** हवाई डाक से **By authority of** के अधिकार से **By command** के समादेश से **By election** उप-निर्वाचन, उप-चुनाव, बाई-इलेक्शन **By-hand** दस्ती **By force** बलात्. जबरदस्ती, जबरन **By instalment** किस्तों में **By means of** के द्वारा **By order** के आदेश से; के हुकम से **—peon** दस्ती चपरासी **By return of post** लौटती डाक से **By special messenger** विशेष सन्देश वाहक/हरकारे द्वारा **By the way (incidentally)** प्रसंगवश **By virtue of** के नाते, की हैसियत से, के आधार पर **By way of** के रूप में **By way of Penalty** शास्ति स्वरूप

Bye-law उपविधि **Bye election** उपनिर्वाचन, उपचुनाव

Cab कोष्ठ, चालक-कोष्ठ **Cabin Man** केबिन वाला **—Master** केबिन मास्टर

Cabinet मंत्रिमण्डल **—Affairs, Department of** मंत्रिमण्डल कार्य-विभाग **Cabinet Councillor** मंत्रिमण्डल सदस्य **Cabinet drawer** अलमारी का खाना **—Minister** मंत्रिमण्डल सदस्य **—responsibility** मंत्रिमण्डल का उत्तरदायित्व **—Secretariat** मंत्रिमण्डल सचिवालय **—Secretary** मंत्रिमण्डल सचिव

Cable Conductor केबल-कडक्टर **—Foreman** केबल-फोरमैन **—Guard** केबल-रक्षक **—Jointer** केबल-योजक **—Supervisor** केबल-पर्यवेक्षक

Cablegram केबुल-तार

Cadastral Surveyor भूकर-सर्वेक्षक

Cadet कैडेट **—Corps** कैडेट कोर

Cadre संवर्ग/काडर **—Emergency** आपात-संवर्ग/आपात-काडर **Cadre, regular** नियमित संवर्ग/काडर

Calculator 1. गणक/परिकलक, 2. गणित्र/परिकलित्र **Calculated to deceive** धोखा देने के ख्याल से

Calculating Machine Operator परिकलन यंत्र प्रचालक **—Supervisor** परिकलन यंत्र पर्यवेक्षक

Calculation गणना/गिनती/परिकलन **Calculations and rates checked by** ने गणना और दरों की जांच की

Calendar पंचांग; तिथिपत्र; कैलेंडर; पंचांग-पद्धति; कार्यसूची **Calendar**

month कैलेंडर मास **—year** कैलेण्डर/पंचांग वर्ष

Call आह्वान, बुलावा **Call bell** घण्टी **Call book** निलंबित मामलों की बही/कॉलबुक **Call for** मंगवाना, बुलवाना **—for an explanation** जबाबतलबी/स्पष्टीकरण मांगना **—for inspection** निरीक्षण की मांग **—for the file** फाइल या मिसिल मांगना **—in question, to** पर आपत्ति करना **—money** अविलंब राशि **—to account** जवाब तलब करना **Called out service** आहूत सेवा

Calligraphist सुलेखकार/खुशनवीस

Calling व्यवसाय/आजीविका **Calling attention** ध्यान दिलाना/आकर्षित कराना, ध्यानाकर्षण **—tax** व्यवसाय कर **Calls in arrears** बकाया मांग

Camera, in बन्द कमरे में, अप्रकाशनीय **camera, Meeting in** गुप्त बैठक/बंद बैठक **Camera-man** कैमरामैन **—Attendant** कैमरा परिचर

Camp शिविर/कैंप **—Comman-dant** कैंप कमांडेंट **camp equipage** शिविर सामग्री **—equipment** शिविर उपस्कर **—office** शिविर/कैम्प कार्यालय **—Officer** शिविर अधिकारी

Campaign Officer विशेष-प्रचार अधिकारी

Camper शिविरक

Canal Officer नहर-अधिकारी

Cancel रद्द करना **Cancellation** मंसूखी; निरसन; मँसूख होना या करना **Cancellation of allot-ment** आबंटन रद्द करना **—indent** इंडेंट रद्द करना/मांगपत्र रद्द करना **Cancelled** रद्द हुआ; मंसूख किया हुआ; मंसूख; निरसित **Cancelling date** रद्द करने की तारीख

Candidate अभ्यर्थी/प्रार्थी/उम्मीद-वार **Candidate, approved** अनुमोदित उम्मीदवार/अभ्यर्थी **Candidature** अभ्यर्थिता/उम्मीद-वारी

Cane Binder बेंतसाज **—Deve-lopment Officer** इक्षु-विकास-अधिकारी

Canon सिद्धान्त; सामान्य नियम **Canon of equality** समता-नियम

Canteen Adviser कैंटीन-सलाह-कार **—Manager** कैंटीन प्रबंधक **—Supervisor** कैंटीन पर्यवेक्षक

Cantonment Executive Officer छावनी-कार्यपालक अधिकारी

Canvass/Canvassing मतार्थन/मत-याचना/वोट मांगना/प्रचार करना

Capable समर्थ **Capable of doing**

करने योग्य

Capacity क्षमता, धारिता **Capacity of, in the** के रूप में, हैसियत से **Capacity, production** उत्पादन क्षमता

Capita, per प्रति व्यक्ति

Capital 1. पूंजी/मूल धन 2. स्तंभ-शीर्ष 3. राजधानी 4. मृत्यु से दंडनीय **—account** पूंजीगत लेखा **—Cost** पूंजीगत लागत **—expenditure** पूंजीगत व्यय **—outlay** पूंजीगत परिव्यय **—tax** प्रतिव्यक्तिकर **—,working** कार्यकर/कार्यशील पूंजी

Capitation (Polltax) व्यक्ति कर **Capitation fee** प्रतिव्यक्ति शुल्क/फीस

Captain कप्तान/कैप्टन

Capitulation आत्म-समर्पण, हार मानना

Capture बंदीकरण

Carbon Paper कार्बन पेपर

Card, Dead बेकार कार्ड **—guide** निर्देश कार्ड **—index** सूचक कार्ड/पत्र **—name** नाम कार्ड

Care 1. सावधानी 2. परवाह/ 3. देखभाल/रखवाली **Care, does not** परवाह नहीं करता **Care, of** के द्वारा, मार्फत

Career वृत्ति/जीविका/जीवन **Career, academic** शैक्षणिक जीवन **—Educational** शैक्षणिक जीवन **Career, question of** वृत्ति/जीविका का प्रश्न

Careful consideration, after सावधानी से विचार करके

Caretaker रखवाल/अवधायक

Cargo स्थोरा **Cargo arrival notice** माल आगमन सूचना **Carpenter** काष्ठकार/कार्पेन्टर/बढ़ई **—Rigger** काष्ठकार-सज्जक/कार्पेंटर रिगर

Car Refreshment Room Manager यान उपाहार कक्ष प्रबंधक **Carriage and Wagon Inspector** सवारी और माल डिब्बा निरीक्षक **—Cleaner** गाड़ी क्लीनर **—Cleaning Inspector** डिब्बा सफाई निरीक्षक **—Supervisor** डिब्बा सफाई पर्यवेक्षक

Carried down तल शेष/अधोनीत **—forward** अग्रेनीत **—over** आगे ले जाया गया

Carrier वाहक

Carry into effect कार्यान्वित करना; अमल में लाना **Carry on** चलाना **Carry out** कार्यान्वित करना/पालन करना

Cartage गाड़ी-भाड़ा/ढुलाई **Carte blanche** कोरा पत्र, पूर्णाधिकार पत्र

Cartographer मानचित्रकार/नक्शा-नवीस

Cartoonist व्यंग-चित्रकार

Case 1. मामला/विषय/ 2. स्थिति **Case, in this** इस मामले/प्रकरण/विषय में **Case of, in** की दशा में, की अवस्था में, स्थिति में **Case of need, in** आवश्यकता पड़ने पर **Case should pend till** तक मामला रोक रखा जाय

Cash 1. रोकड़, नकद 2. नकदी भुनाना **Cash and carry** नकद दो और माल उठाओ **Cash balance** रोकड़ शेष/बाकी **Cash book** रोकड़ बही **—Clerk** रोकड़ क्लर्क **—Counter** 1. रोकड़ पटल/रोकड़ काउंटर 2. रोकड़ संगणक **—Counter Clerk** 1. रोकड़ संगणक क्लर्क 2. रोकड़ पटल क्लर्क **Cash in hand** हाथ रोकड़ **Cash memo** नकद पर्ची, कैश मेमो **—Section** नकदी अनुभाग, रोकड़ अनुभाग **Cashier** रोकड़िया **—, Chief** मुख्य रोकड़िया

Cassab कस्साब/कसाई

Cast मन देना **Caster** ढलाईकार **Casting vote** निर्णायक मत **Castings** ढली वस्तुएं

Casual discussion आकस्मिक-चर्चा **Casual employee** नैमित्तिक-कर्मचारी **Casual employment** सामयिक नियुक्ति/रोज़गार **—labour** नैमित्तिक श्रम/मजदूर **—labourer** नैमित्तिक मजदूर **—leave** आकस्मिक छुट्टी **—vacancy** आकस्मिक रिक्ति

Casualty Officer आपात् अधिकारी कैजुएल्टी अफसर **—report** हताहत रिपोर्ट **—ward** हताहत कक्ष

Casusbelli युद्ध का कारण

Cause वाद; मामला; मुकदमा; केस

Catalogue ग्रंथ-सूची/सूची-पत्र **Catalogue of books** पुस्तक-सूची, ग्रंथ सूची **Cataloguer** सूचीकार

Catch word सूचक शब्द

Category वर्ग/श्रेणी/दर्जा/कोटि **Category of employees** कर्मचारियों का वर्ग/श्रेणी

Caterer भोज-प्रबंधक **Catering** भोजन-प्रबंध **—Inspector** भोजन-प्रबंध निरीक्षक/खानपान निरीक्षक **—Supervisor** खानपान पर्यवेक्षक

Cattle Development Officer पशु-विकास-अधिकारी **—Sterility Officer** पशु-वंध्यता-अधिकारी

Cause and effect कार्य-कारण **Cause of action** वाद का कारण **Cause to be laid** रखवाना

Caused by के कारण हुई, से उत्पन्न

Caution, as a matter of सावधानी के तौर पर **Caution money** अवधान-द्रव्य

Caveat empter क्रेता सावधान

Cease fire युद्ध-विराम **Cease to have effect** प्रभावी न रहना, प्रभावशून्य होना

Ceiling (as of price) उच्चतम सीमा **—money** अवधान-द्रव्य **—price** शिखर मूल्य, अधिकतम मूल्य **—rate** अधिकतम दर

Celebration समारोह

Cell. कोष्ठ/कक्ष/प्रकोष्ठ

Censor सेंसर **—Officer** सेंसर अधिकारी

Censure परिनिन्दा/निन्दा-प्रस्ताव **Censure motion** निन्दा प्रस्ताव **—Vote of** निन्दा-प्रस्ताव

Censured, he was उसकी परिनिन्दा की गई

Census Officer जनगणना-अधिकारी **Census of population** जनगणना

Cent per cent शत प्रतिशत

Central agency section केन्द्रीय एजेंसी अनुभाग **Central Board of Excise and Customs** केन्द्रीय उत्पाद-शुल्क और सीमा-शुल्क मण्डल **—Board of Irrigation and Power** केन्द्रीय सिंचाई और बिजली मण्डल **—Board of Secondary Education** केन्द्रीय माध्यमिक शिक्षा मण्डल **—Building Research Institute** केन्द्रीय भवन-निर्माण अनुसंधान संस्थान **—Bureau of Correctional Services** राष्ट्रीय समाज रक्षक निदेशालय **—Bureau of Educational and Vocational Guidance** केन्द्रीय शिक्षा और व्यवसाय मार्गदर्शन ब्यूरो **—Bureau of Investigation** केन्द्रीय अन्वेषण-ब्यूरो **—Claims Organisation** केन्द्रीय दावा संगठन **—Detective Training School** केन्द्रीय जासूसी प्रशिक्षण स्कूल **—Drug Research Institute** केन्द्रीय औषध-अनुसंधान संस्थान **—Electro-Chemical Research Institute** केन्द्रीय विद्युत-रसायन-अनुसंधान संस्थान **—Electronic Engineering Research Institute** केन्द्रीय इलैक्ट्रॉनिक-इंजीनियरी अनुसंधान संस्थान **—Emergency Relief Training Institute** केन्द्रीय आपात-सहायता प्रशिक्षण संस्थान **—Excise Collectorate** केन्द्रीय उत्पादशुल्क कलक्टरी/केन्द्रीय उत्पादशुल्क समाहर्तालय **—Tariff** केन्द्रीय उत्पादशुल्क दरसूची

—**Finger-print Bureau** केन्द्रीय अंगुलि-छाप ब्यूरो —**Forensic Institute** केन्द्रीय न्यायालयिक संस्थान —**Fuel Research Institute** केन्द्रीय ईंधन-अनुसंधान संस्थान —**Glass and Ceramic Research Institute** केन्द्रीय कांच और मृत्तिका अनुसंधान संस्थान **Central Government** केन्द्रीय सरकार **Central Government Health Service** केन्द्रीय सरकार स्वास्थ्य सेवा —**Hindi Directorate** केन्द्रीय हिन्दी निदेशालय **Indian —Medicinal Plants Organisation** केन्द्रीय भारतीय औषधि पादप संगठन —**Inspectorate** केन्द्रीय निरीक्षालय —**Institute for Training in Industrial Relations** केन्द्रीय उद्योग-संबंध-प्रशिक्षण संस्था **Centre of Education** केन्द्रीय शिक्षा-संस्थान **of Fisheries Operatives** केन्द्रीय मीन-उद्योग परिचालन संस्थान —**of Research and Training in Employment Service** केन्द्रीय अनुसंधान तथा रोजगार प्रशिक्षण-सेवा-संस्थान —**Investigation Agency** केन्द्रीय अन्वेषण-एजेंसी —**Leather Research Institute** केन्द्रीय चर्म-अनुसंधान संस्थान —**Mechanical Engineering Research Institute** केन्द्रीय यांत्रिक - इंजीनियरी - अनुसंधान संस्थान —**Mining Research Station** केन्द्रीय-खनन अनुसंधान केन्द्र —**Ordnance Depot** केन्द्रीय आयुध डिपो/केन्द्रीय आर्डनेन्स डिपो —**Provident Fund Commissioner** केन्द्रीय भविष्य निधि आयुक्त —**Public Health Engineering Research Institute** केन्द्रीय लोक-स्वास्थ्य इंजीनियरी अनुसंधान संस्थान —**Public Works Department** केन्द्रीय लोक-निर्माण विभाग **Central Registry** केन्द्रीय रजिस्ट्री —**Road Research Institute** केन्द्रीय सड़क-अनुसंधान संस्थान —**Revenue** केन्द्रीय राजस्व —**Salt and Marine Chemical Research Institute** केन्द्रीय नमक और समुद्री रसायन अनुसंधान संस्थान —**Scientific Instruments Organisation** केन्द्रीय वैज्ञानिक यंत्र संगठन —**Secretariat** केन्द्रीय सचिवालय **Central Service** केन्द्रीय सेवा —**Social Welfare Board** केन्द्रीय समाज-कल्याण मण्डल —**Statistical Organisation** केन्द्रीय सांख्यिकीय संगठन —**Storage**

Department केन्द्रीय संचयन विभाग **Central Tabulation Unit** केन्द्रीय सारणीयन एकक **—Tasar Research Station** केन्द्रीय टसर अनुसंधान केन्द्र **—Tobacco Research Institute** केन्द्रीय तम्बाकू अनुसंधान संस्थान **—Vigilance Commissioner** केन्द्रीय सतर्कता आयुक्त **—Wage Board for Plantation and Mining Industry** केन्द्रीय पादप-रोपण और खनन-उद्योग मजदूरी परिषद् **—Water and Power Commission** केन्द्रीय पानी और बिजली आयोग

Centralised item केन्द्रीकृत मदद

Centre केन्द्र **Centre, examination** परीक्षा केन्द्र

Ceramic Expert मृत्तिका-शिल्प-विशेषज्ञ **Ceramist** मृत्तिका-शिल्पी

Cerealist धान्यविद्

Ceremony समारोह, गृह्यकर्म **Ceremonial parade** समारोह-परेड **Ceremony, swearing-in** शपथ-समारोह

Certain day, on a किसी नियत/निश्चित दिन

Certainty, with निश्चयपूर्वक

Certificate प्रमाण-पत्र **—Character** चरित्र-प्रमाणपत्र **—,Last pay** अन्तिम वेतन प्रमाणपत्र **—Medical** चिकित्सा-प्रमाणपत्र **—of competence** सक्षमता प्रमाणपत्र **—Officer** प्रमाण-अधिकारी/सर्टिफिकेट अफसर **Certificate of fitness** आरोग्य-प्रमाण पत्र **—of fund** निधि प्रमाण-पत्र **—of identity** पहचान पत्र **—of posting** डाक प्रमाण-पत्र, तैनाती प्रमाण-पत्र

Certification प्रमाणन/प्रमाणीकरण **Certification of shares** शेयरों/अंशों का प्रमाणन **—Centre** प्रमाणीकरण केन्द्र

Certified Copy प्रमाणित प्रति/प्रमाणित नकल **Certified that** प्रमाणित किया जाता है कि

Certify प्रमाणित करना/तसदीक करना/प्रमाण देना **Certifying Surgeon** प्रमाणक सर्जन

Certiorari उत्प्रेषण लेख

Cess उपकर **—Revaluation Officer** उपकर-पुनर्मूल्यन अधिकारी **Cess, sugarcane** गन्ना उपकर

Cessation समाप्ति/विराम

Chainman जरीबी/चेनमैन **Chain of circumstances** परिस्थितियों/घटनाओं की श्रृंखला

Chairman सभापति/अध्यक्ष **Chairman, ex-officio** पदेन सभापति/अध्यक्ष **Chairman, Railway Service Commission**

अध्यक्ष, रेल सेवा आयोग

Challan चालान **Challandar** चालानदार **Chamber of Commerce** वाणिज्य-मण्डल **Chamber of princes** नरेन्द्र मण्डल

Chancellor कुलाधिपति **—Pro-** सम कुलाधिपति **—Pro-Vice-** सम-कुलपति **— Vice-**कुलपति

Chancery चांसरी

Change slip परिवर्तन पर्ची

Channel माध्यम सरणि **Channel of correspondence** पत्र-व्यवहार की सरणि **Channel, through proper** उचित माध्यम से

Chapter अध्याय **Chapter, new** नया अध्याय

Character चरित्र **Character roll** चरित्र-पुरतन

Charge (n.) 1. चार्ज 2. खर्च/प्रभार 3. कार्यभार 4. आरोप (vb.) 1. आरोप लगाना 2. चार्ज **Charge, assumption of** कार्यभार ग्रहण **—contingent** आकस्मिक खर्च, प्रासंगिक खर्च **—free of** निःशुल्क, बिना मूल्य **— freight** भाड़ा प्रभार **—Relinquishment of** कार्यभार-त्याग **— pay** कार्यभार वेवन **—report** कार्यभार-रिपोर्ट **—sheet** आरोप-पत्र **— over** अतिमूल्य; अतिप्रभार **Charge 'd' Affairs (ad interim)** कार्यदूत (अस्थायी) **—(en pied)** कार्यदूत (स्थायी)

Chargeable आदेय **Charged off Stores** वस्तुएं **Chargehand** चार्ज हैंड/कार्यविक्षक **—(lettering)** कार्यविक्षक (अक्षर-लेखन) **Chargeman** चार्जमैन/कार्येक्षक **—Aerated water Factory** कार्येक्षक, वातिल जल कारखाना **—Assistant** सहायक चार्जमैन **— (Inspection)** चार्जमैन (निरीक्षण) **Chargeman (Planning)** चार्जमैन (योजना) **—(Progress)** चार्जमैन (प्रगति) **—(Signal)** चार्जमैन (सिगनल) **—of Fitters** फिटर चार्जमैन

Charges, Convict बंदी संबंधी व्यय **—depreciation** मूल्यह्रास प्रभार **—fixed** नियत प्रभार **—hot & cold weather** मौसमी खर्च **— maintenance** अनुरक्षण व्यय **—overhead** ऊपरी खर्च या खर्च; सामान्य फुटकर खर्च **—Static** निश्चल प्रभार या खर्चे **—water** जल शुल्क

Charitable endowment पूर्त्त अक्षयनिधि **Charitable Trust** पूर्त्त न्यास **Charity Commissioner** पूर्त्त-आयुक्त

Chart चार्ट **Chart, duty** ड्यूटी

का चार्ट

Charter भाड़े पर लेना **Chartered Accountant** सनदी लेखापाल/चार्टरित लेखापाल **Chartered aircraft** भाड़े पर लिया वायुयान

Chaser चेज़र, अनुवीक्षक **Chasing Assistant** अनुवीक्षण सहायक

Chauffeur of Staff Car स्टाफ-कार-चालक

Cheapest route सबसे सस्ता रास्ता, न्यूनतम किराये वाला रास्ता

Check (n.) 1. पड़ताल 2. रोक **(vb.)** 1. पड़ताल करना 2. रोकना **—Clerk** पड़ताल क्लर्क **Check test** जांच परीक्षण **—Measuring Officer** माप-परीक्षण अधिकारी **Check Sheet** पड़ताल-पत्र **—Superviser** पड़ताल-पर्यवेक्षक **—weightment** परीक्षणार्थ तुलाई, पड़ताल के रूप में तोलना **Checked and found correct** पड़ताल की ओर ठीक पाया **Checker** पड़तालकर्ता/चेकर **Checking and scrutiny of indent** इंडेन्ट या मांगपत्र की जांच और छानबीन **Checking Officer** पड़ताल-अधिकारी

Chemical analyser रसायन-विश्लेषक **Chemical and Metallurgical Assistant** रसायन और धातुकर्म सहायक **Chemical division** रसायन प्रभाग **—Examiner** रसायन-परीक्षक **—Examination** रासायनिक परीक्षण **Chemical industry** रसायन उद्योग **Chemist** रसायनज्ञ, रसायनविज्ञानी

Cheque चेक **Cheque, outdated** पूर्वदिनांकित चैक; पूर्व तारीखी चैक **—bearer** धनी जोग चैक **—crossed** शाहजोग चैक, क्रास किया चैक **—order** नाम जोग चैक **—Endorsed** बेचान चैक

Chief मुख्य/प्रमुख **Chief Advertising Assistant** मुख्य विज्ञापन सहायक **—Adviser, Factories** मुख्य फैक्टरी सलाहकार **—Auditor** मुख्य लेखा-परीक्षक **—Auditor, Commercial Accounts** मुख्य लेखा-रीक्षक, वाणिज्य-लेखा **—Cashier** मुख्य खजांची **—and Pay Master** मुख्य खजांची और वेतनपाल **—Paymenter** मुख्य खजांची तथा भुगतान कर्ता **—Cash Witness** मुख्य रोकड़ साक्षी **—Catering Inspector** मुख्य खान-पान निरीक्षक **—Clerk** मुख्य क्लर्क **—Commercial Superintendent** मुख्य वाणिज्य-अधीक्षक **—Conservator of Forests** महावनपाल **—Controller** मुख्य

नियंत्रक —**Printing and Stationery** मुख्य नियंत्रक, मुद्रण तथा लेखन-सामग्री —**of Imports and Exports** मुख्य नियंत्रक, आयात-निर्यात **Chief Crane Inspector** मुख्य क्रेन निरीक्षक —**(Defence)** चीफ (प्रतिरक्षा) —**Design Assistant** मुख्य अभिकल्प सहायक —**Electrical Engineer** मुख्य बिजली इंजीनियर —**Engineer** मुख्य इंजीनियर —**, Central Public Works Department** मुख्यइंजीनियर, केन्द्रीय लोक निर्माण विभाग/मुख्य अभियंता, केन्द्रीय लोक निर्माण विभाग —**, Electric Supply** मुख्य इंजीनियर, बिजली पूर्ति —**Water Supply** मुख्य इंजीनियर, जल पूर्ति —**Enquiry and Reservation Supervisor** मुख्य पूछताछ और आरक्षण पर्यवेक्षक —**Estimator** मुख्य प्राक्कलक —**Good Shed Superintendent** मुख्य माल गोदाम अधीक्षक —**Grainshop Inspector** मुख्य खाद्यान्न दुकान निरीक्षक —**Inspector wireless (Maintenance)** मुख्य निरीक्षक-बेतार (अनुरक्षण) **Chief Inspector, wireless (Transmission)** मुख्य निरीक्षक, बेतार (प्रेषण) —**Jig and Tool Designer** मुख्य जिग और औजार अभिकल्पक —**Judge** मुख्य न्यायाधीश —**Justice** मुख्य न्यायमूर्ति —**Labour Commissioner** मुख्य श्रम-आयुक्त —**Law Assistant** मुख्य विधि सहायक —**Luggage Clerk** मुख्य सामान क्लर्क —**Mechanical Draftsman** मुख्य यांत्रिक प्रारूपकार —**Engineer** मुख्य यांत्रिक इंजीनियर —**(carriage and wagon)** मुख्य यांत्रिक इंजीनियर (सवारी और माल डिब्बा) —**Medical Officer** मुख्य चिकित्सा अधिकारी —**(Locomotive)** मुख्य यांत्रिक इंजीनियर(रेल इंजन)**(workshop)** मुख्य यांत्रिक इंजीनियर(कर्मशाला) **Chief Minister / Secretary** मुख्य मंत्री/सचिव —**Officer (Marine)** मुख्य अधिकारी (समुद्री) —**of Air Staff** वायुसेनाध्यक्ष/चीफ ऑफ एयर स्टाफ —**of Army Staff** थल सेनाध्यक्ष/चीफ ऑफ आर्मी स्टाफ —**of Engineering Services** इंजीनियरी सेवा प्रमुख —**of Materials** सामग्री के प्रमुख/चीफ आफ मेटीरियल्स —**of Naval Staff** नौ-सेनाध्यक्ष/चीफ ऑफ नेवल स्टाफ —**of Protocol** नयाचार-प्रमुख/प्रोतोकोल प्रमुख —**of Staff**

स्टाफ का अध्यक्ष/चीफ ऑफ स्टाफ —**Operating Superintendent** मुख्य परिचालन अधीक्षक—**Parcel Inspector** मुख्य पार्सल निरीक्षक —**Parcel Clerk** मुख्य पार्सल क्लर्क —**Pay and Accounts Officer** मुख्य भुगतान और लेखा अधिकारी **Personnel Officer** मुख्य कार्मिक अधिकारी —**Photographer** मुख्य फोटोग्राफर —**Planner and Estimator** मुख्य योजनाकार और प्राक्कलक **Chief Press Adviser** मुख्य प्रेस-सलाहकार —**Principal Matron** मुख्य प्रधान मैट्रन/चीफ प्रिंसिपल मैट्रन —**Progress Inspector** मुख्य प्रगति निरीक्षक —**Publicity Assistant** मुख्य प्रचार सहायक —**Public Relations Officer** मुख्य जन-संपर्क अधिकारी —**Security Officer** मुख्य सुरक्षा अधिकारी —**Signal and Telecommunication Engineer** मुख्य सिगनल और दूरसंचार इंजीनियर —**Inspector** मुख्य सिगनल निरीक्षक —**Statistical Inspector** मुख्य सांख्यिकी निरीक्षक —**Telecommunication Inspector** मुख्य दूरसंचार निरीक्षक —**Telegraph Inspector** मुख्य तार निरीक्षक —**Ticket Inspector** मुख्य टिकट निरीक्षक —**Traction Power Controller** मुख्य कर्षण शक्ति नियंत्रक —**Trade Instructor** मुख्य व्यवसाय शिक्षक—**Train Examiner** मुख्य गाड़ी परीक्षक —**Transhipment Inspector** मुख्य यानांतरण निरीक्षक —**Transit Inspector** मुख्य परिवहन निरीक्षक —**Travelling Ticket Inspector** मुख्य चल टिकट निरीक्षक —**Vigilance Inspector** मुख्य सतर्कता निरीक्षक —**whip** मुख्य सचेतक —**wireless Mechanic** मुख्य बेतार मेकैनिक —**wireless Traffic Inspector** मुख्य बेतार यातायात निरीक्षक —**Yard Master** मुख्य यार्ड मास्टर

Childhood शैशव **Child welfare** बाल-कल्याण **Child welfare centre** बाल कल्याण केन्द्र

Children education allowance संतान-शिक्षण भत्ता

Chit चिट, पर्ची

Choose चुनना

Chronological order कालक्रम

Cinder keeper सिंडर रक्षक

Cine Cameraman सिने-कैमरामैन **Cine Mechanic** सिने मेकैनिक —**Projector Operator** सिने-प्रक्षेपित्र प्रचालक

Cinema Operator चलचित्र-

प्रचालक/सिनेमा ऑपरेटर/सिनेमा प्रचालक

Cipher Bureau बीज लेख ब्यूरो

Circle इलाका/अंचल **—Commander** सर्किल कमांडर **—Inspector** इलाका निरीक्षक **Circle Service** मण्डल सेवा; परिमण्डल सेवा

Circuit Court दौरा न्यायालय **Circuit House** सर्किट हाउस

Circular गश्ती चिट्ठी/परिपत्र **Circular letter** परिपत्र, गश्ती चिट्ठी **Circular number** परिपत्रांक **Circulate (as a notice)** घुमाना/परिचालित करना **Circulate and then file** परिचालित/घुमा करके इसे फाइल किया गया **Circulated for eliciting Public opinion** जनमत जानने के लिये घुमाया गया **Circulation** परिचालन

Circumstances परिस्थितियाँ **Circumstances exist which render it necessary** ऐसी परिस्थितियां वर्तमान हैं जिनसे यह आवश्यक हो गया है कि **Circumstantial evidence** परिस्थितिगत-साक्ष्य

Citation उद्धरण विरुद पत्र **Citizen** नागरिक

Citizenship नागरिकता; पौरत्व

City नगर/शहर **City allowance** नगर भत्ता **—Father** नगर-पिता **—Magistrate** नगर-मजिस्ट्रेट

Civil सिविल **—Armament and Production Directorate** सिविल आर्मामेंट तथा उत्पादन निदेशालय/सिविल आयुध तथा उत्पादन निदेशालय **—Aviation, Department of** सिविल विमानन विभाग **—authority** सिविल प्राधिकारी; असैनिक प्राधिकारी **—Court** सिविल न्यायालय **Civil Creditnote** सिविल जमा-पत्र **—Defence Officer** सिविल रक्षा अधिकारी/सिविल रक्षा अफसर **—Instructors' Course** सिविल रक्षा शिक्षक पाठ्यक्रम **—Lady Officers' Course** सिविल रक्षा महिला अधिकारी पाठ्यक्रम **—Staff Course** सिविल रक्षा कर्मचारी पाठ्यक्रम **—dispensary** नगर औषधालय; सिविल औषधालय **—Engineer** सिविल इंजीनियर/सिविल अभियंता **Civil List** सिविल सूची **—Judge** सिविल न्यायाधीश **—law** दीवानी विधि/कानून **—liberty** नागरिक स्वतन्त्रता **—list** अधिकारी-सूची, सिविल-सूची **—Obligation** वैध दायित्व **—office** असैनिक/सिविल पद **—procedure** सिविल/दीवानी

प्रक्रिया —**rights** नागरिक अधिकार —**society** सभ्य/समाज —**specification** सिविल विशिष्टि —**Supplies** सिविल रसद/सिविल पूर्ति **Civil Supplies and rationing, department of** सिविल रसद और राशन-विभाग —**Service** सिविल सेवा —**Surgeon** सिविल सर्जन **Civil war** गृह युद्ध **Civilian Passage Officer** सिविल यात्रा अधिकारी

Claim (**n.**) दावा (**vb.**) दावा करना **Claim accepted** दावा स्वीकृत **Claim as right** अधिकार के रूप में मांगना, अधिकार के रूप में दावा करना —**for refund** धन वापसी का दावा —**Officer** दावा-अधिकारी **Claimant** दावेदार/दावी **Claimant, right** सही दावेदार **Claiming under** के अधीन दावा करने वाले **Claims, arrear** बकाया दावे **Claims, double** दोहरे दावे —**erroneous** भ्रांत दावे —**established** स्थापित दावे —**false** झूठे दावे —**genuine** वास्तविक दावे —**genuineness of** दावों की वास्तविकता —**Petty** छोटे दावे **Claims Inspector** दावा निरीक्षक —**Prevention Inspector** दावानिवारण निरीक्षक —**Prevention** दावा निवारण संगठन —**Tracer** दावा खोजकर्ता **Claims, Certified** सत्यापित दावे

Clarification स्पष्टीकरण **clarification sought** स्पष्टीकरण मांगा गया

Class I Central Service प्रथम श्रेणी केन्द्रीय सेवा **Class I Officer** प्रथम श्रेणी अधिकारी **Class I service** प्रथम श्रेणी सेवा **Class of persons** वर्ग-विशेष **Classed with alphabetical slip** वर्णक्रमपर्ची द्वारा वर्गीकृत **Classical Language Teacher** श्रेण्य भाषा शिक्षक **Classification of posts** पदों का वर्गीकरण **Classification of service** सेवा-वर्गीकरण **Classification of stores** सामान का वर्गीकरण **Classified advertisment** वर्गीकृत विज्ञापन

Clause खंड **Clause, under** खंड के अन्तर्गत

Clean copy साफ/स्वच्छ प्रति **Cleaner** क्लीनर —,**Engine** इंजन क्लीनर —,**Loco** लोको क्लीनर

Clear day पूरा दिन **Clear notice of a month** पूरे एक मास की सूचना **Clear notice of a week** पूरे एक सप्ताह का नोटिस

Clear vacancy स्पष्ट रिक्ति, स्पष्ट रूप से खाली जगह **Clearly unjust** स्पष्टतः अन्यायपूर्ण **Clearing Agent** निकासी-अभिकर्ता/निकासी एजेंट

Clerical error लेखन अशुद्धि/लेखन-त्रुटि/लिखाई की भूल **Clerical service/staff** लिपिक सेवा/वर्ग —**Staff** लिपिकवर्ग

Clerk क्लर्क/लिपिक —**, Assistant** सहायक क्लर्क —**,Chief** मुख्य क्लर्क —**,Head** प्रधान क्लर्क

Climate, proper अनुकूल वातावरण/जलवायु **Climatologist** जलवायु-विज्ञानी

Clinic क्लिनिक/निदानशाला

Cloak room क्लोक रूम/यात्री सामान घर

Clock Mechanic घड़ी मेकैनिक

Close समाप्ति **Close an account** लेखा/हिसाब बन्द करना **Close by** निकट **Close co-operation** घनिष्ट/प्रगाढ़ सहयोग —**liasion** गहरा संपर्क **Close of the year** वर्ष की समाप्ति **Close the books** खाते बन्द करना **Closing balance** अंतशेष/रोकड़ बाकी —**date** अन्तिम तारीख **Closure** समाप्ति/समापन

Clothing Factory Foreman वस्त्र फैक्टरी फोरमैन —**Store Inspector** वस्त्र भण्डार निरीक्षक —**Officer** वस्त्र-अधिकारी

Co (as in Co-Chairman) सह **co-administrator** सह-प्रशासक

Coaching Inspector कोचिंग निरीक्षक

Coal कोयला **Coal allotment Inspector** कोयला आवंटन निरीक्षक —**Commissioner** आयुक्त —**Cutter** कोयला-कटर **Distributing Inspector** कोयला वितरण निरीक्षक —**Checker** कोयला पड़तालकर्ता —**Distributor Inspector** कोयला वितरक निरीक्षक —**Inspector** कोयला निरीक्षक **Keeper** कोयला रक्षक **Mining Adviser** कोयला-खनन सलाहकार —**Plant Supervisor** कोयला संयंत्र पर्यवेक्षक —**Tracer** कोयला अनुरेखक —**Transport Officer** कोयला-परिवहन अधिकारी

Coalition Ministry संयुक्त/मिला-जुला मंत्रिमण्डल

Co-arbitrator सह-विवाचक

Coastal तटीय/तटवर्ती

Code 1. संहिता 2. कोड/संकेत —**, Morse** मोर्स कोड

Code, penal दण्ड-संहिता **Code word** संकेत शब्द, कोड शब्द **Codification** संहिताकरण **Codification of rules** नियमों का

संहिताकरण **Codification Officer** संहताकरण-अधिकारी

Co-education सह-शिक्षा

Coercion अवपीड़न/बलप्रयोग/जोर जबर्दस्ती

Co-examiner सह-परीक्षक

Cognizable offence संज्ञेय/हस्त-क्षेप्य अपराध

Coherence संगति/संबद्धता

Coil Winder कुंडली वलयक

Coincidence संपात **Coincidence, as a** संयोग से

Coins Expert सिक्का-विशेषज्ञ **Coins, small** छोटे सिक्के, खरीज

Coir Board Show Room and Sales Depot कॉयर बोर्ड प्रदर्शन कक्ष तथा बिक्री डिपो **Coir Development Officer** कॉयर-विकास अधिकारी

Cold Storage Inspector शीत-संग्रहागार निरीक्षक

Callaboration सहयोग **Collaboration with, in** के सहयोग से

Collateral evidence साम्पार्श्विक साक्ष्य

Collection agent वसूली अभिकर्ता /एजेण्ट **Collection charges** संग्रहण प्रभार, भुनाई/उगाही/वसूली शुल्क **—Tray** संग्रह ट्रे

Collectively सामूहिक रूप से **Collectively responsible** सामूहिक रूप से उत्तरदायी

Collector 1. समाहर्ता/कलक्टर 2. संग्राहक **Collector of Customs** सीमा शुल्क समाहर्ता/कलक्टर **—of Excise** उत्पाद-शुल्क-समाहर्ता

Collectorate समाहर्तालय/कलक्टरी

College महाविद्यालय/कालेज

Colliery Manager कोलियरी मैनेजर

Collusion दुरभिसंधि

Colonel कर्नल **—of the Regiment** रेजिमेंट का कर्नल **in-Chief of the Regiment** रेजिमेंट का कर्नल-इन-चीफ

Colonial Secretary उपनिवेश सचिव **Colonisation** उपनिवेशन

Colony 1. उपनिवेश 2. बस्ती/कॉलोनी

Column स्तंभ/खाना **Columnist** स्तंभ-लेखक **Columns provided in the form** फार्म में दिए स्तम्भों/खानों में

Combined operation संयुक्त क्रिया

Come into force लागू होना **—into operation** चालू होना

Command 1. कमान 2. समादेश **Command, Western** पश्चिमी कमान **Commandant** कमांडेंट **Commander** कमांडर **—of**

Vessel पोत-कमांडर **—in-Chief** कमांडर-इन-चीफ **Commanding Officer** कमान-अफसर

Commemoration स्मारक

Commencement प्रारम्भ **Commencement of session** सत्रारम्भ, सत्र का आरम्भ

Commendatory letter सिफारिशी पत्र

Commensurate अनुरूप **Commensurate with labour** मेहनत के अनुरूप

Comment टीका/टिप्पणी **Commentarv, Running** चल-विवरण/चल-वृत्तांत/आंखों देखा हाल **Commentator** 1. विवरणकार 2. टीकाकार **Comments, for** टीका/टिप्पणी के लिए

Commerce, Ministry of वाणिज्य मन्त्रालय **Commerical Artist** वाणिज्य-कलाकार **—Inspector** वाणिज्य निरीक्षक **—(Ticket)** वाणिज्य निरीक्षक (टिकट) **—Instructor** वाणिज्य शिक्षक **—Publicity Officer** वाणिज्य प्रचार अधिकारी **—,Directorate of** वाणिज्य प्रचार निदेशालय **—Superintendent** वाणिज्य अधीक्षक **—Supervisor** वाणिज्य पर्यवेक्षक **—Tax Department** वाणिज्य-कर-विभाग **—Officer** वाणिज्य-कर-अधिकारी **Commercial wing** वाणिज्य-स्कंध

Commission 1. आयोग/कमीशन 2. दलाली/कमीशन/आढ़त **—(as of crime)** कमीशन करना **—,Bring into** प्रवर्तन करना **Commission, emergency** आपाती कमीशन/आयोग **Commission of enquiry** जांच आयोग **Commission of an offence** अपराध करना **Commission, regular** स्थायी कमीशन; स्थायी समादेश **—Temporary** अस्थायी कमीशन **—Vendor** 1. आढ़ती विक्रेता/कमीशनी विक्रेता 2. कमीशनी खोमचे वाला **Commissionaire** द्वारपाल **Commissioned Officer** आयुक्त-अफसर/कमीशन प्राप्त अधिकारी **Commissioner** आयुक्त/कमिश्नर **—for Departmental Enquiries** विभागीय-जांच-आयुक्त **—for Excess Profit Tax** अतिरिक्त-लाभकर-आयुक्त **—for Linguistic Minorities** भाषाई अल्पसंख्यकों के आयुक्त **—for Scheduled Castes and Scheduled Tribes** अनुसूचित जाति और अनुसूचित आदिम-जाति आयुक्त

Commit 1. करना 2. सुपुर्द करना/भेजना 3. वचनबद्ध होना/वचनबद्ध

करना **Commitment** सुपुर्दगी

Committee समिति **—On Public Undertakings** लोक उपक्रम समिति **Committee, Standing** स्थायी समिति

Commodity पण्य **Commodity Section** पण्य-अनुभाग

Commodore कमोडोर

Common good सार्वजनिक हित/भलाई **—intention** समान इरादा **—interest** पारस्परिक हित **—law** सामान्य-विधि, रूढ़ि विधि **—roster** सामान्य रोस्टर/सामान्य नामावली **—seal** सामान्य मुद्रा **—to all** सर्व साधारण के लिए

Commonwealth राष्ट्रमण्डल; कामनवेल्थ **Commonwealth Secretary** राष्ट्रमंडल-सचिव

Communal सांप्रदायिक **Communal riot** साम्प्रदायिक दंगा

Communicable diseases संचारी-रोग विभाग **Communicated by telegram** तार द्वारा सूचित

Communication 1. संचार 2. संसूचना/संदेश 3. पत्रादि-व्यवहार 4. संप्रेषण **Communication, means of** संचार साधन **—Officer** संचार-अधिकारी **Communications, Ministry of** संचार-मन्त्रालय **Communications received** प्राप्त संसूचनाएं/संदेश

Communique विज्ञप्ति **Communique, press** प्रेस विज्ञप्ति

Community समुदाय। लोक समाज **Community Centre** समुदाय केन्द्र/सामुदायिक केन्द्र **—Development, Department of** सामुदायिक विकास विभाग **—,Block** सामुदायिक विकास खण्ड

Community hall समाज सदन **Community, minority** अल्प संख्यक जाति **Community Project** सामुदायिक प्रायोजना **Community project administration** सामुदायिक प्रायोजना प्रशासन

Commutation परिवर्तन **Commutation of leave into** छुट्टी का···में परिवर्तन **Commutation (of pension or leave etc.)** लघुकरण/परिवर्तन

Commute लघुकरण करना

Company Commandant कम्पनी कमांडेन्ट **—Commander** कम्पनी कमांडर **—Director** कम्पनी संचालक

Comparative तुलनात्मक **Comparative statement** तुलनात्मक विवरण

Comparer मिलानकर्ता **Compared with** की तुलना में, से मिलान किया

Comparing Clerk मिलान-लिपिक **Comparison** 1. तुलना 2. मिलान

Compartment उपखंड/कक्ष/खाना/डिब्बा **Compartment railway** रेल डिब्बा

Compass Adjuster दिक्सूचक समायोजक/कंपास समायोजक

Compassionate Allowance अनुकम्पा भत्ता **Compassionate grounds, on** अनुकम्पा करके, करुणामूलक कारणों से **Compassionate gratuity** अनुकम्पा उपदान

Compatible संकलन **—Inspector** संकलन निरीक्षक **—Officer** संकलन अधिकारी

Compel विवश करना **Compelled to do** करने के लिए विवश

Compendium संग्रह/सार-संग्रह **Compendium of standing orders** स्थायी आदेशों का सारसंग्रह

Compensation प्रतिपूर्ती प्रतिकर/मुआवजा/क्षतिपूर्ति **Compensation for loss** हानि के लिए प्रतिकर/मुआवजा **—Officer** प्रतिकर-अधिकारी/मुआवजा अधिकारी/प्रतिपूर्ति अधिकारी **Compensatory allowance** प्रतिपूरक भत्ता **—holiday** प्रतिपूरक/एवजी छुट्टी **—leave** प्रतिपूरक छुट्टी

Competence सक्षमता/सामर्थ्य/क्षमता **Competency** सक्षमता/सामर्थ्य/क्षमता **Competent** समर्थ/सक्षम **Competent authority** समर्थ/सक्षम अधिकारी **—Financial Author** समर्थ वित्त-प्राधिकारी

Competitive examination प्रतियोगिता परीक्षा **Competitive rate** प्रतियोगी दर

Compilation संगत/अनुरूप **Compilation of data** सामग्री का संकलन **Compiler** संकलन कर्ता

Complaint शिकायत **Complaint book** शिकायत पुस्तक **Complaint Inspector** शिकायत निरीक्षक **—report** शिकायत रिपोर्ट **Complaints Officer** शिकायत-अधिकारी

Complement पूरक **Complementary** पूरक **Complementary to each other** एक दूसरे के पूरक **Complimentary** मानार्थ **Complimentary copy** मानार्थ/उपहार प्रति, सादर भेंट

Complete (adj.) 1. पूर्ण **(vb.)** पूरा करना/समाप्त करना **Complete loss** पूर्ण हानि **Completed statement** पूरा किया गया विवरण **Completed years of Service** सेवा के पूर्ण

वर्ष **Completion certificate** समापन प्रमाण-पत्र **—report** समापन रिपोर्ट

Complex, Industrial औद्योगिक संकुल

Compliance अनुपालन/पालन

Complicated जटिल/उलझनदार **Complicated problem** जटिल समस्या **Complications, serious** गंभीर उलझनें

Complied with पालन किया, कार्यान्वित **—remark** प्रशंसात्मक उक्ति/उल्लेख

Comply with अनुपालन करना/पालन करना **Comply with the requirements** जरूरतें पूरी करना

Composed of मिलकर बनी हुई **Composition** 1. रचना/निर्माण 2. मिश्रण 3. संमिश्रण 4. प्रशमन **Compositor** कम्पोजिटर/अक्षर-योजक

Compost Development Officer कम्पोस्ट-विकास-अधिकारी

Compounder कम्पाउण्डर

Comprehensive data व्यापक सामग्री, सम्पूर्ण जानकारी

Compressor Driver संपीडित्र-चालक

Compromise समझौता **Compromise, as a** समझौते के रूप में

Comptist परिकलन यंत्र-प्रचालक

Comptroller नियंत्रक **Comptroller and Auditor-General** नियंत्रक महालेखा परीक्षक **—of Household** राजभवन-प्रबंधक **— of President's Household** राष्ट्रपति-भवन-प्रबंधक

Compulsory अनिवार्य/बाध्य **Compulsory education** अनिवार्य शिक्षा **—retirement** अनिवार्य सेवा निवृत्ति **—Service** बाध्य सेवा

Computor सगणक **Computing** संगणना करते हुए

Concern 1. प्रतिष्ठान 2. सम्बन्ध **Concern, business** व्यापारिक प्रतिष्ठान **Concerned, I am not** मेरा इससे सम्बन्ध नहीं है **Concerned section** सम्बन्धित अनुभाग **Concerning** संपृक्त

Concession रियायत **Concessional period** रियायत की अवधि **—rate** रियायती दर

Conciliation Officer सुलह-अधिकारी

Concise मिताक्षर, संक्षिप्त

Conclusion 1. समापन 2. निश्चय/परिणाम **Conclusion of, on the** के समापन पर **Conclusions of the conference** सम्मेलन के निश्चय

Conclusive निर्णयात्मक/निर्णायक/

निश्चायक/निश्चयात्मक **Conclusive evidence/proof** निर्णयात्मक/निश्चायक साक्ष्य/प्रमाण

Concrete assets मूर्त परिसम्पत्ति **Concrete cases** प्रत्यक्ष/ठोस उदाहरण **Concrete Depot Foreman** कंक्रीट डिपो फोरमैन **Concrete example** ठोस उदाहरण **—Mixer Driver** कंक्रीट मिश्रक चालक, कंक्रीट मिश्रक ड्राइवर

Concur सहमत होना **Concurrence** सहमति **Concurrent audit** समवर्ती लेखा-परीक्षा **Concurrent jurisdiction** समवर्ती क्षेत्राधिकार **—list** समवर्ती सूची

Condemn 1. अनुपयोगी घोषित करना 2. दंडनीय घोषित करना 3. निन्दा करना **Condemned goods** बेकार/कण्डम माल, अनुपयोगी घोषित किया माल

Condition 1. शर्त/प्रतिबंध 2 दशा/स्थिति **Condition of eligibility** पात्रता की शर्त **Conditional** सशर्त **Conditional acceptance** सशर्त स्वीकृति **Conditions, favourable** अनुकूल परिस्थितियां/अवस्था **Conditions of contract** ठेके की शर्तें/संविदा की शर्तें **—of service** सेवा/नौकरी की शर्तें

Condonation of break भंग माफ/मार्जन करना

Conducive सहायक

Conduct (n.) आचरण **(vb.)** कार्य-संचालन करना **Conduct of business** कार्य संचालन **Conduct rule** आचरण नियम **Conductor** कंडक्टर **—Guard** कंडक्टर गार्ड

Confer 1. प्रदान करना 2. विचार विमर्श करना **Confer on** को प्रदान करना **Confer with** में विचार-विमर्श करना

Conference सम्मेलन **Conference hall** सम्मेलन भवन, कान्फ्रेंस हाल **Conferred** प्रदत्त **Conferred by** द्वारा प्रदत्त

Confession संस्वीकृति

Confidence विश्वास/भरोसा **Confidence, full** पूरा विश्वास/भरोसा **Confidential** 1. **(letter)** गोपनीय 2. **(personal)** अंतरंग **—Assistant** अंतरंग सहायक, गोपनीय सहायक **Confidential Clerk** गोपनीय-लिपिक **—record** गोपनीय अभिलेख **—report** गोपनीय रिपोर्ट

Confined to office कार्यालय तक सीमित

Confirm पुष्टि करना **Confirmation** पुष्टि **Confirmation letter** पुष्टि पत्र **Confirmatory Order** पुष्टि-आदेश **—test** पुष्टि-निरीक्षण **Confirmed report** पुष्टि की गई/

पक्की रिपोर्ट

Confiscate अधिहरण करना/जब्त करना

Confiscated amount जब्त की गई राशि

Conflicting views परस्पर विरोधी विचार

Conformity अनुरूपता/अनुसरण **Conformity with, in** के अनुरूप

Connect संबद्ध करना/जोड़ना **Connected** संबद्ध **Connected papers** सम्बद्ध कागजात **Connecting reference** सम्बन्धी हवाला/संदर्भ **Connection with, in** के सम्बन्ध में **Connection, intimate** घनिष्ठ सम्बन्ध/सम्पर्क

Connivance मौन सहमति/मौनानुकूलता **Connivance of, with the** की मौन सहमति से

Conscientiously शुद्ध अन्तःकरण से

Conscription अनिवार्य सैनिक भर्ती

Consecutive क्रमिक/लगातार **Consecutive days** क्रमिक/लगातार दिन

Consensus of opinion बहुमति, आम राय

Consent (n.) सम्मति/सहमति **(vb)** सहमत होना **Consent, previous** पूर्व सम्मति/सहमति

Consequence परिणाम/फल **Consequence of, in** के परिणाम स्वरूप

Consequent 1. अनुवर्ती 2. परिणामी **Consequent change** परिणामी परिवर्तन **Consequent events** अनुवर्ती घटनाएं **Consequential** आनुषंगिक **Consequently it has been decided that** फलस्वरूप/अतः यह निश्चय हुआ है कि **Conservancy Inspector** मल सफाई निरीक्षक **Conservation** संरक्षण **—Assistant** संरक्षण-सहायक **—Officer** संरक्षण-अधिकारी **—of Wild Life** वनजंतु संरक्षक

Conserve बनाए रखना

Conservation, soil भूमि संरक्षण **Conservator** संरक्षक **Conservator of Forest** वनपाल

Consider विचार करना **Consideration** 1. विचार 2. प्रतिफल **Consideration, after careful** ध्यानपूर्वक विचार करने के पश्चात् **Consideration, under** विचाराधीन **Consideration whether, it is for** विचारणीय है कि क्या

Consign to the record अभिलेखों में डालना/रखना

Consignee परेषिती **Consignee's address** परेषिती का पता

Consignment परेषण
Consignment note परेषण नोट
Consignor परेषक **Consignor's expense, at** परेषक के व्यय पर

Consistent संगत **Consistent with** से संगत के अनुकूल

Consolidated fund संचित निधि, समेकित निधि **Consolidated statement** समेकित/इकट्ठा विवरण **Consolidation of holdings** चकबन्दी **Consolidation Officer** चकबंदी अधिकारी

Conspectus 1. दिग्दर्शन 2. संक्षिप्त विवरण

Constable सिपाही/ कांस्टेबल **—,Head** हवलदार

Constituency निर्वाचन-क्षेत्र **Constitutncy, Parliamentary** संसदीय निर्वाचन-क्षेत्र **Constituent** घटक; अंग **Constituent assembly** संविधान सभा **Constituent Assembly of India** भारतीय संविधान सभा

Constitute संघटन करना/गठन करना **Constituled** गठित **Constituted by** द्वारा गठित

Constitution 1. संघटन/गठन 2. संविधान **Constitution of a Committee** समिति का गठन **Constitution rigid** अनम्य संविधान **Constitutional Convention** संविधान सम्मेलन **—Court** संविधानी न्यायालय **—law** संविधान विधि **—limitation** संविधान बंधन **—officer** संविधान अधिकारी **—process** संविधानी प्रक्रिया **Contitutionalist** संविधानज्ञ

Construct निर्माण करना **Construction Division** 1. निर्माण मंडल 2. निर्माण प्रभाग **—Officer** निर्माण-अधिकारी **Construction work** निर्माण कार्य **Constructive** रचनात्मक **Constructive work** रचनात्मक कार्य

Construe अर्थ लगाना/समझना **Construed, it shall be** इसका यह अर्थ लगाया जायगा, यह समझा जाएगा

Consul कांसुल **—General** महाकांसुल **Consular Attache** कांसुली अताशे **Consular representative** कॉन्सल प्रतिनिधि **Consulate** कांसुलावास **—Generalof India** भारत का महाकांसुलावास

Consult परामर्श करना **Consultant** परामर्शदाता **Consultation** परामर्श **Consultation with, in** से परामर्श करके **Consulting Architect**

परामर्शी स्थपति/परामर्शी वास्तुक **Engineer** परामर्शी अभियंता/ परामर्शी इंजीनियर **—Physician** परामर्शी काय-चिकित्सक/ परामर्शी फिजिशियन

Consume उपभोग करना/उपभोग होना **Consumer goods** उपभोग की/उपभोक्ता वस्तुएं **Consumption** उपभोग **Consumption has increased** खपत बढ़ गई है

Contact संस्पर्श/संपर्क/स्पर्श **Contact with, in** के सम्पर्क में

Contagious सांसर्गिक

Contemplated अवक्षित **Contemplated action** सोची गई कार्रवाई **Cotemplation of, in** को ध्यान में रखते हुए

Contemporary art समकालीन कला

Contempt of court न्यायालय/ अदालत की मानहानि

Contention is untenable तर्क असमर्थनीय है

Contents 1. विषय सूची 2. अंतर्वस्तु 3. अंश **Contents of a letter** पत्र-वस्तु **Contents of the book** पुस्तक की विषय सूची

Context संदर्भ/प्रकरण/प्रसंग **Contingency** विशेष स्थिति/ आकस्मिकता/ प्रासंगिकता **Contingencies** आकस्मिक व्यय/फुटकर व्यय **Contingency fund** आकस्मिकता-निधि **Contingency may arise** आकस्मिकता पैदा हो सकती है, ऐसी विशेष स्थिति आ सकती है

Contingent (adj.) 1. प्रासंगिक 2. समाश्रित (विधि) **(n.)** 3. टुकड़ी (सेना) **Contingent benefit** अनुषंगी लाभ **Contingent bill** फुटकर बिल **Contingent charges** फुटकर/आकस्मिक व्यय **Contingent register** फुटकर खर्च रजिस्टर **Contingent use** सम्भाव्य उपयोग

Continuance of right अधिकार बना रहना **Continuation sheet** अनुवर्ती कागज **Continue in office** पद पर बने रहना **Continue, shall** जारी/चालू रहेगा **Continued from** से आगे **Continued on** शेष पर **Continuing guarantee** अविरत/सतत/ चिरस्थायी प्रत्याभूति/गारन्टी

Continuous acting service अविच्छिन्न कार्यवाहक सेवा **Continuous halt** लगातार अवस्थान

Continuous service अविच्छिन्न/ निरन्तर/ लगातार सेवा **Contraband** निषिद्ध **Contraband goods** निषिद्ध माल

Contract ठेका/संविदा **Contract**

allotment संविदा-नियतन **—Messenger** ठेका-संदेशवाहक/संविदा संदेशवाहक **—Officer** ठेका-अधिकारी/संविदा-अधिकारी **Contract period** ठेके/संविदा की अवधि **Contract Service** संविदा सेवा, इकरारी सेवा **Contractor** ठेकेदार/संविदाकार **Contractual document** ठेका संबंधी प्रलेख/ठेका-प्रलेख/संविदा-प्रलेख

Contradictory विरोधात्मक/विरोधी **Contradictory statements** परस्पर विरोधी कथन, विरोधात्मक बयान

Contrary प्रतिकूल/विपरीत **Contrary to law** कानून/विधि के विपरीत/प्रतिकूल, विधि विरुद्ध

Contravention उल्लंघन

Contribution 1. अंशदान 2. योगदान 3. अभिदान **Contribution, monthly** मासिक अंशदान **Contributory provident fund** अंशदायी भविष्य-निधि **Contribution, valuable** बहुमूल्य योगदान

Control board नियंत्रण-बोर्ड; नियंत्रण-मंडल **Control Cabin Operator** नियंत्रण केबिल प्रचालक **—chart** नियंत्रण चार्ट **—Clerk** नियंत्रण क्लर्क/नियंत्रण लिपिक **Control room** नियंत्रण कक्ष **Control statement** नियंत्रण विवरण **Controlled price** नियन्त्रित मूल्य **Controller** नियंत्रक **—General** महानियंत्रक **—, Defence Production** महा-नियंत्रक, रक्षा-उत्पादन **—, Imports and Exports** महानियंत्रक, आयात और निर्यात

Controller of Capital Issues पूंजी-निर्गम-नियंत्रक **—of Coal Distribution** कोयला वितरण नियंत्रक **—of Communications** संचार नियंत्रक **—of Printing and Stationery** नियंत्रक, मुद्रण तथा लेखन सामग्री **—of Radio Construction and Development Unit** नियंत्रक, रेडियो निर्माण और विकास एकक

Controller of Standardization मानकीकरण-नियंत्रक **—of Stores** भंडार नियंत्रक **—of Telegraph Stores** तार-भंडार-नियंत्रक **—Traffic** तार-यातायात-नियंत्रक **—of Vagrancy** आवारागर्दी नियंत्रक **—of Weights and Measurements** तौल और माप नियंत्रक **Controlling Officer** नियंत्रण अधिकारी

Controversial विवादास्पद **Controversial matter** विवादास्पद मामला, विवादग्रस्त विषय

Convene संयोजन करना/बुलाना

Convene a meeting बैठक बुलाना **Convener** संयोजक

Convenience सुविधा **Convenience, at your** अपनी सुविधानुसार **Conveniently** सुविधापूर्वक

Convention 1. परिपाटी/अभिसमय/रूढि 2. समागम **Convention, according to** परिपाटी के अनुसार **Convention, students** विद्यार्थियों का समागम

Conventional method रूढ़/रूढ़िगत तरीका **Conventional** रूढ़/रूढ़िगत

Conversant with से परिचित **Conversion table** रूपांतरण सारणी, परिवर्तन सारणी

Conveyance allowance सवारी भत्ता/वाहन-भत्ता

Convict Night Guard बंदी रात्रि-रक्षी **—Officer** बंदी-अधिकारी **Convicted** अभिशस्त, सिद्ध-दोष, दोष प्रमाणित **Conviction** अभिशस्ति

Convoy Commander कान्वाय कमांडर **Convoy notes** वहन-पत्र

Cook Instructor रसोइया शिक्षक

Co-operation, Department of सहकारिता-विभाग **Co-operation, full** पूर्ण सहयोग **Co-operative Officer** सहकारिता-अधिकारी **—Societies Inspector** सहकारी समिति निरीक्षक **Co-operative Society** सहकारी समिति

Co-opt सहयोजित करना **Co-opted member** सहयोजित सदस्य

Coordination समन्वय/तालमेल **Coordination officer** समन्वय/अधिकारी **Coordination and Complaint Section** समन्वय और शिकायत अनुभाग **Co-ordination committee** समन्वय समिति **Coordination supplies branch** संभरण-समन्वय-शाखा

Co-pilot सह-विमान-चालक/को-पाइलट

Copy 1. प्रतिलिपि/नकल 2. प्रति **Copy enclosed for ready reference** तत्काल हवाले/संदर्भ के लिए प्रतिलिपि संलग्न **Copy forwarded to** को प्रति/प्रतिलिपि प्रेषित **Copyholder** मूलवाचक/कापी होल्डर **Copy Writer** वृत्त लेखक **Copying** नकल करना **Copying Slate-bed** नकल स्लेट **Copyist** प्रतिलिपिक, नकलनवीस **Copyright** कापीराइट/स्वत्वाधिकार

Cordoning Officer परिवेष्टन-अधिकारी

Core Maker गुल्ली-निर्माता

Coroner मृत्यु-समीक्षक

Corporation निगम/कार्पोरेशन **—Officer** निगम-अधिकारी **—tax** निगम कर

Corps Commander कोर-कमांडर **—of Volunteers** स्वयं सेवक-कोर/स्वयं सेवक दल **Corps pay** कोर वेतन **Corrected copy** शोधित प्रति, भूल-सुधार की गई प्रति **Correction slip** शुद्धि-पत्रक

Correspond पत्र-व्यवहार करना समरूप होना/मेल खाना/समान होना **Correspond with** के सदृश होना से पत्र-व्यवहार करना **Correspondence** पत्र-व्यवहार **—Clerk** पत्र-व्यवहार-लिपिक **—resting with** पर निलम्बित पत्र ब्यवहार **Correspondent** संवाददाता संपर्की **Correspondent, press** पत्र सम्वाददाता **Corresponding** तदनुरूप **—entry** तत्सम्बन्धी, तदनुरूप, मुकाबले की प्रविष्टि

Corrigendum शुद्धि-पत्र **Corrigendum may be put up** शुद्धि-पत्र प्रस्तुत करें **Corroborate** संपुष्टि करना **Corroborative evidence** संपुष्टिकर साक्ष्य

Corrupt means भ्रष्ट साधन **practice** भ्रष्टाचार **Corruption** भ्रष्टाचार **Corruption, anti** भ्रष्टाचार-निरोधी **—practice** भ्रष्टाचार

Cost लागत **—Accountant** लागत लेखापाल **—Account Officer** लागत-लेखा-अधिकारी **Cost Accounts Branch** लागत-लेखा शाखा **Cost, insurance and freight** लागत-बीमा-भाड़ा (सहित मूल्य) **Cost of living** निर्वाह व्यय, खर्च **—of production** उत्पादन व्यय, लागत **price** लागत मूल्य **—plus profit basis** लाभ-सहित लागत-आधार **working** चालन व्याय; संचालन-व्याय

Cottage Industries कुटीर उद्योग **Cottage Industries Department** कुटीर-उद्योग-विभाग

Council of Medical Registration चिकित्सक-पंजीकरण-परिषद् **Council of Ministers** मंत्रि-परिषद **—of States** राज्य-सभा **—of Scientific & Industrial Research** वैज्ञानिक तथा औद्योगिक अनुसंधान परिषद्

Counsel, standing स्थायी परामर्शदाता, कांउसेल **Councillor** पार्षद **Counsel** परामर्शी, काउंसेल **Counsellor** परामर्शदाता, सलाहकार

Count गिनना, गणना करना **Counter** काउंटर/पटल, प्रति, गणित्र, गणक **Counter**

affidavit प्रति-शपथपत्र **Counter balance** प्रतितोलन, बराबर करना —**charge** प्रत्यारोप —**claim** प्रति दावा, जवाबी दावा —**Clerk** काउंटर क्लर्क **Counterfeit coin** जाली सिक्का **Counterfeiting** कूटकरण **Counterfoils** प्रतिपर्ण, अधपन्ना, मुसन्ना **Counter, on the** काउंटर, पटल पर **Counterpart** प्रति-स्थानी, प्रतिरूप, प्रति वस्तु **Counter signature** प्रति-हस्ताक्षर —**statement** प्रति कथन **Countervailing duties** प्रति शुल्क **Counting of votes** मतों को गिनना, मत गणना

Country of Origin उद्गम-देश

Coup d'etat राज्य क्रांति, राज्य का तख्ता उलट देना

Coupon कूपन **Coupon, money order** मनीआर्डर का कूपन

Courier वार्ताहार

Course मार्ग/दिशा, क्रम, विधि, प्रक्रिया, पाठ्यक्रम **Course of, in the** के अनुक्रम, दौरान —**employment, during the** नियुक्ति-पर्यन्त, नियुक्ति काल में —**studies** पाठ्यक्रम **Course, right** सही मार्ग, दिशा

Court न्यायालय, कोर्ट —**civil** दीवानी न्यायालय; अर्थ न्यायालय दीवानी अदालत —**Inspector** कोर्ट इंस्पेक्टर, न्यायालय निरीक्षक —**martial** सैनिक न्यायालय —**of appeal** अपील न्यायालय —**of inquiry** जांच न्यायालय

Courteous भद्र; सुशील

Cover आवरण लिफाफा **Cover, sealed** मुहरबन्द लिफाफा **Covering letter** प्रावरण पत्र

Coxswain नाव सुकानी, कनहार

Craft Teacher शिल्प शिक्षक —**Designer** शिल्पी अभिकल्पक **Craftsman** शिल्पकार, शिल्पी

Cranage क्रेन-भाड़ा **Crane Driver** क्रेन-चालक, क्रेन ड्राइवर —**Inspector** क्रेन निरीक्षक —**Jamadar** क्रेन जमादार —**Mechanic** क्रेन मेकैनिक

Credence, Letter of प्रत्यय-पत्र

Credential प्रत्यय-पत्र **Credentials committee** प्रत्ययपत्र समिति

Credibility विश्वसनीयता **Credibility of news** समाचार की विश्वसनीयता

Credit श्रेय/मान्यता, उधार, साख जमा, **Credit and thrift society** उधार और बचत समिति **Credit goes to** इसका श्रेय···को है **Credit, leave at his** उसके हिसाब में जमा छुट्टी **Credit marks** श्रेय अंक —**note** जमा-

पत्र —**Note Cash Clerk** जमा-पत्र रोकड़ क्लर्क, जमा-पत्र रोकड़ लिपिक

Crematory श्मशान

Creosoting Plant Superintendent क्रिओसोट संयंत्र अधीक्षक

Crew कर्मी दल **Crew, ship's** जहाज का कर्मी दल

Crime अपराध **Crime statistics** अपराध सम्बन्धी आंकड़े **Criminal** दांडिक-अपराधी —**breach of trust** आपराधिक-विश्वास भंग —**Investigation Department** खुफिया पुलिस-विभाग

Criterion मानदंड, कसौटी **Criterion for** के लिए मानदंड, कसौटी

Critical situation नाजुक परिस्थिति/हालत

Crop Competition Officer फसल प्रतियोगिता अधिकारी —**Physiologist** शस्यक्रिया-विज्ञान —**Season Observer** फसल-मौसम-प्रक्षक —**Specialist** फसल-विशेषज्ञ

Cross गुणन चिह्न, काट देना —**examination** प्रति परीक्षा, जिरह —**movement** वहन-प्रतिवहन —**out** काट देना —**reference** प्रति निर्देश, अन्योन्य संदर्भ **Crossing of efficiency bar** दक्षता रोध को पार करना

Crown prince युवराज

Cultivation Assistant जुताई-सहायक

Cultural Affairs, Department of सांस्कृतिक-कार्य विभाग —**Division** सांस्कृतिक प्रभाग —**relations** सांस्कृतिक सम्बन्ध —**Relations Officer** सांस्कृतिक संपर्क अधिकारी

Cumulative संचित, उपचित, उपचयी, संचयी **Cumulative benefits** उपचित/उपचयी लाभ

Cupolaman गुंबदिया —**in-charge** गुंबदिया इंचार्ज

Curator संग्रहालय-अध्यक्ष, क्यूरेटर —**of Herbarium** वनस्पति-संग्रहालय-अध्यक्ष

Currency, foreign विदेशी मुद्रा **Currency of, during the** के दौरान

Current चालू/प्रचलित —**expenses** चालू व्यय —**price** वर्तमान मूल्य —**session** चालू सत्र/अधिवेशन

Cursory glance सरसरी निगाह

Curtail कम करना **Curtail expenses** व्यय कम करना, व्यय घटाना

Custodian अभिरक्षक **Custodian General** महा परिरक्षक —**of Deposits** निक्षेप-अभिरक्षक —**of Evacuee property**

निष्क्रांत सम्पत्ति-परिरक्षक **—of property** संपत्ति अभिरक्षक **Custody** अभिरक्षा

Custom duty सीमा-शुल्क **—examination** सीमा-शुल्क परीक्षा **—House Officer** सीमाशुल्कालय-अधिकारी, जकात-खाना अधिकारी **—Officer** सीमाशुल्क-अधिकारी

Customary law प्रथागत विधि, कानून **Customs department** सीमाशुल्क-विभाग **—document** शुल्क-छूटपत्र

Cut कर्तन/कटौती **Cut motion** कटौती प्रस्ताव

Cyclostyle साइक्लोस्टाइल करना **Cyclostyle machine** साइक्लो-स्टाइल-मशीन **Cyclostyled material** साइक्लोस्टाइल की हुई सामग्री

Cylinder Mate सिलिंडर मेट

Cypher (Cipher) बीज लेख, शून्य, सिफर **—Inspector** बीज लेख निरीक्षक, साइफर निरीक्षक **—Operator** बीजलेखित प्रचालक, साइफर आपरेटर **—telegram** बीजलेख, साइफर तार

Cytogeneticist कोशिकाजनन-विज्ञानी, कोशिकानुवंशिक विज्ञानी

Cytologist कोशिकाविज्ञानी **Cytological Assistant** कोशिकाविज्ञान-सहायक

Czarism जारशाही, जार समर्थन

Dafadar Major दफादार मेजर

Daftry दफ्तरी

Daily दैनिक **—allowance** दैनिक भत्ता **—attendance** दैनिक हाज़िरी **—balance** दैनिक अतिशेष, दैनिक बाकी **—diary** दैनिकी, दैनंदिनी **—note** दैनिक नोट/दैनिक टिप्पणी **—register** दैनिक रजिस्टर **—routine** दैनिक कार्य, रोज का काम **—wages** दिहाड़ी, दैनिक मज़दूरी

Dairy Development Officer डेरी-विकास-अधिकारी **development section** डेरी-विकास अनुभाग **Dairyman** डेरी वाला

Dak book डाक पुस्तक **—register** डाक रजिस्टर **—runner** हरकारा

Dam and Designs Engineer बांध और रूपांकन-इंजीनियर

Damage feasant नुकसान करने वाला **Damage, serious** गंभीर क्षति **Damaged and unserviceable stores** टूटा-फूटा और बेकार सामान **Damages** क्षति, नुकसान, हर्जाना **—,assessment of** हर्जाना निर्धारण, क्षति, नुकसान का मूल्यांकन

Dandyman डांडीवाला

Danger खतरा, विपद, संकट

Dangerous situation खतरनाक स्थिति **Dangerously** भयानक रूप से

Darkroom Assistant अंधकक्ष-सहायक

Data आधार सामग्री, आँकड़े, सांख्यिकी **Data, statistical** सांख्यकीय आधार-सामग्री, आंकड़े

Date दिनांक, तिथि, तारीख **and time of receipt (D T. R.)** आवती मिलने की तारीख और समय **—of arrival** आगमन तारीख **—out of** पुराना, गतावधि, अप्रचलित **—stamp** तारीख की मोहर **—upto** आज तक का, अद्यतन **Dated** दिनांकित, तारीख **Dated signature** दिनांकित, दिनांक सहित हस्ताक्षर

Day दिन **—Book** रोजनामचा, दैनिक पंजी **- by day** दिन प्रतिदिन **—Republic** गणतन्त्र दिवस **--to day work** दिन-प्रतिदिन, नित्य प्रति का कार्य **Days of grace** रियायती दिन

Dead body मृत शरीर, शव **—card** बेकार कार्ड **—Letter Office (D. L. O.) (Returned Letter Office)** पुनः प्रेषण-केन्द्र **—loss** पूर्ण हानि **—weight** कुल भार

Dealer, authorised प्राधिकृत व्यापारी **Dealing Assistant** संबंधित सहायक **—fair** ईमानदारी का व्यवहार, लेन-देन **—with** से सम्बन्धित **Dealings** व्यवहार, लेन देन

Dean (of a Faculty) डीन, संकाय-अध्यक्ष **—of the Faculty of Arts** कला संकाय-अध्यक्ष **—of the Faculty of Science** विज्ञान संकाय-अध्यक्ष

Dearness allowance महंगाई-भत्ता **pay** मंहगाई वेतन

Dear Sir/Madam प्रिय महोदय, महोदया

Death anniversary मृत्यु दिवस, पुण्यतिथि, बरसी **Death-cum-retirement gratuity** मृत्यु तथा निवृत्ति आनुतोषिक, मृत्यु तथा निवृत्ति उपदान **Death in service** नौकरी करते हुए मृत्यु

Debar रोकना, वर्जन करना **Debar from** से रोकना, वर्जन करना **Debarment** रोक, वर्जन, वारण **Debarred from service** सेवा वारित

Debate बहस **Debenture holder** ऋण पत्र धारक

Debit नामे, नामे डालना, नामे खर्च, डालना **—advice** नामे संज्ञापन **—balance** नामे शेष **—entry** नामे टीप **Debited to**

के नामे डाला गया

Debt ऋण **—public** लोक ऋण **—Settlement Board** ऋण निपटारा-मंडल

Deceased मृत **—depositor** मृत जमाकर्ता **—person** मृत व्यक्ति

Decency शिष्टता **Decency, with** शिष्टतापूर्वक **Decennial** दश-वार्षिक **Decennium** दशक, दशाब्द

Decentralisation विकेन्द्रीकरण **—of industries** उद्योगों का विकेन्द्रीकरण **Decentralised item** विकेन्द्रीकृत मद

Decided on merits of गुण-दोष के आधार पर निर्णीत **— that, it has been** यह निर्णय, फैसला हुआ है कि **Decidedly** निश्चित रूप से **—the best** निश्चित रूप से सर्वोत्तम **Deciding vote** विनिश्चायक मत

Decimal coinage दशमिक सिक्का प्रणाली

Decision 1. विनिश्चय 2. निर्णय **Decision, pending** निर्णय होने तक **Decisive** निश्चायक

Deck डेक **—Serang** डेक सेरांग

Declaration घोषणा **—form** घोषणा-पत्र **— of war** युद्ध घोषणा

Declare घोषणा करना/घोषित करना **Declare ineligible** अपात्र घोषित **— on oath** सशपथ घोषित करना/शपथपूर्वक घोषणा करना

Declared घोषित **Declarer** घोषक **Declaring authority** घोषक अधिकारी

Decontrol विनियंत्रण **Decontrol, complete** पूर्ण विनियंत्रण

Decoration अलंकरण सजावट **Decorations, military** सैनिक अलंकरण

Decorum शिष्टता, शालीनता

Decrease घटती, कमी **Decreased amount** घटी, कम हुई राशि

Decree डिगरी, डिक्री **Decree, amount of** डिगरी, डिक्री की राशि **—Writer** डिगरी-लेखक

Decypher बीजलेखवाचन

Dedicate समर्पण **Dedicated** समर्पित

Deduction कटौती, घटाना **Deduction from** से कटौती, घटौती

Deed विलेख **Deed, sale** बिक्री विलेख **Deeds** विलेख

Deem समझना **Deemed to be** समझा जायगा

Deface विरूपित करना/मुहर लगाना

De facto वस्तुतः, वास्तविक, यथार्थ

में तथ्येन

Defalcation गबन

Defamation मानहानि **—case** मान हानि का मामला

Default 1. त्रुटि, चूक, व्यतिक्रम 2. बकाया **—and Accident Department** चूक और दुर्घटना विभाग **—in payment** भुगतान में चूक, अदायगी न करना **—of, in** के अभाव में, की चूक, करने पर, न करने पर **Defaulter** 1. चूक करने वाला, त्रुटिकारी, व्यतिक्रामी 2. बकायादार, बाकीदार

Defeat, crushing करारी हार **—the purpose** प्रयोजन को निष्फल करना

Defective plan दोषपूर्ण/त्रुटिपूर्ण योजना

Defence रक्षा **Defence accounts** रक्षा लेखा **—Accounts Department** रक्षा-लेखा विभाग **—Cataloguing Authority** रक्षा-सूची प्राधिकारी **Defence, in his** अपने बचाव में **—Inspection Organisation** रक्षा-निरीक्षण संगठन **—Institute of Physiology & Allied Sciences** शरीर क्रिया विज्ञान तथा संबद्ध विज्ञानों का रक्षा संस्थान **—,Ministry of** रक्षा-मंत्रालय **—Production** रक्षा उत्पादन **Research and Development Council** रक्षा अनुसंधान और विकास-परिषद् **—Organization** रक्षा-उत्पादन संगठन **—Science Laboratory** रक्षा-विज्ञान-प्रयोग-शाला **— Services Staff College** रक्षा-सेवा स्टाफ-कालेज **— Specification** रक्षा (मन्त्रालय) विशिष्टि

Defend प्रतिवाद करना; बचाव करना **Defendent** प्रतिवादी **Defendant's statement** प्रतिवादी का बयान **Defending Officer** प्रतिवाद-अधिकारी/प्रतिवाद-अफसर

Defer आस्थगित करना **Deferred** आस्थगित **— annuity** आस्थगित वार्षिकी **—expenditure** आस्थ-गित व्यय **—payment** आस्थगित भुगतान/आस्थगित अदायगी

Defiance उद्धतता/ अवज्ञा **Defiance of, in** की अवज्ञा करते हुए

Deficiency, to make good कमी पूरा करना

Deficit घाटा/कमी **Deficit area** कमी वाला क्षेत्र **—budget** घाटे का बजट **Deficiency** कम

Define निश्चित करना/परिभाषा देना **Defined** परिभाषित **—properly** ठीक तरह से परिभाषा/निश्चित किया

Definite period निश्चित/नियत अवधि **Definitely attributable** निश्चित रूप से आरोप्य

Deformity विरुपता

Defrayable किये जाने वाले

Defunct निष्क्रिय **Defunct company** निष्क्रिय, निश्चेष्ट, बन्द कम्पनी

Defy अवज्ञा करना

Degradation पद घटाना, ग्रेड घटाना

Degree 1. डिग्री, उपाधि 2. मात्रा 3. कोटि 4. डिग्री/अंश/अंशांक **Degree centigrade** अंश सेंटीग्रेड **Degree of priority** पूर्वता की मात्रा **Degree of utility** उपयोगिता की मात्रा **Degree, university** विश्वविद्यालय की डिग्री

De jure विधित: **De jure officer** विधित: अधिकारी

Delay विलम्ब **Delay is regretted** देरी/विलम्ब के लिए खेद है **—report** विलम्ब-रिपोर्ट **Delayed tender** विलम्बित टेंडर/विलम्बित निविदा

Delegate (n.) प्रतिनिधि, **(vb.)** प्रत्यायोजित करना/दे देना/सौपना **Delegation** 1. प्रतिनिधि मंडल 2. प्रत्यायोजन **—cultural** सांस्कृतिक प्रतिनिधि मण्डल **—of financial powers** वित्तीय अधिकार सौंपना, वित्तीय शक्तियों का प्रत्यायोजन **—of powers** शक्तियों का प्रत्यायोजन

Delete the following lines नीचे की पंक्तियों को निकाल/हटा/काट दीजिए

Deliberate जानबूझ कर किया हुआ **Deliberately** जानबूझकर **—done** जान बूझकर किया गया, विमर्शपूर्वक किया गया

Deliberation विचार-विमर्श/विमर्श **Deliberation, after due** उचित विचार-विमर्श के बाद **Deliberative body** विचारक निकाय

Delicate question/situation नाजुक सवाल/हालत (स्थिति) **Delicate Situation** नाजुक हालत; नाजुक स्थिति

Delimitation परिसीमन **—of constituencies** निर्वाचन क्षेत्रों का परिसीमन

Delinked, file has been मिसिल अलग कर ली गई है

Delivery परिदान/वितरण/सुपुर्दगी **—Clerk** वितरण-लिपिक/वितरण-क्लर्क/सुपुर्दगी क्लर्क **—Examiner** वितरण-परीक्षक **—of dak** डाक-वितरण **—of goods** माल की सुपुर्दगी, माल-परिदान **—date**

दाति-तारीख; देने की तारीख

Demand अभियाचना/मांग **—and Collection Clerk** मांग और संग्रह लिपिक/मांग और संग्रह क्लर्क **— an explanation** स्पष्टीकरण मांगना **— Control Officer** माँग नियंत्रण अधिकारी **—notice** माँग नोटिस **—note** मांग पत्र **—operational** सांग्रमिक मांग **— restricted** सीमित मांग **—supplementary** अनुपूरक मांग **—for notice** मांग नोटिस

Demarcation (Demarkation) सीमांकन **Demarcation, line of** सीमांकन रेखा

Demi-official letter (D.O.) अर्ध-सरकारी पत्र **Demi-official reminder** अर्ध-सरकारी तकाजा

Demobilizalion सैन्यवियोजन

Democratic लोकतंत्रात्मक **Democratic Government** लोकतन्त्रात्मक सरकार, लोकतन्त्री शासन

Demonstration 1. **(Show)** निदर्शन/प्रदर्शन 2. **(Proof)** प्रमाण

Demonstration, ample पर्याप्त प्रमाण **—Officer** निदर्शन अधिकारी **—public** सार्वजनिक प्रदर्शन

Demonstrator निदर्शक

Demote पदावनत करना/पद घटाना

Demoted persons पदावनत व्यक्ति

Demotion पदावनति.

Demurrage विलम्ब-शुल्क/डेमरेज

Demurrage charge विलम्ब शुल्क, डेमरेज **—Inspector** विलम्ब-शुल्क निरीक्षक/डेमरेज निरीक्षक

Denial अस्वीकार/इन्कार **Denial, flat** साफ इन्कार

Denomination अभिधान

Denote बताना, सूचित करना

De novo नए सिरे से

Dental Hygienist दंत-स्वास्थ्य-विज्ञानी **—Mechanic** दंत-मेकैनिक/दंत यांत्रिक **—Officer** दंत-उपचार-अधिकारी **—Surgeon** दंत-सर्जन **Dentist** दंत-चिकित्सक

Deny इन्कार करना/अस्वीकार करना

Depart 1. प्रस्थान करना/रवाना होना 2. विचलित होना/हटना 3. दिवंगत होना/मरना **Depart from** से हटना, से विचलित होना **Departed soul** दिवंगत आत्मा

Department विभाग **Department, Govt.** सरकारी विभाग **—of Agriculture** कृषि विभाग **—of Atomic Energy** परमाणु ऊर्जा विभाग **—of Aviation** विमानन विभाग **—of Cabinet Affairs** मंत्रिमंडल - कार्य विभाग **— of Chemicals**

रसायन विभाग **—of Communications** संचार विभाग **—of Community Development** सामुदायिक-विकास विभाग **—of Company Affairs** कंपनी-कार्य विभाग **—of Coordination** समन्वय विभाग **—of Cooperation** सहकारिता विभाग **—of Economic Affairs** आर्थिक-कार्य विभाग **—of Expenditure** व्यय विभाग **—of Food** खाद्य विभाग **—of Foreign Trade** विदेश व्यापार विभाग **—of Heavy Engineering** भारी इंजीनियरी विभाग **– of Health** स्वास्थ्य विभाग **—of Industrial development** औद्योगिक विकास-विभाग **—of Information and Broadcasting** सूचना और प्रसारण विभाग **—of Internal Trade** आंतरिक व्यापार विभाग **—of Iron and Steel** लोहा और इस्पात विभाग **—of Labour and Employment** श्रम और रोजगार विभाग **—of Legal Affairs** विधि-कार्य विभाग **—of Materials Planning** पदार्थ योजना विभाग **—of Mines and Metals** खान और धातु विभाग **—of Parliamentary Affairs** संसदीय-कार्य विभाग **—of Petroleum** पैट्रोलियम विभाग **—of Revenue** राजस्व विभाग **— and Insurance** राजस्व और बीमा विभाग **—of Rehabilitation** पुनर्वास विभाग **—of Social Welfare** समाज-कल्याण विभाग **—of Statistics** सांख्यिकी विभाग **— of Supply** पूर्ति विभाग **—of Technical Development** तकनीकी-विकास विभाग **—of Transport, Shipping and Tourism** परिवहन, पोतपरिवहन और पर्यटन विभाग **—of Works, Housing & Urban Development** निर्माण, आवास और नगर विकास विभाग

Departmental charges विभागीय प्रभार **Departmental enquiry** विभागीय जांच **—inspection** विभागीय निरीक्षण **—order** विभागीय आदेश **—permission** विभागीय अनुमति **— promotion** विभागीय पदोन्नति / विभागीय तरक्की **— Stamp Vendor** विभागीय टिकट विक्रेता

Departure 1. प्रस्थान 2. विचलन/हटाना **Departure time** रवाना होने/प्रस्थान का समय

Depend upon, it would यह इस बात पर निर्भर करेगा **Dependent** परतंत्र/ आश्रित **— country**

परतन्त्र देश —**relations** आश्रित सम्बन्धी/रिश्तेदार **Depending upon the circumstances of each case** हर मामले की परिस्थितियों के अनुसार

Deposit निक्षेप/जमा **Deposit at call receipt** मांग पर जमा की रसीद **Deposited in record room** अभिलेखकक्ष/रिकार्ड रूम में जमा किया गया **Deposit office** जमा कार्यालय **Depository** निक्षेपागार

Depot डिपो —**Assistant** डिपो सहायक —**Superintendent** डिपो अधीक्षक —**Clerk** डिपो क्लर्क —**Guard** डिपो गार्ड **Keeper** डिपो पाल —**Manager** डिपो मैनेजर —**Store Keeper** डिपो भण्डारी —**Store Keeper, Catering** डिपो भण्डारी, खानपान —**Supervisor** डिपो पर्यवेक्षक

Depreciated value ह्रसित मूल्य **Depreciation charges** मूल्य-ह्रास प्रभार, अवक्षय प्रभार —**cost** मूल्य-ह्रास लागत – **in value** मूल्य-ह्रास

Depressed class दलित/शोषित वर्ग

Deprive वंचित करना **Deprived of a right** अधिकार से वंचित

Deputation 1. प्रतिनियुक्ति 2. शिष्ट-मण्डल —**allowance** प्रतिनियुक्ति भत्ता —**of citizens** नागरिकों का शिष्टमण्डल —**on** प्रतिनियुक्ति पर, डेपूटेशन पर **Deputation** प्रतिनियुक्त

Deputy उप —**Chairman** उपसभापति, उपाध्यक्ष — **Chief Accounts Officer** उप मुख्य लेखा अधिकारी —**Chief Account Officer (General)** उप मुख्य लेखा अधिकारी (सामान्य) —**Chief Accounts Officer (Traffic Accounts)** उप मुख्य लेखा अधिकारी (यातायात लेखा) **Chief Auditor (Administration)** उप मुख्य लेखा परीक्षक (प्रशासन) **Chief Auditor (Division)** उप मुख्य लेखा परीक्षक (मण्डल) —**Chief Commercial Superintendent** उप मुख्य वाणिज्य अधीक्षक — **Chief Commerical Superintendent (General)** उप मुख्य वाणिज्य अधीक्षक (सामान्य) —**Chief Commerical Superintendent (Research and Development)** उप मुख्य वाणिज्य अधीक्षक (अनुसंधान और विकास) — **Chief Controller** उप मुख्य नियंत्रक **Chief Controller of Standardization** उप मुख्य नियंत्रक,

मानकीकरण **Chief Electrical Engineer** उप मुख्य बिजली इंजीनियर **—Chief Engineer** उप मुख्य इंजीनियर **—Chief Engineer (Bridges)** उप मुख्य इंजीनियर (पुल) **—Chief Engineer (Construction)** उप मुख्य इंजीनियर (निर्माण) **—Chief Engineer (Special)** उप मुख्य इंजीनियर (विशेष) **—Chief Engineer (Works)** उप मुख्य इंजीनियर (संकर्म) **—Chief Mechanical Engineer** उप मुख्य यांत्रिक इंजीनियर **—Chief Operating Superintendent** उप मुख्य परिचालन अधीक्षक **—Chief Operating Superintendent (Coaching)** उप मुख्य परिचालन अधीक्षक (कोचिंग) **—Chief Operating Superintendent (Goods)** उप मुख्य परिचालन अधीक्षक (माल) **—Chief Operating Superintendent (Planning)** उप मुख्य परिचालन अधीक्षक (योजना) **Deputy Chief Operating Superintendent (Rolling Stock)** उप मुख्य परिचालन अधीक्षक (चल स्टाक) **—Chief Personnel Officer** उप मुख्य कार्मिक अधिकारी **—Chief Signal and Tele-communication Engineer (Construction)** उप मुख्य सिगनल और दूरसंचार इंजीनियर (निर्माण) **—Chief Signal and Tele-communication Engineer (Maintenance)** उप मुख्य सिगनल और दूरसंचार इंजीनियर (अनुरक्षण) **—Chief Traction Power Controller** उपमुख्य कर्षण शक्ति नियंत्रक **—Chief Traffic Superintendent** मुख्य यातायात अधीक्षक **— Chief Transportation Superintendent** उप मुख्य परिवहन अधीक्षक **—Chief Whip** उप मुख्य सचेतक **—Collector** उप समाहर्ता/डिप्टी कलक्टर **—Commissioner** उपायुक्त **Controller (—Deputy Chief Controller)** उप मुख्य नियंत्रक **—Controller Stationery Supply (- Deputy Chief Controller Stationery Supply)** उप मुख्य नियंत्रक, लेखन सामग्री पूर्ती **—Controller, Stores (- Deputy Chief Controller Stores)** उप मुख्य नियंत्रक, भण्डार **— Controller of Stores** उप भण्डार नियंत्रक **—Controller of Stores (Construction)** उप भण्डार नियंत्रक

(निर्माण) **—Controller of Stores (Maintenance)** उप भण्डार नियंत्रक (अनुरक्षण) **—Controller of Stores (Planning and Works)** उप भण्डार नियंत्रक (योजना और सकर्म) **—Director** उपनिदेशक **—Financial Adviser** उप वित्त सलाहकार **—Financial Adviser and Chief Accounts Officer (Construction)** उप वित्त सलाहकार और मुख्य लेखा अधिकारी (निर्माण) **—General Manager** उप महाप्रबंधक

Deputy General Manager (Administration) उप महाप्रबंधक (प्रशासन) **—General Manager (General)** उप महा प्रबंधक (सामान्य) **—Inspector General (Police) (D.I.G.)** उप महानिरीक्षक (पुलिस) **—Inspector of Stores and Clothing** उप निरीक्षक, भण्डार और वस्त्र **—Minister** उप मंत्री **—Secretary** उप सचिव **—Speaker** उपाध्यक्ष **—Station Master** उप स्टेशन मास्टर **—Superintendent** उप स्टेशन अधीक्षक **—Superintendent of Police (D.S.P.)** पुलिस उपाधीक्षक **—Yard Master** उप यार्ड मास्टर

De-requisition अधिग्रहण-मोचन/अधिग्रहण से छुड़ाना

Dereliction of duty कर्तव्य-विमुखता

Derogate अल्पीकरण करना **Derogate from the powers of** की शक्तियों का अल्पीकरण, का अधिकार घटाना **Derogation** 1. अनादर 2. अल्पीकरण **Derogatory** अनादर सूचक **Derogatory statements** अनादर-सूचक कथन/वक्तव्य

Descending order, in अवरोही/उतरते क्रम से

Descent उद्भव उतार, अवरोहण

Description वर्णन/विवरण **Described as** जैसा वर्णित/लिखा है **Descriptive** वर्णनात्मक **—Descriptive form, in** वर्णनात्मक रूप में **Descriptive roll** विवरणी, विवरण-नामावली

Desertion from duty काम/कर्तव्य छोड़कर भाग जाना

Deserving योग्य **Deserving person** योग्य व्यक्ति, सुपात्र

Design (n.) अभिकल्प/डिजाइन/अभिकल्पना, रूपांकन **—Assistant** अभिकल्पक सहायक **—competition** अभिकल्प/डिजाइन प्रति-

योगिता —**Engineer** रूपांकन अभियंता/डिजाइन इंजीनियर

Designate नामोद्दिष्ट करना/अभिहित करना **Designated** नामोद्दिष्ट **Designation** पद/पदनाम **Designation, official** सरकारी पदनाम **Designer** रूपकार/डिजाइनकार

Desirability वांछनीयता **Desirable** अभीष्ट, वांछनीय

Desk calender डेस्क कैलेंडर

Despatch (n.) प्रेषण/रवानगी **(vb.)** प्रेषित करना/रवाना करना भेजना —**,advice of** प्रेषण-सूचना —**Clerk** प्रेषण क्लर्क —**instruction** प्रेषण-अनुदेश —**memo** प्रेषण-ज्ञापन —**mode of** प्रेषण-रीति —**note** प्रेषण-पत्र/रवानगी-पत्र —**register** प्रेषण-पंजी/रजिस्टर —**,Proof of** प्रेषण-प्रमाण —**Rider** सवार हरकारा **Despatcher** प्रेषक/भेजने वाला

Despite this इसके होते हुए, बावजूद

Destination गंतव्य/लक्ष्य **Destination, has reached the** गंतव्य स्थान पर पहुंच गया

Destitutes Home निराश्रित-गृह

Destroying Machine Operator नाशन-मशीन प्रचालक **Destruction Assistant** नाशन-सहायक **Destruction of old records** पुराने अभिलेखों/रिकार्डों को नष्ट करना

Detail ब्योरा **Detailed budget bill** विस्तृत बजट प्राक्कलन — **contingent bill** ब्यौरेवार फुटकर बिल —**inspection** विस्तृत निरीक्षण —**report** विस्तृत रिपोर्ट/प्रतिवेदन —**statement** ब्यौरेवार विवरण **Details, full** पूरा ब्यौरा

Detaining Officer निरोध अधिकारी

Detect 1. पता लगाना 2. पकड़ना **Detection** 1. निरूपण 2. जासूसी 3. पता लगाना **Detective** गुप्तचर/जासूस

Detention निरोध **Detention Quarters Officer** निरोधगृह अधिकारी

Deteriorating situation बिगड़ती हुई हालत/स्थिति

Determination 1. अवधारण 2. संकल्प —**of priorities** अग्रता निर्धारण —**with firm** दृढ़ संकल्प के साथ **Determined, as** जैसा निर्धारित/निश्चित किया है

Detriment अहित **Detrimental** अहितकर —**action** हानिकारक/अहितकर कार्य

Devaluation अवमूल्यन **—of currency** मुद्रा का अवमूल्यन

Development विकास **—block** विकास खण्ड **—Board** विकास बोर्ड **—Commissioner, Small Scale Industries** विकास आयुक्त, लघु उद्योग **—Inspector** विकास निरीक्षक **Minister** विकास-मंत्री **—Officer** विकास अधिकारी **— Overseer** विकास ओवरसियर **Plan** बिकास-आयोजना **— Project** विकास-प्रायोजना **—schemes** विकास योजनाएं **—wing** विकास-स्कंध

Deviate विचलित होना **Deviate from** से विचलित होना **Deviation** विचलन/भेद/अंतर/फर्क **—minor** मामूली भेद/अन्तर/फर्क/विचलन

Devoid of से रहित, के बिना

Devote निरत रहना **Devote one's time in** में अपना समय लगाना **Devotion to duty** कर्त्तव्य-निष्ठा, कर्त्तव्य-परायणता

Dexterity निपुणता; कौशल

Diagonal stroke तिरछी रेखा

Diagram आरेख **—as shown in** आरेख में दिखाया गया

Diarise डायरी करना **Diarised, letters have been** पत्र डायरी कर लिए गए हैं **Diarising** डायरी में चढ़ाना; दैनिकी में चढ़ाना

Diarist डायरी लेखक

Diary डायरी/दैनिकी/दैनंदिनी **—Daily** दैनिकी, दैनिक डायरी **—register** डायरी रजिस्टर

Dictation श्रुतलेख **—speed** श्रुतलेख गति

Diesel Car Foreman डीजल कार फोरमैन **—Car Inspector** डीजल कार निरीक्षक **—Checker** डीजल पड़तालकर्ता **—Driver** डीजल ड्राइवर/डीजल चालक **—Engine Driver** डीजल इंजन ड्राइवर/डीजल इंजन चालक **Foreman** डीजल फोरमैन **—Rail Car Driver** डीजल रेल-कार ड्राइवर/डीजल रेल-कार चालक **—Shunter** डीजल शंटर

Dietallowance आहार भत्ता **—Distributor** आहार-वितरक

Dietician आहारविद्

Digest सार-संग्रह

Digest, weekly साप्ताहिक सार संग्रह

Difference of opinion मतभेद **Different places** भिन्न/विभिन्न/अन्य/पृथक स्थान

Dignitory उच्च पदधारी/उच्च-पदस्थ/महिमान्वित

Dignity गौरव/मर्यादा/गरिमा **Dignity, with** गौरव/मर्यादा सहित

Dilatory बिलम्बकारी; विलम्बी **Dilatory motion** विलम्बकारी प्रस्ताव

Dinner रात्रि भोजन/डिनर

Diploma उपाधि-पत्र/डिप्लोमा/ सनद **Diploma, recognised** मान्यता प्राप्त सनद/डिप्लोमा **Diplomatic** राजनयिक **Diplomatic bag** राजनयिक डाक-थैला **—body** राजनयिक निकाय **Corps** राजनयिक कोर **—Protest** राजनयिक विरोध

Diplomatic relations राजनयिक संम्बन्ध **—Service** राजनयिक सेवा **—Status** राजनयिक हैसियत

Direct (adj.) प्रत्यक्ष/सीधा (**vb.**) निदेश दना **—action** सीधी/प्रत्यक्ष कार्रवाई **—charges** प्रत्यक्ष आरोप; प्रत्यक्ष आवेश **—demanding officer** सीधी मांग करने वाला अधिकारी **—nomination** प्रत्यक्ष नामन **—report** प्रत्यक्ष रिपोर्ट/सीधी रिपोर्ट **—revenue** प्रत्यक्ष राजस्व **Direct to, may be sent** को सीधा भेज दिया जाए **Directed, as** यथा निदेशित, जैसा निदेश दिया गया **Directed to, I am** मुझे निदेश हुआ है **Direction** निदेश/निदेशन **Direction and control** निदेशन और नियंत्रण **—Officer (Naval)** निदेशन-अफसर (नौसेना) **Directive (n.)** निदेश (**adj.**) निदेशात्मक

Directive Principles निदेश सिद्धान्त; निदेशक सिद्धान्त या तत्व

Directly or indirectly प्रत्यक्ष या परोक्ष रूप से

Director निदेशक/संचालक **—,Assistant** सहायक/निदेशक **—,Deputy** उपनिदेशक **Director General** महानिदेशक **—,Joint** संयुक्त निदेशक **—,Assistant** संयुक्त सहायक निदेशक **—,Advertising and Visual Publicity** निदेशक, विज्ञापन और दृश्य प्रचार **—,Agricultural Implements** कृषि औजार निदेशक **—Budget-Finance & Coordination** निदेशक, बजट-वित्त और समन्वय **—,Establishment** निदेशक, स्थापना **—,Labour Bureau** निदेशक, श्रम ब्यूरो **—,Locust Control** निदेशक, टिड्डी नियंत्रण **—,Malariology** निदेशक, मलेरिया-विज्ञान **—,Movements** निदेशक, संचलन **—,Ports and Depots** निदेशक, पत्तन और डिपो **—,Procurement** निदेशक, आसादन **—,Storage and Inspection** निदेशक, संचयन और निरीक्षण **—,Storage**

Construction निदेशक, संचयन-निर्माण —,**Telecommunications Research** निदेशक, दूरसंचार अनुसंधान —,**Telegraph Services** निदेशक, तार-व्यवस्था —**of Accounts** लेखा-निदेशक —**of Archives** अभिलेखागार-निदेशक —**of Audit** लेखा परीक्षा-निदेशक —**of Commercial Audit** वाणिज्य-लेखा परीक्षा निदेशक —**of Consumer's Goods** उपभोक्ता-वस्तु-निदेशक **Director of Controlled Commodities** नियंत्रित-पण्य-निदेशक —**of Coordination (Police Wireless)** समन्वय-निदेशक (पुलिस बेतार) —**of Education** शिक्षा निदेशक —**of Enforcement** प्रवर्त्तन-निदेशक —**of Estates** संपदा निदेशक —**of Extension and Training** विस्तार तथा प्रशिक्षण निदेशक —**of Field Publicity** क्षेत्र-प्रचार-निदेशक —**of Historical Monuments** ऐतिहासिक-स्मारक-निदेशक —**of Industrial Cooperation** औद्योगिक सहकारिता निदेशक —**of Industries** उद्योग-निदेशक —**of Information** सूचना-निदेशक —**of National Archives** राष्ट्रीय अभिलेखागार निदेशक —**of Public Relations** जनसंपर्क-निदेशक —**of Personnel** कार्मिक-निदेशक —**of Plant Protection, Quarantine & Storage** वनस्पति रक्षण, संगरोध तथा संचयन निदेशक —**of Public Instructions (Director of Education)** शिक्षा निदेशक —**of Physical Education** व्यायाम शिक्षा निदेशक —**of Publicity** प्रचार-निदेशक —**of Railway Mail Service (Director R. M. S.)** रेलडाक निदेशक —**of Sericulture** रेशम उत्पादन निदेशक **of Statistics** साँख्यिकी-निदेशक —**of Telegraphs** तार-निदेशक —**of Zoo** चिड़ियाघर-निदेशक **Director General** महानिदेशक —,**Civil Aviation** महानिदेशक, सिविल विमानन —,**Indian Supply Mission** महानिदेशक, भारत पूर्ति मिशन —,**Relief** महानिदेशक, सहायता —,**Shipping** महानिदेशक, जहाजरानी —,**Supplies and Disposal** महानिदेशक, पूर्ति और निपटान

Director General of Civil Defence सिविल-रक्षा-महानिदेशक —**of Employment and Training** रोजगार और प्रशिक्षण

महानिदेशक —of Health Services स्वास्थ्य सेवा महानिदेशक —of Inspection निरीक्षण-महानिदेशक

Directorate निदेशालय/संचानालय —**of Advertising & Visual Publicity** विज्ञापन और दृश्य प्रचार निदेशालय —**of Coordination** समन्वय निदेशालय —**of Electronics** इलेट्रानिकी निदेशालय —**of Enforement** प्रवर्तन निदेशालग्र —**of Engineering** इंजीनियरी निदेशालय —**of Estates** संपदा निदेशालय —**of Exhibitions** प्रदर्शनी निदेशालय —**of Field Publicity** क्षेत्र प्रचार निदेशालय —**of Inspection (Customs and Central Excise)** निरीक्षण निदेशालय (सीमा-शुल्क और केन्द्रीय उत्पाद-शुल्क) —**of National Sample Survey** राष्ट्रीय नमूना सर्वेक्षण निदेशालय —**of Plant Protection, Quarantine and Storage** वनस्पति-रक्षण, संगरोध तथा संचयन निदेशालय —**of Production and Inspection (Electronics)** उत्पादन और निरीक्षण निदेशालय (इलेक्ट्रॉनिकी) —**of Psychological Research** मनोवैज्ञानिक अनुसंधान निदेशालय —**of Research** अनुसंधान निदेशालय —**of Revenue Intelligence** राजस्व-आसूचना निदेशालय **of Standardisation** मानकीकरण निदेशालय —**of Statistics** सांख्यिकी निदेशालय —**of Stores Production (Navy)** सामग्री उत्पादन निदेशालय (नौसेना) —**of Sugar and Vanaspati** चीनी और वनस्पति निदेशालय —**of Technical Development and Production (Air)** तकनीकी विकास और उत्पादन निदेशालय (हवाई)

Directorate General महानिदेशालय —**of Border Roads** सीमा-सड़क महानिदेशालय **Directorate General of Civil Defence** सिविल रक्षा महानिदेशालय —**of Employment & Training** रोजगार तथा प्रशिक्षण महानिदेशालय —**of Health Services** स्वास्थ्य सेवा महानिदेशालय —**of Supplies & Disposals** पूर्ति तथा निपटान महानिदेशालय —**of Technical Development** तकनीकी विकास महानिदेशालय

Directory निर्देशिका **Directory, telephone** टेलीफोन निर्देशिका/डायरेक्टरी

Disability 1. विकलांगता 2. निर्योग्यता **Disability pension** विकलांगता पेंशन

Disabled अंगहीन **Disablement** अंगहानि, विकलांगता

Disadvantage हानि/अहित **Disadvantage, position of** हानि की स्थिति **Disadvantageous** अलाभकारी

Disagree असहमत होना **Disagree, I** मैं असहमत हूं

Disallow अस्वीकार करना, मना करना

Disapprobation अननुमोदन/नापसन्दी

Disapproval अननुमोदन/नापसन्दी **Disapprove** निरनुमोदन करना

Disband तोड़ देना/भंग करना

Disbar निर्वाजित करना

Disbursement संवितरण/बांटना **Disbursement of pay** वेतन का संवितरण, वेतन बांटना **Disbursing officer** संवितरण अधिकारी **—Authority** संवितरणअधिकारी

Discard अमान्य करना/अलग करना /हटा देना

Discharge (as of duty) निर्बहन/पालन **—(as from debt)** उन्मोचन **Discharge certificate** सेवा-मुक्ति/कार्य-मुक्ति प्रमाण-पत्र

Discharged from hospital अस्पताल से छुट्टी **—from service** सेवा से मुक्त करना, नौकरी से हटाना/अलग करना **—of duties** कर्तव्य-पालन, कर्तव्य-निर्वहन **—slip** छुट्टी की पर्ची **Discharged quantity** निकाली/उतारी गई मात्रा

Discipline अनुशासन **—officer** अनुशासन अधिकारी **Disciplinary** अनुशासनीय; अनुशासन सम्बन्धी **—action** अनुशासनिक कार्रवाई **—measure** अनुशासनिक उपाय

Disclaim responsibility जिम्मेदारी अस्वीकार करना

Disclose प्रकट करना **Disclosure** प्रकटन

Discontent, wide व्यापक असन्तोष /क्षोभ

Discontinue बंद करना **Discontinuance** बन्द कर देना **Discontinued, should be** बन्द कर दी जाए

Discount बट्टा **Discount, at a** बट्टे पर

Discover पता लगाना **Discovered, it has been** यह पता लगा है **Discovery** प्रकट करना

Discrepancy विसंगति **Discrepancy may be reconciled**

विसंगति का समाधान कर लिया जाए, अन्तर ठीक किया जाए, त्रुटि दूर की जाए

Discretion विवेक **Discretionary power** विवेकाधिकार, स्वेच्छा निर्णय अधिकार

Discriminate against से विभेद करना, भेदभाव बरतना **Discrimination** विभेद

Discussion 1. विचार-विमर्श/चर्चा 2. बहस **Discussed with** से बात/विचार-विमर्श/चर्चा कर ली है **Discussion, during the course of** चर्चा/बातचीत/बहस के दौरान

Disfigurement विरूपन

Disgraceful conduct लज्जास्पद/अपयशकर आचरण

Dishonest बेईमान **Dishonest means, by** बेईमानी से

Dishonour (a cheque) अस्वीकार करना/नकारना **Dishonur, notice of** अनादर सूचना **Dishonoured cheque** अनादृतचैक, अस्वीकृत चैक

Dislocation of work काम में बाधा/गड़बड़

Dismiss 1. पदच्युत करना/बरखास्त करना 2. खारिज करना **Dismissal** पदच्युति/बरखास्तगी **—from service** नौकरी से निकाला जाना, पदच्युति, बर्खास्तगी **—of case** मामला खारिज होना

Disobedience अवज्ञा **Disobedience of orders** आदेशों की अवज्ञा **Disobey** आज्ञा न मानना/अवज्ञा करना

Disorder 1. अव्यवस्था/गड़बड़ी 2. शांति भंग **Disorder, in the event of** शांति-भग होने पर **—serious** गम्भीर गड़बड़ी/अव्यवस्था **Disorderly behaviour** उच्छृंखल व्यवहार **—fashion, in** अव्यवस्थित रूप में

Disparity असमानता **Disparity in rates** भावों/दरों में असमता/अन्तर

Dispassionate opinion निष्पक्ष राय, निरपेक्ष मत

Dispel doubts संशय दूर करना

Dispensary औषधालय/डिस्पेन्सरी **Dispensary, Government** सरकारी औषधालय/डिस्पेन्सरी

Dispense with अलग करना **—services** नौकरी/सेवा से अलग करना, नौकरी खत्म करना

Dispersal Officer विसर्जन अधिकारी **Disperse** विसर्जन करना/तितर-बितर करना **Dispersed, crowd was** भीड़ को तितर-बितर किया गया **—meeting** सभा विसर्जित हुई

Displace विस्थापित करना **Displaced** विस्थापित **Displaced**

government servant विस्थापित सरकारी कर्मचारी

Display प्रदर्शित करना/सजावट करना **Display advertisement** प्रदर्शन/सजावटी विज्ञापन

Displeasure अप्रसाद

Disposal 1. निपटान/निवर्तन 2. व्ययन — **of business** काम निपटाना —**of cases** मामलों का निपटान/निवर्तन —**Officer** व्ययन-अधिकारी/निपटान अधिकारी —**order** निपटानआदेश **Disposals wing** निपटान स्कंध

Dispose of निपटाना

Dispute विवाद **Disputed matter** विवाद-ग्रस्त/झगड़े वाला मामला

Disqualification अयोग्यता/अनर्हता **Disqualified** अयोग्य/अनर्ह —**will be declared** अयोग्य/अनर्ह घोषित कर दिया जाएगा **Disqualify** अनर्ह करना/अनर्ह होना

Disregard अवहेलना **Disregarding the facts** तथ्यों की उपेक्षा करते हुए —**the orders** आदेशों की अवहेलना करते हुए

Disrespect अनादर/अविनय **Disrespectful** निरादरपूर्ण —**behaviour** अनादर/अविनय का वर्ताव

Dissection Room Assistant विच्छेदन-कक्ष-सहायक

Dissent विसम्मति/विमति/असहमति **Dissent, note of** विमति/विसम्मति लेख **Dissenting opinion** विमति

Disservice अपकार —**rendering** अपकार करते हुए

Dissolution भंग/विघटन —**of society** संस्था/समिति का विघटन/भंग

Distillery Inspector मद्यनिर्माण-शाला-निरीक्षक

Distinct 1. भिन्न/अलग 2. सुस्पष्ट/सुव्यक्त —**from** से भिन्न/अलग —,**made it quite** यह बिलकुल साफ/सुस्पष्ट कर दिया गया **Distinction** 1. विभेद 2. विशेष योग्यता —**in, with** विशेष योग्यता से —,**there is no** में कोई विभेद नहीं है **Distinctive** 1. विशिष्ट 2. पृथक/भिन्न

Distinguished विशिष्ट **Distinguished guest** विशिष्ट अतिथि

Distribute वितरण करना/बांटना **Distributed** वितरित **Distributing shelf** वितरक खाना **Distribution** वितरण —**list** वितरण सूची —**Officer** वितरण-अधिकारी **Distributor** वितरक/डिस्ट्रिब्यूटर —**sole** एकमात्र

वितरक

District जिला **—Controller of Stores** जिला भण्डार नियंत्रक **District Council** जिला-परिषद् **—Court** जिला-न्यायालय **—Demanding Officer** जिला मांग अधिकारी **—intelligence staff** जिला खुफिया कर्मचारी वर्ग **—Judge** जिला न्यायाधीश **—Magistrate** जिला-मजिस्ट्रेट **—Manager, Telephones** जिला प्रबंधक, टेलीफोन **—Office** जिला कार्यालय **—Officer** जिला-अधिकारी **—Traction Power and Traction Controller** जिला कर्षण शक्ति तथा कर्षण नियंत्रक

Ditto यथोपरि/जैसे ऊपर

Divide भाग देना **Divided responsibility** विभाजित जिम्मेदारी/उत्तरदायित्व

Dividend लाभांश **Dividend, annual** वार्षिक लाभांश **Dividend-warrant** लाभांश-अधिपत्र; लाभांश-वारण्ट

Division Bench खण्ड (न्याय) पीठ **Division, Budget** बजट प्रभाग **—Commander** डिवीजन कमांडर **Division Court** खण्ड न्यायालय **Division, lower** नीचे की श्रेणी, निम्न श्रेणी **—of labour** श्रम-विभाजन **Divisional Accounts Officer** मण्डल लेखा अधिकारी **—Accounts Officer (Construction)** मण्डल लेखा अधिकारी (निर्माण) **—Accountant** मण्डल लेखापाल **—Assistant Security Officer** मण्डल सहायक सुरक्षा अधिकारी **—Audit Officer** मण्डल लेखा-परीक्षा अधिकारी **—Boiler Maker** मण्डल बॉयलर मेकर **—Boiler Maker Chargeman** मण्डल बॉयलर मेकर कार्येक्षक **—Cashier** मण्डल रोकडिया **—Clerk** मण्डल क्लर्क **—Commercial Inspector** मण्डल वाणिज्य निरीक्षक **—Commercial Officer** मण्डल वाणिज्य अधिकारी **—Commercial Superintendent** मण्डल वाणिज्य अधीक्षक **—Electrical Engineer** मण्डल बिजली इंजीनियर **—Electrical Engineer (Development)** मण्डल बिजली इंजीनियर (विकास) **—Electrical Engineer (General)** मण्डल बिजली इंजीनियर (सामान्य) **—Electrical Engineer (Overhead Equipment)** मण्डल बिजली इंजीनियर (ऊपरी उपस्कर) **—Electrical Engineer (Railway Stores)** मण्डल बिजली इंजीनियर (रेल भण्डार)

—**Engineer** मण्डल इंजीनियर —**head** प्रभाग-अध्यक्ष **Divisional headquarter** मण्डल-मुख्यालय —**Inspector** मण्डल निरीक्षक —**Manager** मण्डल प्रबंधक — **Mechanical Engineer** मण्डल यांत्रिक इंजीनियर **Divisional office** मण्डल-कार्यालय —**Medical Officer** मंडल चिकित्सा अधिकारी —**office** मण्डल/डिवीजन कार्यालय — **Operating Superintendent** मण्डल परिचालन अधीक्षक —**Pay Clerk** मण्डल वेतन क्लर्क — **Personnel Officer** मण्डल कार्मिक अधिकारी —**Safety Officer** मण्डल संरक्षा अधिकारी **Divisional Signal and Telecommunication Engineer** मण्डल सिगनल और दूरसंचार इंजीनियर —**Signal and Telecommunication Engineer (Construction)** मण्डल सिगनल और दूरसंचार इंजीनियर (निर्माण) —**Signal and Telecommunication Engineer (Headquarter)** मण्डल सिगनल और दूरसंचार इंजीनियर (मुख्यालय) —**Superintendent** मण्डल अधीक्षक —**Traffic Manager** मण्डल यातायात प्रबंधक

Draft प्रारूप/मसौदा; नक्शा

Dock गोदी, डाक, डग **Dock labour** गोदी मजदूर **Docketting** संदर्भ-देना **Docketing of papers** कागजों को संदर्भित/डॉकेट करना

Document लेख्य **Documentary proof** लिखित प्रमाण, दस्तावेजी/कागजी सबूत

Documentation centre प्रलेख केन्द्र —**of sale** बिक्री लेख-बन्ध

Documents produced जो प्रलेख/दस्तावेज प्रस्तुत किए गए हैं

Domestic purposes घरेलू प्रयोजन/काम

Domicile अधिवास; अधिवासी **Domicile by birth** जन्माधिवास -- **certificate** अधिवास प्रमाणपत्र **Domiciled** अधिवासी

Dormant case प्रसुप्त मामला

Dote मूर्खता पूर्ण बातें करना

Double account दुहरा लेखा/हिसाब — **dated** द्वि-दिनांकित

Doubt, benefit of संदेह लाभ

Dowry दहेज

Draft as amended is put up for approval यथा संशोधित मसौदा/प्रारूप अनुमोदन के लिए प्रस्तुत है – **as directed** निदेशानुसार मसौदा बनाइए -- **brief**

संक्षिप्त मसौदा **—for approval** अनुमोदनार्थ मसौदा **Draft put up, reply may be sent as per** प्रस्तुत मसौदे/प्रारूप के अनुसार उत्तर भेज दिया जाए **Drafting and noting** प्रारूपण/आलेखन और टिप्पणी **Draftsman** प्रारूप-कार; नक्शानवीस

Draw attention ख्याल दिलाना, ध्यान आकर्षित करना **—(a) cheque** चैक काटना, चैक से धन निकालना **—back claim** वापसी का दावा **— conclusion** निष्कर्ष निकालना **—up a scheme** योजना बनाना **Drawing officer** आदान-अधिकारी **Drive, Small Savings** अल्प बचत अभियान

Drying book सोख्ता कापी

Due 1. देय/प्राप्य 2. नियत **—amount** देय/प्राप्य राशि **—authority** उचित प्राधिकार **—course, in** यथासमय उचित समय **—date, on** नियत तारीख/तिथि को **—notice** नईमत सूचना/नोटिस **—performancc of agreement** करार का उचित पालन **—regard** उचित ध्यान/सम्मान/लिहाज

Duly विधिवत्/यथाविधि **—complied** विधिवत/उचित पालन किया गया **—performed** विधिवत/यथाविधि/यथोचित/यथासमय किया गया, सही रूप से किया गया **—qualified** यथोचित योग्यता रखने वाले

Dummy (n) डमी **(adj.)** नकली

Dunnage निभार

Duplicate अनुलिपि; दुपर्ती; दूसरी प्रति **—copy** अनुलिपि, दूसरी प्रति, नकल **—, In** अनुलिपि सहित/दो प्रतियों में **—Clerk** अनुलिपि-क्लर्क / अनुलिपिक **Duplicating** अनुलिपिकरण **— machine** अनुलिपित्र **Duplicator, typesetting** टाइप-लिपित्र **Durable goods** टिकाऊ सामान **Duration** अवधि **—of sanction** मंजूरी की अवधि/मियाद

Duress दबाव **— under** दबाव में आकर

During the discussion चर्चा के समय / दौरान, चर्चा में **—the pendency of the case** मुकदमे/मामले की विचार अवधि में **— the pleasure of the President** राष्ट्रपति के प्रसाद पर्यन्त **– the term of office** पदावधि में, पदावधि पर्यन्त, कार्य काल में **—this period** इस अवधि में

Duty काम/कर्तव्य भार, शुल्क **—allowance** ड्यूटी-भत्ता **—bill** शुल्क बिल **—chart** ड्यूटी-चार्ट

—death मरण-शुल्क **—devotion to** कर्तव्य-निष्ठा **—excise** उत्पाद शुल्क **—free** शुल्क मुक्त **—inspection** निरीक्षण-ड्यूटी **—,off** ड्यूटी/कार्य-समय के बाद **—Officer** ड्यूटी-अधिकारी **—on** काम/ड्यूटी पर **—,on special** विशेष ड्यूटी/काम पर **—,officer on special** विशेष कार्य अधिकारी, विशेषाधिकारी **—,Protective** संरक्षी शुल्क **—,recall to** ड्यूटी पर वापस बुलाना **—roster** ड्यूटी-रोस्टर/ड्यूटी पंजिका **—,sense of** कर्तव्य भावना **—,shift** पारी ड्यूटी **—,sphere of** ड्यूटी-क्षेत्र, कर्तव्य-क्षेत्र

Dyeing and Finishing Instructor रंजन और परिष्करण-शिक्षक **—Teacher** रंजन-शिक्षक/रंगाई-शिक्षक

Dyke तटबन्ध, बांध; नहर

Dynamo Car Officer डायनमो यान अधिकारी

Each हरएक; प्रत्येक प्रति **Each and every** एक और प्रत्येक

Earlier assessment year पूर्ववर्ती निर्धारण वर्ष

Earmark चिह्नित करना/अलग करना **Earmarked** चिह्नित **—funds** चिह्नित निधि

Earlier, whichever is जो भी पहले/पूर्वतर हो **Earliest opportunity** शीघ्रतम अवसर, अवसर मिलते ही **Early orders are solicited** शीघ्र आदेशों की प्रार्थना है

Earned leave अर्जित छुट्टी **—leave granted** अर्जित छुट्टी/अवकाश मंजूर **Earnest money** बयाना/अग्रिम धन **Earnings, daily** दैनिक कमाई/आमदनी

Earthgraphic Assistant भूमिलेखाचित्रीय सहायक/भू-लेखाचित्रिक सहायक

Easements annexed thereto उससे संलग्न सुखभोग

Ease, the position will स्थिति सुधरेगी **Easily influenced** आसानी/सरलता से प्रभावित, सहज प्रभावित **Easy reference** सुलभ संदर्भ **—terms** सुकर/आसान शर्तें

Ecclesiastic Commissioner चर्च कमिश्नर

Ecologist पारिस्थितिकीविज्ञ/परिस्थिति विज्ञानी

Economic अर्थ सम्बन्धी, आर्थिक **—Adviser** आर्थिक सलाहकार **—crisis** आर्थिक संकट **—Affairs**

Department आर्थिक-कार्य विभाग **—and Statistical Adviser** आर्थिक और सांख्यिकीय सलाहकार

Economy 1. अर्थ-व्यवस्था 2. किफायत **Economic boycott/crisis** आर्थिक बहिष्कार/संकट **Economy, effect on** अर्थ व्यवस्था पर प्रभाव **—Intelligence Inspector** आर्थिक-आसूचना-निरीक्षक **—Investigator** आर्थिक-अन्वेषक

Economical 1. सस्ता 2. मितव्ययी **—measures** मितव्यय/किफायत के उपाय **—slip** किफायत पर्ची

Editor संपादक **—,Chief** मुख्य संपादक **—,General** प्रधान संपादक **—in-Chief** प्रमुख संपादक **—,Managing** प्रबंध-संपादक **—News** समाचार-संपादक **—Sub** उप संपादक **Editorial comments** सम्पादकीय टिप्पणी **—Section** संपादकीय अनुभाग

Education Directorate शिक्षा-निदेशालय **—Officer** शिक्षा अधिकारी **Educational Adviser** शिक्षा-सलाहकार **—Service** शिक्षा-सेवा

Effect 1. प्रभाव 2. परिणाम **—from such date, with** इसी तारीख से **—from, with** से, से लागू, से प्रभावी **—give** प्रभावशील करना; प्रभावी करना; कार्यान्वित करना **—of** का परिणाम/प्रभाव **—shall not be given** प्रभावशील न किया जाएगा **Effect, shall have** प्रभावी/लागू होगा **—,take** प्रभावशील होना; **Effect, to that** उस उद्देश्य का/से **—,with immediate** जो तुरन्त प्रभावशील होगा; जो तुरन्त प्रभावी होगा, **Effective** प्रभावी/कार्यकारी **—control** प्रभावी नियंत्रण **Effects** चीज वस्तु/मालमत्ता

Efficiency दक्षता/कार्य-पटुता **— bar** दक्षता रोध/रोक **—Bureau** कार्यकुशलता-केन्द्र / कार्यकुशलता ब्यूरो **—Inspector** दक्षता निरीक्षक **—of administration** प्रशासन की दक्षता/कार्यपटुता **Efficiently done** दक्षता, कुशलता से किया गया **e. g.** उदाहरणार्थ, जैसे

Elaborate examination सविस्तार परीक्षा

Elapse (as of time) बीतना/बीत जाना **Elapsed, much time has** काफी समय बीत गया है

Elected निर्वाचित **—member** निर्वाचित सदस्य **—Representative** निर्वाचित प्रतिनिधि

Election निर्वाचन —**Agent** निर्वाचन-अभिकर्त्ता —**booth** चुनाव-कोष्ठ —**Commission** निर्वाचन-आयोग —**Commissioner** निर्वाचन - आयुक्त —**indirect** अप्रत्यक्ष चुनाव, परोक्ष निर्वाचन —**Officer** चुनाव अधिकारी —**petition/tribunal** निर्वाचन-याचिका / अधिकरण —**Tribunal** निर्वाचन-अधिकरण **Electoral Officer** निर्वाचन-अधिकारी —**Registration Officer** निर्वाचन-पंजीयन-अधिकारी **Electoral roll** निर्वाचन सूची —**Rolls Inspector** निर्वाचन - नामावली - निरीक्षक —**Supervisor** निर्वाचन-पर्यवेक्षक

Electric Inspector बिजली निरीक्षक —**Shunter** बिजली शंटर —**Supervisor** बिजली पर्यवेक्षक **Electrical Engineer** विद्युत् अभियंता/बिजली-इंजीनियर —**in-Chief** प्रमुख बिजली-इंजीनियर —**Measuring Instrument Fitter** विद्युत्मापी फिटर —**Signal Maintainer** बिजली सिगनल अनुरक्षक —**Works Division** बिजली-निर्माण-प्रभाग **Electrician** बिजली मिस्त्री / इलेक्ट्रीशियन/ बिजली वाला **Electroplater** विद्युतलेपक

Elementary प्रारंभिक —**education** प्रारंभिक शिक्षा **Elementary stage** प्रारंभिक अवस्था, आरम्भ

Eligible पात्र —**for** के लिए पात्र **Eligibility** पात्रता —**certificate** पात्रता प्रमाणपत्र

Elucidate स्पष्ट करना —**the reasons** कारण खोलकर बताइए

Elucidation स्पष्टीकरण

Embankment Officer तटबंध-अधिकारी

Embarrassing situation आकुलकारी स्थिति, परेशानी/असमंजस की स्थिति

Embassy राजदूतावास **Embassy of** का राजदूतावास

Embezzlement गबन —**of money** धन का गबन

Emblem प्रतीक/चिन्ह

Emergency आपात/आपतिक/ आपात-स्थिति —**action** आपाती कार्रवाई —**measures** आपातिक उपाय —**Officer** आपात-अधिकारी —**Production Committee** आपात-उत्पादन समिति —**Relief Organisation** आपात-सहायता-संगठन —**state of** आपातकाल की स्थिति, आपातकालीन स्थिति, आपात स्थिति

Emigrant उत्प्रवासी —**control** उत्प्रवास-नियंत्रण **Emigration Commissioner** उत्प्रवास-आयुक्त

Emoluments परिलब्धियां —**total** कुल परिलब्धियां

Employ 1. नियुक्त करना/नियोजित करना 2. प्रयोग करना/काम में लाना **Employed** नौकरी में लगे हुए — **on daily wages** दिहाड़ी पर नियुक्त **Employee** कर्मचारी —,**government** सरकारी कर्मचारी

Employees State Insurance Corporation कर्मचारी राजकीय बीमा-निगम **Employer** नियोक्ता —**contribution** नियोक्ता का अंशदान

Employment नौकरी/रोजगार/सेवायोजन व्यवसाय/नियोजन —**exchange** रोजगार कार्यालय —**Liaison Officer** रोजगार-संपर्क-अधिकारी —**Officer** रोजगार-अधिकारी —,**part time/whole-time** अंशकालिक/पूर्णकालिक रोजगार/नौकरी —**tax** रोजगार कर

Emporium भण्डार, पण्यशाला

Empower शक्ति देना/अधिकार देना **Empowered to** के लिए शक्ति/अधिकार दिया गया

Enabling Act समर्थकारी अधिनियम

Enact अधिनियम बनाना/अधिनियमित करना

Enactment अधिनियमन

En bloc एक साथ, सामूहिक रूप से

Encashment भुनाना/तुड़ाना —,**premature** समय-पूर्व भुनाना

En clair स्पष्ट शब्दों में

Enclave विदेशी अंत:क्षेत्र

Enclose 1. बंद करना 2. साथ रखना **Enclosed letter** साथ का पत्र, संलग्न पत्र —,**statement is** विवरण संलग्न है **Enclosure** 1. अनुलग्नक 2. बाड़ा, अहाता —**to the letter** पत्र का अनुलग्नक

Encourage प्रोत्साहन देना

Encroachment अधिक्रमण —**Inspector** अधिक्रमण-निरीक्षक —**on Govt. land** सरकारी भूमि का अधिक्रमण

Endanger संकटापन्न

Endeavour प्रयास करना

Ending, period को समाप्त होने वाली अवधि

Endorse 1. पृष्ठांकन करना/सही करना 2. समर्थन करना **Endorsed** अंकित, पृष्ठांकित —,**these views are** इन विचारों का समर्थन किया जाता है **Endorsement** 1. पृष्ठांकन/सही करना 2. समर्थन —**put up for signature**

पृष्ठांकन हस्ताक्षर के लिए प्रस्तुत

Endow प्रदान करना **Endowment** 1. विन्यास 2 धर्मस्व/धर्मदा/धर्मदाय/अक्षय निधि **—Commissioner** अक्षयनिधि-आयुक्त

Enforce प्रवर्तन-करना/प्रवर्तन कराना **Enforceable** प्रवर्तनीय **—by any court** किसी न्यायालय द्वारा लागू करने योग्य **Enforcement** प्रवर्तन **—department** प्रवर्तन विभाग **—Officer** प्रवर्तन-अधिकारी **—staff** प्रवर्तन-अमला

Engage 1. लगाना/नियुक्त करना 2. वचनबद्ध करना/वचनबद्ध होना **Engagement** आबंध/वचन-बंध **—diary** कार्य-डायरी **—of labour** मजदूर लगाना/नियुक्त करना

Engine Driver इंजन ड्राइवर, इंजन चालक **—Examiner** इंजन परीक्षक **—Fitter** इंजन फिटर **Engine room** इंजिन का कमरा **—Room Artificer** इंजन-कक्ष-परिशिल्पी **—Operator** इंजन कक्ष प्रचालक **—Supervisor** इंजन पर्यवेक्षक

Engineer अभियंता/इंजीनियर **—, Chief** मुख्य अभियंता/मुख्य इंजीनियर **—, Sewage Disposal** मल-अपवहन-इंजीनियर **—, Switch Room** स्विचकक्ष-इंजीनियर **—, Telemaintenance Group** इंजीनियर, दूरसंचार-अनुरक्षण-दल **—in-Chief** प्रमुख इंजीनियर **Engineering** इंजीनियरी/अभियांत्रिकी **—college** इंजीनियरी कालेज **—division** इंजीनियरी प्रभाग **—Stores Inspector** इंजीनियरी भण्डार निरीक्षक **—Supervisor —(Carrier Maintenance/Trunk Faults)** इंजीनियरी पर्यवेक्षक (वाहक अनुरक्षण इंजीनियरी/ट्रंक-दोष) **—, Telegraphs-Trunk-Maintenance Group** इंजीनियरी पर्यवेक्षक, तार ट्रंक-अनुरक्षण दल

Engraver उकेरक/उत्किरक

Enhanced rent बढाया हुआ किराया, वर्धित किराया **— powers** वर्धित/बढ़ाए हुए अधिकार

Enjoy the benefit लाभ उठाना, उपभोग करना

Enlarged jurisdiction प्रवर्धित क्षेत्राधिकार

Enlist 1. भर्ती करना/भर्ती होना/सूची में चढ़ाना 2. नाम लिखना/नाम लिखाना **—soldiers** सैनिक भर्ती करना **—support** समर्थन प्राप्त करना **—volunteers** स्वयं सेवकों के नाम लिखना/सूची में चढ़ाना

Enquiry 1. पूछताछ 2. जांच **—and Reservation Clerk** पूछताछ और आरक्षण क्लर्क **—Supervisor** पूछताछ और आरक्षण पर्यवेक्षक **—Clerk** पूछताछ क्लर्क **—,departmental** विभागीय जांच **—,office** पूछताछ कार्यालय **—Officer** जांच अधिकारी **—,Secret** गुप्त जांच **(secret)** गुप्त जाँच कार्यालय, पूछताछ दफ्तर **-- to be completed and report submitted** जांच पूरी की जाए और रिपोर्ट प्रस्तुत की जाए

Enrolment नामांकन/नाम दर्ज करना **—number** नामांकन-संख्या

Enroute मार्ग में, रास्ते में, बरास्ता

Ensuing आगामी **—year** आगामी वर्ष

Ensure आश्वस्त करना **—that rules are properly observed in future** यह सुनिश्चित कर लिया जाए कि भविष्य में नियमों का उचित पालन हो

Enter (to make an entry) दर्ज करना/प्रविष्टि करना **—(upon an office)** कार्यभार संभालना/कार्यभार ग्रहण करना **—by force** बलात् प्रवेश, जबरदस्ती घुसना **—in register** रजिस्टर में चढ़ाना/दर्ज करना/प्रविष्टि करना **—into a bond** बांड लिख देना **—into an agreement** समझौता/करार करना **—upon an office** पद ग्रहण करना, पद संभालना

Enthetain 1. मनोरंजन करना 2. सत्कार करना 3. ग्रहण करना **—an appeal** अपील ग्रहण करना

Entertainment मनोरंजन **—allowance** सत्कार भत्ता **—Officer** मनोरंजन-अधिकारी **—tax** मनोरंजन कर **—tax commission** मनोरंजन-कर-आयोग, मनोरंजन-कर-कमीशन **– Tax Officer** मनोरंजन कर-अधिकारी

Entire cost of haulage कुल ढ़ुलाई **—service** सम्पूर्ण/सारी सेवा

Entitle हकदार होना/हकदार बनाना **Entitled** हकदार **—to** के लिए अधिकारी/हकदार **Entitlement criteria** हकदारी की कसौटी

Entomologist कीटविज्ञानी/कीटज्ञ **Entomological Assistant** कीटविज्ञान-सहायक

Entrance 1. प्रवेश 2. प्रवेश-द्वार

Entrust सौंपना/न्यस्त करना **—with** सौंपना, न्यस्त करना

Entry 1. इंदराज/प्रविष्ट 2. प्रवेश

—,**adverse** प्रतिकूल इन्दराज/प्रविष्टि —,**no** प्रवेश निषिद्ध, आना मना है

Enumeration गणना/गिनना **Enumerated above, for the reasons** ऊपर बताए/गिनाए गए कारणों से **Enumerator** गणनाकार

Envelope, Sealed मुहरबन्द लिफाफा

Envoy दूत —**Extraordinary** असाधारण दूत —**Extraordinary and Minister Plenipotentiary** असाधारण दूत और मूर्खाधिकारी मंत्री

Ephemeral file अल्पकालिक मिसिल —**roll** अल्पकालिक पंजी

Epidemic महामारी —**form, in** महामारी के रूप में **Epidemiologist** महामारीविद्

Epigraphist पुरालेखवेत्ता

Epitome निष्कर्ष/सार

Equal in all respects सर्वांगसम, हर तरह से बराबर **Equality** समता —**of opportunity** अवसर समता, समान अवसर **Equally entitled** समान रूप से हकदार

Equipage सामग्री

Equipment उपस्कर —,**modern** आधुनिक उपस्कर —**Officer** उपस्कर-अधिकारी / इक्विपमेंट अफसर —, **Preservation Officer** उपस्कर-संरक्षण-अधिकारी **Equipped, well** सुसज्जित

Equitable साम्ययुक्त —**distribution** साम्ययुक्त वितरण

Equivalent **(n.)** 1. तुल्यांक/तुल्यमान 2. पत्र पर्याय **(adj.)** तुल्य, समकक्ष —**Hindi** हिन्दी पर्याय —**post** समकक्ष पद —**rank** समान पद —**to** के समान/तुल्य/बराबर **Equivalents** पर्याय

Eradicate उन्मूलन करना/मूलोच्छेदन करना —**Eradication** मूलोच्छेदन —**malaria** मलेरिया उन्मूलन

Eraser रबर

Errata शुद्धि-पत्र

Erroneous views भ्रममूलक/गलत विचार

Error त्रुटि/भूल/गलती —**is regretted** त्रुटि/भूल/गलती के लिए खेद है —**of fact** तथ्य की भूल **Errors and Omissions** भूल-चूक —**excepted** भूल-चूक लेनी देनी

Escheat राजगामी

Escort अनुरक्षक

Essential अनिवार्य/आवश्यक —**qualification** अनिवार्य/आवश्यक/लाजमी योग्यता

—services अनिवार्य सेवाएं
Establish स्थापना करना, संस्थापन **Established procedure** संस्थापित प्रक्रिया **Establishment** स्थापना —,**authorised** प्राधिकृत सिब्बंदी —,**industrial** उद्योग —**Instructor** स्थापना शिक्षक —**Section** स्थापना अनुभाग
Estate संपदा —**duty** संपदा शुल्क —**Department** संपदा-विभाग —**Manager** संपदा-प्रबंधक —**non-Pensionable** गैर पेंशनी सिब्बंदी —**Peace** शांति (कालीन) सिब्बंदी —,**regular** नियमित सिब्बंदी —**return** सिब्बदी विवरण —**work charged** निर्माण मद की सिब्बंदी —**office** राजसम्पत्ति कार्यालय —**officer** संपदा-अधिकारी —**Supervisor** संपदा पर्यवेक्षक —**Duty Officer** संपदा-शुल्क अधिकारी
Estimate (n.) प्राक्कलन/आकलन/अनुमान **(vb.)** आकलन करना/आंकना/कूतना —**Officer** प्राक्लन-अधिकारी —,**over** अधिक कूतना/आंकना —,**preliminary** प्रारम्भिक प्राक्कलन/आकलन/अनुमान **Estimated** प्राक्कलित —**budget** बजट प्राक्कलन, बजट अंदाजा —**cost** अनुमानित लागत, अनुमानिक खर्च —**Committee** प्राक्कलन समिति —**of Expenditure** व्यय-अनुमान —**revised** पुनरीक्षित प्रक्कलन, पुनरीक्षित अंदाजा **Estimator** प्राक्कलन
Ethnologist मानवजाति-विज्ञानी
Etiquette शिष्टाचार —,**by way of** शिष्टाचार के नाते
Evacuee निष्क्रांत/निष्क्राम्य **Evacuee property** निष्क्रान्त सम्पत्ति —**Property, Custodian of** निष्क्रांत-संपत्ति अभिरक्षक —**Department** निष्क्रांत संपत्ति-विभाग
Evaluation मूल्यांकन —**Committee** मूल्यांकन समिति —,**work** काम का मूल्यांकन —**Officer** मूल्यांकन-अधिकारी
Evasive replies टालू उत्तर
Even distribution सम/समान वितरण —**if he agrees** यदि वह सहमत भी हो जाए —**number** युग्म संख्या, सम संख्या
Event of, in the के होने पर
Eventually this is bound to happen अन्ततः/अन्ततोगत्वा यह होकर रहेगा
Ever since जब से, तब से **Every now and then** बार-बार, समय-समय पर
Eviction बेदखली/निष्कासन

—**Inspector** बेदखली-निरीक्षक/निष्कासन निरीक्षक **Eviction proceedings** बेदखली की कार्यवाही

Evidence साक्ष्य/गवाही/प्रमाण —**,oral** मौखिक गवाही/साक्ष्य —**,there is enough** इसका काफी प्रमाण/साक्ष्य है **Evident, it is quite** यह बिलकुल स्पष्ट है

Evolve 1. विकसित करना 2. (शब्द) निर्माण करना

Exactly this is what was stated there यह ठीक वही है जो वहां कहा गया था

Examination परीक्षण/परीक्षा —**,after proper** समुचित परीक्षण/जांच के बाद —**,competitive** प्रतियोगिता परीक्षा **Examine** जांच करना **Examine the proposal in the light of observation at 'A'** 'क' पर व्यक्त विचारों को दृष्टि में रखते हुए प्रस्तावों की जांच कीजिए **Examiner** परीक्षक —**, Local Fund Accounts** स्थानीय-निधि-लेखा-परीक्षक —**of Books and Publications** पुस्तक और प्रकाशन परीक्षक —**of Central Excise Accounts** केन्द्रीय उत्पाद-शुल्क लेखा परीक्षक —**of Documents** प्रलेख-परीक्षक/दस्तावेज परीक्षक

Example उदाहरण —**,for** उदाहरण के लिए, उदाहरणार्थ

Ex-cadre post संवर्गबाह्य पद

Excavator उत्खनक **Excavation Assistant** उत्खनन-सहायक

Exceeding, not से अनधिक, से अधिक नहीं

Except as otherwise provided for exception, as an इस विधान/संविधान की किसी अन्य अपवाद स्वरूप **Exceptional** विशिष्ट/अपवादात्मक —**case** विशिष्ट/अपवादात्मक मामला —**measure** विशेष/आपवादिक/असाधारण उपाय/कार्रवाई

Excess अति/अधिकता/ज्यादती —**committed on** पर हुई ज्यादती —**duty** अधिक शुल्क —**of, in** से अधिक —**profit** अधिक लाभ/अधिक मुनाफा

Exchange 1. विनिमय 2. केन्द्र —**Control** विनिमय-नियंत्रण —**Controller** विनिमय-नियंत्रक —**Inspector (Telephone)** केन्द्रनिरीक्षक (फोन) —**Mast Lascar** टेलीफोन केन्द्र स्तंभ-लस्कर **Exchange rate** विनिमय दर —**Switch Board Mechanic** टेलीफोन केन्द्र-स्विच बोर्ड मेकैनिक **Exchange, Telephone** टेलीफोन केन्द्र

Exchequer राजकोष

Excise 1. उत्पादन शुल्क 2. आबकारी **—Commissioner** 1. उत्पादन शुल्क-आयुक्त 2. आबकारी आयुक्त **—duty** उत्पाद-शुल्क

Exclude वर्जित करना/निकालना/ अपवर्जन **Excluding the cost of** की लागत को छोड़कर

Exclusive 1. अनन्य 2. रहित **—of** को छोड़कर को सम्मिलित न करके, के रहित **—powers** अनन्य शक्तियां/एकमात्र अधिकार **—right** अनन्य अधिकार, एकमात्र अधिकार **Exclusively** अनन्य रूप से **—for** अनन्य रूप से…के लिए

Execute निष्पादन करना **Executed** निष्पादित

Execution निष्पादन **—of contract** ठेका-निष्पादन **—of works** निर्माण-कार्य पूरे करना

Executive 1. कार्यपालिका 2. कार्यपालक/प्रबंधक **—authority** कार्यकारी प्राधिकारी, कार्यकारी-प्राधिकार, कार्यकारी प्राधिकरण **—Council** कार्य-परिषद् **—Engineer** कार्यपालक इंजीनियर/कार्यकलाप अभियंता **—Engineer (Stores)** कार्यपालक इंजीनियर (भण्डार) **—(Bridges)** कार्यपालक इंजीनियर (पुल) **—(Design)** कार्यपालक इंजीनियर (अभिकल्प) **—(Floods)** कार्यपालक इंजीनियर (बाढ़) **—(General)** कार्यपालक इंजीनियर (सामान्य) **—(Metric)** कार्यपालक इंजीनियर (मीटर प्रणाली) **—(Planning) and** कार्यपालक इंजीनियर (योजना) और **—(Survey)** कार्यपालक इंजीनियर (सर्वेक्षण) **—(Vigilance)** कार्यपालक इंजीनियर (सतर्कता) **—(Water Supply)** कार्यपालक इंजीनियर (जलपूर्ति) **—(Workshop)** कार्यपालक इंजीनियर (कर्मशाला) **—officer** कार्यपालक अधिकारी कार्यपालक **—power** कार्यकारी अधिकार/शक्ति **—staff** कार्यपालक कर्मचारी-वर्ग

Executor निष्पादन

Exemplary punishment निवारक/ शिक्षाप्रद/उदाहरणात्मक दंड

Exempt विमुक्त करना/छूट देना/ माफी देना **Exempted person** छूट-प्राप्त/विमुक्त व्यक्ति **Exemption** छूट/माफी **—from payment** अदायगी से छूट/(रकम) देने से छूट **Exemption from Police** पुलिस के अधिकार क्षेत्र से छूट

Exercise प्रयोग करना **—due**

discretion उचित स्वविवेक का प्रयोग करना —of functions कृत्यों का सम्पादन —of, in का प्रयोग करते हुए —of power शक्ति-प्रयोग

Ex-gratia payment अनुग्रह-पूर्वक अदायगी

Exhibit No. प्रदर्श संख्या **Exhibition** प्रदर्शनी —**Officer** प्रदर्शनी-अधिकारी —**staff** प्रदर्शनी कर्मचारी वर्ग

Exigency अनिवार्य आवश्यकता/अत्यावश्यकता **Exigencies of public service** लोक सेवा की आवश्यकताएं

Ex-India भारत के बाहर

Existence अस्तित्व **Existing law** वर्तमान विधि/कानून

Exit 1. निर्गम/निकास 2. निकास द्वार/निर्गम द्वार —**Gate Checker** निकास द्वार चेकर/निकास द्वार पड़तालकर्ता

Ex-officio पदेन —**Secretary** पदेन सचिव

Exonerate दोषमुक्त करना **Exonerated, has been** दोष मुक्त कर दिया गया है

Expansion विस्तार/प्रसार/प्रसरण —**programme** विस्तार/प्रसार का कार्यक्रम

Ex-parte इकतरफा, एक पक्षीय

Expatriation 1. देश निकाला 2. देश त्याग 3. राष्ट्रीयता त्याग

Expected time अपेक्षित समय

Expediency कालोचितता/समीचीनता

Expedient कालोचित/समीचीन —**it is** यह कालोचित/समीचीन है

Expedite शीघ्र कार्रवाई करना/शीघ्र निबटान —**action** कार्रवाई शीघ्र करें, कार्रवाई में शीघ्रता करें**Expeditious action** अति-शीघ्र कार्रवाई

Expedition खोज यात्रा/अभियान

Expell निकाल देना/निष्कासित करना **Expel from** से निकाल देना/निष्कासित करना

Expenditure व्यय/खर्च ,**antici-pated** प्रत्याशित खर्चा —,**capital** —पूंजीगत खर्चा —**control form** —खर्च का नियंत्रण फार्म —,**irregular** अनियमित खर्च —,**new** नया खर्च —,**recurring** आवर्ती व्यय/खर्च **Expenses** व्यय

Experiment प्रयोग/परीक्षण —**as an** प्रयोग/परीक्षण के रूप में

Experimental measure प्रयोगात्मक उपाय

Expert विशेषज्ञ —**Committee**

विशेषज्ञ समिति

Expiry समाप्ति **Expiration** समाप्ति **—date** कालावधि समाप्त होने की तारीख **—of, on the** की समाप्ति पर

Explain the circumstances under which वे परिस्थितियां बताइए जिनके कारण **Explained in your letter, as** जैसा आपके पत्र में स्पष्ट किया गया है **Explaining** स्पष्ट करते हुये **Explanation** 1. व्याख्या 2. स्पष्टीकरण **—from the defaulter** चूककर्ता/दोषी से स्पष्टीकरण मांगा जाए

Explanatory व्याख्यात्मक **—note** व्याख्यात्मक टिप्पणी

Explicitly told स्पष्टतया बता दिया गया

Exploit 1. शोषण करना 2. समुपयोग करना **Exploitation** शोषण क्षेत्रवर्धन **—Officer** समपयोजन-अधिकारी **—Assistant** समन्वेषण-सहायक/खोज-सहायक

Export निर्यात **—application** निर्यात आवेदन-पत्र **—division** निर्यात प्रभाग **—duty** निर्यात शुल्क **—tax** निर्यात-कर

Exporter निर्यातक, निर्यातकर्ता

Expost facto कार्योत्तर

Ex-post facto sanction कार्योत्तर मंजरी **Ex-President** भूतपूर्व राष्ट्रपति/अध्यक्ष

Express 1. तुरंत 2. अभिव्यक्त 3. **(vb.)** व्यक्त करना/प्रकट करना / अभिव्यक्त करना **—acceptance** अभिव्यक्त/स्पष्ट स्वीकृति **—delivery** तुरत विवरण, एक्सप्रेस डाक **Expression** अभिव्यक्ति

Expressly स्पष्टता पूर्वक **—made known** प्रत्यक्ष/स्पष्ट बताया गया

Expulsion निष्कासन/निर्वासन/निकाल देना/बहिष्करण **—from** से निष्कासन/निकाल देना

Extend 1. बढ़ाना/विस्तार करना 2. प्रचलित होना/लागू होना **Extension** विस्तार/बढ़ाना **—of delivery date** परिदान की तारीख बढ़ाना **—of leave** छुट्टी बढ़ाना

Extension of service सेवावधि बढ़ाना **—Officer** विस्तार-अधिकारी **—services** विस्तार सेवाएं

Extensive व्यापक/विस्तृत/विस्तीर्ण **—form, in** व्यापक/विस्तृत रूप से

Extent विस्तार/सीमा **—of, to the** की सीमा/हद तक

Extenuating circumstances उपशामक स्थितियां/परिस्थितियां

External Affairs Ministry विदेश मंत्रालय **—Relation Division (Min. of Education)** बाह्य-संपर्क प्रभाग (शिक्षामंत्रालय)

Extra (as in Extra Magistrate) अतिरिक्त **—Departmental Branch Post Master** अतिरिक्त विभागीय शाखा पोस्टमास्टर **—curricular** पाठ्येतर/पढ़ाई के अतिरिक्त **—duty pay** अतिरिक्त कार्य वेतन **—ordinary** असाधारण **—leave** विशेष छुट्टी, असाधारण छुट्टी **—meeting** असाधारण बैठक **—work/payment** अतिरिक्त कार्य/अदायगी **—territorial** राज्यक्षेत्रातीत

Extract उद्धरण **—of indent** मांगपत्र का उद्धरण **Extract taken** उद्धरण ले लिए गए

Extraditing state प्रत्यर्पण, राज्य-क्षेत्रातीत वर्तन

Extradition officer प्रत्यर्पण-अधिकारी

Extraneous matter असंगत/अप्रासंगिक विषय, बाह्य तत्त्व

Extremely good बहुत ही अच्छा

Fabricate 1. गढ़ना 2. निर्माण करना **Fabricated evidence** झूठी/रचित साक्ष्य, गढ़ी हुई गवाही **Fabrication (construction)** रचना/निर्माण **—of charges** (आरोप) गढ़ना

Face of it, on the प्रत्यक्षत:, स्पष्ट है कि **Face value** अंकित मूल्य

Facilitate सरल बनाना/सुकर बनाना **—it will** यह सरल/सुकर बना देगा **Facilitating commission of offence** अपराध करने में सहायता करना **Facilities, reasonable** उचित सुविधाएं

Facility आसानी/सुविधा **—with** आसानी/सुविधा से

Facsimile अनुलिपि / प्रतिकृति **—signature** प्रतिकृति हस्ताक्षर, अनुलिपि हस्ताक्षर

Fact तथ्य **—in** वस्तुत:, वास्तव में **—, question of** तथ्य सम्बन्धी प्रश्न **Facts of the case may kindly be furnished** कृपया मामले के तथ्य भेज दें

Factory Inspector फैक्टरी-निरीक्षक / कारखाना निरीक्षक **—Manager** फैक्टरी-मैनेजर/कारखाना-प्रबन्धक

Factual data तथ्यपूर्ण आधार-सामग्री

Faculty संकाय **—of Arts** कला

संकाय —**of Engineering** इंजीनियरी संकाय —**of Science** विज्ञान संकाय

Failing which न हुआ तो, न होने होने पर —**serious action will be taken** ऐसा न करने पर कठोर कार्रवाई की जाएगी

Fail to appear उपस्थित न होना

Failure विफल, असफल —**of crops** फसल न होना

Fair 1. स्वच्छ 2. उचित 3. निष्कपट 4. पर्याप्त/साधारण —**copy** स्वच्छ प्रति —**deal** उचित व्यवहार, निष्कपट व्यवहार —**Grading :** कोटि : साधारण —**knowledge** पर्याप्त ज्ञान/अच्छा ज्ञान/साधारण ज्ञान —**letter/copy** स्वच्छ पत्र/प्रति —**measure, in** पर्याप्त मात्रा में —**price** उचित मूल्य —**treatment** उचित व्यवहार/उचित बर्ताव

Fairness औचित्य/न्याय —**in** औचित्य/न्याय की दृष्टि से

Faith धर्म, श्रद्धा —**acting in good** सद्भाव से कार्य करते हुए —**breach of** विश्वासघात **Faithful employee** निष्ठावान कर्मचारी —**Service** वफादारी से सेवा, निष्ठापूर्वक सेवा **Faithfully yours** भवदीय

Fallacious argument भ्रान्तिमूलक तर्क, गलत दलील

Fall due देय होना —**into arrears** बाकी पड़ना, बकाया इकट्ठा होना —**short of** कम होना —**through** निष्फल होना

False charge मिथ्या/झूठा आरोप

Familiar with, to become से परिचित होना

Family परिवार/कुटुंब/कुल —**allowance** कुटुंब-भत्ता/परिवार-भत्ता —**members** परिवार-सदस्य – **pension** परिवार पेन्शन —**Planning Centre** परिवार नियोजन केन्द्र —**Welfare Officer** परिवार-कल्याण-अधिकारी/ कुटुम्ब कल्याण अधिकारी

Famine दुर्भिक्ष/अकाल —**relief** अकाल सहायता/राहत —**Relief Officer** अकाल-सहायता अधिकारी

Fare किराया/भाड़ा —**rail** रेल किराया/भाड़ा **Farewell address** विदाई भाषण —**function** विदाई समारोह

Farm, agricultural कृषि फार्म —**Manager** फार्म-मैनेजर

Farming खेती/कृषि —**Inspector** खेती-निरीक्षक /फार्मिंग निरीक्षक

Fatal accident घातक दुर्घटना

Fathom-line फैदम लाइन

Fault दोष/चूक — **finding** छिद्रान्वेषण, दोष निकालना —**Inspector** दोष-निरीक्षक **Faultless** दोष-

रहित **Faulty** दोषपूर्ण/सदोष **—action** दोषपूर्ण कार्रवाई

Favour 1. अनुग्रह/कृपा 2. पक्षपात/पक्ष **—, he has done a great** उसने बड़ा अनुग्रह/कृपा की है **—, in his** उसके पक्ष में **—of necessary action, for** उचित कार्रवाई के लिए **—(favouritism), undue** अनुचित पक्षपात **Favourable** अनुकूल **—action, for** अनुकूल कार्रवाई के लिए **—attitude** अनुकूल रुख **Favouritism** पक्षपात

Feasible शक्य **Feasible, it is not** यह शक्य/व्यवहार्य/साध्य/सम्भव नहीं है

Feature writer रूपक लेखक **Features, special** विशेष लक्षण, विशेष बातें

Federal संघन्यायालय

Federation 1. संघीकरण 2. महासंघ **—, employees'** कर्मचारी महासंघ **—of Insurance** बीमा-संस्थान-महासंघ

Fee शुल्क/फीस **—, admission** प्रवेश शुल्क, प्रवेश फीस **—, Tuition** शिक्षा शुल्क

Feeling 1. भाव/अनुभूति/भावन 2. संवेदन **—expressed in the meeting** बैठक में व्यक्त हुई भावना

Feigned issue कल्पित वादपद, कल्पित तनकीह

Fellow (a member) अधिसदस्य **—(of an Academy)** रत्न-सदस्य **—, research** अध्येता **— ship** अध्येतावृत्ति

Female स्त्री / नारी / महिला **—dependent** आश्रित नारी/स्त्री **—Dresser** महिला ड्रेसर **—ward** महिला वार्ड

Ferro Printer फैरो मुद्रक/लौह-मुद्रक **—Clerk** नौघाट लिपिक **—Engineer** नौघाट इंजीनियर **—Superintendent** नौघाट अधीक्षक **—Toll Collector** घाट-तहसीलदार **—Wagon Inspector** नौघाट मालडिब्बा निरीक्षक

Fertiliser Association of India भारत का उर्वरक संघ **—Controller** उर्वरक नियंत्रक **—Corporation of India** भारत का उर्वरक निगम

Festival advance उत्सव-अग्रिम/त्यौहार पेशगी

Fettler संवारने वाला

Fibre Expert तंतु-विशेषज्ञ

Fictitious काल्पनिक/फर्जी/कल्पित **—claim** फर्जी दावा **—story** काल्पनिक/कल्पित कहानी/समाचार

Fidelity निष्ठा/वफादारी **—guarantee policy** निष्ठा

गारन्टी-बीमा

Field क्षेत्र **—Agency** क्षेत्र अभिकरण/क्षेत्र एजेंसी **—, in the** मैदान में, कार्य क्षेत्र में **—Manure Officer** खेत-खाद अधिकारी **—man (Horticulture)** क्षेत्रिक (बागवानी) **—Marshal** फील्ड मार्शल **—Research Station** क्षेत्र अनुसंधान केन्द्र **—Security Officer** क्षेत्र-सुरक्षा अधिकारी

Figure 1. अंक 2. आकृति

Figures आंकड़े **—correct** सही आंकड़े **—in** अंकों में

File 1. संचिका/मिसिल/फाइल 2. फाइल करना/दाखिल करना **—a suit** दावा दायर करना **—an application** अर्जी देना, आवेदन-पत्र देना **—board/cover** फाइल बोर्ड/आवरण **—cabinet** फाइल कैबिनेट **—cover** फाइल-आवरण **—flap** फाइल पट्टी/फाइल फ्लैप **—keeper** फाइल रक्षक **—movement register** फाइल संचलन-रजिस्टर **—number** फाइल संख्या, मिसिल संख्या **—order** फाइल क्रम, मिसिल क्रम **Filed, may be** फाइल कर दिया जाय, फाइल/संचिका/मिसिल में रख दिया जाय **Filing** मिसिलबंदी/फाइल करना **Filing date** फाइल करने की तारीख **—system** फाइल पद्धति **—up of posts** पदों को भरना

Film censor फिल्म सेंसर **—Checker** फिल्म चेकर **—division** फिल्म प्रभाग **—Editor** फिल्म- संपादक/चलचित्र - संपादक **—Joiner** फिल्मयोजक **—Librarian** फिल्म लाइब्रेरियन **—Officer** फिल्म अधिकारी **—Production Officer** फिल्म-निर्माण अधिकारी

Filter Plant Operator निस्यंदक संयंत्र प्रचालक **—Overseer** निस्यंदक संयंत्र ओवरसियर

Final अन्तिम **—decision** अन्तिम निर्णय/फैसला **—report** अन्तिम रिपोर्ट **Find write off** अन्तिम रूप से बट्टे खाते डालना

Finalised, report is being रिपोर्ट को अन्तिम रूप दिया जा रहा है

Finance (n.) वित्त **(vb.)** रुपया लगाना **—Administration** वित्त-प्रशासन **—Commission** वित्त आयोग **—Minister** वित्त मंत्री **—ministry of** वित्त मंत्रालय **—Officer** वित्त अधिकारी

Financed by द्वारा रुपया लगाया गया **Financer** वित्तदक्ष, रुपया लगाने वाला, पूंजीपति **Financial** वित्तीय / वित्त संबंधी / वित्त **—advice** वित्तीय सलाह

—**Advisor** वित्त-सलाहकार —**and Chief Accounts Officer** वित्त सलाहकार एवं मुख्य लेखा अधिकारी —**certificate** वित्तीय प्रमाण पत्र —**commitment** वित्तीय बद्धता —**Commissioner** वित्त-आयुक्त —, **Railways** रेल वित्त आयुक्त —**concurrence** वित्तीय सहमति —**control** वित्तीय नियंत्रण —**irregularity** वित्तीय अनियमितता —**legislation** वित्त विधान —**liability** वित्तीय-दायिता —**obligation** वित्तीय दायित्व/वित्तीय आभार —**powers** वित्तीय शक्तियाँ/वित्तीय अधिकार —**Proceedings** वित्तीय कार्यवाही —**Propriety** वित्तीय औचित्य —**sanction** वित्तीय मंजूरी/वित्तीय संस्वीकृति —**statement** वित्तीय विवरण —**system** वित्तीय पद्धति —**transaction** वित्तीय व्यवहार —**year** वित्तीय वर्ष

Finding of the Enquiry Officer जांच अधिकारी का निष्कर्ष

Findings निष्कर्ष

Fine दंड/जुर्माना —, **collective** सामूहिक जुर्माना/दंड —**person** अच्छा व्यक्ति

Finger print अंगुलि-छाप —**Examiner** अंगुली-छाप परीक्षक —**Expert** अंगुली-छाप-विशेषज्ञ

Finished goods निर्मित माल, तैयार वस्तुएं

Fire 1. आग 2. फायर/गोलाबारी —**arms** अग्न्यस्त्र —**Arms Expert** अग्निशस्त्र-विशेषज्ञ —**Brigade Inspector** दमकल दल निरीक्षक —**Engine Driver** दमकल ड्राइवर/दमकल चालक —**extinguisher** अग्निशामक/दमकल —**fitter** अग्नि-शामक फिटर —**Inspector** अग्निशमन निरीक्षक — **Insurance** अग्नि-बीमा—**Officer** 1. अग्निशमन-अधिकारी/अग्निशमन अफसर 2. फायर-अफसर/गोलाबारी अफसर —, **Chief** मुख्य अग्निशमन-अधिकारी —**proof** अग्निसह — **risk** आग का खतरा —**services** अग्निशमन सेवा —**Station Office** दमकल केन्द्र कार्यालय —**Officer** दमकल केन्द्र अधिकारी **Fire services** अग्निशमन सेवा, आग बुझाने का दल —**Unit commander** फायर यूनिट कमांडर **Fireman** आग-वाला/फायरमैन **Firing, police** पुलिस द्वारा गोली वर्षा/गोली चलाना

Firm action दृढ़ कार्रवाई

First aid प्रथम उपचार, प्रथमोपचार —**Aider** प्रथमोपचारक — **appointment** प्रथम नियुक्ति

—**Class Magistrate** प्रथम श्रेणी मजिस्ट्रेट —**information report** प्रथम सूचना-रिपोर्ट —**Lieutenant** फर्स्ट लेफ्टिनेंट —**round** प्रथम/पहला दौर —**Preference** प्रथम अधिमान, प्रथम वर्यता, प्रथम तरजीह —**reading** प्रथम वाचन —**reprint** प्रथम पुनर्मुद्रण

Fiscal राजस्व संबंधी —**policy** राजस्व सम्बन्धी नीति

Fisheries 1. मीन-उद्योग 2. मीनक्षेत्र —**development** मीन-उद्योग-विकास —**Development Advisor** मीन - उद्योग-विकास - सलाहकार —**Officer** मीन-उद्योग-विकास-अधिकारी —**Extension Officer** मीन - उद्योग-विस्तार - अधिकारी —**Research & Investigation Officer** मीन-उद्योग अनुसंधान और अन्वेषण अधिकारी —**Warden** मीनक्षेत्रपाल **Fish Farm Supervisor** मीनकेन्द्र-पर्यवेक्षक

Fit for consumption उपभोग्य **Fit for use** उपयोग/काम के लायक **Fitness certificate** आरोग्य प्रमाण पत्र **Fitter** फिटर —**(Electric)** फिटर (बिजली) —**Chargeman** फिटर कार्येक्षक

Fixation of pay वेतन नियत/स्थिर करना

Fixed deposit आवधिक निक्षेप, आवधिक जमा —**deposit receipt** मियादी जमा रसीद, आवधिक जमा रसीद —**hours of work** काम के नियत घण्टे —**monthly allowance** नियत मासिक भत्ता —**pay** नियत वेतन —**point** नियत स्थल —**price** निश्चित मूल्य, एक दाम —**(value)** निश्चित/नियत

Fixtures जुड़नार

Flag पताका —**Flag 'A'** पताका/पर्ची 'क' —**Lieutenant** फ्लैग लेफ्टिनेंट — **nation** राष्ट्रीय झंडा —**man** झंडीवाला

Flat denial साफ इनकार —**file** चपटी फाइल —**rate** समान दर, एक दर

Flight फ्लाइट/उड़ान —**Commander** फ्लाइट कमांडर —**Instructor** उड़ान-शिक्षक

Float (a company/bond/loan etc.) प्रवर्तन करना

Flood control बाढ़ नियन्त्रण —**Investigation Division** बाढ़-अन्वेषण-प्रभाग

Floor area तल क्षेत्रफल, फर्श क्षेत्र-फल —**price** निम्नतम मूल्य

Floriculturist पुष्पविज्ञानी

Flotilla Supervisor बेड़ा-पर्यवेक्षक

Fluctuation उच्चावचन/घट-बढ़/

चढ़ाव —in prices मूल्यों के उतार - चढ़ाव, कीमतों में घट-बढ़

Flying Officer फ्लाइंग अफसर **—squad** द्रुतगामी दल, उड़न-दस्ता **—Inspector** द्रुतगामी दल, निरीक्षक

Flyleaf कोरा पन्ना

Fodder Development Officer चारा-विकास-अधिकारी **—Inspector** चारा-निरीक्षक

Fogman कुहासिया **Fogman's Hut** कुहासिए की गुमटी

Folder फोल्डर/पुटक **—, Expansion** बिस्तारी फोल्डर **—, Straightened** सीधा फोल्डर **—, tab** टैब फोल्डर

Folio पन्ना/फोलियो **—, ledger** खाता पन्ना

Follow up action अनुवर्ती कार्रवाई **—negotiation** अनुवर्ती बातचीत **Following** 1. निम्नलिखित/नीचे लिखा/नीचे दिया 2. अनुगामी **—facts** निम्नलिखित तथ्य **—paragraph** अनुवर्ती/आगे का पैरा **—year** आगामी वर्ष

Foment उत्तेजित करना

Food, Department of खाद्य विभाग **—and Agriculture Division** खाद्य और कृषि प्रभाग **—Controller** खाद्य - नियंत्रक **—Corporation of India** भारत का खाद्य निगम **—Fermentation and Forest Products Department** खाद्य-किण्वन और वन-उपज विभाग **—Inspector** खाद्य निरीक्षक **—minister** खाद्य मंत्री **—ministry** खाद्य मंत्रालय **—position** खाद्य - स्थिति **—Supply Inspector** खाद्य पूर्ति निरीक्षक **Foodgrains** खाद्यान्न **—Inspectors** खाद्यान्न निरीक्षक **—Production Drive Department** खाद्यान्न-उत्पादन-अभियान विभाग

Foot note पाद टिप्पणी, फुट नोट **Foot prints** पद-छाप **—Prints Expert** पद-छाप-विशेषज्ञ

For a total period कुल मिलाकर कालावधि के लिये **For and on behalf of** के लिए और उनकी ओर से **For approval** अनुमोदन के लिए **For consideration** विचारार्थ **For disposal** निपटान के लिए **—expression of opinion** मत/राय प्रगट करने के लिए **—favour of doing the needful** यथावश्यक कार्रवाई के लिए, आवश्यक कार्रवाई करने की कृपा की जाय **—favour of orders** कृपया आदेश दें, आदेशार्थ **—favourable action** अनुकूल कार्रवाई के लिए

further action आगे की कार्रवाई के लिए, अगली कार्रवाई के लिए **—guidance** संदर्शन/मार्ग-दर्शन के लिए **—instance** उदाहरण के लिए, उदाहरणार्थ **—interim information** अन्तरिम सूचना के लिए **For non-residential Purpose** आवासेतर प्रयोग के लिए **—onward transmission** आगे भेज़ने के लिए **—perusal and return** देखकर लौटाने के लिए **—private use** निजी प्रयोग के लिए **—public purpose** सार्वजनिक प्रयोग के लिए **—ready reference** तत्काल निर्देश/हवाले के लिए **—signature** हस्ताक्षर के लिए **—such action as may be necessary** ऐसी कार्रवाई के लिए जो आवश्यक प्रतीत हो **—suggestions** सुझावों के लिए **—sympathetic consideration** सहानुभूतिपूर्वक विचार के लिए **—the present** अभी, फिलहाल **—the purpose of the Act** अधिनियम के प्रयोजन के लिए **—the time being** सम्प्रति, फिलहाल **—the time being in force** तत्समय प्रवृत्त, उस समय लागू

Forbid निषेध करना

Forbidden निषिद्ध

Forecast पूर्वानुमान **—, crop** फसल का पूर्वानुमान **Forecaster** पूर्वानुमानकर्ता

Fore-going पूर्वगत/पूर्ववर्ती **—provisions** पूर्ववर्ती/पहले उपबन्ध

Foreign exchange विदेशी मुद्रा **—Minister** विदेश मंत्री **—Secretary** विदेश-सचिव **—Service** विदेश-सेवा **—Service, conclusion of** विदेश सेवा की समाप्ति **—Service, reversion from** विदेश से परावर्तन **—Tourist Organisation** विदेशी पर्यटक-संगठन **service** विदेश सेवा, इतर सेवा **Foreman** फोरमैन **—(Inspection)** फोरमेन (निरीक्षण) **—(Planning)** फोरमैन (योजना) **—(Production)** फोरमैन (उत्पादन) **—(Progress)** फोरमैन (प्रगति) **—, Timber Section** प्रकाष्ठ अनुभाग फोरमैन

Forenoon पूर्वाह्न/दोपहर से पहले **—, in the** पूर्वाह्न में, दोपहर से पहले

Forensic Science Laboratory न्यायालयिक विज्ञान प्रयोगशाला

Forest department वन विभाग **—Guard** वन सिपाही **—Officer** वन अधिकारी **—Ranger** वन रेंजर/वन राजिक **—research institute** वन अनुसंधान शाला

—**Settlement Officer** वन-बदोबस्त-अधिकारी —**Utilization Officer** वन-उपयोजन-अधिकारी **Forester** वन-दरोग

Forfeited Service अमान्य सेवा

Forfeiture समपहरण **Forged** कूटरचित —**Note Expert** जाली-नोट-विशेषज्ञ

Forgerer जालसाज **Forgery** कूट रचना/जालसाजी **Forging of signature** जाली हस्ताक्षर बनाना, कूटरचित हस्ताक्षर

Form 1. प्रपत्र/फार्म 2. रूप —, **admission** प्रवेश-पत्र —,**in another** दूसरे रूप में —**Keeper** फार्मवाला / प्रपत्रवाला / प्रपत्री —, **prescribed** विहित/निर्धारित फार्म/प्रपत्र —**Supervisor** फार्म-पर्यवेक्षक/प्रपत्र / पर्यवेक्षक —**Supplier** फार्मदाता/प्रपत्रदाता **Formal** औपचारिक —**sanction** औपचारिक मंजूरी —**warning** औपचारिक चेतावनी **Formation** निर्माण/रचना —**of ring** गुटबन्दी —**Pressman** फर्मा-प्रूफ प्रेसमैन **Form Proof Inkman** फर्माप्रूफ-स्याहीवाला **Formerly** पहले, इससे पूर्व **Forms Carrier** फर्मा-वाहक —**Issuer** फार्म निर्गामक, फार्म जारी कर्ता

Formula सूत्र **Formulate** 1. बनाना 2. रूप देना **Formulate plan** योजना बनाना, योजनाओं को रूप दना

Forthcoming आगामी — **meeting** आगामी बैठक के लिए

Forthwith तत्काल —, **action should be taken** कार्रवाई तत्काल/इसी समय की जानी चाहिए

Fortnight पक्ष/पखवाड़ा —, **small savings** अल्प बचत पखवाड़ा **Fortnightly** पाक्षिक —**progress** पाक्षिक प्रगति

Fortuitous event दैवी/दैवकृत/ अनपेक्षित घटना

Forward (adj.) अग्रवर्ती **(vb.)** अग्रेषित करना —**Air Controller** अग्रवर्ती हवाई-नियंत्रक —**area** अग्रवर्ती क्षेत्र —**Programme-indent** भावी कार्यक्रम सम्बन्धी इण्डेंट; भावी कार्यक्रम सम्बन्धी माँग-पत्र **Forwarded and recommended** अग्रेषित और संस्तुत/अभिशंसित, सिफारिश के साथ आगे प्रेषित **Forwarding Letter** अग्रेषण-पत्र —**note** अग्रेषण-टिप्पणी

Foundation 1. शिलान्यास 2. नींव/आधार 3. प्रतिष्ठान —, **laying of** शिलान्यास करना नींव रखना, आधारशिला रखना

—, **peace** शान्ति-प्रतिष्ठान

Founder संस्थापक **Founder's Day** संस्थापक दिवस

Foundry Expert ढलाई-विशेषज्ञ

Frame charges आरोप लगाना **Frame work** ढांचा

Fraternity भ्रातृत्व; बन्धुता

Fraud कपट; धोखा; जालसाजी —**Clerk** कपट-कार्य लिपिक **Fraudulent action** कपटपूर्ण कार्य, धोखेबाजी

Free 1. निःशुल्क 2. अलग्न/मुक्त —**baloon pilot** मुक्त गुब्बारा चालक —**competition** मुक्त/अबाध प्रतियोगिता —**delivery** निःशुल्क वितरण —**distribution, for** निःशुल्क वितरण के लिए —**education** निःशुल्क शिक्षा —**on Board (F.O.B.)** पोतपर्यन्त निःशुल्क —**on board Contract** नौतल तक निष्प्रभार ठेका; —**on Rail (F.O R.)** रेलपर्यन्त निःशुल्क —**of tax** कर मुक्त —**Service Clerk** निःशुल्क सेवा क्लर्क/निःशुल्क सेवा लिपिक

—**Service Checker** निःशुल्क सेवा पडतालकर्ता —**transit** निःशुल्क पारगमन **Freely, can be approached** बिना रोक-टोक मिला जा सकता है

Freight मालभाड़ा/ढुलाई —**paid** भाड़ा दिया **Freight to pay** भाड़ा देना है

French Interpreter फ्रेंच भाषांतरकार

Frequency आवृत्ति /बारंबारता —**of requests** अनुरोध की आवृत्ति **Frequent** बारंबार —**absence** बारम्बार अनुपस्थिति —**demands** बारम्बार की मांगें

Fresh fruits ताजा फल —**goods** नया माल —**receipt (F.R.)** नई आवती

Frivolous argument तुच्छ/असार/तर्क

From (in letters) प्रेषक **From ...to...** प्रेषक···सेवा में··· —**time to time** समय समय पर

Frontier सीमा/सीमान्त क्षेत्र —**area** सीमा/सीमान्त क्षेत्र

Fruit Development Officer फल विकास-अधिकारी —**Preservation Officer** फल-संरक्षण-अधिकारी

Fuel Checker ईंधन पड़तालकर्ता —**consumption** ईंधन की खपत —**Distributor** ईंधन वितरक —**Inspector** ईंधन निरीक्षक —**(Landing and Statistical)** ईंधन निरीक्षक (अवतरण और सांख्यिकी) —**Keeper** ईंधन रक्षक —**Supervisor** ईंधन पर्यवेक्षक

Verification Inspector ईंधन सत्यापन निरीक्षक —**Watcher** ईंधन रखवाल **Fuelling Officer** ईंधन-अधिकारी

Full tariff rate पूर्ण टैरिफ दर **Fulitime** पूर्णकालिक

Fumigator धूमक

Function 1. कार्य/कृत्य 2. समारोह —, **official** सरकारी समारोह **Functionaries** अहलकार **Functionary** कार्यकर्ता **Functioning** कृत्यकारिणी **Functions and powers** कार्य/कृत्य और शक्तियां/अधिकार

Fund निधि —, **allotted** नियत निधि —, **Benevolent** हितकारी निधि —, **civil compassionate** सिविल अनुकम्पा निधि —, **provident** भविष्य निधि —, **regional** प्रादेशिक निधि —, **Small Saving** अल्प बचत-निधि

Fundamental मूल/मौलिक/आधारिक/आधारभूत —**features** आधारभूत विशेषताएं —**principles** आधारभूत/मूलभूत सिद्धान्त —**rule** मूल नियम

Furnaceman भट्टीवाला

Furnish 1. देना 2. सज्जित करना/सजाना **Furnished information, has** ने सूचना दे दी है **Furnished residence, free** किरायामुक्त सज्जित मकान

Further action आगे की कार्यवाही/अगली कारंवाई —**action, for** आगे कारंवाई के लिए —**orders will follow** आगे और आदेश भेजे जाएंगे —**Proceedings** आगे की कार्यवाहियां

Furlough फरलो

Future भविष्य —**date** भविष्यवर्ती तारीख —, **in the near** निकट भविष्य में —**maintenance** भावी भरण पोषण —**market** वायदा बाजार —**position** भावी स्थिति

Gage बन्धन; गिरवी; रहन

Gain लाभ; लब्धि **Gains of learning** विद्याधन

Gallantry award शौर्य पुरस्कार

Gallery दीर्घा/गैलरी/वीथी —**assembly** सभा वीथी; सभा गैलरी —**Assistant** दीर्घा-सहायक/गैलरी-सहायक —**General** सामान्य वीथी; सामान्य गैलरी —**ladies** महिला वीथी; महिला गैलरी —**official** सरकारी वीथी; सरकारी गैलरी —**press** पत्रकार दीर्घा/गैलरी —**Pressman** गैली प्रेस मैन **Gallery speeker's** अध्यक्ष वीथी, अध्यक्ष गैलरी —**visitor's** दर्शक वीथी; दर्शक

अध्यक्ष गैलरी

Galvaniser जस्तकार/गैल्वनाइजर

Games खेल **—Inspector** आखेट-निरीक्षक / शिकार-निरीक्षक **—Master** खेल शिक्षक

Gang Inspector टोली-निरीक्षक/ गैंग-निरीक्षक

Gantry Operator गैन्ट्री प्रचालक

Garage Supervisior गराज-पर्यवेक्षक

Garden Party उद्यान-भोज

Garrison Engineer गैरिजन इंजीनियर **—Field Officer** गैरिजन फील्ड अफसर

Gas Cutter गैस कटर **Gasman** गैस वाला/गैस मिस्त्री

Gate Guard द्वार-रक्षक **—main** मुख्य द्वार **—Keeper** द्वारपाल/ दरबान/फाटक वाला **—pass** प्रवेश-पत्र, द्वार-पत्र **—Pass Collector** प्रवेश-पत्र-संग्राहक **—Sergeant** द्वार-सारजेंट **—Supervisor** द्वार-पर्यवेक्षक

Gauge Checker गेज चेकर **—Reader** गेज वाचक

Gazette राजपत्र/गजट **—extra-ordinary** असाधारण गजट/राजपत्र **—notification** गजट अधिसूचना **Gazetted** राजपत्रित **—holiday** राजपत्रित अवकाश/राजपत्रित छुट्टी **—Officer** राजपत्रित अधिकारी **—post/service** राज-पत्रित अधिकारी/पद/सेवा **—post** राजपत्रित पद **—service** राज-पत्रित सेवा **Gazetteer** गजेटियर **G.C. Note keeper** सरकारी मुद्रा नोट रक्षक

Gear up कसना, तेज करना

General (in Defence) जनरल **—(as in General Editor)** प्रधान **—(as in Director General)** महा **—(as in General admn.)** सामान्य **—(as in General meeting)** साधारण **—(as in General election)** आम **—administration** सामान्य प्रशासन **—application** सामान्य प्रयोग **—Central Service** सामान्य केन्द्रीय सेवा **—circular** सामान्य परिपत्र **—elections** आम चुनाव **—conditions of contract** ठेके की सामान्य शर्तें/संविदा की सामान्य शर्तें **—diary** सामान्य दैनिकी **—Duties Clerk** जनरल ड्यूटी-क्लर्क/सामान्य कर्तव्य लिपिक **—Editor** प्रधान सम्पादक **—fund** सामान्य निधि **—inspection** सामान्य निरीक्षण **—Liaison Inspector** सामान्य संपर्क निरीक्षक **—Manager** प्रधान प्रबंधक/ महाप्रबंधक **—meeting** साधारण सभा बैठक **— Office Inspector**

सामान्य कार्यालय निरीक्षक —**Officer** जनरल अफसर —**Commanding** जनरल अफसर कमांडिंग —**in-chief (G.O.C. in-C)** जनरल अफसर कमांडिंग-इन-चीफ (जी० ओ० सी० इन-सी०) —**practice** सामान्य प्रथा —**principles and rules** सामान्य सिद्धांत और नियम —**procedure** सामान्य कार्यविधि/सामान्य प्रक्रिया —**proposal/rule** सामान्य प्रस्ताव/नियम —**Provident Fund** सामान्य भविष्य निधि —**reserve** सामान्य रक्षित निधि —**reserve fund** सामान्य रक्षित निधि —**rule** सामान्य नियम —**revenues** सामान्य राजस्व —**Secretary** महासचिव —**Service** सामान्य सेवा —**Staff Officer** जनरल स्टाफ अफसर —**ward** सामान्य वार्ड

Geneticist आनुवंशिक विज्ञानी/आनुवंशिकीविद्

Genius 1. प्रतिभा 2. प्रतिभाशाली 3. प्रकृति —**of language** भाषा की प्रकृति

Genuine 1. प्रामाणिक 2. यथार्थ/वास्तविक/ सच्चा/असली 3. विशुद्ध —**signature** वास्तविक हस्ताक्षर, असली दस्तखत —**statement** यथार्थ कथन —**text** प्रामाणिक पाठ

Geologist भूविज्ञानी **Geological Adviser** भूविज्ञान-सलाहकार

Gestetner Machine Operator गेस्टेटनर मशीन प्रचालक —**Operator** गेस्टेटनर ऑपरेटर/गेस्टेटनर प्रचालक

Ghat Inspector घाट निरीक्षक —**Serang** घाट सेरांग

Gift उपहार/भेंट —**as a** उपहार/भेंट के रूप में

Gin Fitter जिन फिटर

Girding Officer परितक्षण-अधिकारी

Gist भावार्थ —**of the proposals** प्रस्तावों का भावार्थ

Give effect to को प्रभावी करना, आरम्भ करना, अमल में लाना, कार्यान्वित करना **Give order** आदेश देना **Give up** छोड़ देना

Glance through, may पर निगाह डाल लें, सरसरी तौर से देख लें

Glaring mistake अति स्पष्ट भूल, भारी गलती/अशुद्धि

Glass Technologist काच उद्योग-विज्ञानी

Glaze Instructor काचक-शिक्षक

Glazier काचक/शीशागर

Global tender विश्व टेंडर/विश्व-निविदा

Glossary शब्दावली/शब्द-संग्रह —**technical** तकनीकी शब्दावली/

शब्द-संग्रह

Godown गोदाम **—Keeper** गोदाम-रक्षक **—Manager** गोदाम प्रबंधक **—(Catering)** गोदाम प्रबंधक (खानपान)

Good and sufficient reason समुचित और पर्याप्त कारण **—behaviour** सद्व्यवहार/अच्छा चलन **—books, in one's** किसी की कृपा होना,…का कृपा पात्र होना **—character** सुचरित्र, अच्छा चरित्र, सच्चरित्रता **—conduct** सदाचरण **—faith** सद्भाव **—offices** मध्यस्थता **—order, in** अच्छी स्थिति में **—reason** पर्याप्त कारण **—service pay** सुसेवा वेतन, प्रशस्त सेवा वेतन **—will** सुनाम, सद्भावना **Goods** वस्तुएं **—Clerk** माल क्लर्क/माल बाबू **—Jetty serang** माल घाट सेरांग **—train** माल गाड़ी **—with care** संभाल कर

Govern 1. शासन करना 2. नियंत्रण रखना **Governance** अभिशासन/शासन **Governed** शासित

Governing body शासी निकाय

Government शासन/सरकार **—advocate** सरकारी अधिवक्ता; सरकारी ऐडवोकेट **—affairs** राजकाज, सरकारी मामले **—agency** सरकारी एजेंसी **—business** सरकारी काम **—Estate** राज-संपदा **—House** राज भवन **—land** सरकारी भूमि **—of India** भारत सरकार **—Concern** भारत सरकार का प्रतिष्ठान **—Undertaking** भारत सरकार उपक्रम **—pleader** सरकारी वकील **—Press** सरकारी प्रेस/राजकीय मुद्रणालय **—Provident Fund** सरकारी भविष्य-निधि/सरकारी निर्वाह-निधि **—regulation** सरकारी विनियम **—securities** सरकारी प्रतिभूतियां **——Servants' Conduct Rules** सरकारी कर्मचारी आचरण नियमावली **—Service** सरकारी सेवा **—Solicitor** सरकारी प्रति-पुरुष; सरकारी सालीसिटर **—undertaking** सरकारी उपक्रम

Governor 1. राज्यपाल 2. अभि-शासक/गवर्नर/शासक 3. सूबेदार (मुगल काल) **—General** महा राज्यपाल **Governor's box** राज्यपाल कक्ष

Grace 1. अनुग्रह/प्रसाद 2. रियायत **—, Day of** रियायती दिन **—period** रियायत की अवधि

Gradation list पदक्रम सूची **—Clerk** पदक्रम-सूची-लिपिक

Grade श्रेणी/पदक्रम/ग्रेड/कोटि

—junior अवर कोटि/पदक्रम, जूनियर ग्रेड —, Junior administrative अवर प्रशासन-ग्रेड/अवर प्रशासनकोटि —pay पदक्रम/ग्रेड वेतन --senior वरिष्ठ कोटि, सीनियर ग्रेड —, Senior administrative प्रवर प्रशासन-ग्रेड/प्रवर प्रशासन कोटि **Graded Specialist** वर्गीकृत विशेषज्ञ **Grader** ग्रेडर/श्रेणी-निर्धारिक **Grading Inspector** श्रेणीकरण निरीक्षक **Gradual increase** क्रमश:/क्रमिक वृद्धि

Graduate स्नातक —clerk स्नातक लिपिक

Grain Inspector खाद्यान्न निरीक्षक —shop खाद्यान्न दुकान —Shop Inspector खाद्यान्न दुकान निरीक्षक —Manager खाद्यान्न दुकान प्रबंधक —Storage,, Research and Training centre अनाज संचयन, अनुसंधान तथा प्रशिक्षण केन्द्र

Grand total महायोग, कुल जोड़ —Parents महाजनक

Grant (n.) अनुदान **(vb.)** स्वीकार करना, प्रदान करना —, Extra अतिरिक्त अनुदान —, Fixed नियत अनुदान **Grant-in-aid** सहायक अनुदान —, Interim अंतरिम अनुदान —, Maintenance अनुरक्षण अनुदान/भरण-पोषण अनुदान —Non-recurring अनावर्ती अनुदान —Pardon क्षमा प्रदान करना —, Preliminary प्रारंभिक अनुदान करना —Recurring आवर्ती अनुदान —, Special विशेष अनुदान —, Supplementary अनुपूरक अनुदान

Granted स्वीकृत **Granted leave** छुट्टी स्वीकृत

Granter अनुदाता

Graph ग्राफ/आलेख/लेखा चित्र —Supervisor लेखा चित्र-पर्यवेक्षक/ग्राफ पर्यवेक्षक

Gratification, Illegal अवैध परितोषण

Gratis नि:शुल्क/मुफ्त **Gratis given** नि:शुल्क मुफ्त दी गई

Gratuitous 1. आनुग्रहिक 2. मुफ्त —advice बिना मांगे सलाह, मुफ्त सलाह

Gratuity उपदान/आनुतोषिक —, retirement निवृत्ति उपदान आनुतोषिक

Grave गम्भीर —disorder गम्भीर/व्यापक/भीषण अव्यवस्था/गड़बड़

Greaser ग्रीजर —, Incharge ग्रीजर प्रभारी **Greasing Supervisor** स्नेहन पर्यवेक्षक

Greeting 1. शुभ कामना/बधाई

2. अभिवादन

Grievance शिकायत **Procedure** शिकायत-निवारण क्रियाविधि; शिकायतें दूर करने का तरीका **redress of** व्यथा निवारण शिकायत दूर करना **Grievous injury** गहरी चोट

Gross 1. सकल/कुल 2. घोर/भारी —**abuse** घोर दुरुपयोग —**amount** सकल राशि, कुल रकम —**assets** कुल परिसम्पत्ति/कुल आस्तियाँ —**error** घोर त्रुटि/भारी गलती —, **income** कुल आमदनी/सकल आय —, **mis-conduct** घोर दुराचरण —, **mis-take** भारी भूल —, **neglect** घोर उपेक्षा —**negligence** भारी गफलत, घोर प्रमाद, असाधारण लापरवाही/उपेक्षा —**revenue** कुल राजस्व —**total** सकल योग —**value** कुल मूल्य/सकल मूल्य

Ground Engineer स्थल-अभियंता/ग्राउंड इंजीनियर —**rent** जमीन का भाड़ा —, **Traffic Controller** भू-यातायात-नियंत्रक **Grounds** आधार —**of, on** के आधार पर

Group Captain ग्रुप कैप्टेन —, **Commander** ग्रुप कमांडर —, **Engineer** समूह इंजीनियर —, **Incharge** ग्रुप इंचार्ज —, **Officer** समूह-अधिकारी —, **(Defence)** ग्रुप अफसर —**Testing Officer (G.T.O)** ग्रुप टेस्टिग अफसर(जी० टी० ओ०)

Grouping and grading वर्गीकरण और कोटिकरण/पदक्रमण

'Grow More Food' Officer अधिक-अन्न-उत्पादन-अधिकारी

Guarantee गारंटी —**written** लिखित गारण्टी **Guarantor** गारण्टीकर्त्ता

Guard रक्षक/गार्ड —, **(of a train)** गार्ड —**against, to** से बचाव करना/रखना —, **book** रक्षक-पुस्तक —**file** रक्षक मिसिल, निदेश फाइल, गार्ड फाइल —**of honour** सम्मान गारद

Guardian अभिभावक/वली/संरक्षक **Guardianship certificate** अभिभावकता प्रमाण-पत्र

Guest house अतिथि-गृह —, **Superintendent** अतिथि-गृह-अधीक्षक

Guidance मार्ग दर्शन/निर्देशन —**Checking Clerk** मार्ग दर्शन पड़ताल लिपिक **Guidance, for** संदर्शन/मार्ग दर्शन के लिए

Guide (n.) परिदर्शक, गाइड **(vb.)** संदर्शन, करना/मार्ग-दर्शन करना/मार्ग दिखाना **Guide book**

संदर्शिका, गाइड पुस्तक **Guide keys** निर्देश कुंजियां **Guiding price** निर्देशक मूल्य

Guilt अपराध/दोष **Guiltless** निरपराध **Guilty** दोषी
—of delay विलम्ब का दोषी
—of fraud कपट का दोषी
—of, found के लिए दोषी पाया गया

Guise ब्याज, बाना; भेष; वेश

Gummer गोंदवाला

Gunman गनवाला/गनमैन

Gunner तोपची/गनर

Habeas corpus बन्दी प्रत्यक्षीकरण

Habit 1. स्वभाव/आदत 2. अभ्यास
—by स्वभाव/आदत से
Habitable वास योग्य; रहने योग्य, निवास; निवास योग्य
—condition, in रहने योग्य दशा/हालत में **Habitation** वास; निवेश; निवास **Habitual** आभ्यासिक; स्वभावत; स्वाभाविक; अभ्यस्त **—Criminal** अभ्यस्त अपराधी; आभ्यासिक अपराधी **—cruel and inhuman treatment** स्वभावत: क्रूर और अमानुषिक व्यवहार; आभ्यासिक क्रूर **—defaulter** 1. आभ्यासिक व्यतिक्रमी/आभ्यासिक दोषी 2. आभ्यासिक बकायादार **—offender** आभ्यासिक / आदतन अपराधी **Hackney carriage** भाड़े की गाड़ी; भाटक वाहन; भाड़ा गाड़ी; किराये की गाड़ी

Hail insurance ओला बीमा; उपल झंझा-आगोप

Half holiday आधी छुट्टी
—mast झुका, अर्धनत **—monthly Payments** अर्ध मासिक संदाय **—pay** आधा वेतन/अर्द्ध वेतन **—pay leave** अर्ध वेतन छुट्टी **—timer** अर्द्ध कालिक सहित
—yearly अर्द्ध वार्षिक/छमाही
—yearly inspection अर्धवार्षिक निरीक्षण, छमाही मुआयना
Halftone Engraver हाफटोन एन्ग्रेवर/बिंदुचित्र उकेरक
Hand, under my मेरे हस्ताक्षर

Hall हॉल/भवन **—, conference** कांफ्रेंस हाल, सम्मेलन भवन
—, Jamadar हाल-जमादार

Halt विराम/अवस्थान **Halt at...** ...में विराम/रुकना **—Conductor** व्यवधान-कंडक्टर **Halting allowance** विराम-भत्ता

Hammerman हथौड़े वाला, हथौड़िया

Hand हस्त, हाथ **—bill** परचा
—book पुस्तिका, हस्तक
—Press Operator (Hand

Pressman) हाय छाईकार बाधा

Handicap दस्तकारी/हस्तकला/हस्तशिल्प **Handicaps inspite of** वाधाओं के बावजूद **Handicraft** दस्त/मूठहत्था **—exhibition** हस्तकला/दस्तकारी प्रदर्शनी

Handle (vb.) संभालना **Handled the situation** स्थिति संभाल ली **Handling (of dak)** (डाक पर) कार्यवाई करना **Handling charges** चढाई-उतराई खर्च/प्रभार **Handloom** हाथ करघा

Handloom industry हाथ करघा उद्योग **—Inspector** हाथकरघा-निरीक्षक

Hand-over सौंपना/देना **—charge** कार्यभार सौंपना **Hands, additional** अतिरिक्त कर्मचारी

Handwriting Expert लिखावट-विशेषज्ञ/हस्तलेख विशेषज्ञ

Hanging Paragraph दूर शेष पैरा

Harbour बंदरगाह/पत्तन **—dues** बंदरगाह के देय **—, Master** बंदरगाह-मास्टर / पत्तन मास्टर **Harbouring an offender** अपराधी को आश्रय देना

Hard and fast rules पक्के-नियम **—cash** नकदी **—currency area** दुर्लभ मुद्रा-क्षेत्र **Hardness test** कठोरता-परीक्षण

Hardware Unit धातु-वस्तु एकक

Harsh treatment कठोर/रूखा व्यवहार

Haulage charges ढुलाई खर्च

Havildar हवलदार **—, Major** हवलदार मेजर

Having force of law विधिसम्मत होना **Having satisfied myself** अपना समाधान करके

Hazardous संकटमय **—act** जोखिम वाला काम, संकटमय कार्य

Head 1. प्रधान 2. शीर्ष/मद **—account** प्रधान लेखाकार **—, Assistant** प्रधान सहायक **— Barman** प्रधान बारमैन **—, Block Instrument Mistry** प्रधान ब्लॉक उपकरण मिस्त्री **—, Bromide Printer** प्रधान ब्रोमाइड मुद्रक **—Cash Counter** प्रधान रोकड़ गणक **—Witness** प्रधान रोकड़ साक्षी **—Clerk** प्रधान लिपिक/प्रधान क्लर्क **—Constable** प्रधान हवलदार **—Crane Inspector** प्रधान क्रेन निरीक्षक **—Design Assistant** प्रधान अभिकल्प सहायक **—Despatcher** प्रधान प्रेषक **—of account** लेखा-शीर्ष, लेखा मद्द **—office** प्रधान कार्यालय **—office account**

प्रधान कार्यालय लेखा —**of department/office** विभाग/कार्यालय अध्यक्ष —**of State** राष्ट्र का प्रधान —**quarters** मुख्यालय, मुख्य कार्यालय —**,sub-** उपशीर्ष —, **Technical Section** प्रधान, तकनीकी अनुभाग

Heading, standard मानक शीर्षक —**sub** उपशीर्षक —**subject** विषय शीर्षक **Headway, making** प्रगति होना, आगे बढ़ना

Health certificate स्वास्थ्य प्रमाण-पत्र

Hearing of the suit वाद/मुकदमे की सुनवाई

Heavy equipment भारी उपस्कर

Heir वारिस —**apparent** प्रत्यक्ष दायाद / वारिस / उत्तराधिकारी —**(of a State)** युवराज **appointed** नियुक्त दायाद; नियुक्त वारिस —**Collateral** सांपार्श्विक दायाद; सांपार्श्विक वारिस —**expectant** प्रत्याशी दायाद, प्रत्याशी वारिस —**legal** वैध दायाद; वैध वारिस —**presumptive** संभावित दयाद प्रकल्पित उत्तराधिकारी —**Prospective** भावी दायाद; भावी वारिस

Held in abeyance रोक रखी गई, स्थगित रखी गई **Held, it was** यह निर्णय किया गया, यह पाया/ठहराया गया

Helminthiasist कृमिरोग-विज्ञानी

Helper मददगार

Henceforth अब से, आगे से

Her Excelleney परमश्रेष्ठ (स्त्री)

Her Majesty महामहिम (स्त्री)

Herbarium Keeper वनस्पति-संग्रहपाल

Hereafter इसके बाद **Hereby acknowledged** इसके द्वारा प्राप्ति की सूचना दी गई, एतद्द्वारा अभि-स्वीकृत

Hereditary पैतृक / मौरूसी/आनुवंशिक —**right** पैतृक/मौरूसी अधिकार **Hereinafter** इसके आगे **Hereinbefore** इसके पहले **Herein provided for** इसमें उपबन्धित, इसमें दिए अनुसार **Heretofore** अब तक **Herewith enclosed** इसी के साथ संलग्न **Herewith please** साथ प्रस्तुत है

Hesitation, without any बिना हिचकिचाहट के, निस्संकोच

Hide Development Officer चर्म-विकास अधिकारी

Hierarchy 1. उत्क्रम/सोपान 2. धर्मसत्ता

High Commission उच्चायोग/हाई कमीशन —**Commissioner**

उच्चायुक्त / हाई कमिश्नर **—Court** उच्च न्यायालय **—power committee** उच्चशक्ति/ उच्चाधिकार समिति **—Pressure Boiler Operator** उच्च दाब बॉयलर प्रचालक **—treason** महा राज्यद्रोह, महा अभिद्रोह **Higher authority** उच्चतर प्राधिकारी **Highest bid** सब से ऊँची बोली **Highly objectionable** अत्यन्त/बहुत आपत्तिजनक **Highly Skilled Mechanic** अतिकुशल मेकैनिक **Highway** राजपथ/राजमार्ग **Division** राजपथ प्रभाग/राजमार्ग प्रभाग **Highway, National** राष्ट्रीय राजपथ, राष्ट्रीय मुख्य मार्ग

Hill allowance पहाड़-भत्ता/पर्वतीय स्थान-भत्ता **—station** पर्वतीय स्थान

Hindi Inspector हिन्दी निरीक्षक **—Instructor** हिन्दी शिक्षक **—officer** हिंदी अधिकारी **—Section** हिन्दी अनुभाग **—Teacher** हिन्दी अध्यापक

Hindrance बाधा/अड़चन **—, without** बिना अड़चन

Hindu Religious and Charitable Endowment Department हिन्दू धर्मस्व और पूर्त-अक्षयनिधिविभाग

Hint संकेत/इशारा **Hinted, as** यथा संकेतित, इशारे के अनुसार

Hire (n.) भाड़ा **(vb.)** भाड़े पर लेना **—charges** भाड़ा **—purchase** भाड़ा-क्रय **—Purchase Division** भाड़ा क्रय-प्रभाग

His Excellency परम श्रेष्ठ **His Majesty** महामहिम

History sheet इतिवृत्त, वृत्त-पत्र

Hold (Office) (पद) ग्रहण करना **Hold a meeting** बैठक करना **Hold an office** पद धारण/ग्रहण करना, पदासीन **Hold brief** वकालत करना, पक्ष लेना **Hold office during the pleasure of the authority** प्राधिकार के प्रसाद पर्यन्त पद धारण करना **Hold over** स्थगित करना, रोक लेना **Hold up** रोकना **Holdings, consolidation of** चकबन्दी

Holiday अवकाश छुट्टी **—public** सार्वजनिक अवकाश/छुट्टी

Hollerith Punch Operator हौलरिथ पंचित्र प्रचालक

Holograph स्वलेखन

Homage श्रद्धांजलि **—, pay** श्रद्धांजलि अर्पित करना

Home गृह **—Affairs, Ministry of** गृह-मन्त्रालय **—Guard** होम गार्ड **—Science Assistant**

गृहविज्ञान-सहायक **—Secretary** गृह-सचिव **—town** मूल निवास स्थान

Honest ईमानदार **—person** ईमानदार व्यक्ति **Honoraria, allowances and** भत्ते तथा मानदेय **Honorarium** मानदेय

Honorary अवैतनिक **Honorary capacity, in an** अवैतनिक रूप में **—Air Aide-de-camp** अवैतनिक हवाई ए डी सी **—degree** साम्मानिक उपाधि **—Dental Adviser** अवैतनिक दन्त-सलाहकार **—Life Aide-de-camp** अवैतनिक आजीवन ए डी सी **—Secretary** अवैतनिक सचिव **—Statistical Adviser** अवैतनिक सांख्यिकीय सलाहकार **Honourable** 1. माननीय 2. सम्मानपूर्ण **Honourable Member** माननीय सदस्य

Honorific prefix सम्मान-शब्द

Horticulture department उद्यान विभाग **—Inspector** बागबानी निरीक्षक **—Mistry** बागवानी मिस्त्री **—Superintendent** बागवानी अधीक्षक **—Supervisor** उद्यान-कृषि पर्यवेक्षक **Horticulturist** उद्यान-कृषि-विशेषज्ञ

Hospitality fund आतिथ्य/सत्कार निधि

Hospital leave अस्पताली छुट्टी **—Steward** चिकित्सालय स्टूवर्ड/अस्पताल स्टूवर्ड **—Store Keeper** चिकित्सालय भंडारी

Host आतिथेय **Hostess** सत्कारिणी **Hostess, air** वायुयान-सत्कारिणी

Hostel Superintendent छात्रावास अधीक्षक **—Warden** छात्राबास-पाल, छात्रपाल

Hours of business कार्य समय **Hours of employment** काम के घण्टे

House building advance गृह निर्माण अग्रिमधन/पेशगी **House, Leader of the** सदन का नेता **—of Correction** सुधार-गृह **—of legislature** विधान मण्डल सदन, विधान मण्डल **—of People** लोकसभा **—rent** मकान-किराया **—rent allowance** मकान किराया भत्ता **—Surgeon** हाउस-सर्जन/स्थानीय सर्जन **—tax** गृह कर **—Tax Collector** गृहकर-समाहर्ता

Housing आवास **—Adviser** आवास सलाहकार **—Commissioner** आवास आयुक्त **facilities** आवास सुविधाएं **—schemes** आवास योजनाएं

Hue and cry शोर, दुहाई

Human Ecologist मानव परिस्थिति-विज्ञानी/मानव परिस्थितिकी-विज्ञ **Humanitarian grounds, on** मानवीय आधार पर

Hypothetical question काल्पनिक प्रश्न

Hutment अस्थायी मकान

Hydraulic Research Station जलीय अनुसंधान-केन्द्र

Hygiene Officer स्वच्छता अफसर/स्वच्छता अधिकारी

I agree मैं सहमत हूँ **I am directed to** मुझे निदेश हुआ है कि **I am to add** मुझे यह भी लिखना है कि **I authorise you** मैं आपको अधिकार देता हूं **I beg to submit** निवेदन है कि **I have no instructions** मुझे कोई हिदायत नहीं मिली है **I have not the least hesitation** मुझे जरा भी संकोच नहीं है **I have satisfied myself** मैंने अपना समाधान कर लिया है **I have the honour to** सादर

Ibid, (Ibidem) तत्रैव/वहीं

Identical case एक सा मामला **—scale** एकरूप / समान वेतनमान **Identical scale of pay** एकरूप वेतनमान **—time-scale of pay** वेतन का समान समय-मान

Identification पहचान/शिनाख्त **—certificate** पहचान प्रमाणपत्र **—card** पहचान पत्र **—mark** पहचान चिह्न **—number** पहचान संख्या **Identity card** पहचान-पत्र

If and when यदि और जब **If and whenever** यदि और जब कभी **If any** यदि कोई हो **If necessary** यदि आवश्यक हो

If possible यदि संभव हो

If required यदि अपेक्षित हो

Ignorance अनभिज्ञता **—of law** कानून/विधि की अनभिज्ञता, कानून न जानना

Illegal अवैध **—dealings** अवैध व्यवहार **—gratification** अवैध परितोषण **—practice** अवैध आचरण/अवैधाचार **—war** अवैध युद्ध

Illegible अपाठ्य **—signature** अपाठ्य हस्ताक्षर **Illegitimate** अवैध/अधर्मज **-- action** अवैध कार्य

Illicit निषिद्ध **Illiteracy** निरक्षरता **Ill-treatment** दुर्व्यवहार **Ill-will** वैमनस्य

Illustration निदर्शन/निदर्शना/उदाहरण **— as an**

उदाहरणस्वरूप **Illus trative lts** दृष्टान्त/निदर्शी सूची

Image बिम्ब, प्रतिमा, प्रतिबिम्ब

Immediate 1. तत्काल 2. अव्यवहित/आसन्न **—action** तत्काल/अविलम्ब / फौरन कार्रवाई **—annuity due** तत्कालदेय वार्षिकी **—danger** आसन्न संकट **—employer** आसन्न नियोक्ता **—officer** आसन्न अधिकारी **—slip** तत्कालपर्ची

Immediately before तुरन्त पहले/पूर्व **below** ठीक नीचे

Immigration Authority आप्रवास प्राधिकारी

Imminent आसन्न **—danger** सन्निकट संकट

Immoral act अनैतिक कार्य

Immovable property अचल सम्पत्ति

Immune from से मुक्त, से प्रतिरक्षित

Immunity प्रतिरक्षा

Impartial निष्पक्ष **—judgement** निष्पक्ष निर्णय / फैसला

Impartiality निष्पक्षता

Impeachment अधिक्षेप

Impediment अड़चन / बाधा **—serious** गम्भीर अड़चन

Impending आसन्न **—danger** आसन्न खतरा

Impersonation प्रतिरूपण **—, charge of** प्रतिरूपण का आरोप

Impertinence, gross घोर धृष्टता

Implement कार्यान्वित करना/अमल में लाना/परिपालन करना

Implementing the decision, in निर्णय को कार्यान्वित करते हुए, फैसले पर अमल करते हुए **Implementation Cell** कार्यान्वयन एकक **—officer** परिपालन अधिकारी/कार्यान्वयन अधिकारी

Implicated, falsely झूठे फंसा दिया

Implication 1. विवक्षा/मंशा 2. फंसा जाना फंसना/फंसाना **—of rule** नियम का आशय/मंशा/विवक्षा

Implied विवक्षित **—, it is** आशय/मंशा यह है, यह विवक्षित है

Import 1. आयात 2. अभिप्राय **—policy** आयात नीति **— recommendation certificate** आयात-सिफारिश-प्रमाण पत्र **—Trade Controller** आयात-व्यापार नियंत्रक

Importance महत्त्व **Important** महत्वपूर्ण **—call** आव-

श्यक कॉल —**matter** महत्त्वपूर्ण बात —**papers** महत्वपूर्ण कागजात

Imported stores आयात माल

Imports and Exports, Chief Controller of मुख्य नियन्त्रक, आयात-निर्यात

Impose अधिरोपित करना **Imposed, conditions** अधिरोपित/थोपी गई शर्तें

Imposition अधिरोपण

Impossible असंभव

Impost लाभकर

Impracticable अव्यावहारिक —**suggestions** अव्यावहारिक सुझाव

Impression 1. छाप २. मन पर प्रभाव —**deep** गहरी छाप —**thumb** अंगूठा-निशानी —**wrong** गलत धारणा

Imprest अग्रदाय/उचंत —**account** अग्रदाय लेखा —**holder** उचंतधारी —**money** अग्रदाय धन

Imprison कारावासी करना

Improper अनुचित —**way** अनुचित ढंग/तरीका

Improve सुधार करना/समुन्नति करना **Improved** उन्नत, संशोधित, सुधरा, सुसंस्कृत —**draft** सुधारा हुआ प्रारूप, बेहतर मसौदा

Improvement 1. सुधार/संशोधन 2. समुन्नति/अभिवृद्धि —**Trust** नगर-सुधार-मण्डल

Improvisation काम चलाऊ/तात्कालिक (व्यस्था) **Improvise** काम चलाना/व्यवस्था करना/तात्कालिक व्यवस्था करना

Improvised काम चलाऊ —**arrangement** काम चलाऊ/तात्कालिक व्यवस्था

Impute लांछन लगाना

In abeyance निलंबित/आस्थगित —**held** आस्थगित/निलंबित रखा गया

In accordance with के अनुसार —**prescribed chanels** विहित प्रणाली के अनुसार —**the requirement** अपेक्षाओं के अनुसार

In addition to के अतिरिक्त

In advance अगाऊ, पहले से, अग्रिम

In aid of की सहायता में, के सहायतार्थ

In all recepts सब बातों में

In an exemplary manner अनुकरणीय रूप में; अनुकरणीय रीति से

In anticipation के भरोसे पर, की प्रत्याशा में **In** —**of your approval** आपके अनुमोदन/

मंजूरी की प्रत्याशा में (के भरोसे पर)

In any case किसी अवस्था में भी, हर हालत में

In any form किसी भी रूप में

In as much as जहां तक कि

In breach of Contract संविदा भंगकारी **—his official duties** अपने पदीय कर्त्तव्यों के भंग में

In camera बन्द कमरे में, गुप्त, गुप्त बैठक

In case it appears यदि प्रतीत होता हो **In case of need** आवश्यकता पड़ने/होने पर **In case of doubt** संशय की दशा में, संशय होने पर **In case of failure** यदि कार्य न हो सका तो, विफल हो जाने पर, चूक जाने पर **In case or instance** किसी भी दशा या अवस्था में

In cash नकद

In certain cases कुछ अवस्थाओं में कुछ मामलों में

In charge भार साधक, प्रभारी

Inconclusive discussion अनिर्णीत चर्चा/बहस

In compliance with का पालन करते हुए

In confirmation of की पुष्टि में **In confirmity with** के अनुरूप

In connection with के सम्बन्ध/सिलसिले में

In consultation with से परामर्श करके

In continuation of this Ministry's इस मंत्रालय के तारीख के पत्र

In contravention of के विपरीत, का उल्लंघन

In course of के दौरान **—of business** काम करते हुए **—of time** यथा समय समय से, समय बीतने पर

In default of के अभाव में, न करने पर, चूक करने पर, न होने पर

In detail सविस्तार/ब्यौरेवार

In due course यथा समय, समय से **—of law** यथोचित विधि प्रक्रिया में

In excess of से अधिक

In exercise of का प्रयोग करते हुए, के प्रयोग में, से काम लेते हुए

In extenso सविस्तार, विस्तार में/से

In fact वस्तुतः, वास्तव में

In favour of के पक्ष में, के नाम में

In force लागू , प्रवृत्त

In full पूरा, पूर्णतः

In general सामान्य रूप से, आमतौर पर

In his discretion अपनी समझ से

In his view उनकी दृष्टि में, उनके विचार में

In keeping with के अनुरूप

In kind वस्तु रूप में

In lieu of के स्थान में/पर, के बदले में

In like manner समान रीति से, उसी ढंग से

In lump sum एक मुश्त, एक बार में

In matter of के विषय में

In memorium स्मृति में

In official capacity पद की हैसियत से

In operation अमल में

In order विधिवत्, सही, यथाक्रम, क्रम से, व्यवस्थित **In order of merit/priority** योग्यता/अग्रता क्रम से **In order to** के लिए

In other respects अन्य बातों/प्रकरण में

In Pari Causa समान दशा में; समान स्थिति में, समदशा में **In Pari delicto** समदोषी; समान दोषी **In pari materia** समान विषय में समविषयक

In part अंशत:, आंशिक **In parts** कई भागों में, भागश:

In pay वेतन पाने वाला

In Pendent निलंबित

In Perpetuity शाश्वत; सदैव के लिये

In person स्वयं **In Personal Capacity** वैयक्तिक हैसियत से **In Parsonam** व्यक्तिलक्षी

In particular विशेषत:

In Perpetnity सदा के लिए शाश्वत

In practice व्यवहार में

In preference to की अपेक्षा

In Presence of के समक्ष; के सामने

In public interest लोकहित में; लोकहित की दृष्टि में

In pursuance of के अनुसरण में, के अनुसार

In question प्रश्नास्पद, सम्बन्ध में, सम्बन्धित

In reference to के प्रति निर्देश से

In regard/relation to के बारे में **In relation to** के सम्बन्ध में

In reply to के उत्तर में

In respect of के बारे में

In so far as जहां तक कि

In supersession of का अधिक्रमण करते हुए, को निष्प्रभाव करते हुए

In that respect तद् विषयक, उस बारे में

In the case of की स्थिति में, के विषय में **In the circumstances** इस परिस्थिति में, इन हालतों में

In the course of के दौरान

In the event of के होने पर, की अवस्था में **In the following manner** निम्नलिखित प्रकार/रीति/ढंग से **In the light of** को ध्यान में रखते हुए **In the nature of** के प्रकार/स्वरूप का, के रूप में **In the presence of** के समक्ष, के सामने, की उपस्थिति में **In the prescribed manner** विहित रीति से, नियत/निर्धारित ढंग से **In the same way** उसी भांति/तरह

In that behalf उस विषय में, उसके लिए, उस प्रयोजन के लिए

In this behalf इस बारे में, इस सम्बन्ध में

In theory सिद्धान्त रूप में

In time समय पर

In toto पूर्णतः, पूरी तरह से

In transit मार्ग में, मार्गस्थ, मार्ग-वर्ती, आने जाने में

In view of को ध्यान में रखकर, को देखते हुए, के अनुसार

Inability अयोग्यता

Inability to agree सहमति प्रकट करने में असमर्थता

Inaccuracy अयथार्थता/अशुद्धि **Inaccurate figures** अयथार्थ/अशुद्ध/गलत आंकड़े

Inadequate funds अपर्याप्त धन

Inadmissible अस्वीकार्य/अग्राह्य **—claim** अस्वीकार्य/अग्राह्य दावा

Inadvertence अनवधानता **—through** अनवधानता में, असावधानी से, अनजाने

Inadvertently अनजाने/असावधानीं से

Inapplicable अप्रयोज्य **—it is** यह लागू नहीं है

Inauguration उद्घाटन **—ceremony** उद्घाटन समारोह

Incapable of में असमर्थ, के अयोग्य, अक्षय

Incapacity असमर्थता

Incentive प्रोत्साहन **—proper** उचित प्रोत्साहन /उत्प्रेरक

Inception, since आरम्भ से, जन्म से

Incidental आनुषंगिक/प्रासंगिक **—charges** प्रासंगिक प्रभार **– expenditure** प्रासंगिक व्यय **—order** प्रासंगिक आदेश **Incidentally it may be stated** प्रसंगवश यह कहा जा सकता है

Incited mob भड़काई/उकसाई गई भीड़

Include अन्तर्गत होना

Inclusive सहित **—of** को सम्मिलित करके, को मिलाकर, सहित

Incognito 1. अज्ञात 2. गुप्त रूप से

Income आय **—tax** आय-कर **Income tax clearance certificate** आयकर शोधन-पत्र **— Officer** आयकर अधिकारी

Incoming call आवक काल **Incoming dak** आने वाली डाक, आवक डाक

Incompatible बेमेल **Incompatible with** से मेल न खाता हुआ, बेमेल

Incompetency अक्षमता **Incompetent hands** अक्षम कर्मचारी

Incomplete अधूरा **—Sample** अधूरा नमूना **—work** अधूरा काम

Inconclusive अनिर्णीत

Incongruous असंगत/बेतुका

Inconsistency असंगति, अननुरूपता **Inconsistent** असंगत **statement** असंगत कथन

Inconvenience असुविधा **—caused to you is much regretted** आपको हुई असुविधा के लिए बहुत खेद है

Incorporated in the draft प्रारूप/मसौदे में समाविष्ट/शामिल **Incorporation** निगमन

Incorrectly stated गलत रूप से कहा/बनाया हुआ

Increment वेतन-वृद्धि/वेतन-तरक्की **—annual** वार्षिक वेतन-वृद्धि **—certificate** वेतन वृद्धि-पत्र/वेतन-तरक्की पत्र

Incumbent पदस्य/पदधारी **—of an office** पदधारी, पदस्थ **—upon, it would be** पर यह लाजिम/आवश्यक होगा **Incumbrance** अधिभार

Incurred (व्यय) किया हुआ

Indebtedness ऋणता, ऋणग्रस्तता

Indefinite अनिश्चित **—period** अनिश्चित काल/अवधि

Indemmify क्षतिपूर्ति करना **Indemnification** क्षतिपूरण **Indemnity** हर्जाना, क्षतिपूर्ति **—bond** क्षतिपूर्ति बन्ध-पत्र

Indent मांग पत्र/इंडेंट **—, annual** वार्षिक मांग-पत्र / इंडेन्ट **—item** इंडेंट मद/मांग-पत्र-मद **— transfer memo** मांग हस्तांतरण ज्ञापन **Indented paragraph** दूरारम्भ पैरा **Indentor** मांग कर्ता **Indentor's instructions** मांग-कर्ता की हिदायतें **Sample** मांग का नमूना **Indenture** कोष्ठक, इन्डेन्चर, करारनामा, अनुबन्धपत्र

Independent note स्वतन्त्र/टिप्पणी **—opinion** स्वतन्त्र राय

Index सूचक / अनुक्रमणी **—card/slip** सूचक कार्ड/पर्ची

—number अनुक्रमणी अंक/सूचक अंक —, Simple सरल सूचक —sheet सूचक पत्र —slip सूचक पर्ची **Indexer** अनुक्रमणीकार **Indexing** सूची बनाना/अनुक्रमणी बनाना —, alphabetical वर्णानुसार सूची बनाना —vowel स्वरानुसार सूचक बनाना

India Supply Mission भारत पूर्ति मिशन

Indian Administrative Service भारतीय प्रशासन सेवा —Agricultural Research Institute भारतीय कृषि अनुसंधान संस्थान —Airlines corporation भारतीय हवाई कम्पनी निगम —Bureau of Mines भारतीय खान ब्यूरो **Indian Civil Service** भारतीय सिविल सेवा —Council of Agricultural Research भारतीय कृषि अनुसंधान परिषद् —of Cultural Relations भारतीय सांस्कृतिक सम्पर्क परिषद् — of Medical Research भारतीय चिकित्सा अनुसंधान परिषद् —Custom Tariff भारतीय सीमा-शुल्क दर —Delegation Office भारतीय शिष्टमण्डल कार्यालय **Indian Educational Service** भारतीय शिक्षा सेवा — Foreign Service भारतीय विदेश सेवा —Institute of Biochemistry and External Medicine भारतीय जीव-रसायन और प्रयोगिक भेषज-संस्थान —Institute of Petroleum भारतीय पेट्रोलियम संस्थान —Police Service भारतीय पुलिस-सेवा —Railways Standard भारतीय रेलवे मानक **Indian Revenue Service** भारतीय राजस्व सेवा —Service Pay भारतीय सेवा वेतन

Indication संकेत/सूचना **Indicated above, as** जैसा ऊपर संकेत किया बताया गया है **Indication, according to** संकेत/सूचना के अनुसार

Indicator संकेतक

Indifferent attitude उपेक्षापूर्ण रुख/रवैया, उदासीन भाव

Indigenous Medicine Department देशी औषध-विभाग **Indigenous production** देशी उत्पादन

Indirectly परोक्ष रूप से **Indirect election** परोक्ष निर्वाचन, अप्रत्यक्ष चुनाव

Indiscipline अनुशासनहीनता —, act of अनुशासनहीनता का कार्य

Indiscretion अविवेक —act of

अविवेक का कार्य

Indispensable अपरिहार्य **—, he is** वह अपरिहार्य है, उसके बिना काम नहीं चल सकता

Individual व्यक्तिगत **—cases will be decided on merits** हरेक मामले पर अलग-अलग उसके गुणदोषों के आधार पर निर्णय किया जायगा **inspection** पृथक-पृथक निरीक्षण **Individuals, several** अनेक व्यक्ति

Indoor patient भरती हुआ रोगी, अन्तरंग रोगी **Indoor Patients Department** अन्तरंग रोगी विभाग

Indulgence shown by you आपने जो अनुग्रह किया है

Industrial complex औद्योगिक संकुल **—relations** औद्योगिक सम्बन्ध **—Finance Corporation of India** भारतीय औद्योगिक वित्त निगम **Industries department** उद्योग विभाग

Industry उद्योग **—and Supply Division** उद्योग और पूर्ति प्रभाग **Industrial and Technological Museum** औद्योगिक और शिल्पविज्ञानीय संग्रहालय **—Civil Defence Staff Course** औद्योगिक सिविल रक्षा कर्मचारी पाठ्यक्रम **—Development and Company Affairs, Ministry of** औद्योगिक विकास तथा कम्पनी कार्य मन्त्रालय **—Economist** उद्योग-अर्थशास्त्री **—estate** उद्योग-सम्पदा **—Extension Centre** उद्योग-विस्तार केन्द्र **—relations** औद्योगिक सम्पर्क **Industry, small scale** लघु उद्योग **—staff** उद्योग-कर्मचारी वर्ग **—Statistician** उद्योग-सांख्यिकीविद् **—tribunal** औद्योगिक अधिकरण **—X-Ray Superintendent** औद्योगिक एक्सरे अधीक्षक **—X-Ray Technical Assistant** औद्योगिक एक्सरे तकनीकी सहायक

Inefficiency अदक्षता **Inefficient** अदक्ष **—hand** अदक्ष कर्मचारी

Ineligible अपात्र **—for** के लिए अपात्र **Ineligibility** अपात्रता

Inexpedient असमीचीन **—, it will be** यह असमीचीन होगा

Infection संक्रमण **Infectious disease** संक्रामक रोग **—Disease Hospital** संक्रामक रोग अस्पताल

Inference अनुमति/अनुमान

Inferior निम्न / अवर / छोटा **—quality, of** घटिया किस्म का

—**service** अवर सेवा, निम्न सेवा —**to** से घटिया **Inferiority complex** हीनता की भावना, हीन भाव

Infirmity अशक्तता/दौर्बल्य

Inflated rate of pay वेतन की स्फीत दर

Inflationary tendency स्फीतिकारी प्रवृत्ति, मुद्राबाहुल्य के लक्षण

Influence, undue अनुचित प्रभाव

Informal अनौपचारिक

—**discussion** अनौपचारिक चर्चा/बातचीत **Informally ascertained** अनौपचारिक रूप से पता कर लिया है

Information सूचना/वार्ता —**and Broadcasting, Ministry of** सूचना और प्रसारण मन्त्रालय —**Bureau Supervisor** सूचना कार्यालय पर्यवेक्षक —**department** सूचना-विभाग —**for** सूचना/जानकारी के लिए, सूचनार्थ —**Officer** सूचना-अधिकारी —**Services of India** भारतीय-सूचना-सेवा **Informative note** सूचनाप्रद टिप्पणी

Infringement अतिलंघन

Inquire जांच करना

Inhabitant निवासी **Inhabited** बसे हुए

Inherit दाय प्राप्त करना

Initial प्रारंभिक —**pay** प्रारम्भिक वेतन **Initials** आद्यक्षर

Initiate प्रारम्भ करना/उपक्रमण/पहल करना —**action, to** कार्रवाई आरम्भ/शुरू करना, कार्य-वाही का सूत्रपात करना **Initiated** सूत्रपात किया जाना **Initiative** सत्रपात-क्षमता/पहल **Initiative, he is full of** उसमें बहुत पहल-शक्ति/सूत्रपात-क्षमता है, वह पहल-शक्ति से भरपूर है **Initiative, took the** पहल की, सूत्रपात किया

Injunction व्यादेश

Injurious हानिकारक

Inking stale-bed स्याही स्लेट

Inkman स्याही वाला/मसि वाला

Inland अंतर्देशीय —**letter** अंतर्देशीय पत्र

Inn पान्थशाला **Inn-keeper** पन्थिशाला-पाल

Inoculator टीका लगाने वाला

Inoperative प्रवर्तनहीन अप्रवृत्त —**sanction has become** मंजूरी/संस्वीकृति निष्प्रभावी हो गई है

Inordinate delay अत्यधिक देरी, असाधारण विलम्ब

Inquire into the offence अपराध की जांच करना **Inquiry** 1. पूछताछ 2. जांच —**Clerk** पूछताछ

लिपिक/पूछताछ क्लर्क
—departmental विभागीग्र जांच
—Inspector जांच निरीक्षक
—Office पूछताछ कार्यालय
—, Preliminary प्रारंभिक जांच
—, Secret गुप्त जांच

Insecticide Attendant कीटनाशक-परिचर

Insignia लक्ष्म

Insignificant amount तुच्छ/नगण्य राशि, बहुत थोड़ी रकम

Insolvency दिवाला —**Clerk** दिवाला क्लर्क **Insolvent, declared** दिवालिया घोषित किया गया

Inspect निरीक्षण करना

Inspection निरीक्षण —**after execution** निष्पादन के बाद निरीक्षण —**and Progress Supervisor** निरीक्षण और प्रगति पर्यवेक्षक —**at site** मौके/स्थल पर निरीक्षण —**Authority** निरीक्षण प्राधिकारी —**certificate** निरीक्षण प्रमाण-पत्र —**circle** निरीक्षण अंचल/निरीक्षण इलाका —, **Directorate of (Armament),** निरीक्षण निदेशालय (आयुध) —**equipment** निरीक्षण उपस्कर —**fee** निरीक्षण-शुल्क/निरीक्षण की फीस —**note** निरीक्षण टिप्पणी —**Officer** निरीक्षण अधिकारी —,**Periodical** आवधिक निरीक्षण **Inspecting officer** निरीक्षण अधिकारी **Inspection report** निरीक्षण रिपोर्ट —**wing** निरीक्षण स्कंध

Inspector निरीक्षक —**(Debit)** निरीक्षक (नामे) —**(Steel)** निरीक्षक (इस्पात) —**(Telegraph and Phones)** निरीक्षक (तार और फान) —, **Carriage and Wagon** सवारी और माल डिब्बा निरीक्षक —, **Finishing** परिष्करण निरीक्षक —, **Manufacturing** विनिर्माण निरीक्षक —, **Self Printing Ticket Machine** निरीक्षक, स्वतः मुद्रण टिकट मशीन —**of Drugs Control** औषध-नियंत्रण निरीक्षक —**of Explosives** विस्फोटक-निरीक्षक —**of Grain Godowns** अन्न-गोदाम-निरीक्षक —**of Notified Factories** अधिसूचित कारखानों का निरीक्षक —**of Pay Clerk** वेतन क्लर्क निरीक्षक —**of plantation** —पादपरोपण-निरीक्षक —**of Post Offices** डाकघर-निरीक्षक —**of Printing** मुद्रण निरीक्षक/छपाई-निरीक्षक —**of Schools** विद्यालय-निरीक्षक/स्कूल निरीक्षक —**of Station Accounts** स्टेशन लेखा निरीक्षक —**of Stores** भण्डार निरीक्षक

—of Training प्रशिक्षण निरीक्षक —of Weights and Measures बाट और माप निरीक्षक —of Works संकर्म निरीक्षक —of Works (Sanitation) संकर्म निरीक्षक (स्वच्छता) —on Special Duty विशेष कार्य निरीक्षक —General महानिरीक्षक —of Forests वन महानिरीक्षक —of Police पुलिस-महानिरीक्षक —of Prisons कारागार महानिरीक्षक —of Registration पंजीयन महानिरीक्षक/रजिस्ट्री-महानिरीक्षक—of Special police Establishment विशेष पुलिस स्थापना महानिरीक्षक

Inspectorate निरीक्षणालय —, **Dock Safety** गोदी-संरक्षा-निरीक्षणालय —**General** महानिरीक्षणालय

Inspectress निरीक्षिका

Instability, layer of अस्थिरता-परत

Install (also Instal) 1. नियुक्त करना/संस्थापित करना 2. लगाना **Installation (in Office)** संस्थापन/अधिष्ठापन —**electric** बिजली संस्थापन —**Engineer** संस्थापन इंजीनियर/संस्थापन अभियंता **Installed, newly** नया लगाया गया

Instalment किस्त **Instalments, in** किस्तों में

Instance of, at the की प्रेरणा पर, के कहने पर **Instance, for** उदाहरणार्थ, मिसाल के तौर पर **Instance, in the first** प्रथमतः, पहले तो **Instance, in this** इस मामले में

Instantaneous action तत्क्षण/तुरन्त कार्रवाई

Instead of के स्थान में, की बजाय

Instigated by द्वारा उकसाया गया

Instigation उकसाना

Institute (n.) संस्थापन **(vb.)** 1. स्थापित करना/संस्थापित करना 2. चलाना/प्रारंभ करना **Institute an inquiry** जांच करना **Institute, educational** शैक्षणिक संस्थान, शिक्षा-संस्था —**of Agricultural Research Statistic** कृषि-अनुसंधान-सांख्यिकी-संस्थान —**of Physiology** शरीर-क्रिया-विज्ञान संस्थान **Institution** संस्था

Instruction अनुदेश/हिदायत **Instructions are solicited** अनुदेश/हिदायत दीजिए **Instructor** शिक्षक/अनुदेशक — **Captain** इंस्ट्रक्टर कैप्टेन —**Commander** इंस्ट्रक्टर कमांडर —**Lieutenant** इंस्ट्रक्टर लेफ्टिनेंट —**Commander** इंस्ट्रक्टर लेफ्टिनेंट कमांडर —**Officer** इंस्ट्रक्टर अफसर

Instrument 1. यंत्र/उपकरण/औजार 2. लेख पत्र/लिखत 3. साधन **—Inspector** यंत्र-निरीक्षक/औजार-निरीक्षक **—Tester** यंत्र परीक्षक/औजार-परीक्षक **Instruments, moderu** आधुनिक यंत्र/उपकरण/औजार

Insubordination अनधीनता **Insubordination, charge of** अवज्ञा करने का आरोप, अनधीनता का आरोप

Insufficient अपर्याप्त **Insufficient cause** अपर्याप्त कारण

Insurance बीमा **Insurance charges** बीमा खर्च **Insurance Medical Officer** बीमा चिकित्सा अधिकारी **—Officer** बीमा-अधिकारी **Insurance Pool** बीमा निकाय, बीमा पूल **Insurance premium** बीमे की किस्त **Insured letter** बीमा किया हुआ पत्र **—on rail** रेल-बीमा किया

Integral part अभिन्न/अविभाज्य अंग **Integration** एकीकरण/समाकलन/समेकीकरण, समेकन/संकलन **Integration of states** राज्यों का एकीकरण/समेकन

Integrity 1. सत्यनिष्ठा/ईमानदारी 2. अखंडता **Integrity is beyond doubt** सत्यनिष्ठा/ईमानदारी संदेह से परे है

Intelligence 1. गुप्तवार्ता/खुफिया 2. आसूचना **—Bureau** गुप्तवार्ता विभाग **—Officer** गुप्तवार्ता अधिकारी

Intended leave आशयित छुट्टी

Intensive गहन/प्रकृष्ट/तीव्र **Intensive drive** गहन प्रयास, तीव्र आंदोलन **Intent** आशय

Intention अभिप्राय/आशय **—is** अभिप्राय/आशय/मंशा यह है **Intentionally** साभिप्राय/साशय **Intentionally done** जान-बूझकर किया गया, साभिप्राय किया गया

Inter alia अन्य/दूसरी बातों के साथ-साथ

Interception अंतर्ग्रहण/बीच में पढ़ लेना/रोक लेना/सुन लेना/अंतरावरोध

Interchange Stock Verifier विनिमय सामान सत्यापक/अंतर्बदल स्टाक सत्यापक

Inter communication अंतरा संचारण

Intercourse समागम, वृद्धि

Inter-departmental अंतर्विभागीय/अंतर-विभागीय **—reference** अंतराविभागीय पत्राचार **—sectional references** अंतरानुभागीय पत्राचार **—movement register** अंतरानुभागीय संचलन

रजिस्टर

Inter set आपस में परस्पर

Inter-state अन्तर-राज्य **—State Transport Commission** अंतर राज्य परिवहन आयोग **—Unit** अंतरा एकक

Interest ब्याज **Interest, in his own** अपने हित में **—, in public** लोक-सार्वजनिक हित में **Interest recoverable** ब्याज जो वसूल करना हैं

Interfere हस्तक्षेप करना **Interference** हस्तक्षेप **Inference, undue** अनुचित हस्तक्षेप

Interim अंतरिम **Interim arrangement** अन्तरिम प्रबन्ध **—award** अंतरिम पंचाट **—order** अंतरिम आदेश **Interim relief** अन्तरिम सहायता **—reply** अंतरिम उत्तर

Intermediary मध्यवर्ती

Intermediate मध्यवर्ती

Intermediate station मध्यवर्ती स्टेशन

Internal आंतरिक/आभ्यांतरिक **—arrangement** आंतरिक व्यवस्था, स्थानीय प्रबन्ध

International organisation अंतर्राष्ट्रीय संगठन

Interpolation प्रक्षेप

Interpretation 1. निर्वचन 2. व्याख्या **Interpretation, correct** ठीक निर्वचन, सही अर्थ लगाना **Interpreter** दुभाषिया/भाषांतरकार

Interrogate पूछताछ करना/परिप्रश्न करना **Interrogation** परिप्रश्न/पूछताछ **Interrogation, police** पुलिस द्वारा पूछताछ/परिप्रश्न **Interrogator** परिप्रश्नक

Interruption बाधा/विघ्न/व्यवधान/क्रमभंग **Interruption in service** सेवा क्रमभंग

Interse परस्पर/आपस में **Intersectional references** अंतरानुभागी पत्राचार

Interval अंतरावधि/अंतराल

Interval regular नियमित अंतराल/अंतरावधि

Interview साक्षात्कार/इंटरव्यू/प्रत्यक्ष भेंट **—, call for** साक्षात्कार/इंटरव्यू के लिए बुलावा

Intestacy इच्छापत्र-हीनत्व निर्वसीयता

Intimate 1. सूचना देना 2. प्रज्ञापित करना **Intimation** प्रज्ञापन/सूचना/इत्तिला **Intimation, timely** समय से सूचना/इत्तिला/प्रज्ञापन **Intimation to us, under** हमें सूचना देते हुए

Intimidation अभित्रास

Intra vires विधिवत्

Intricacy जटिलता

Intricate जटिल

intricate matter जटिल/पेचीदा मामला

Introduce 1. प्रस्तुत करना 2. परिचय कराना 3. समाविष्ट करना **Introduce a bill** विधेयक प्रस्तुत करना **Introduced, a new procedure has been** एक नई पद्धति चालू की गई है

Introduction, as an परिचय के रूप में **Introduction to the book** पुस्तक की प्रस्तावना

Invalid 1. अशक्त 2. अविधिमान्य **Invalid action** अविधिमान्य **—pension** अशक्तता पेंशन

Invalidate अमान्य होना

Invalidation अमान्यकरण

Invalidation of proceedings कार्यवाही का अमान्यकरण **Invalidity** असमर्थता/अशक्तता

Inventions Promotion Board आविष्कार-वर्धन-मंडल

Inventory सूची/फर्द/फेहरिस्त **—of furniture** फरनीचर की सूची/फर्द/फेहरिस्त

Investigating officer जांच पड़ताल अफसर

Investigation अन्वेषण/जांच/जांच-पड़ताल/तफतीश **—and Vigilance Division** अन्वेषण और सतर्कता प्रभाग **—Inspector** अन्वेषण निरीक्षक **Investigation of the case** मामले की जांच/तफतीश **Investigator** अन्वेषक

Investment पूंजी लगाना/निवेश

Invigilator निरीक्षक

Invitation 1. निमंत्रण 2. मांगना/आमंत्रण **—is accepted** आमन्त्रण स्वीकार **Invitation of tender** टेण्डर मांगना **Inviting a reference to** का हवाला देते हुए **Inviting your attention to** की ओर आपका ध्यान आकर्षित करते/दिलाते हुए

Invoice बीजक **—of receipts** आवती बीजक

Involved अन्तर्ग्रस्त **Involving question of policy** जिसमें नीति का प्रश्न (निहित) हो

Irrespective of विचार किए बिना, लिहाज किए बिना

Inward clerk आवक लिपिक/क्लर्क **Inward register** आवक रजिस्टर/आवक पंजी **—returns** आवक विवरणियाँ

Ipso facto यथातथ्यत:/इसी बात से **Ipso Jure** विधित:

Iron and Steel Controller लोहा और इस्पात नियंत्रक **Iron Ore Mines Cess Commissioner** लोहा अयस्क खान उपकर आयुक्त

Irrecoverable अप्रत्युद्धरणीय/लावसूल/नावसूल **Irrecoverable amount** लावसूल/अशोध्य राशि, न वसूल होने योग्य रकम

Irregular अनियमित **Irregular action** अनियमित कार्रवाई/काम

Irrelevant असंबद्ध/विसंगत

Irrespective of का विचार किए बिना/का लिहाज किए बिना **Irrespective of the fact** इस बात का विचार/लिहाज किए बिना

Irrespective of whether or not चाहे···हो या न हो

Irresponsible अनुत्तरदायी/बेजवाबदार/गैर जिम्मेदार **Irresponsible person** अनुत्तरदायी/गैर जिम्मेदार व्यक्ति

Irrevocable अटल **Irrevocable decision** अटल निर्णय

Irrigation and Power, Ministry of सिंचाई और बिजली मंत्रालय **—Adviser** सिंचाई सलाहकार

Is hereby informed सूचित किया जाता है

I shall be obliged मैं अनुगृहीत होऊँगा

Issue (n.) 1. निर्गम 2. वाद-पद **(vb.)** जारी करना/भेजना/देना/ निकालना **— as modified** यथा संशोधित पत्र भेजिए, संशोधन के अनुसार जारी कीजिए **Issue clerk** निर्गम लिपिक/क्लर्क **—department** निकासी विभाग **—diary** निर्गम-डायरी **—note** निर्गम-टिप्पणी **—of store** सामान देना **—of this is authorised** इसका निर्गमन अधिकृत है, इसके जारी करने की इजाजत है **—order** निर्गम-आदेश **—price** निर्गम-कीमत **Issue register** निर्गम रजिस्टर **Issue to-day** आज ही जारी करें **—voucher** निर्गम-वाउचर **Issued certificate** दिया गया प्रमाण पत्र **Issues of the case** मामले के वाद-पद **Issuing an order** आदेश निकालना

It is highly objectionable यह बहुत ही आपत्तिजनक है **It is requested** यह निवेदन है, निवेदन है **It is suggested** यह सुझाव दिया जाता है

It may further be added यह भी बताया जाता है/बता दिया जाए

It will be construed इस का यह अर्थ लगाया जाएगा

Item मद्द/मद **Item by item (itemwise)** मदवार, मद्दवार **—veto** मद निषेधाधिकार

Itinerary 1. यात्रा कार्यक्रम 2. मार्गनिर्देशिका

Its own motion स्वयं अपनी प्रेरणा से; स्वप्रेरणा से

Jactitation झूठी आत्मश्लाघा विकथन, असत्य कथन- गलत दावा

Jail जेल/बंदीगृह **Jailor** जेलर

Jemadar जमादार **—Adjutant** जमादार एडजटेंट **—Quarter-Master** जमादार क्वार्टर मास्टर

Jettison फेंक देना

Jetty घाट/जेटी

Jig and Tool Designer जिग-औजार अभिकल्पक **Jig borer** जिग-वेधक

Job नौकरी **—Analyst** कार्य-विश्लेषक **—card** कार्य-कार्ड/जॉब कार्ड **—full-time** पूर्णकालिक काम/नौकरी **—Inspector** कार्य निरीक्षक **—work** छुटपुट काम, फुटकर काम **Jobbery** क्षुद्र कर्म/स्वार्थाचार

Join 1. कार्यभार ग्रहण करना/नौकरी शुरू करना । 2. सम्मिलित होना 3. संयोजित करना **Joined a little latter** कुछ देर से सम्मिलित हुआ **Joining date** कार्यग्रहण तारीख/कार्यारंभ तारीख **—pay** कार्यारंभ-काल वेतन **—period** कार्यारंभ-अवधि/पद ग्रहण अवधि **Joining report** कार्यारम्भ प्रतिवेदन, कार्य-ग्रहण रिपोर्ट, काम पर आने की सूचना **Joining time** कार्यारम्भ काल, कार्य-ग्रहण अवधि, योग काल

Joint संयुक्त **—annuity** संयुक्त वार्षिकी **—application** संयुक्त आवेदनपत्र **—attestation** संयुक्त साक्ष्यांकन **—Chief Controller** संयुक्त मुख्य नियंत्रक **—committee** संयुक्त समिति **—Communications Electronics Committee** संयुक्त संचार इलेक्ट्रॉनिकी समिति **—concurrence** संयुक्त सहमति **—consultation** सम्मिलित परामर्श **—Control** संयुक्त नियंत्रण **—Controller** संयुक्त नियंत्रक **—Deputy Director** संयुक्त उपनिदेशक **—draft** संयुक्त मसौदा **—Educational Adviser** संयुक्त शिक्षा सलाहकार **—electorate** संयुक्त निर्वाचक-मंडल **—family system** संयुक्त परिवार प्रथा **—funds** संयुक्त निधि **—intelligence staff** संयुक्त गुप्तवार्ता कर्मचारीवर्ग/संयुक्त खुफिया स्टाफ, **—liabilities** संयुक्त दायिता/संयुक्त दायित्व **—life annuity** संयुक्त जीवन वार्षिकी **—life Policy**

सम्मिलित-जीवन बीमा पालिसी —**planning staff** संयुक्त योजना स्टाफ —**representation** 1. संयुक्त प्रतिनिधान 2. संयुक्त अभिवेदन —**resolution** संयुक्त संकल्प **Secretary** संयुक्त सचिव —**Select committee** संयुक्त प्रवर समिति —**services wing examination** सम्मिलित सेवा स्कन्ध परीक्षा —**supervision** संयुक्त पर्यवेक्षण —**tenants** संयुक्त काश्तकार/संयुक्त किरायेदार मुश्तर्का असामी

Jointly संयुक्त रूप से —**and severally** संयुक्त और पृथक रूप से, एक साथ और अलग-अलग

Journal 1. दैनिकी/रोजनामचा 2. पत्रिका जरनल **Journal, Daily** रोजनामचा **Journal, Monthly** मासिक पत्रिका,जनरल

Journalist पत्रकार **Journalist, working** श्रमजीवी पत्रकार

Journey, break of यात्रा-विश्राम, यात्रा के बीच रुक जाना **Journey man** जर्नी मैन **Journey, return** वापसी यात्रा

Jubilee जयंती —**diamond** हीरक जयन्ती —, **golden** स्वर्ण जयन्ती —**silver** रजत जयन्ती

Judge न्यायाधीश **Judge, additional** उपर न्यायाधीश; अपर जज —**Advocate** न्यायाधीश अधिवक्ता / जज-एडवोकेट —**General** न्यायाधीश महाधिवक्ता/जज एडवोकेट जनरल **Sessions** सत्र न्यायाधीश; सैशन जज

Judgment —**Judgement,** निर्णय —**deliver** निर्णय देना

Judicial न्यायिक/अदालती —**Commissioner** न्यायिक आयुक्त —**department** न्याय-विभाग —**enquiry** अदालती जांच —**Magistrate** न्यायिक मजिस्ट्रेट —**Officer** न्यायिक अधिकारी —**service** न्यायिक सेवा **Judiciary** न्यायपालिका

Jump Assistant जंप असिस्टैंट

Junction Stock verifier जंकशन स्टॉक सत्यापक —**Verifier** जंकशन सत्यापक

Junior (as in Junior Inspector) कनिष्ठ **Junior (as in Junior Training College)** अवर —**Accountant** कनिष्ठ लेखापाल —**Account Officer, Establishment** कनिष्ठ लेखा अधिकारी, स्थापना — **Accounts Officer, Establishment, Gazetted** कनिष्ठ लेखा अधिकारी,

राजपत्रित स्थापना —**Accounts Officer Provident Fund, Pension and Inspection (Accounts)** कनिष्ठ लेखा अधिकारी, भविष्य निधि, पेंशन और निरीक्षण (लेखा) —**Binder** कनिष्ठ जिल्दसाज —**Cashier** खजांची —**Chargeman** कनिष्ठ चार्जमैन/कनिष्ठ कार्येक्षक —**Chemical and Metallurgical Assistant** कनिष्ठ रसायन और धातुकर्म सहायक —**Commander** जूनियर कमांडर —**Commissioned Officer (J.C.O.)** जे० सी० ओ० —**Compositor** कनिष्ठ कंपोजिटर/कनिष्ठ अक्षर योजक —**Co-operative Societies Inspector** कनिष्ठ सहकारी समिति निरीक्षक —**Design Assistant** कनिष्ठ अभिकल्प सहायक —**Fitter** कनिष्ठ फिटर —**Grains Inspector** कनिष्ठ खाद्यान्न निरीक्षक —**Grainshop Manager** कनिष्ठ खाद्यान्न-दुकान प्रबन्धक —**in rank** पद में कनिष्ठ/छोटा —**Inspector** कनिष्ठ निरीक्षक —**Inspector of Station Accounts** कनिष्ठ स्टेशन लेखा निरीक्षक —**Law Assistant** कनिष्ठ विधि सहायक —**Lecturer** कनिष्ठ प्राध्यापक —**Machineman** कनिष्ठ मशीनमैन —**Machinery Maintenance Inspector** कनिष्ठ मशीन अनुरक्षण निरीक्षक —**Mechanic** कनिष्ठ मेकैनिक —**Non-Commissioned Officer** जूनियर ओहदेदार —**Planner** कनिष्ठ योजनाकार —**Progressman** कनिष्ठ प्रगतिवीक्षक —**Publicity Assistant** कनिष्ठ प्रचार सहायक —**Reader** कनिष्ठ वाचक —**Roller Caster** कनिष्ठ रोलर ढलाईकार —**Special Inspector** कनिष्ठ विशेष निरीक्षक —**Staff Council** कनिष्ठ कर्मचारी परिषद् —**Statistical Inspector** कनिष्ठ सांख्यिकी निरीक्षक —**Stereo Typer** कनिष्ठ स्टीरियो टाइपकर्ता —**Telegraph Overseer** कनिष्ठ तार ओवरसियर —**Ticket Counter** कनिष्ठ टिकट गणक —**time scale** अवर समय-मान —**Trade Instructor** कनिष्ठ व्यवसाय-शिक्षक —**Training College** अवर प्रशिक्षण कालेज —**Water and Drainage Inspector** कनिष्ठ जल और जल निकासी निरीक्षक

Junicrity अवरता

Jurisdiction अधिकार-क्षेत्र/क्षेत्रा-

धिकार/अधिकारिता —outside his उनके क्षेत्राधिकार के बाहर

Jurist विधि शास्त्री **Juror (Juryman)** जूरी-सदस्य **Jury** जूरी

Just न्याय्य/उचित/ठीक —**and reasonable** उचित/न्याय्य और युक्ति संगत —**below** ठीक नीचे **Just now** अभी, तुरन्त

Justice 1. न्याय 2. न्यायमूर्ति **Justifiable** 1. न्यायोचित 2. समर्थनीय **Justification** तर्कसंगति/औचित्य **Justification for the proposal** प्रस्ताव का औचित्य

Justify न्यायोचित ठहराना/सफाई देना/न्यायसंगत सिद्ध करना/उचित सिद्ध करना

Jute Development Officer पटसन विकास अधिकारी

Juvenile बाल/बाल्य/किशोर **Juvenile convict** किशोर अपराधी —**court** किशोर-न्यायालय —**delinquency** किशोर अपचार —**employment** किशोर सेवायोजन —**Jail** किशोर कारागार —**offender** किशोर दोषी

Kabuliyat कबूलियत

Keep रखैल —**direction** ठीक दिशा में बढ़ना **Keeper** पालक रक्षक; पाल; चलाने वाला **Keeper of Archaeology** अध्यक्ष, पुरातत्त्व —**of Archives** (शासकीय) अभिलेखाध्यक्ष —**of Records** अभिलेखपाल **Keeping the Peace** परिशान्ति **Keeping with in** के अनुरूप —**Kept in abeyance** आस्थगित/मुल्तवी रखा गया —**pending** निर्णयार्थ रोका गया, निलम्बित रखा गया —**with the file** इसे मिसिल के साथ रखा गया था

Key board कुंजीपटल/की-बोर्ड —**industry/post** खास/मूलभूत/प्रमुख उद्योग/पद —**map** मूल नक्शा —**Punch Machine Operator** कुंजी छिद्रक-मशीन प्रचालक

Khadi and Village Industries Commission खादी और ग्रामोद्योग आयाग

Kid मेमना

Kindergarten teacher बालबाड़ी शिक्षक

Kinship बंधुता

Knowingly जान-बूझकर; ज्ञानपूर्वक —**and unlawfully** जान-बूझ कर और अवैध रूप से

Knowledge ज्ञान; जानकारी **Knowledge and belief, to the**

best of अधिकतम ज्ञान और विश्वास के अनुसार **Knowledge, I have no** मुझे कोई जानकारी नही, मुझे कुछ मालूम नहीं

Known defects ज्ञात/विदित दोष

Known Shri... for two years, I have मैं श्री······को दो वर्ष से जानता हूँ

Label लेबल

Laboratory प्रयोगशाला **—Assistant** प्रयोगशाला सहायक **—Bearer** प्रयोगशाला-परिचर **—, scientific** वैज्ञानिक प्रयोगशाला **—Superintendent** प्रयोगशाला अधीक्षक

Laborious work श्रमसाध्य काम, मेहनत का काम

Labour 1. श्रम 2. श्रमिक-वर्ग **—and Employment Adviser** श्रम और रोजगार सलाहकार **—Commissioner** श्रम आयुक्त **—department** श्रमविपत्तन **Lahour, hard** कड़ी मेहनत **—Intelligence Officer** श्रम आसूचना अधिकारी **— involved in gathering** सूचना एकत्रित करने में लगने वाला श्रम **—Officer** श्रमिक अधिकारी/श्रम अधिकारी **—relations** श्रम-संपर्क श्रमिक-संपर्क **—Supervisor** श्रमिक पर्यवेक्षक **Labour union** श्रमिक संघ, मजदूर संघ**—welfare** श्रम कल्याण, श्रमिक कल्याण

Labourer श्रमिक/मजदूर

Laches सुस्ती; ढील; शैथिल्य

Lack न्यूनता **— of discipline** अनुशासन का अभाव/की कमी

Lacuna कमी

Lady Attendant परिचारिका **—doctor** महिला डाक्टर **—President** महिला अध्यक्ष **—Staff officer** महिला स्टाफ आफिसर **—Superintendent** अधीक्षिका **—Supervisor** पर्यवेक्षिका **—Welfare Superindent** कल्याण अधीक्षिका

Lag behind पिछड़ जाना, पीछे रह जाना

Laid down अधिकथित **Laid down in** में निर्धारित **—on the table of Parliament, Shall be** संसद के पटल पर रखे जाएँगे

Lampman बत्तीवान

Lampson निन्दात्मक लेख; व्यंग्य लेख; निन्दा-रचना

Lance Daffadar लांस दफादार **—Naik** लांस नायक

Land and development office भूमि और विकास कार्यालय **—Acquisition Officer** भूमि

अर्जन अधिकारी **—Adviser** भूमि सलाहकार **—cess** लगान उपकर **—compensation** भूमि प्रतिकर/मुआवजा **—Compensation Officer** भूमि प्रतिकर अधिकारी **—Control Inspector** भूमि-नियंत्रण-निरीक्षक **—Control Officer** भूमि-नियंत्रण अधिकारी **—Hirings and Disposal Directorate** भूमि भाड़ा और निपटान निदेशालय **—Leasing Inspector** भूमि पट्टा निरीक्षक **Landmark** सीमा चिह्न, युगान्तरकारी घटना **—Mortgage Bank** भूमि बंधक बैंक **—record** भू-अभिलेख **—Reforms Officer** भूमि-सुधार अधिकारी **—revenue** मालगुजारी, भू-राजस्व **—route** स्थल-मार्ग **—tenure** पट्टेदारी/भू-धृति

Landed cost उतरे हुए की लागत **Landing date** उतरने की तिथि; उतारने की तिथि

Language भाषा **—Division** भाषा प्रभाग **—Expert** भाषा विशेषज्ञ **—official** राज भाषा

Lapse (n.) लय/बीतना/व्यपगमन **(vb.)** लय होना/बीत जाना/व्यपगत होना **—administrative** प्रशासनिक चूक/भूल **—of time** समयावसान, समय बीतने पर **Lapsed and Cancelled Policies book** गतावधि तथा रद्द पालिसी बही **—sanction** व्यपगत मंजूरी **Lapsing of deposit** जमा का व्यपगमन

Large scale, on बड़े पैमाने पर

Lascar लश्कर/खलासी

Last month गत मास **Last pay certificate (LPC)** अंतिम वेतन पत्र **—purchase price** अंतिम क्रय मूल्य **—source of supply** प्रदाय का अन्तिम स्रोत

Late 1. विलंब/देर 2. स्वर्गीय **Late arrival** देरी से आना/आगमन **Late coming** विलम्ब से आना **Late Department of...** भूतपूर्व विभाग **Late fee** विलम्ब शुल्क, देर-फीस **—payment** देर से अदायगी **Late Shri......**स्वर्गीय श्री **Latest, at the** देर से देर **Latest decision** नवीनतम निर्णय

Latheman खरादिया

Latter पश्चात् कथित **Latter part** पिछला भाग

Laundry Supervisor धुलाईघर पर्यवेक्षक

Law विधि/कानून **Law, administrative** प्रशासनिक विधि **Law and order** विधि और व्यवस्था, शान्ति **Law**

Commission विधि आयोग **—Constitutional** सांविधानिक विधि, सांविधानिक कानून; संविधान-विधि **—,Ministry of** विधि मंत्रालय **—Officer** विधि अधिकारी **—Superintendent** विधि अधीक्षक **Lawyer** वकील **Lawful action** विधि संगत कार्रवाई

Lay before समक्ष रखना, सामने रखना **lay down** निर्धारित करना त्यागना **Lay off** लामबन्दी **Lay on the table of Sabha** सभा-पटल पर रखना **Lay out** अभिन्यास, नक्शा, खाका

Leader of the House सदन का नेता **—of the Opposition** विरोधी दल का नेता

Leading article अग्र लेख **Leading case** निदर्शक वाद **—Counsel** प्रमुख कौंसल **— question** संकेतक प्रश्न

Leap year लौंद वर्ष

Lease (n.) पट्टा **(vb.)** पट्टे पर देना **—for life** आजीवन पट्टा **—from month to month** मासानुमास पट्टा **Lease-hold** पट्टे पर **Lease hold System** पट्टाधारिता **Lease holder** पट्टाधारी **—for life** आजीवन पट्टा **—, mortgage** बंधक-पट्टा **—system** पट्टाधारिता **—, sub** उप पट्टा/शिकमी पट्टा **—without term** निरवधि पट्टा

Leave (n) 1. छुट्टी/अवकाश 2. अनुमति **(vb.)** छोड़ना **—account** छुट्टी का लेखा **—allowance** छुट्टी भत्ता **—, Average** औसत छुट्टी **—casual** आकस्मिक छुट्टी **—commuted** परिणत छुट्टी **—compensatory** प्रतिपूरक छुट्टी **—, Converted** परिवर्तित छुट्टी/रूपांतरित छुट्टी **—duty** कार्यार्थ छुट्टी **—, earned** अर्जित छुट्टी **—,Ex-India** भारत बाह्य अवकाश/भारत बाह्य छुट्टी **—, Extraordinary** असाधारण छुट्टी **Leave it here** इसे यहां छोड़ दीजिए **—, maternity** प्रसूति छुट्टी **—, Medical** चिकित्सा छुट्टी **—not due** अर्जनशोध्य छुट्टी **—not earned** अनर्जित छुट्टी **—of absence** अनुपस्थिति की अनुमति **Leave on average pay (L.A.P)** औसत वेतन छुट्टी **—on half average pay** अर्द्ध औसत वेतन छुट्टी **—on medical grounds** रोग-कारण छुट्टी, बीमारी की छुट्टी, चिकित्सा-छुट्टी **—Pay** छुट्टी वेतन **—, Preparation** तैयारी के लिए छुट्टी **—preparatory to**

retirement सेवा निवृत्तिपूर्व छुट्टी **Leave, quarantine** संगरोध छुट्टी **—reserve** छुट्टी रिजर्व **—Reserve Clerk** छुट्टी रिजर्व क्लर्क **Restricted** प्रतिबंधित छुट्टी **—salary** छुट्टी का वेतन **Leave, study** अध्ययनार्थ छुट्टी **Leave to appeal** अपील करने की अनुमति **Leave vacancy** अवकाश रिक्ति **—with pay** वैतनिक छुट्टी/सवेतन छुट्टी **—without pay** बिना वेतन छुट्टी

Leaving tomorrow कल जा रहा हूं

Lecture Hall भाषण भवन/लेक्चर हाल

Lecturer प्राध्यापक / लेक्चरर **—Guide** व्याख्याता परिदर्शक **Ledger** खाता **—balance** खाता बकाया/शेष **—Clerk** खाता क्लर्क **—folio** खाता पन्ना **—Keeper** खातानवीस

Legal कानूनी; वैध **Legal action** वैध/कानूनी कार्रवाई **—Adviser** विधि सलाहकार **—Affairs** विधि विषयक मामले **—Remembrancer** विधि परामर्शी **—representative** विधि-प्रतिनिधि **Legation** दूतावास **—of India** भारतीय दूतावास

Legible सुवाच्य/पढ़ा जाने योग्य **—handwriting** सुवाच्य लिखाई/लेख

Legislation विधान **Legislative Assembly** विधान सभा **—business** विधायी कार्य **—Council** विधान परिषद् **—Department** विधायी विभाग **—function** विधायी कार्य **—measure** विधायी कार्य/विधायी उपाय

Legislator विधिकर्ता **Legislature** विधान मंडल **—bicameral** द्विसदनी विधानांग **—department** विधानांग विभाग **—Secretary** विधानांग सचिव **—, State** राज्य का विधान-मंडल **—, unicameral** एकसदनी विधानांग

Legitimate 1. उचित/विधिसम्मत/विधि संगत 2. धर्मज **Legitimate child** धर्मज सन्तान/बच्चा **—claim** विधिसंगत/उचित/वैध दावा **—purpose** वैध प्रयोजन

Leisure अवकाश/फुरसत **Leisure, at** फुरसत में

Length of service सेवा काल

Leniency पट्टाधारी Leniency, to show नरमी बरतना/दिखाना

Lese meeste राजद्रोह; राजापमान

Leskari तश्करी

Less than से कम

Lessee पट्टेदार —, Permanent स्थायी पट्टेदार

Lessor पट्टादाता, पट्टाकर्ता

Let him come उसे आने दीजिए

Let him see me वह मुझसे मिले

Let on hire भाटक पर देना

Let or hinderance, without बेरोक-टोक

Let out किराए पर दिया हुआ

Let, to किराए के लिए खाली है

Let us wait for some time हम कुछ देर और प्रतीक्षा करें

Letter पत्र —book पत्र पुस्ती —Box Peon लेटर बक्स चपरासी —, covering व्याख्या पत्र —head सरनाम/शीर्षनामा —of acceptance स्वीकृति-पत्र —of advice सूचना-पत्र —of authority प्राधिकार-पत्र —of credence प्रत्यय-पत्र —of credit साख-पत्र —of guarantee गारण्टी-पत्र —of introduction —pad पत्र-बंध/पत्र पैड —of request अनुरोध पत्र —Press पत्र टीका

Level, decided at a high उच्च स्तर पर निर्णीत

Levy उद्ग्रहण/महसूल/उगाही

Lexicographer कोशकार Lexicography कोश विज्ञान

Lexicon कोश

Liability दायिता/देयता/दायित्व/उत्तरदायित्व Liability, joint संयुक्त दायिता/देयता/दायित्व

Liable दायी/दायित्व के अधीन —to pay देनदार —to punishment दंड का भागी

Liaison संपर्क —Inspector संपर्क निरीक्षक —Officer संपर्क अधिकारी

Libel अपमान लेख

Liberal interpretation उदार अर्थ-निर्णय/निर्वचन

Liberty, Personal दैहिक स्वाधीनता

Librarian पुस्तकाध्यक्ष —and Storekeeper पुस्तकाध्यक्ष और भण्डारी

Library पुस्तकालय

License (Licence) अनुज्ञप्ति/लाइसेंस —Collector लाइसेंस संग्राहक/लाइसेंस कलक्टर – holder अनुज्ञप्तिधारी/लाइसेंसदार —Inspector लाइसेंस निरीक्षक —Officer लाइसेंस अधिकारी/अनुज्ञप्ति अधिकारी Licensed अनुज्ञप्त/अनुज्ञापित / लाइसेंस-प्राप्त

—**Porter Inspector** लाइसेंस-प्राप्त भारिक निरीक्षक **Licenced shop** अनुज्ञप्त दुकान, लाइसेंस प्राप्त दुकान **Licensee** अनुज्ञप्ति-धारी **Licensing Inspector** अनुज्ञापन निरीक्षक —**Officer** अनुज्ञापन अधिकारी

Lien 1. पुनर्ग्रहणाधिकार 2. धारणाधिकार —**on post** पद पर हक/पुनर्ग्रहणाधिकार/लियन —**right of** धारणाधिकार

Lieu of, in के स्थान पर, की जगह

Lieutenant लेफ्टिनेंट — **Colonel** लेफ्टिनेंट कर्नल —**Commandar** लेफ्टिनेंट कमांडर —**General** लेफ्टिनेंट जनरल —**Governor** उप राज्यपाल

Life annuity आजीवत वार्षिकी **Life insurance** जीवन बीमा **Insurance Corporation** जीवन बीमा निगम **Life-long** आजीवन, यावज्जीवन

Lift Attendant (Lift-man) लिफ्ट परिचर

Light house दीप घर, प्रकाश स्तम्भ **Light House Department** दीपघर विभाग/प्रकाशस्तंभ-विभाग —**Houses and Light Ships Department** दीपघर तथा दीपपोत विभाग **Light of in the** को ध्यान में रखते हुए **Light responsibility** हल्की जिम्मेदारी **Light, to throw** प्रकाश डालना

Like amount उतनी/समान राशि **Like-wise** वैसी ही, उसी प्रकार **Likely to arise** उत्पन्न होने की सम्भावना

Limitation 1. सीमा 2. अवधि

Limited concern सीमित दायिता प्रतिष्ठान **Limited liability** सीमित दायित्व **Limited Period** सीमित कलावधि; परिसीमित कालावधि **Limited tender** सीमित टेंडर **Limited time** परिसीमित समय

Line Inspector लाइन निरीक्षक **Lineman** लाइनमैन —**Munshi (Lining Munshi)** लाइन मुंशी **Line of communication** संचार-पथ **Line of promotion** पदोन्नति का क्रम **Line, railway** रेल की लाइन —**Rider** सवार लाइन मैन

Linen Supervisor वस्त्र पर्यवेक्षक **Lines, on these** इस तरह से, इन बातों के आधार पर

Link (adj.) संलग्न/संबद्ध **(n.)** 1. कड़ी/शृंखला/बंध/लिंक 2. संपर्क —**language** सम्पर्क भाषा **Linked file** संलग्न/सम्बद्ध फाइल, साथ लगी मिसिल

Lino Attendant लिनो परिचर —**Operator** लिनो ऑपरेटर

Liquidated damages निर्धारित हानिपूर्ति (हरजाना) **Liquidation** 1. परिसमापन 2. शोधन 3. निर्धारण **Inspector** परिसमापन निरीक्षक **Liquidation of debt** ऋण का समापन

Liquidator परिसमापक **Liquidator, official** सरकारी परिसमापक **Liquor** मद्य, मदिरा, सुरा, शराब

List सूची **—, Concurrent** समवर्ती सूची; संवर्ती सूची **—of business** कार्य सूची

Listeners Research Officer श्रोता अनुसंधान अधिकारी

Literacy साक्षरता **Literacy campaign** साक्षरता अभियान

Literal शाब्दिक **—translation** शाब्दिक अनुवाद **Literate** साक्षर **Literate person** साक्षर व्यक्ति

Litho Artist लीथो कलाकार **Lithograph** शिला मुद्रक **Litho Machine Operator** लीथो मशीन ऑपरेटर **Litho Polisher** लीथो पॉलिशर **Lithographer (Litho Printer)** शिला मुद्रक/लीथो मुद्रक

Litigant वादकारी/मुकदमा करनेवाला

Litigation मुकदमेबाजी **—Litigation Officer** मुकदमा अधिकारी **Litigation, under** मुकदमेबाजी हो रही है

Live Stock Development Adviser पशुधन विकास सलाहकार **Live Stock Officer** पशुधन अधिकारी **Livelihood** जीविका **Livelihood, means of** जीविका/आजीविका का साधन **Living expense** निर्वाह खर्च

Loading and unloading लदान और उतराई **Loading Assistant** लदान सहायक

Loan ऋण, उधार **Loan Inspector** उधार निरीक्षक **—, long term** दीर्घकालीन/दीर्घकालिक कर्जा/ऋण

Lobby लॉबी **—Clerk** लॉबी क्लर्क

Local board स्थानीय बोर्ड स्थानीय मण्डल **Local body** स्थानीय निकाय **Local council** स्थानीय परिषद् **Local Government** स्थानीय सरकार **— purchase** स्थानीय खरीद/स्थानीय क्रय **—Self-Government** स्थानीय स्वशासन/स्थानीय स्वायत्त शासन **—stock** स्थानीय स्टॉक **Locally recruited** स्थानीय रूप से भर्ती किया हुआ

Lock-up बंदीखाना **Lock out** तालाबंदी

Loco Gunner लोको गनर **Loco Inspector** लोको-निरीक्षक **Loco Pressure Boiler Operator** लोको दाब बॉयलर प्रचालक

Loco shed लोको शैड **—Store-keeper** लोको भण्डारी **—Training School** लोको प्रशिक्षण विद्यालय

Locus standi अधिस्थिति **Locust department** टिड्डी विभाग **Locust Warning Officer** टिड्डी-चेतावनी-अधिकारी

Lodging वास **—house** वास-गृह

Log-book लाग-बुक, कार्य-पंजी

Logical action तर्क संगत कार्रवाई

Long term plan दीर्घकालीन योजना

Lord स्वामी

Lorry Cleaner लॉरी क्लीनर **—Driver** लॉरी चालक **—Sircar** लॉरी सरकार

Loss in transit मार्ग में हानि **—of resale** पुनर्विक्रय में हानि

Lost and found खोया-पाया **Lost Property Office** खोया-सामान-कार्यालय

Lot of work बहुत-सा काम, बहुत काम

Loud speaker ध्वनि-विस्तारक, लाउडस्पीकर

Lounge विश्राम कक्ष

Lower age limit निम्न आयु सीमा **Lower chamber** अवर सदन **—Division clerk** निम्न श्रेणी लिपिक **Lower house** अवर सदन **Lower Selection grade** निम्न वरण ग्रेड **Lower Selection Grade Clerk** निम्न प्रवरण कोटि लिपिक **Lower tender** न्यूनतर टेंडर, न्यूनतर निविदा **Lowest rate** न्यूनतम दर/निम्नतम दर

Lowest offier न्यूनतम निवेद, न्यूनतम प्रस्ताव **Lowest price** निम्नतम मूल्य **Low income group** अल्प-आय वर्ग, कम आमदनी वालों का वर्ग

Loyal स्वामिभक्त; राजभक्त **Loyalty** भक्ति, निष्ठा; वफादारी

Lubricating Supervisor स्नेहन पर्यवेक्षक **Lubrication Supervisor** स्नेहन पर्यवेक्षक/स्नेहन सुपरवाइजर

Lucid सुबोध, स्पष्ट **Lucit interval** स्वस्थ अन्तराल; निरुन्माद अन्तराल

Lucrative लाभदायक; लाभकर

Ludlow Operator लुडलो प्रचालक

Luggage Inspector सामान-निरीक्षक **—room** सामान घर **—Room Attendant** सामान घर-परिवार **—Weigher** सामान तोलक

Lun.p sum एक राशि, एक मुश्त

Lunacy पागलपन; उन्माद

Lunar month चन्द्र मास

Lunatic पागल; उन्मत्त **Lunatic asylum** पागलखाना **Lunatic Prisoner** पागल कैदी

Lunch मध्याह्न-भोजन/लंच

—**party** मध्याह्न-भोजन/लंच पार्टी

Lurking प्रच्छन्न; गुप्त

Machine, Adding जोड़ मशीन —, **Calculating** परिकलन यंत्र/परिकलित्र **Machine, Copying** प्रतिलिपि यंत्र —**Foreman** मशीन फोरमैन —, **Invoice** बीजक मशीन —**man** मशीन मैन/मशीन चालक —**operator** मशीन प्रचालक —**Perforating** छिद्रक मशीन —**Punching** बेधनी मशीन —, **Recording** अभिलेखन मशीन/अभिलेखित्र —**Setter** मशीन सेटर **Machine Shop** यंत्रालय —, **Stapling** तार-सिलाई मशीन —**Supervisor** मशीन पर्यवेक्षक —, **Time recording** समय-लेखी मशीन/समयलेखित्र **Machine tool** उपयंत्र —, **Transcribing** प्रतिलेखन मशीन/प्रतिलेखित्र

Machinery मशीनरी, साधन; यांत्र —**Maintenance Inspector** मशीन अनुरक्षण निरीक्षक —**of Government** शासन-व्यवस्था

Machinist मशीन-मिस्त्री —,**Miller** घिसाई मशीन-मिस्त्री

Madam, Dear प्रिय महोदया

Made known विदित कराया गया **Made to order** आदेशानुसार निर्मित, आर्डर से बनाया गया

Magazine 1. गोदाम 2. बारूदघर/आयुधागार 3. पत्रिका —,**monthly** मासिक पत्रिका

Magisterial functions मजिस्ट्रेट के कृत्य **Magistracy** दण्डाधिकारीगण **Magistrate** मजिस्ट्रेट **Magistrate, Additional chief presidency** अपर मुख्य प्रेसिडेन्सी मजिस्ट्रेट **Magistrate, chief Judicial** मुख्य न्यायिक मजिस्ट्रेट **Magistrate chief presidency** मुख्य प्रेसिडेन्सी मजिस्ट्रेट —,**City** नगर-मजिस्ट्रेट **Mugistrate, committing** सुपुर्द करने वाला मजिस्ट्रेट **Magistrate, cantonment** छावनी मजिस्ट्रेट **Magistrate, District** जिला मजिस्ट्रेट **Magistrate, Executive**, कार्यपालिक मजिस्ट्रेट **Magistrate, first class** प्रथम वर्ग मजिस्ट्रेट; मजिस्ट्रेट वर्ग एक **Magistrate, Metropolitan** महानगर मजिस्ट्रेट **Magistrate presidency** प्रेसीडेन्सी मजिस्ट्रेट **Magistrate, Second class** द्वितीय वर्ग मजिस्ट्रेट **Magistrate, Special**

विशेष मजिस्ट्रेट **Magistrate, specially empowered** विशेषत: सशक्त मजिस्ट्रेट **Magistrate, stipendiary** वैतनिक मजिस्ट्रेट **Magistrate, sub-divisional** उप-खण्ड मजिस्ट्रेट **Magistrate, subordinate** अधीनस्थ मजिस्ट्रेट **Magistrate superior** वरिष्ठ मजिस्ट्रेट

Mail Agent डाक एजेंट/रेल-डाक क्लर्क **—Carrier** डाक वाहक **—Clerk** डाक-क्लर्क/डाक बाबू **—Contractor** डाक-ठेकेदार **—Escort** डाक-अनुरक्षी **—Guard** डाक-रक्षक **—Motor Organisation Staff** डाक-मोटर-व्यवस्था स्टाफ **—Office** डाक-कार्यालय **—Opener** डाक-खोलने वाला **—Overseer** डाक-ओवरसियर **—Peon** डाक-पियन **Mail train** डाक गाड़ी **Mailing list** डाक सूची

Main Office मुख्य/प्रधान कार्यालय **Main Purpose** मुख्य प्रयोजन **Mains Inspector** मुख्य तार निरीक्षक

Maintain (account) (लेखा) रखना **—(a family)** (परिवार का) भरण-पोषण करना **—(a garden)** (बाग का) अनुरक्षण करना **(law and order)** (कानून और व्यवस्था) बनाए रखना **Maintained, account is being** लेखा (हिसाब) रखा जा रहा है

Maintenance 1. अनुरक्षण 2. रखना/भरण-पोषण **Maintenance allowance** निर्वाह/पोषण भत्ता, रोटी-कपड़ा भत्ता **—Inspector** अनुरक्षण निरीक्षक **—Officer** अनुरक्षण अधिकारी **Maintenance of building** इमारत का अनुरक्षण **Maintenance of discipline** अनुशासन बनाए रखना

Major 1. वयस्क/प्राप्तवय 2. मुख्य 3. मेजर **—General** मेजर जनरल **Major, has become** वयस्क/बालिग हो गया है **Major head** मुख्य शीर्ष **Major repairs** बड़ी मरम्मत **Major works** बड़े निर्माण-कार्य, मुख्य कर्म

Majority 1. बहुमत 2. वयस्कता/बालिगपन/प्राप्त वर्धता 3. बहुसंख्यक **Majority, age of** वयस्कता **Majority community** बहुसंख्यक समुदाय **Majority of** अधिकांश **Majority vote** बहुमत

Make available जुटाना, देना उपलब्ध करना **Make over** हवाले करना; सौंपना **Make Public** लोक विदित करना **Make-up man** मेकअप वाला **Make up the cash** रोकड़ का मिलान करना

Mala fides कदाशयता, दुर्भावना से

Malaria Inspector मलेरिया निरीक्षक **—Overseer** मलेरिया ओवरसियर

Malicious act दुर्भावनापूर्ण कार्य

Malpractice अनाचार

Man (Defence) सैनिक/जवान **— days** श्रम दिन **—hours** श्रम घण्टे

Man of ordinary prudence मामूली अक्ल का आदमी

Manager प्रबंधक/मैनेजर/व्यवस्थापक **Management** प्रबंध **—, General** प्रधान प्रबंधक **—, Mail Motor Service** प्रबंधक, डाक मोटर व्यवस्था **—cum-Clerk (Catering)** प्रबंधक-व-लिपिक (खानपान) **—of Publications** प्रकाशन प्रबंधक/प्रकाशन मैनेजर **—of Works** प्रबंधक, निर्माण-कार्य **Managerial work** प्रबन्धकीय कार्य **Managing Committee** प्रबंध-समिति **Managing Director** प्रबन्ध निदेशक **—Editor** प्रबन्ध संपादक

Mandamus परमादेश

Mandate अधिदेश **Mandate, according to** अधिदेश के अनुसार **Mandatory** 1. अधिदेशात्मक 2. अधिदेश प्राप्त (राज्यशक्ति) 3. अनिवार्य 4. आज्ञापक

Manifesto घोषणा-पत्र **Manifesto, election** चुनाव घोषणा-पत्र

Manipulate 1. चलाना 2. जोड़-तोड़ करना **Manipulated, it was** जोड़-तोड़ कर लिया गया था **Manipulation** 1. हस्त-कौशल 2. जोड़-तोड़/हेर-फेर

Manner, prescribed विहित रीति/ढंग/तरीका

Manpower मनुष्य-शक्ति **—Directorate** मनुष्य-शक्ति निदेशालय **—Officer** मनुष्य-शक्ति अधिकारी

Manual (adj.) शारीरिक/हस्त **(n.)** 1. गुटका/पुस्तिका 2. नियम-पुस्तक/ नियमावली**—Instructor** हस्तकला-शिक्षक/ दस्तकारी-शिक्षक **—Labour** शारीरिक श्रम **Manual, Office** कार्यालय नियम-पुस्तक **—Training Instructor** शारीरिक-प्रशिक्षण शिक्षक

Manufacture विनिर्माण/औद्योगिक निर्माण/व्यापारिक निर्माण **Manufactured articles** निनिर्मित वस्तुएं **Manufacturer** विनिर्माता **Manufacturer's organisation** विनिर्माता संगठन

Manure Inspector खाद-निरीक्षक

Manuscript Officer पांडुलिपि-अधिकारी **Manuscript, original** मूल पांडुलिपि

Map Mounter नक्शा मढ़ाईकार
Map, political राजनैतिक नक्शा
Mapper नक्शाकार

Margin 1. हाशिया 2. गुंजाइश 3. उपांत **Margin, it leaves no** इसमें कोई गुंजाइश नहीं है
Marginal adjustment उपांतिक समायोजन **—note** हाशिया टिप्पणी

Marine Engineer नौ-इंजीनियर
Marine insurance परिवहन/समुद्री बीमा **Marine Inspection Officer** समुद्र निरीक्षण-अधिकारी **—Superintendent** नौ अधीक्षक **survey report** समुद्री सर्वेक्षण रिपोर्ट **—workshop foreman** नौ-कर्मशाला फोरमैन **Marine** समुद्रीय **Marine officer** समुद्री अधिकारी **Mariner** नाविक/जहाजी

Mark, absent अनुपस्थिति चिह्न
Mark, he has left a उसने अपनी छाप छोड़ी है **Mark sheet** अङ्क-सूची **Marked absent** गैर हाजिरी/अनुपस्थिति लगा देना
Marker मार्कर/निशानकर्ता

Market Reporter बाजार रिपोर्टर/बाजार-प्रतिवेदक **Marketing Officer** पणन अधिकारी **Market rate** बाजार भाव **—Superintendent** बाजार-अधीक्षक **—value** बाजार मूल्य

Marking 1. नम्बर देना/नम्बर डालना 2. अंकन/चिह्न लगाना 3. निशाना लगाना **—and sorting** चिह्न लगाना और छांटना/निशान लगाना और छांटना

Marks अङ्क **Marks obtained** प्राप्त अङ्क/नम्बर

Marshal मार्शल

Martial law सैनिक शासन/कानून

Mason राज/राज मिस्त्री

Mast मस्तूल **Master** 1. अध्यापक 2.मास्टर **—at-Arms** मास्टर-एट-आर्म्स **—General of Ordinance** मास्टर-जनरल ऑफ आर्डनैन्स/आयुध का मास्टर-जनरल **—of Vessel (Master of ship)** पोत-मास्टर **—Warrant Officer** मास्टर वारण्ट अफसर

Mast Leskari मस्तूल लश्करी

Mate मेट

Material change खास/बड़ा/महत्वपूर्ण परिवर्तन **Material Chaser** सामग्री चेजर **—Checker** सामग्री-पड़तालकर्ता **Material for reply** उत्तर के लिए सामग्री **—Inspector** सामग्री-निरीक्षक
Materialise, is not likely to कार्यरूप में परिणत (कार्यान्वित) होने की सम्भावना नहीं है

Maternity प्रसूति/मातृत्व **—and**

Child Welfare Centre मातृ और शिशु-कल्याण-केन्द्र —Assistant प्रसूति-सहायक —leave प्रसूति-छुट्टी

Mathematical adviser गणित-परामर्शदाता

Matron मैट्रन **Matron's office** मैट्रन का दफ्तर

Matter विषय/मामला **Matter is under consideration** विषय/मामला विचाराधीन है **Matter of fact, as a** वास्तव में, वस्तुतः **Matter of fact statement** यथातथ्य कथन **Matter of Public or general Interest** लोक या साधारण हित की बात **Matter of regret** खेद का विषय **Matter of right, as a** अधिकार के रूप में **Matter, subject** विषय वस्तु, विषय

Maximum अधिकतम/ज्यादा से ज्यादा **—average pay** अधिकतम औसत वेतन **Maximum pay** अधिकतम वेतन **Maximum price** अधिकतम मूल्य

May be added जोड़ा जा सकेगा **May be called** कहा जा सकेगा **May be cited** कहा जा सकेगा **May be considered** विचार किया जाए **May be convened** बुलाया जा सकेगा **May be discharged** उन्मोचित किया जा सकेगा **May be disposed of** निपटारा किया जा सकेगा **May be excused** क्षमा किया जाए **May be filed** फाइल कर दिया जाए **May be informed, accordingly** तदनुसार सूचित कर दिया जाए **May be obtained** प्राप्त किया जाए **May be permitted** अनुमति/अनुज्ञा दी जाए **May be regretted** खेद प्रकट किया जाए **May be requested to clarify** स्पष्टीकरण के लिए निवेदन किया जाए **May be returned when done with** काम हो जाने पर लौटा दिया जाए **May be sworn** शपथित किया जा सकेगा **May be treated as urgent** इसे अविलम्बनीय समझा जाए

May by law determine, he वह विधि द्वारा निर्धारण करे

May call for मांग सकेगा **May consider proper** उचित समझें **May seem necessary** आवश्यक समझे **May draw inference** अनुमान कर सकेगा **May I know when reply can be expected** कृपया बतलाइए कि उत्तर कब तक मिल सकेगा **May please see** कृपया देखें **May Presume**

उपधारणा कर सकेगा **May receipt** प्रतिक्षेपित कर सकेगा **May repudiate** निराकृत कर सकेगा **May take up-steps** कार्यवाही कर सकेगा

Mayor महापौर/मेयर

Means साधन/उपाय **Means, by all** निस्सन्देह, अवश्यमेव **Means by any** किसी भी प्रकार/उपाय से, कैसे भी **Means, by no** कभी नहीं, कदापि नहीं **Means, of communication** संचार-साधन **Mean time, in the** इस बीच

Measure 1. उपाय 2. माप 3. मान 4. कार्रवाई/कार्यवाही **Measure, Compulsive** बाध्यकारी उपाय **Measure legislatvie** विधानीय अनुपाय **Measure of damages** क्षति-माप —, **Precautionary** पूर्वोपाय/एहतियाती कार्रवाई —, **Preventive** निवारक उपाय/रोकथाम सम्बन्धी उपाय

Measurement माप **Measuring Officer** मापन-अधिकारी **Measures, please take suitable** कृपया उचित कार्रवाई करें **Measures, weights and** तौल और माप

Mechanic यांत्रिक/मेकैनिक —, **Carrier** वाहक मेकैनिक —, **Motor Vehicle** मोटर-गाड़ी मैकेनिक **—Examiner** मैकेनिक परीक्षक **Mechanical assistant** यान्त्रिक सहायक **Mechanical Boiler Inspector** यांत्रिक बॉयलर निरीक्षक **Mechanical defect** यान्त्रिक दोष मशीन की खराबी **--Engineer** यांत्रिक अभियंता/यांत्रिक इंजीनियर **Engineering** यांत्रिक अभियांत्रिकी **—Department** यांत्रिक इंजीनियरी विभाग **—Foreman** यांत्रिक फोरमैन **—Mistry** यांत्रिक मिस्त्री **—Signal Maintainer** यांत्रिक सिगनल अनुरक्षक **— Supervisor** यांत्रिक पर्यवेक्षक/यांत्रिक सुपरवाइजर **—Tabulation Unit** यांत्रिक सारणीयन एकक **—Testing Inspector** यांत्रिक परीक्षण निरीक्षक **Mechanician** मेकेनिशयन **Mechanist** यांत्रिक/मेकैनिस्ट

Mediation मध्यस्थता/बीच-बचाव **Mediation, offer of** मध्यस्थता का प्रस्ताव

Medical चिकित्सा **—aid** चिकित्सा-सहायता **—and Para-Medical Section** चिकित्सा और पराचिकित्सा अनुभाग **—benefit** चिकित्सा-सुविधा **—certificate of fitness** स्वस्थता-प्रमाणपत्र **—of sickness** बीमारी का प्रमाणपत्र

—**Examination** स्वास्थ्य-परीक्षा
—**Officer** चिकित्सा-अधिकारी
—**record card** चिकित्सा-अभिलेखपत्र/चिकित्सा-अभिलेख-कार्ड
—**report** चिकित्सा की रिपोर्ट

Medium of examination/instruction परीक्षा/शिक्षण का माध्यम

Meeting बैठक/सभा/मीटिंग **Meeting, extraordinary** असाधारण बैठक

Member सदस्य —, **Associate** सह-सदस्य **Member, co-opted** सहयोजित सदस्य —, **Corresponding** संवादी सदस्य —, **Engineering** अभियांत्रिकी सदस्य/इंजीनियरी सदस्य —**for Finance** वित्त सदस्य —**of Legislative Assembly** विधान सभा सदस्य —**of Legislative Council** विधानपरिषद् सदस्य —**of Parliament** संसद-सदस्य (संसद-सदस्य) —, **Railway Service Commission** सदस्य, रेल सेवा आयोग —**Secretary** सदस्य सचिव —, **Transportation** परिवहन सदस्य

Memo याची, ज्ञापक **Memorandum** ज्ञापन **Memorandum of objection** आपत्ति ज्ञापन **Memorandum, office** कार्यालय ज्ञापन

Memorial 1. स्मारक 2. अभ्यावेदन **Memorialist** अभ्यावेदक

Mensuration Officer क्षेत्रमिति-अधिकारी

Mental defficiency मनोवैकल्य **Mental Hospital** मानसिक चिकित्सालय

Mentioned against each प्रत्येक के सामने लिखा हुआ **Mentioned above** उपर्युक्त, उपरिलिखित **Mentioned therein** उसमें उल्लिखित

Mere supposition कल्पना मात्र

Merger विलयन **Merger of grades** पदक्रमों/ग्रेडों का विलयन

Merit गुण **Meriting consideration** विचार करने योग्य है **Merit, in order of** गुणक्रम के अनुसार **Merits** गुण **Merits and demerits** गुणावगुण, गुण दोष **Merits, on its** इसके गुणावगुण/गुण-दोषों के आधार पर

Message संदेश —**Checker** संदेश पड़तालकर्ता **Message, oral** मौखिक संदेश **Messenger** संदेश वाहक **Messenger, by special** विशेष वाहक/संदेशवाहक द्वारा

Messman मैसमैन

Metalled road पक्की सड़क

Metallurgist धातुकर्मी

Meteorological Assistant मौसम-सहायक **Meteorological office** मौसम कार्यालय **—Observer** मौसम-प्रेक्षक **Meteorologist** मौसम-विज्ञानी

Meter Inspector मीटर-निरीक्षक **—Mechanic** मीटर-मैकेनिक **—Reader** मीटर-वाचक **Meter reading** मीटर वाचन **Meter repairer and tester** मीटर की मरम्मत और जांच करने वाला **—Testing Superintendent** मीटर-परीक्षण अधीक्षक **Metering Clerk** मीटर-क्लर्क

Method of procedure प्रक्रिया-रीति, प्रक्रिया-पद्धति

Mica-Mines Labour Welfare Fund Advisory Committee अभ्रक - खान - श्रम-कल्याण- निधि सलाहकार समिति

Micro-biologist सूक्ष्मजीव-विज्ञानी

Midshipman मिडशिपमैन **Midwife** धात्री/दाई/धाय

Migrant प्रवासी **Migration** प्रवास **—Certificate** प्रवास-प्रमाणपत्र

Milch दुधारु

Mileage (Milage) 1. मील-दूरी 2. मील **Mileage allowance** भत्ता मील-दूरी भत्ता, मील--भत्ता

Military सेना-सम्बन्धी; सैनिक **Military adviser** सैनिक सलाहकार **Military area/duty** सैनिक क्षेत्र/ड्यूटी **Military Engineering Service (M.E.S.)** सैनिक इंजीनियरी-सेवा **—Estate Officer** सेना संपदा-अधिकारी **— Lands and Cantonments Directorate** सैनिक भूमि और छावनी निदेशालय **Military officer** सेना अधिकारी

Military rates of pay वेतन की सैनिक दर **Military received order** सेना-प्राप्त आदेश **Military regulations and forms** सैनिक विनियम और फार्म **— Secretary to the President** राष्ट्रपति का सैनिक-सचिव **Military service** सैन्य सेवा **Military wing examination** सेना-स्कन्ध-परीक्षा

Milk Collection and Chilling Centre दुग्ध-संग्रह तथा द्रुतशीतन केन्द्र **—Dispenser** दुग्ध-वितरक **—Supply Scheme** दुग्ध-पूर्ति-योजना

Millwright मिलराइट **—Inspector** मिलराइट निरीक्षक

Mine खान-खनि

Mineral counsel खनिज परामर्शदाता **Mineral Technologist** खनिज-शिल्पविज्ञानी **—Technology Laboratory** खनिज-शिल्प

विज्ञान- प्रयोगशाला **Minerals and Metals Trading Corporation** खनिज तथा धातु व्यापार निगम **Mineralogist** खनिज विज्ञानी

Mines and Metals, Department of खान और धातु विभाग

Minimum न्यूनतम/कम से कम **Minimum amount** न्यूनतम राशि कम से कम रकम **Minimum pay** न्यूनतम वेतन **—wages** कम से कम मजदूरी

Minister मंत्री **Minister, Chief** मुख्य मंत्री **—, Deputy** उप मंत्री **—, Prime** प्रधान मंत्री **—Envoy** मंत्री दूत **—of State** राज्य मंत्री **—Without Portfolio** निर्विभाग-मंत्री

Ministerial लिपिक-वर्गीय/अनुसचिवीय **Ministerial inteference** मंत्री द्वारा हस्तक्षेप; मंत्रियों द्वारा हस्तक्षेप **Ministerial officer** लिपिक वर्गीय आफिसर **Ministerial Service** लिपिक-वर्गीय सेवा **—Staff** लिपिक वर्गीय कर्मचारी/दफ्तरी स्टाफ

Ministry मंत्रालय **Ministry, Coalition** सम्मिलित मंत्रि-मंडल; मिला-जुला मंत्रि-मंडल **—of Commerce** वाणिज्य मंत्रालय **—of Defence** रक्षा मंत्रालय **—of Education and Youth Service** शिक्षा और युवक सेवा मंत्रालय **—of Education and Social Welfare** शिक्षा और समाज कल्याण मंत्रालय **—of External Affairs** विदेश मंत्रालय **—of Finance** वित्त मंत्रालय **—of Food, Agriculture, Community Development & Co-operation** खाद्य, कृषि, सामुदायिक विकास और सहकारिता मंत्रालय **—of Foreign Trade and Supply** विदेश व्यापार और पूर्ति मंत्रालय **—of Health and Family Planning** स्वास्थ्य और परिवार नियोजन मंत्रालय **—of Home Affairs** गृह-मंत्रालय **—of Industrial Development, Internal Trade and Company Affairs** औद्योगिक विकास, आंतरिक व्यापार और कम्पनी कार्य मंत्रालय **—of Information, Broadcasting and Communications** सूचना, प्रसारण और संचार मंत्रालय **—of Irrigation and Power** सिंचाई और विद्युत् मंत्रालय **—of Labour, Employment and Rehabili-**

tation श्रम, रोजगार और पुनर्वास मंत्रालय —of Law विधि मंत्रालय **Ministry of Parliamentary Affairs** संसदीय कार्य मंत्रालय —of Petroleum and Chemicals पेट्रोलियम और रसायन मंत्रालय —of Railways रेल मंत्रालय —of Shipping and Transport पोत परिवहन तथा परिवहन मंत्रालय —of Steel, Mines and Metals इस्पात, खान और धातु मंत्रालय —of Tourism and Civil Aviation पर्यटन और सिविल विमानन मंत्रालय —of Works, Housing and Supply निर्माण, आवास और पूर्ति मंत्रालय

Minor 1. अवयस्क/अप्राप्त व/नाबालिग 2. लघु/गौण —head लघु शीर्ष/गौण शीर्ष —children अवयस्क / नाबालिग बच्चे —irregularities मामूली अनियमितताएँ **Minority** 1. अल्पसंख्यक/अल्पसंख्या / अल्पसंख्यक-वर्ग 2. अल्पमत 3. अवयस्कता **Minority opinion** अल्पसंख्यकों का मत/राय, अल्पमत

Mint (n.) टकसाल (vb.) सिक्के ढालना/ढलाई करना – Superintendent टकसाल अधीक्षक

Minute of dissent विसम्मति-टिप्पण **Minutes** कार्यवृत्त —book कार्यवृत्त पुस्तक **Minutes of meeting** बैठक का कार्य-वृत्त

Misappropriation दुर्विनियोग/दुर्विनियोजन **Misappropriation of money** धन का गबन/दुर्विनियोग

Misbehaviour दुर्व्यवहार/कदाचार

Miscellaneous फुटकर/विविध –- Clerk विविध-कार्य लिपिक **Miscellaneous demand** विविध/फुटकर/प्रकीर्ण मांग

Misconduct अवचार/कदाचार **Misconduct, on grounds of** अवचार के आधार पर

Misleading statement भ्रामक बयान/कथन

Mismanagement कुप्रबंध **Mismanagment, gross** घोर कुप्रबन्ध

Misrepresentation अन्यथा-कथन **Misrepresentation of facts** तथ्यों की गलत बयानी, तथ्यों का गलत ढंग से प्रस्तुतीकरण, अन्यथा-कथन

Mission मिशन **Mission, diplomatic** राजनयिक मिशन **Mistry** मिस्त्री —(Traffic Workshop) मिस्त्री (यातायात कर्मशाला) —Fitter (Carriage) मिस्त्री फिटर (सवारी डिब्बा)

Misuse (n.) कदुपयोग/दुरुपयोग (vb.) कदुपयोग करना/दुरुपयोग

करना **Misuse of powers** अधिकारों का दुरुपयोग

Mobile Civil Emergency Force चल सिविल आपात दल **Mobile squad** चल जत्था **—Squad Inspector** चल जत्था निरीक्षक/चलस्क्वाड निरीक्षक **Mobilisation Section** लामबन्दी अनुभाग

Mode of dispatch प्रेषण-प्रकार **Mode of payment** भुगतान की रीति, अदायगी का तरीका

Model Room प्रतिरूप कक्ष **Model rules** आदर्श नियम **Modelling Teacher** प्रतिरूपण-शिक्षक

Moderate means साधारण साधन, मामूली हैसियत **Moderate views** नरम विचार, संयत दृष्टिकोण

Modification आशोधन/तरमीम/रूप-भेद रूपान्तर **Modification of, in** में आशोधन/तरमीम करते हुए

Modus operandi कार्य-प्रणाली

Momentary importance क्षणिक महत्त्व

Momentum, to gain तेजी पकड़ना, वेग में आना, गतिमात्रा बढ़ना

Monetary grant आर्थिक अनुदान **— limit** आर्थिक सीमा

Money Bill धन विधेयक **Money lending** साहुकारी **Money order** मनीआर्डर

Month to month मासानुमासी

Monitoring Department मानीटरी विभाग/अनुश्रमण विभाग **Monitoring officer** अनुश्रवण अधिकारी

Monthly arrear statement हुए काम का मासिक विवरण **Monthly instalment** मासिक किश्त **—progress report** मासिक प्रगति-रिपोर्ट **Monthly rate** मासिक दर **—statement** मासिक विवरण

Monument स्मारक

Mooring नौ-बन्ध, लंगर स्थल

Moral obligation नैतिक दायित्व/बंधन **Moral turpitude** नैतिक पतन **Morality** सदाचार

More convenient अधिक सुविधाजनक, सुकर **More or less** न्यूनाधिक

Morgue Supervisor शवागार-पर्यवेक्षक

Morse Signaller मोर्स-संकेतक, मोर्स स्गिनलर

Mortgage बंधक/गिरवी/रेहन **Mortgaged property** बन्धक सम्पत्ति, गिरवी जायदाद **Mortgager** बंधक कर्त्ता

Mortor Non-Commissioned Officer मोर्टर ओहदेदार **—Position Controller** मोर्टर

पोजीशन कंट्रोलर/मोर्टर पोजीशन नियंत्रक

Mortuary शवागार **—Clerk** शवागार क्लर्क

Most immediate अति तात्कालिक **Most favoured nation treatment** परमानुगृहीत राष्ट्र का सा व्यवहार **—urgent** अति तुरंत परम आवश्यक

Mother tongue मातृभाषा

Motion प्रस्ताव **Motion, adjonrnment** स्थगन-प्रस्ताव, काम रोको प्रस्ताव **—of confidence** विश्वास प्रस्ताव **Motion, of his own** स्वप्रेरणा से **—of no-confidence** अविश्वास-प्रस्ताव

Motor-car allowance कार भत्ता **—Chargeman** मोटर कार्येक्षक/मोटर चार्जमैन **—Controller** मोटर नियंत्रक **—Foreman** मोटर फोरमैन **—Mistry** मोटर मिस्त्री **—Regulator** मोटर नियामक **Vehicle Inspector** मोटर-निरीक्षक/मोटर गाड़ी निरीक्षक **—Vehicles Department** मोटर गाड़ी विभाग **Motorman** मोटरमैन

Mounted Police सवार पुलिस

Mounter मढ़ाईकार/माउंटर

Movable चल जंगम/अस्थिर **Movable property** चल सम्पत्ति

Move प्रस्ताव रखना/प्रस्तावित करना **Move a resolution** प्रस्ताव रखना **Move of offices** कार्यालयों का स्थानान्तर/बदली

Movement Clerk संचलन क्लर्क **Movement Controller** संचलन-नियंत्रक **—Director** संचलन निदेशक **—Inspector** संचलन निरीक्षक **—register** संचलन पंजी/संचलन रजिस्टर **Movement of files** फाइलों की आवाजाही, फाइलों का संचलन **Mover** उपस्तावक

Municipal board नगरपालिका

Mr. President अध्यक्ष महोदय

Mucudam (Mukadam) मुकद्दम

Mukadam मुकद्दम

Multifarious duties विविध/अनेक/बहुमुखी कर्तव्य **Multigrapher Attendant** बहुलेखित्र-परिचर **Multigraph Operator** बहुलेखित्र प्रचालक **Multipurpose** बहूद्देशीय **—Co-operative Society** बहूद्देशीय सहकारी समिति **Multipurpose project** बहूद्देशीय/बहुमुखी/बहूपयोजनी परियोजना

Municipal नगरपान्चिका/नगरपालिका संबंधी **—Commissioner** 1. नगरपालिका-आयुक्त 2. नगरपालिका-सदस्य **Municipal Corporation** नगर निगम **Municipal funds** नगरपालिका निधि **Municipality**

नगरपालिका

Museum संग्रहालय **—Keeper** संग्रहपाल

Music Teacher संगीत-शिक्षक/संगीत-अध्यापक **Musician** संगीत-कार/म्यूजिशियन

Muster Clerk उपस्थिति लिपिक/उपस्थिति **Muster-roll** उपस्थिति नामावली/हाजिरी रजिस्टर

Mutation नामांतरण/दाखिल-खारिज **—Clerk** नामांतरण-लिपिक/दाखिल-खारिज क्लर्क **—of names** नामपरिवर्तन; नामांतरण **proceeding** नामांतरण दाखिल – खारिजकी कार्यवाही **—Surveyor** नामांतरण-सर्वेक्षक /दाखिल-खारिज सर्वेक्षक

Mutatis mutandis यथोचित परि-वर्तन करके

Mutilate विकृत करना; अंगभंग करना **Mutilated cheque** विकृत चेक

Mutual agreement पारस्परिक/परस्पर करार

Mycologist कवकविज्ञानी **Myco-logical Assistant** कवक-विज्ञान सहायक

Nadir, reached its अधोबिन्दु तक पहुंच गया

Name plate नाम-पट्ट

Narrow majority थोड़ा सा बहुमत **Narrow mentality** संकीर्ण मनोवृत्ति

National (adj.) राष्ट्रीय **(n.)** राष्ट्रिक **—Academy of Administration** राष्ट्रीय प्रशासन-अकादमी **—Aeronautical Laboratory** राष्ट्रीय वैमानिकी-प्रयोगशाला **—anthem** राष्ट्र-गान **—Archives of India** भारत का राष्ट्रीय अभिलेखागार **—Buildings Organisation** राष्ट्रीय भवन संग-ठन **—Cadet Corps, Directo-rate of** राष्ट्रीय कैडेंट कोर निदे-शालय **—Calendar** राष्ट्रीय कैलंडर/राष्ट्रीय पंचांग **—Chemical Laboratory** राष्ट्रीय रसायन-प्रयोगशाला **Council of Educational Re-search and Training** राष्ट्रीय शिक्षा-अनुसंधान और प्रशिक्षण परिषद् **—debt** राष्ट्रीय ऋण **—Defence Academy** राष्ट्रीय रक्षा-अकादमी **—Defence College** राष्ट्रीय रक्षा कॉलेज **—Extension Development Block** राष्ट्रीय विस्तार-विकास-खंड **—Film Archives of India** भारत का राष्ट्रीय फिल्म अभिले-

खागार —**Fire Service College** राष्ट्रीय अग्निशमन-सेवा कालेज —**flag** राष्ट्र-ध्वज/राष्ट्रीय-झंडा —**Food Technological Research Institute** राष्ट्रीय खाद्य प्रौद्योगिकी अनुसंधान संस्थान —**Fundamental Education Centre** राष्ट्रीय मूलभूत-शिक्षा-केन्द्र —**Geophysical Research Institute** राष्ट्रीय भूभौतिकी-अनुसंधान-संस्थान —**guild** राष्ट्रीय शिल्पिक संघ —**income** राष्ट्रीय आय —**Industrial Development Corporation** राष्ट्रीय औद्योगिक विकास निगम —**Institute of Audio-visual Education** राष्ट्रीय दृश्य-श्रव्य-शिक्षा संस्थान —**of Basic Education** राष्ट्रीय बुनियादी शिक्षा-संस्थान —**of Education** राष्ट्रीय शिक्षा संस्थान **National Institute of Medical Research** राष्ट्रीय चिकित्सा-अनुसंधान संस्थान —**Insurance Scheme** राष्ट्रीय बीमा योजना —**language** राष्ट्र भाषा —**Metallurgical Laboratory** राष्ट्रीय धातुकर्म-प्रयोगशाला —**Museum** राष्ट्रीय संग्रहालय —**Physical Laboratory** राष्ट्रीय भौतिक-प्रयोगशाला —**Plans Savings Certificate** राष्ट्रीय योजना-बचत-पत्र —**Productivity Council** राष्ट्रीय उत्पादकता-परिषद् —**Project Construction Corporation** राष्ट्रीय परियोजना-निर्माण-निगम —**Research Development Corporation of India** भारत का राष्ट्रीय, अनुसंधान विकास निगम —**Savings Certificate** राष्ट्रीय बचत-पत्र/राष्ट्रीय बचत प्रमाण-पत्र —**Commissioner** राष्ट्रीय बचत-आयुक्त —**Scheme** राष्ट्रीय बचत-योजना —**Small Industries Corporation** राष्ट्रीय लघु उद्योग निगम —**Song** राष्ट्र-गान/राष्ट्र-गीत

Nationalisation of industries उद्योगों का राष्ट्रीयकरण **Nationalism** राष्ट्रीयता **Nationality** राष्ट्रिकता **Nationality, question of** राष्ट्रीयता का प्रश्न **Nationalization** राष्ट्रीयकरण

Native (adj.) 1. प्राकृतिक/प्राकृत/सहज 2. देशी/देशज (**n.**) मूल, मूल निवासी —**language** देशीय भाषा

Natural, it is यह स्वाभाविक है **Natural resources** प्राकृतिक संसाधन **Naturalization** देशीयकरण

Nature of work कार्य का स्वरूप/

प्रकार

Naval Adviser नौ-सेना-सलाहकार **Attache** नौ-सेना अताशे/नौ-सेना-सहचारी **Naval officer** नौ-सेना अफसर/अधिकारी

Navigator 1. मार्ग-निर्देशक (वायु-सेना) नैविगेटर 2. नौचालक (नौसेना) नेविगेटर

Near निकट **Near relative** निकट सम्बन्धी

Necessary जरूरी, आवश्यक **Necessary action** आवश्यक कार्रवाई **Necessary draft put up** आवश्यक/अपेक्षित मसौदा प्रस्तुत है **Necessary Powers** आवश्यक शक्तियाँ **Necessary Precaution** आवश्यक पूर्वविधानी **Necessary report is still awaited** अपेक्षित रिपोर्ट की अभी तक प्रतीक्षा है **Necessary steps should be taken** आवश्यक कार्रवाई की जाए, आवश्यक कदम उठाए जाएं

Needful आवश्यक कार्रवाई **Needful, do the** आवश्यक कार्रवाई करें **Needful done** आवश्यक कार्रवाई की जा चुकी है, अपेक्षित कार्रवाई हो चुकी है

Needs close supervision सूक्ष्म पर्यवेक्षण आवश्यक है, बहुत ध्यान से देख-भाल होनी चाहिए **Needs no comments** टिप्पणी की आवश्यकता नहीं

Negative निषेधात्मक **Negative reply** नकारात्मक उत्तर

Neglect of duty कर्तव्य की उपेक्षा **Neglecting his legitimate duties** अपने वैध कर्तव्यों से विमुख होकर **Negligence** उपेक्षा/प्रमाद/गफलत **Negligence, gross** घोर प्रमाद, भारी गफलत

Negotiable instruments परक्राम्य लिखतें

Negotiate परक्रमण करना/बातचीत करना **Negotiated Contract** बातचीत से तय किया गया ठेका/बातचीत से तय की गई संविदा **—sale** बातचीत से तय की गई बिक्री/वार्ता-तय बिक्री **Negotiation** 1. (समझौते की) बातचीत 2. परक्रमण **Negotiation, bilateral** द्विपक्षी वार्ता/बातचीत

Neighbouring पड़ौसी **Neighbouring country** पड़ौसी देश

Neither...nor न तो···और न

Nepotism स्वजन पक्षपात/भाई-भतीजावाद **Nepotism and corruption** स्वजन-पक्षपात/भाई-भतीजावाद और भ्रष्टाचार

Net amount निवल राशि/शुद्ध राशि **—assests** निवल परिसंपत्ति/शुद्ध परिसंपत्ति **—total** शुद्ध जोड़

—weight निवल भार/शुद्ध भार/ नेट भार

Neutral तटस्थ **Neutral country** तटस्थ देश

Nevertheless तो भी, तथापि

News agents समाचार-पत्र एजेंट **News Editor** समाचार-संपादक **—paper** समाचार पत्र/अखबार **—Reader** समाचार वाचक **—Reel Unit** समाचारदर्शन एकक **—Reporter** समाचार-दाता

Next below अगला निचला, उससे नीचे **Night Duty Section** रात्रि ड्यूटी अनुभाग **—shift** रात की पारी

No action necessary कोई कार्रवाई आवश्यक नहीं है **No admission** प्रवेश निषिद्ध, अन्दर आना मना है **No bar** कोई रोक नहीं **No-confidence motion** अविश्वास प्रस्ताव **No confidence vote** अविश्वास मत **No demand certificate** बेबाकी (प्रमाण) पत्र **No exit** बाहर जाने का रास्ता नहीं है **No instruction** कोई अनुदेश/हिदायत नहीं **No objection certificate** अनापत्ति (प्रमाण) पत्र **No profit no loss basis** लाभालाभ आधार **No reason to doubt** सन्देह का कोई कारण नहीं

Nomadic अस्थिर वासी **Nomadic Tribes Welfare Officer** यायावरी-जाति-कल्याण अधिकारी

Nomenclature नाम पद्धति

Nominal inspection नाममात्र का निरीक्षण **—member** नाममात्र का सदस्य **—value** अंकित मूल्य **Nominal rent** नाममात्र/सांकेतिक किराया **Nominal roll** नामावली, कर्मचारी सूची

Nominate नामित करना/मनोनीत करना **Nominated** नामित/मनोनीत **Nominated member** नामित/नामजद/मनोनीत सदस्य **Nomination** 1. नाम-निर्देशन 2. मनोनयन / नामन / नामांकन **—paper** नामन-पत्र/नामजदगी-पत्र **Nominator** नामनकर्ता, नामजद करने वाला **Nominee** नामिती/मनोनीत व्यक्ति/नामित व्यक्ति

Non-acceptance अस्वीकृति **Non-age** अवयस्कता **Non agriculture purposes** कृषितर प्रयोजन **Non-cognizable offence** अहस्तक्षेप्य/असंज्ञेय अपराध **Non-combatant** अयोधी, गैर लड़ाकू **Non-commercial** अव्यापारिक **Non-commissioned** अ-राजादिष्ट **Non-commissioned Officer**

ओहदेदार (एन० सी० ओ०) **Non-compliance** अपालन **Non-confidential** अगोपनीय **Non-consent** असहमति **Non-continuous Service** विच्छिन्न सेवा **Non-delivery** अवितरण **Non-Departmental Telegraphist** अविभागीय तार-संकेतक **Non-divisible expenditure** अविभाज्य व्यय **Non-earning** अनर्जक, बेकार **Non-edible** अभक्ष्य **Non-employment certificate** बेरोजगारी-पत्र **Non-essential services** निवार्य सेवाएं **Non-ferrous Metal Section** अलोह-धातु-अनुभाग **Non-Gazetted** अराजपत्रित **Non-gazetted service** अराजपत्रित सेवा **Non-government delegate** गैर-सरकारी/अराजकीय प्रतिनिधि **Non-Indian Supplier** विदेशीय प्रदायक **Non-military** असैनिक **Non-ministerial** अलिपिक वर्गीय/अनुसचिवीय **Non-ministerial service** अलिपिक वर्गीय सेवा **Non-observance** अपालन **Non-official** गैर-सरकारी / अशासकीय / अनधिकारिक **Non-payment certificate** अशोधन (प्रमाण)-पत्र/अदनगी (प्रमाण) पत्र **Non-party** निर्दलीय, पक्षातीत **Non-pensionable** अपेंशनी/ **Non-pensionable Service** अपेंशनी सेवा **Non-petitioner** अप्रार्थी **Non-practising allowance** प्रैक्टिसबंदी भत्ता **Non-productive consumption** अनुत्पादी उपभोग **Non-recurring expenditure** अनावर्त-व्यय/अनावर्ती व्यय **Non-reckonable service** असंगणनीय सेवा **Non-residential** अनिवासी **Non-residential University** अनिवासी विश्वविद्यालय **Non-saleable** अविक्रेय **Non-selection post** अप्रवरण पद **Non-standard** अमानक/मानक के अनुसार नहीं **Non-statutory** विधीतर **Non-technical post** अप्रविधिक पद/अतकनीकी पद **Non-voted** अदत्तमत **Non-working day** अवकाश/छुट्टी का दिन

Normal expenditure सामान्य व्यय

North Eastern Railway, Out Patient Block पूर्वोत्तर रेलवे बहिरंग रोगी खंड

N. B. (Note Bane) विशेष ध्यान दीजिए

Not advertised अविज्ञापित **Not competent** अक्षम **Not essential** आवश्यक नहीं **Not exceeding** से अनधिक, से अधिक नहीं, अधिक

से अधिक···तक **Not guilty** निर्दोष **Not later than** तारीख के बाद नहीं, तारीख···से पहले **Not less than** से कम नहीं अन्यून, कम से कम **Not more than** से अधिक नहीं, से अनधिक **Not-negotiable** अपरक्राम्य **Not only—but also** इतना ही नहीं··· बल्कि **Not otherwise provided for** जिसके बारे में दूसरे उपबन्ध न हों (या दूसरी व्यवस्था न हो) **Not payable before Ist of the nexth month** अगले मास कीं पहली तारीख के पूर्व अदेय **Not subject to** के अनधीन **Not subject to jurisdiction** क्षेत्राधिकार के अधीन न हो **Not to be tolerated** सहन नहीं किया जा सकता **Not traceable** पता नहीं लग रहा है, अप्राप्य **Not transferable** दूसरे को नहीं दिया जा सकता, अहस्तान्तरणीय, बदली अयोग्य **Notwithstanding to the contrary** किसी बात के अन्यथा होते हुए भी

Nota bene ध्यान दीजिए

Notary public नोटरी पब्लिक

Note टिप्पणी/नोट **—book** नोटबुक **—of dissent** असहमति-नोट **Note of protest** विरोध पत्र **Note-sheet** टिप्पणी-पत्र, नोट कागज **Noted** नोट कर लिया **Noted, thanks** नोट कर लिया, धन्यवाद **Noter** टिप्पणी लेखक **Noters and drafters** टीपक और मसौदाकार **Notes cover** टिप्पणी आवरण **Notes at page—may please be seen in this connection** इस सम्बन्ध में कृपया पृष्ठ···पर की टिप्पणी देख ली जाए

Nothing in clause (2) shall effect खण्ड (2) की किसी बात का प्रभाव नहीं होगा **Nothing in this article shall prevent** इस अनुच्छेद की किसी बात से बाधा नहीं होगी **Nothing in this clause be construed** इस खण्ड की किसी बात का यह अर्थ नहीं किया जाए **Nothing shall derogate from the power of Parliament** कोई बात संसद की शक्ति को कम नहीं करेगी

Notice सूचना/नोटिस **—board** सूचना पट्ट/नोटिस बोर्ड **Notice inviting tender** टेंडर/निविदा मंगाने के लिए सूचना **Notice in writing** लिखित सूचना **—of discharge** कार्यमुक्ति सूचना/कार्यमुक्ति नोटिस **—of motion** प्रस्ताव-सूचना **Notice to admit** स्वीकृति के लिये नोटिस; स्वीकृति

के लिये सूचना

Notification अधिसूचना **Notification, gazette** राजपत्र/गजट अधिसूचना **Notified** अधिसूचित **Notified area** अधिसूचित क्षेत्र/नोटीफाइड एरिया **Notified for general information** जनसाधारण की जानकारी के लिए अधिसूचित **Noting** टिप्पणी लिखना **Noting and drafting** टिप्पणी और मसौदा-लेखन

Nuclear headquarters नाभीय/अन्तरंग मुख्यालय

Null बातिल **—and void** बातिल और शून्य **Nullify** बातिल करना/अकृत करना

Number संख्या **Number, even** समसंख्या **Number, odd** विषम संख्या **Number, of even** इसी संख्या का, समसंख्यक **—Taker** नंबर लेखक/नंबर टेकर **Numbered paragraph** संख्यांकित पैरा **Numbering stamp** अंकन मोहर, नम्बर लगाने वाली मोहर

Numeral संख्यांक/अंक **Numerical abstract** संख्यात्मक सार **Numerical data** संख्यात्मक आंकड़े **Numerical order** संख्या क्रम, संख्यात्मक क्रम **Numerical Strength** संख्या बल, संख्या

Numismatist मुद्राविद्

Nuncupative मौखिक

Nuptial वैवाहिक; विवाह सम्बन्धी

Nurse नर्स/परिचारिका/उपचारिका **—(Male)** परिचारक/उपचारक **Nursery development** पौधशाला विकास **Nursery Development Officer** पौधशाला विकास-अधिकारी/नर्सरी विकास-अधिकारी **Nursing Orderly** उपचर्या-अर्दली **—Sister** उपचर्या-सिस्टर

Nutrition पोषण; पुष्टि **Nutrition Research Laboratory** पोषण-अनुसंधान-प्रयोगशाला

Oar चप्पू

Oath शपथ **—Commissioner** शपथ आयुक्त **—of allegiance** निष्ठाशपथ/राजनिष्ठा-शपथ **—of office** पद-शपथ **—of secrecy** गोपनीयता-शपथ

Obedience आज्ञापालन/आज्ञानुवर्तन

Obedient आज्ञापालक

Obiter dictum प्रासंगिक विचार अप्रकृतोक्ति; अनन्वितोक्ति

Obituary निधन-सूचना

Object (n.) वस्तु (vb.) आपत्ति उठाना/आपत्ति करना **Object of legislation** विधान का उद्देश्य **Objection** आपत्ति **Objection statement** आपत्ति विवरण

Objectionable action आपत्तिजनक कार्रवाई **Objectionable, it is highly** यह बहुत ही आपत्तिजनक है **Objections have been dealt with** आपत्तियों पर विचार कर लिया गया है **Objective** वस्तुनिष्ठ, निष्पक्ष; तटस्थ

Obligation बाध्यता/दायित्व/आभार/बंधन **Obligation for, there is no** के लिए कोई बाध्यता/बंधन नहीं है **Obligatory** बाध्यकर अनिवार्य **Obligatory attendance** अनिवार्य/बाध्यकर उपस्थिति **Obligatory, it is** यह अनिवार्य/बाध्यकर है

Obliged, I shall be मैं अनुगृहीत हूंगा **Obliged to answer** उत्तर देने के लिए बाध्य

Obscene अश्लील **Obscene literature** अश्लील साहित्य

Observance पालन **Observance of rule** नियम पालन **Observation** 1. प्रेक्षण/संप्रेक्षण 2. लेखा टिप्पणी/समुक्ति **Observation post** प्रेक्षण चौकी **Observation Superintendent** प्रेक्षण-अधीक्षक **— Supervisor (P. & T.)** अनुश्रवणक **Observation made above** ऊपर कही गई बातें उपर्युक्त विचार/टिप्पणी **Observatory, Astronomical** वेधशाला **—, Meteorological** मौसम-प्रेक्षणालय

Observer प्रेक्षक **Observer delegate** प्रेक्षण प्रतिनिधि

Obsolete लुप्त/अप्रचलित **Obsolete equipment** अप्रचलित उपस्कर

Obstruction बाधा **Obstruction caused** उत्पन्न बाधा

Obtain formal sanction औपचारिक मंजूरी प्राप्त करें **Obtain signature** हस्ताक्षर करवाइए **Obtainable, easily** आसानी से प्राप्य

Obvious स्पष्ट **Obvious, it is** यह स्पष्ट है

Occasional यदा कदा/अनियत/प्रासंगिक **Occasion arises, when** जब अवसर/समय आएगा **Occasional check** यदाकदा पड़ताल **Occasioned by** से उत्पन्न, से जनित

Occupation 1. उपजीविका/व्यवसाय/धंधा 2. अधिभोग 3. अधिग्रहण **Occupation, wholetime** पूर्णकालिक व्यवसाय/धंधा **Occupation, under my** मेरे कब्जे/अधिकार में **Occupational Therapist** व्यवसाय चिकित्सक

Occupy 1. अधिकार में करना/दखल करना 2. स्थान घेरना **Occupying so much space**

इतनी जगह घेरे हुए

Occurred to me मुझे सूझा

Occurrence घटना **Occurrence of, on the** के घटित होने पर, के होने पर

Ocean freight समुद्री भाड़ा

Oceanographist समुद्र-विज्ञानी

Octroi duty चुंगी **—Inspector** चुंगी-निरीक्षक

Off day छुट्टी का दिन, खाली दिन

Off duty 1. काम के बाद/काम पर न होना 2. खाली दिन

Of no avail व्यर्थ, निष्फल, निष्प्रयोजन **Of the like amount** उतनी राशि/मूल्य का

Offence अपराध **Offence, serious** गंभीर अपराध

Offender अपराधी

Offensive 1. आक्रमणात्मक 2. अप्रिय/कटु 3. उपघातक **Offensive action** आक्रमणात्मक कार्रवाई **Offensive, enemy's** शत्रु का आक्रमण **Offensive expressions** अप्रिय/कटु/आक्षेपयुक्त वचन

Offer नियुक्ति-प्रस्ताव **Offer of appointment** नियुक्ति-प्रस्ताव **Offer to perform** पालन करने की प्रस्थापना

Office 1. कार्यालय/दफ्तर 2. पद **—, Acceptance of** पद-स्वीकृति **—, Attached** संलग्न कार्यालय/संलग्न दफ्तर **—Bearer** पदाधिकारी **Office considered that** कार्यालय का विचार था कि **—copy** कार्यालय प्रति/दफ्तर की प्रति **Office expenses** कार्यालय व्यय **- hours** कार्यालय-समय **—memorandum** कार्यालय-ज्ञापन **— note** कार्यालय-टिप्पणी/कार्यालय नोट **Office of issue** निर्गम-कार्यालय **Office of profit** लाभ पद **—of the appellate controller of estate duty** कार्यालय, नियंत्रक, संपदाशुल्क-अपील **— of the Chief Pay and Accounts Officer** कार्यालय, मुख्य वेतन तथा लेखा अधिकारी **—of the Commissioner of Income Tax** आयकर-आयुक्त का कार्यालय **— of the Custodian of Deposits** कार्यालय, निक्षेप अभिरक्षक **—of the Director of Inspection** कार्यालय, निरीक्षण-निदेशक **—of the Inspecting Officer** कार्यालय, निरीक्षण-अधिकारी **—of the Inspector (Sugar)** कार्यालय, निरीक्षक (शर्करा) **Office of the Narcotics Commissioner** कार्यालय, संवेदनमंदक आयुक्त/नार्कोटिक्स आयुक्त का कार्यालय **—of the Registrar General of India**

कार्यालय, भारत के महापंजीयक **—of the Superintendent of Census operation** कार्यालय, जनगणना परिचालन अधीक्षक **—order** कार्यालय आदेश **Office proposes** कार्यालय का प्रस्ताव है **—Superintendent** कार्यालय अधीक्षक **—Supervisor** कार्यालय पर्यवेक्षक **—, Subordinate** अधीनस्थ कार्यालय/अधीन कार्यालय **Office to note and comply** कार्यालय ध्यान दे और पालन करे **Officer** अधिकारी/अफसर

Officer addressed सम्बोधित अधिकारी / पदाधिकारी / अफसर **—Commanding** अफसर कमांडिंग/ कमान अफसर **Officer, Commissioned** आयुक्त आफिसर **—in-charge** प्रभारी अधिकारी **in-Tactical Command (Naval)** सामरिक कमान अफसर (नौसेना) **Officer, inspecting** निरीक्षक आफिसर; निरीक्षक अधिकारी **—on Special Duty (O.S.D)** विशेष-कार्य अधिकारी **—Supervisor (O.S.)** पर्यवेक्षक अफसर (ओ० एस०) **—(Traffic Survey)** विशेष कार्य अधिकारी (यातायात **—Under Training** प्रशिक्षणाधीन अधिकारी

Official 1. शासकीय/सरकारी 2. आधिकारिक **Official administrator** सरकारी प्रशासक; राजकीय प्रशासक **—benches** सरकारी पक्ष **—business** सरकारी काम **Official capacity, in** आधिकारिक/पदीय हैसियत से **Official communication** शासकीय संसूचना **—correspondence** सरकारी पत्र-व्यवहार / आधिकारिक पत्र-व्यवहार **—duty** पदीय कर्तव्य **official envelope** शासकीय लिफाफा **official function** पदीय कृत्य **—Gallery** सरकारी दीर्घा **official Gazette** शासकीय राजपत्र; आफिशियल गजट **official, Government** सरकारी पदाधिकारी **—Incharge, LPO** आधिकारिक प्रभारी, खोया सामान घर **—language** राजभाषा **official member** शासकीय सदस्य **official Publication** सरकारी प्रकाशन **official rank** शासकीय पद **official reason** शासकीय कारण **Official reply** सरकारी उत्तर **—report** सरकारी रिपोर्ट **Official residence** पदावास; सरकारी निवास **—secret** सरकारी गुप्ति **Official trustee** सरकारी न्यासधारी **—version** सरकारी कथन/आधिकारिक कथन

Officiate 1. स्थानापन्न होना

2. स्थानापन्न रूप में काम करना **Officiating** स्थानापन्न **—allowance** स्थानापन्न-भत्ता **—pay** स्थानापन्न-वेतन **—post** स्थानापन्न पद **—rank** स्थानापन्न पदवी; स्थानापन्न ओहदा **– service** स्थानापन्न सेवा

Offset Printer आफसैट मुद्रक

O H E Maintainer शिरोपरि बिजली तार अनुरक्षक

Oil and Natural Gas Commission तेल तथा प्राकृतिक गैस आयोग **—Engine Inspector** तेल इंजन निरीक्षक **—Seeds Specialist** तिलहन-विशेषज्ञ **Oiler** तेल देने वाला

O. K. (correct alright) सब ठीक, अच्छा

Omission अकरण; लुप्ति **—to pay** देने/भुगतान में चूक **Omit** छोड़ना; छूटना; लुप्त करना **Omitted from the list, shall be** सूची में से छोड़ दिया जायेगा

On a trial विचारण में, विचारण पर **—account of** के कारण **account payment** लेखे पर देना, खाते पर देना **—active service** सक्रिय सेवा पर **—all fours** सर्वांगसम **—an average** औसतन **On approval** अनुमोदनार्थ **—behalf of** की ओर से **—ceasing to be such member** ऐसे सदस्य न रहने पर **—compassionate grounds** दया के आधार पर **—deputation** प्रतिनियुक्ति पर **—duty** काम पर, ड्यूटी पर **—grounds of** के आधार पर **—his behalf** उसकी ओर से **—his own motion** स्वप्रेरणा से **—India Government Service** भारत सरकार के सेवार्थ **On medical grounds** रोग के कारण **—merits** गुण-दोष/गुणावगुण के आधार पर **—no account** किसी अवस्था में नहीं **—or about** को या उसके आसपास **—or after the day** उस दिन या उसके पश्चात् **—perusal of the application** आवेदन पत्र के देखने/अवलोकन करने पर **—probation** परिवीक्षाधीन / परखाधीन **—probation of good conduct** सदाचरण की परिवीक्षा पर **—receipt of** के मिलने पर **—relief by** द्वारा पदमुक्त किए जाने पर **—such terms and conditions as he thinks fit** ऐसे निबन्धों और शर्तों के साथ जिन्हें वह उचित समझें **—the advice of** की सलाह पर **—the contrary** इसके प्रतिकूल, इसके विपरीत **—the face of it**

प्रत्यक्षत: **—the ground that** के आधार पर **—the lines of** की शैली पर, के समान **—the part of the candidate** अभ्यर्थी की तरफ से **—these points** इन मुद्दों पर **—the spot** घटनास्थल पर; तत्स्थान **—the subject noted above** उपर्युक्त विषय पर

One way traffic इकतरफा रास्ता

Onus भार/दायित्व **—of proof (burden of proof)** सिद्धि-भार, सिद्ध करने का दायित्व **—pro-bandi** प्रमाण-भार; सिद्धिभार

Onward transmission/despatch, for आगे भेजने के लिए

Open delivery खुला परिदान, खुली सुपुर्दगी

Open fire, to गोली चलाना **—general licence** निर्बाध आम लाइसेन्स **—letter** खुला पत्र **—mind** निष्पक्ष मन **—part file** खण्ड फाइल खोलें **—secret** खुला रहस्य **—session** खुला अधिवेशन **—tender** खुला टेंडर/खुली निविदा **—the case/discussion** वाद/बहस आरम्भ करना **Opening balance** आदि शेष, रोकड़ जमा **—entry** प्रारम्भिक प्रविष्टि

Operating staff परिचालन अमला, प्रचालन स्टाफ **—Superintendent** प्रचालन-अधीक्षक **Operation** 1. प्रचालन 2. संक्रिया 3. शल्यकर्म कॉपरेशन **—directorate** सैनिक आर्रवाई निदेशालय **—is in** जारी है, चालू है **—mechanical** मशीनी संक्रिया **—officer** सैनिक कार्रवाई अधिकारी **—room** आपरेशन का कमरा **Operative Telegraphist** कर्मी तार संकेतक **Operator** प्रचालक/ऑपरेटर **—, Electrical machine** मशीन प्रचालक/आपरेटर

Opinion राय **—in my** मेरी राय में **—of expert** विशेषज्ञ की राय **—of the majority** बहुसंख्या की राय

Opium Officer अफीम अधिकारी **—Section** अफीम अनुभाग

Opportune moment उपयुक्त समय

Opportunity अवसर **—to be heard** सुनवाई का अवसर

Opposite direction effect विरुद्ध दिशा/प्रभाव **—party** प्रतिपक्षी, विपक्ष दल, विरोधी दल **—side** सामने, दूसरी ओर

Opposition 1. विरोध 2. विरोधी दल **—Leader of** विरोधी दल का नेता **—strong** कड़ा विरोध

Opticist दृष्टि विज्ञानी

Optimistic estimate आशावादी अनुमान

Optimum point अनुकूलतम बिन्दु

Option विकल्प **—for** के लिए

विकल्प **Optional** वैकल्पिक **—medium** वैकल्पिक माध्यम

Oral मौखिक/जबानी **—agreement/contract** मौखिक करार/संविदा **—consultation** मौखिक परामर्श, जबानी सलाह-मशविरा **—evidence / examination** मौखिक साक्ष्य/परीक्षा **Orally** मौखिक रूप से

Orchestrator वाद्यवृन्दकार

Order आदेश; व्यवस्था **—,conditional** सशर्त आदेश **—, in** ठीक कम में; नियमित **—in writing** लिखित आदेश **—is restored** शान्ति/व्यवस्था स्थापित की गई **—, issuing an** आदेश निकालना **—, making an** आदेश करना **—, office** कार्यालय आदेश **—of merit** योग्यता क्रम, गुणानुक्रम **—of priority** अग्रता क्रम **—of transfer** अन्तरण का आदेश **—passed on appeal** अपील पर दिया गया आदेश **—, Standing** स्थायी आदेश **—that, in** जिससे कि **—this is in** यह ठीक/नियमित है **—to set the dismissal aside** खारिजी को अपास्त करने का आदेश

Orderly अर्दली **—proceedings** व्यवस्थित कार्यवाही

Orders are solicited कृपया आदेश दें **—communicated** आदेश भेजे/बताए गए

Ordinance अध्यादेश **—, by** अध्यादेश से **Ordinance Officer** आयुध अधिकारी/आर्डनेंस अफसर **—factory** आयुध निर्माणी, आयुध निर्माणी, आयुध फैक्ट्री

Ordinarily सामान्यतया; आम तौर पर **Ordinary call** साधारण कॉल **—repair** साधारण/मामूली मरम्मत

Organisation संघटन; संस्था **—and methods** संगठन और पद्धति **—Division** संगठन और पद्धति-प्रभाग **Organiser** आयोजक **—successful** सफल आयोजक

Orientation and Study Centre अभिविन्यास तथा अध्ययन केन्द्र

Original (n.) मूल प्रति **(adj.)** मूल/मौखिक **—auction Purchaser** मूल नीलाम क्रेता; मूल नीलाम खरीदार **—copy** मूल प्रति **—. returned in** मूल रूप से/में वापस **—work** मौलिक कार्य

Ostensible means of subsistence निर्वाह के ज्ञात साधन

Other part दूसरा पक्ष/दल **—ranks** जवान, अन्य श्रेणियां **—than** के अतिरिक्त, से भिन्न, को छोड़कर

Otherwise action will be taken

वरना/ अन्यथा कार्रवाई की जाएगी **—than** से अन्यथा

Out and out पूर्णतः **—door patient** बहिरंग/बाहरी रोगी **—of bounds** वर्जित क्षेत्र **—of date** पुराना/गतावधिक/अप्रचलित **—of order** 1. खराब/चालू नहीं/ बिगड़ी दशा में 2. अव्यवस्थित/ अनियमित **—of stock** स्टॉक में नहीं **—of turn allotment** बिना पारी आबंटन **—of use** उपयोग में नहीं, बेकार **—to day** आज ही भेजिए **—turn** उपज, निकासी, उत्पादन, काम **Outfit allowance** परिधान भत्ता **Outgoing files** जाने वाली फाइलें, निर्गामी फाइलें/ मिसिलें **Outlay** 1. परिव्यय 2. प्रारूप/खाका **—,of** का प्रारूप/ खाता **—on the plan** योजना पर होने वाला परिव्यय **Outlying areas** दूरवर्ती/बाहरी क्षेत्र **Outpost** सीमा चौकी **—, police** पुलिस सीमा चौकी **Output** उत्पादन/ उत्पाद **— , total** कुल उत्पादन **Outstanding** उत्कृष्ट/प्रकृष्ट **—work** उत्कृष्ट कार्य **Outward clerk** जावक लिपिक; जावक क्लर्क **—register** जावक रजिस्टर **—returns** जावक विवरणियां

Over-age अधिक आयु **—all** समस्त/समग्र/कुल **—all expenditure** समस्त/समग्र/कुल व्यय **—due** 1. अतिशोध्य 2. पुराना/बाकी **—estimate (n.)** अधिप्रावकलन/ अधिक अनुमान **(vb.)** अधिक आंकना/अधिक कूतना **—head charge** ऊपरी खर्च

Overlapping परस्परव्यापी **—functions** परस्पर व्यापी काम/ कृत्य **—payment** अधिक भुगतान/ अधिक अदायगी **Overriding** अधिभावी/अध्यारोही **—decisions** अधिभावी निर्णय **Overhauling** 1. जीर्णोद्धार 2. पूरी मरम्मत/ ओवरहाल **Overrule** उलटना; विरुद्ध व्यवस्था देना

Overseas allowance समुद्रपार-भत्ता **—service** समुद्र पार सेवा **Overseer** ओवरसियर **—(Drainage)** ओवरसियर (जल निकासी) **Overstayal of leave** छुट्टी से अधिक ठहरना **Overtime** अतिरिक्त समय **—allowance** अतिरिक्त समय भत्ता/समयोपरि भत्ता **— bill** समयोपरि बिल

Owing to के कारण

Own स्वामित्व रखना; स्वामी होना **—motion** स्वप्रेरणा **Owner** स्वामी **Owner's risk, at** मालिक के दायित्व पर **Owning authority** स्वामी प्राधिकारी/मालिक प्राधिकारी

Oyer and termine सुनना और निर्णय करना

Pacify शान्त करना; विरोध मिटाना **Pacification** शान्ति-स्थापन

Pack पिट्ठू; बांधना **Package** पैकेज **—proposal** एक मुश्त प्रस्ताव **Packer** पैकर **Packet** पुलिंदा/पैकेट **Packing** पैक करना/बांधना **—and marking** पैक करना और चिह्न लगाना **—list** पैकिंग-सूची

Pact समझौता **—, bilateral** द्विपक्षीय समझौता

Pad गद्दी/पैड **—, Ink** स्याही-पैड/मसि-पैड **—, Letter** पत्र-पैड **—, Writing** लेखन-पैड

Paddy Specialist धान विशेषज्ञ

Page 8 notes पृष्ठ 8 टिप्पणी **Pagination** पृष्ठ-संख्या डालना **Pagination has not been done correctly** पृष्ठ-संख्या ठीक नहीं डाली गई है

Paid 1. प्रदत्त/दत्त 2. सवेतन 3. भुगतान किया हुआ/अदा किया हुआ **—apprentice** सवेतन शिक्षु **—articles** दत्त वस्तुएं **—, bill has been** बिल का भुगतान हो गया है **—freight** भाड़ा चुकाया

Painter 1. रंगसाज 2. चित्रकार

Pamphlet पुस्तिका **—, Publicity** प्रचार पुस्तिका

Panchayat Raj Department पंचायत-राज विभाग

Panel नामिका **—of experts** विशेषज्ञ नामिका, विशेषज्ञों का पैनल

Paper Currency Department कागजी-मुद्रा-विभाग **—for disposal** निपटान के लिए कागज **—particulars** कागजी ब्यौरा **—transaction** कागजी लेन-देन **—under consideration (P.U.C.)** विचाराधीन कागज/पत्र, (वि० का०) **—under disposal** निकासी के कागज; निपटान के अधीन कागज

Par value सम मूल्य

Paragraph 2 पैरा 2

Parasitologist परजीव-विज्ञानी

Parcel पार्सल **—and Luggage Supervisor** पार्सल और सामान पर्यवेक्षक **—Clerk** पार्सल क्लर्क **—, Chief** मुख्य पार्सल क्लर्क **—, Head** प्रधान पार्सल क्लर्क **—-Office** पार्सल कार्यालय **—Supervisor** पार्सल पर्यवेक्षक, पार्सल सुपरवाइजर

Parent office मूल कार्यालय

Parents, dependant आश्रित माता-पिता

Par-excellence श्रेष्ठ/उत्कृष्ट

Pari Pasu (at equal pace) समगति से, समभाव से, समरूप

Parity समानता/बराबरी **—rate** समता दर

Parliament संसद **Parliamentary** संसदीय **Parliamentary Committee** संसदीय समिति **—and legal affairs committee** संसदीय और वैधानिक मामलों की समिति **—affairs** संसदीय कार्य **—Assistant** संसदीय सहायक **—correspondent** संसद-सम्वाददाता **—democracy** संसदीय लोकतंत्र **—Secretary** संसदीय सचिव

Part file खंड-फाइल/खंड मिसिल/खंड-संचिका **—time** अंशकालिक **—time worker** अंशकालिक कर्मचारी; अंशकालिक कार्मिक **—two order** भाग दो आदेश

Partiality, obvious स्पष्ट पक्षपात

Partial modification आंशिक संशोधन/तरमीम

Particular, In विशेषत: **Particulars** ब्यौरा/विशिष्टियां

Partiality पक्षपात **—with full** पूरे ब्यौरे/विवरण सहित

Partition विभाजन/बंटवारा **—council** विभाजन परिषद **—Secretariat** विभाजन सचिवालय

Partly in order अंशत: ठीक

Partner भागी; साझेदार; साझी **Partnership deed** साझा-पत्र/भागिता विलेख

Parts, in several कई भागों में

Party inferior Service अंशत; अवर सेवा; अंशत: अवर नौकरी **Party in power** सत्तारूढ़ दल **—spirit** दलगत भावना. पार्टीबाजी

Pass (n.) 1. पास 2. पारण **(vb.)** 1. पास करना 2 पार जाना/गुजारना - **bills** बिल पास करना **—book** पास-बुक **—order** आदेश पारित करना **—service** पूर्व-सेवा **—word** संकेत शब्द

Passage 1. मार्ग/गली/गलियारा 2. किराया 3. अंश/उद्धरण 4. यात्रा **—, air** हवाई यात्रा/किराया **—from this book** इस पुस्तक का अंश/उद्धरण **– of a bill** बिल पास करना

Passed for payment अदायगी/भुगतान के लिए स्वीकृत/पास किया गया **—resolution was** संकल्प पारित हुआ

Passenger Attendent यात्री परिचर **—Guide** यात्री-परिदर्शक

Passing of train गाड़ी गुजरना

Passport पार सत्र/पासपोर्ट **—and Visa** पारपत्र/पासपोर्ट और बीजा

—**authority** पासपोर्ट-प्राधिकारी/ पारपत्र-प्राधिकारी **office** पारपत्र/ पासपोर्ट कार्यालय —**Visa Attache** पासपोर्ट और बीजा अताशे/ पार-पत्र और बीजा-सहचारी

Past service पूर्व-सेवा, पिछली नौकरी/सेवा —**weather** विगत मौसम

Patent पेटेंट/एकस्व **Patent's Officer** एकस्व अधिकारी/पेटेंट अधिकारी — **Inspection Centre** एकस्व निरीक्षण केन्द्र

Patrolman पैट्रोलमैन

Patron 1. संरक्षक 2. प्रश्रयदाता —**in-Chief** मुख्य संरक्षक

Patronage संरक्षण —**under his** उसके संरक्षण में

Pattern Keeper प्रतिमान-पाल —**Maker** नमूनाकार/ नमूनासाज

Pay वेतन —, **Advance** अग्रिम वेतन —**and Accounts Officer** भुगतान और लेखा अधिकारी —**Assistant** वेतन-बिल सहायक —, **Basic** मूल वेतन —**bill** वेतन-बिल/वेतन-विपत्र —**Clerk** वेतन क्लर्क/वेतन लिपिक — **day** वेतन दिवस —, **Fixed** नियत वेतन —**head** वेतन-मद्द —**Master** वेतन मास्टर/वेतन-पाल —**of appointment** नियुक्ति वेतन —**of rank** ओहदा वेतन —**of substantive oppointment** मौलिक नियुक्ति वेतन —**order** अदायगी-आदेश —, **Overseas** समुद्रपार वेतन —, **Personal** वैयक्तिक वेतन —**Presumptive** प्रकल्पित वेतन —**roll** वेतन पत्रक —**scale** वेतन-मान —**self** स्वयं देय —**slip** वेतन पर्ची —, **Special** विशेष वेतन —, **substantive** मूल पद-वेतन —, **Time Scale** काल-मान वेतन **Payable** देय/ भुगतानी —, **to** को देय

Payee पाने वाला/आदाता **Payee's receipt** पाने वाले की रसीद, आदाता की रसीद

Payer 1. भुगतान कर्ता 2. दाता

Payment भुगतान/संदाय/देना —**Office** पेंशन-भुगतान कार्यालय —**of money into** में धन जमा करना —**terms** भुगतान की शर्तें; अदायगी की शर्तें

Peace time Surplus शान्तिकालीन अधिशेष

Pecuniary धन-संबंधी **Pecuniary interest** आर्थिक हित/स्वार्थ

Pediatrician बाल-चिकित्सक

Penal code दंड-संहिता —**interest** दंड-स्वरूप ब्याज —**rent** दंड-स्वरूप किराया

Penalty 1. दंड 2. अर्थ दंड/जुर्माना 3. शास्ति **—for contravention of orders** आदेशों के उल्लंघन का दण्ड

Pend till decision is taken on the main file मुख्य मिसिल पर निर्णय होने तक इसे रोक रखिए

Pending 1. अनिर्णीत/पड़ा हुआ/रुका हुआ/लंबित 2. तक/पर्यंत **—cases** अनिर्णीत/रुके हुए मामले **—till the conclusion of enquiry** जांच समाप्त होने तक

Penologist दंडशास्त्री

Pension पेंशन **—card** पेंशन-कार्ड **—Clerk** पेंशन-क्लर्क **—, Extra-ordinary** असाधारण पेंशन **Pensionable** पेंशन योग्य/पेंशनी **—service** पेंशनी सेवा **Pensionary charges** पेंशन संबंधी प्रभार **Pensioner** पेंशन भोगी **—,Govt.** सरकारी पेंशन भोगी **—Post** पेंशनी-पद

Pen-tray कलमदान

Peon चपरासी **—book** पत्रवाह-पंजी/चपरासी-बही

Per annum प्रतिवर्ष / वार्षिक / सालाना **—bearer** वाहक द्वारा/पत्र-वाहक द्वारा **—capita** प्रति-व्यक्ति **—diem** प्रतिदिन **Per mensem** प्रतिमास, माहवार

Percent प्रतिशत / फीसदी

Percentage प्रतिशतता/प्रतिशत दर **—increase** प्रतिशत वृद्धि, प्रतिशतता वृद्धि

Performance निष्पादन / पालन **—register** निष्पादन रजिस्टर

Period अवधि/कालावधि **—, for short** थोड़ी अवधि के लिए **—, of service** सेवावधि, सेवाकाल

Periodical (n.) 1. पत्र/सामयिकी/पत्रिका **(adj.)** 2. आवधिक/समय-समय पर सामयिक/कालिक **check** आवधिक जांच, समय-समय पर पड़ताल **—inspection** आवधिक निरीक्षण/समय-समय पर निरीक्षण **—report** आवधिक रिपोर्ट **—return** आवधिक विवरणी **—review** सामयिक समीक्षण

Perishable विनाशवान **—goods** विनाशवान माल

Permanence स्थायित्व **Permanency** स्थायित्व

Permanent स्थायी **—Joint Planning Committee** स्थायी संयुक्त योजना समिति **—post** स्थायी पद **—Service** स्थायी सेवा

Permissible 1. अनुमेय/अनुज्ञेय 2. क्षम्य **Permission** अनुज्ञा/अनुमति **Permit (n.)** अनुज्ञा-पत्र परमिट **(vb.)** अनुज्ञा देना **—card** अनुज्ञा पत्र, परमिट **Permitted** 1. अनुज्ञप्त/अनुमति प्राप्त 2. अनु-

मति दी जाती है —**cannot be** अनुमति/अनुज्ञा/इजाजत नहीं दी जा सकती

Perpetual शाश्वत —**arrangement** शाश्वत प्रबंध

Personal वैयक्तिक —**Assistant** वैयक्तिक सहायक —**capacity in** वैयक्तिक रूप मे —**Pay** वैयक्तिक वेतन —**Staff** निजी कर्मचारी वर्ग, निजी अमला **Personality test** व्यक्तित्व परीक्षण

Personnel कार्मिक —**Inspector** कार्मिक निरीक्षक —**Officer** कार्मिक अधिकारी —**Relation Officer** कार्मिक संपर्क अधिकारी

Persons to be attested व्यक्ति जिन्हें अनुप्रमाणित किया जाएगा

Perspective संदर्श/परिप्रेक्ष्य —, **In proper** सही परिप्रेक्ष्य में

Persuade 1. समझाना/मनाना 2. सहमत करना **Persuasion, after great** बहुत समझाने/मनाने के पश्चात

Pertaining to से सम्बन्धित, के सम्बन्ध में

Perusal अवलोकन/देखना —, **for** अवलोकनार्थ, देखने के लिए **Perused, may be** अवलोकन कर लें, देख लिया जाय

Pest Control Officer नाशकजीव-नियंत्रण-अधिकारी

Petition याचिका/अर्जी —,**election** चुनाव याचिका —**Writer** याचिका-लेखक **Petitioner** याचिकादाता/प्रार्थी

Petroleum and Chemicals, Ministry of पेट्रोलियम और रसायन मंत्रालय —**division** पैट्रोलियम प्रभाग —**Geologist** पैट्रोलियम भूविज्ञानी —**Officer** पैट्रोलियम अधिकारी **Petrol Pump Keeper** पैट्रोल पंप रक्षक —**Rail-car Driver** पैट्रोल रेल-कार ड्राइवर —**Viewer** पैट्रोल वीक्षक

Petty cash खुदरा रोकड़ —**Officer** पेटी अफसर—**repairs** छोटी-मोटी मरम्मत

Pharmaceutical Enquiry committee भेषज - जाँच - समिति **Pharmaceutist** औषध-निर्माण-विज्ञानी **Pharmacist** भेषजज्ञ **Pharmacologist** औषधविज्ञानी

Photo and Cinema Officer फोटो तथा सिनेमा अधिकारी —**Artist** छविकार —**Division** फोटो प्रभाग —**Litho Operator** फोटो लिथो-प्रचालक —**Printer** फोटो-मुद्रक **Photographed** फोटो-चित्रित **Photographer** फोटोग्राफर **Photostat** फोटोस्टैट —**machine**

फोटोस्टेट मशीन —**Operator** फोटोस्टैट मशीन प्रचालक

Physical check प्रत्यक्ष/वस्तुगत पड़ताल **Physical count** वस्तुश: गणन **Physical Culture Instructor** व्यायाम-शिक्षक —**Education and Research Division** व्यायाम शिक्षा और अनुसंधान प्रभाग —**Fitness and Drill Instructor** शारीरिक स्वस्थता और कवायद शिक्षण —**fitness certificate** शारीरिक स्वस्थता (प्रमाण) पत्र, शारीरिक क्षमता (प्रमाण) पत्र —**Training Instructor** व्यायाम-शिक्षक **verification of stock** स्टाक का प्रत्यक्ष सत्यापन

Physician काय-चिकित्सक/फिजीशियन **Physicist** भौतिकी-विज्ञानी

Physiologist शरीर-क्रिया-विज्ञानी/शरीर वृत्ति-विज्ञानी **Physiotherapist** भौतिक-चिकित्साविद्

Piece and time worker ठेका और अमानी कामगर —**work rate** उजरत-दर **Piece wages** उजरत/खदरे काम की मजदूरी —**work** उजरती काम **Pickler** परिष्कारक

Pilot विमान-चालक/पाइलट/यान चालक —**Officer** पाइलट अफसर —**Scheme** पुरोगामी योजना —**survey** प्रायोगिक सर्वेक्षण

Pin cushion पिन कुशन/पिन गद्दी

Pipeline Inspector नल-निरीक्षक

Pisciculturist मत्स्यपालनविद्/मीनपालनविद्

Place of enquiry जाँच स्थान **Placed at the disposal of** को सौंपा गया —**below** नीचे रखा —**under suspension** मुअत्तिल/निलम्बित रखा गया

Plainer (Planer) रंदाकार **Plain language, in** सादा/सीधी/साधारण भाषा में

Plaintiff वादी **Plaintiff failed to appear** वादी हाजिर/उपस्थित नहीं हुआ

Plan योजना —**according to** योजना के अनुसार —**Recorder** योजना अभिलेखक

Planner योजनाकार **Planning** 1. योजना 2. योजना बनाना —**and Procurement** योजना और आसादन —**and Statistics** योजना और सांख्यिकी —**circle** आयोजना·समिति —**Commission** योजना आयोग —**Office** योजना अधिकारी

Plant and machinery संयंत्र और मशीनें —**Breeder** पौधा-संवर्धक —**in-Charge, Water Softening** संयंत्र प्रभारी, जल मृदूकरण

—Inspector संयंत्र निरीक्षक —Introduction Sub-Station पादप-प्रवर्तन उपकेन्द्र —Pathologist पादप-विकृति-विज्ञानी/पादप-रोग-विज्ञानी —Physiologist पादप-क्रियाविज्ञानी —Protection Adviser वनस्पति रक्षण सलाहकार —Officer वनस्पति-रक्षण-अधिकारी **Plantation Enquiry Commission** बागान-जाँच-आयोग, बागान-जाँच-कमीशन

Plasma Officer प्लाविका अधिकारी/प्लाजमा अफसर

Plate Laying Inspector प्लेट लेयिंग निरीक्षक **Plater** प्लेटर

Platform Assistant प्लेटफार्म सहायक **—Inspector** प्लेटफार्म निरीक्षक **—Porter** प्लेटफार्म भारिक **—Supervisor** प्लेटफार्म पर्यवेक्षक

Platoon Commander प्लाटून कमांडर

Plea advanced by him उसके द्वारा प्रस्तुत तर्क **Pleader** अधिवक्ता/प्लीडर

Please acknowledge receipt कृपया पावती भेजिए, पहुंचने की सूचना दीजिए, कृपया प्राप्ति सूचना दें **—appear in person before** कृपया···के समक्ष स्वयं उपस्थित होइए **—discuss** चर्चा कीजिए **—hand over charge to** कृपया श्री···को कार्यभार सौंप कर··· **Shri···and report yourself at**···उपस्थित हो जाइए **—put up precedent** कृपया दृष्टान्त दीजिए, पूर्वोदाहरण प्रस्तुत कीजिए **—reconcile the discrepancy in the entries** कृपया प्रविष्टियों का अन्तर ठीक कीजिए **—speak** कृपया चर्चा/बात कीजिए **—treat as most urgent** कृपया अत्यन्त जरूरी समझें **—treat this as strictly confidential** इसे कृपया सर्वथा गोपनीय समझें

Pleasure प्रसाद **—of, during the** के प्रसाद पर्यन्त

Pledge गिरवी, बंधक

Plenary पूर्ण **—conference** पूर्ण सम्मेलन **—session** पूर्ण अधिवेशन

Plinth area निम्न स्थल

Plumber नलसाज

Plus amendments and minus amendments वृद्धि के संशोधन और कमी के संशोधन

Poaching Guard शिकार-चोरी निरोधक

Point for determination अवधारण के लिए प्रश्न; अवधार्य प्रश्न **Points** मुद्दे **—, involved** निहित

—, raised in उठाए गए मुद्दे
Police आरक्षी/पुलिस Police Post पुलिस चौकी Policy, acceptable स्वीकार्य नीति —, Joint, life सम्मिलित-जीवन-पालिसी —of insurance बीमा-पत्र
Political officer राजनीतिक अधिकारी
Polling station पोलिंग-स्थान, वोट डालने का स्थान
Pontsman पैटमैन/कांटेवाला
Port quarantine पत्तन निरोध —and dcpots directorate पत्तन और डिपो निदेशालय --trust dues पत्तनप्रबन्ध समिति के देय
Post copy डाक प्रति —dated उत्तर दिनांकित, उत्तर तारीखी —deposit parties बाद में जमा करने वाले मांगकर्ता —, dereservation of पद-निराकरण, पद अनारक्षण —, duty ड्यूटी-पद —, excluded वर्जित-पद —facto Sanction कार्योत्तर मंजूरी —graduate स्नातकोत्तर —, higher temporary उच्चतर अस्थायी-पद —, included समाविष्ट पद —, independent पृथक् पद, अलग पद —Master General महापोस्टमास्टर/पोस्टमास्टर जनरल —mortem (examination) शव परीक्षा —, non-selection गैर-सेलेक्शन-पद, वरणेतर पद —,permanent/ pensionable स्थायी/पेंशनी पद —office डाक घर —,police पुलिस चौकी --, Probation परिवीक्षाधीन पद —regular नियमित पद —, regularly constituted नियमित निर्मित पद —, reservation of पद-आरक्षण —reserved आरक्षित पद —, retention of पद कायम रखना —, selection सेलेक्शन पद, प्रवरण पद —script (P.S.) पुनश्च, पश्च-लेख —, specialist's विशेषज्ञ पद —, substantive मौलिक पद —and Telegraph Department डाक-तार-विभाग —, temporary अस्थायी पद —, unreserved अनारक्षित पद —, vacant रिक्त पद
Postal address डाक-पता Postal certificate डाक प्रमाण-पत्र—dak पोस्टल डाक Postage stamp डाक टिकट Posted in due course सम्यक् अनुक्रम में डाक से भेजा गया
Posthumous award मरणोपरांत पुरस्कार
Posting of figures अंक दर्ज करना, चढ़ाना Posting orders तैनाती के आदेश

Postman डाकिया/पोस्टमैन

Postpone मुल्तवी करना **Postponed meeting** मुल्तवी हुई बैठक **Postponement** मुल्तवी

Pottery Supervisor मृद्भांड-पर्यवेक्षक

Poultry Development Officer कुक्कुट-विकास-अधिकारी **—farming** कुक्कुट पालन

Power 1. शक्ति 2. बिजली **—Controller** मशीन नियंत्रक/यंत्रनियंत्रक **—, financial** वित्तीय अधिकार/शक्ति **—, general** सामान्य शक्ति **—House** बिजली-घर

Power, in his उसके शक्त्यधीन; उसकी शक्ति में **—of appropriation** विनियोजन शक्ति **—of Attorney** मुख्तारनामा **—of reappropriation** पुनर्विनियोजन **—of Sanction** मंजूरी की शक्ति **—Recorder** 1. शक्ति-अभिलेखी 2. बिजलीअभिलेखी **—Room Attendant** विद्युत्‌कक्ष-परिचर **—Station Operator** बिजली-घर प्रचालक

Practice 1. पद्धति, 1. कर्म/पेशा **Practicable, as far as** जहां तक व्यवहार्य हो/हुआ **Practical experience** व्यावहारिक अनुभव **—, in** व्यवहार में **—, Legal** वकालत **—, Medical** चिकित्सा-कर्म/डाक्टरी पेशा **—, regular** नियमित अभ्यास/कार्य प्रणाली

Practise आचरण करना **Practising** वृत्ति करने वाला

Prayin the alternative अनुकल्पतः प्रार्थना करना **Prayer for relief** अनुतोष के लिए प्रार्थना

Preamble प्रस्तावना/उद्देशिका

Precaution पूर्वावधान/पूर्वोपाय/एहतियात **Precautionary measures** ऐहतियाती उपाय/कार्रवाई

Precedence पूर्वता/अग्रता **—, Order of** पूर्वता-क्रम **—, Warrant of** पूर्वता-अभिपत्र/पूर्वता-वारंट **Precedent** पूर्व उदाहरण/नजीर **Precedents, past** पिछले उदाहरण, पूर्वनिर्णय, पिछली नजीर

Preceding पूर्वगत **Preceding notes** पूर्वगामी टिप्पणियाँ

Precise meaning ठीक-ठीक अर्थ

Precision Miller सूक्ष्म तराशक **—Turner** सूक्ष्म कर्म खरादी

Precondition पूर्व शर्त

Predecessor 1. पूर्वज 2. पूर्वाधिकारी 3. पूर्ववर्ती **—, as said by me** जैसा मेरे पूर्ववर्ती/पूर्व वक्ता ने कहा है **—, decision** पूर्वाधिकारी का निर्णय **Predecessors,**

our हमारे पूर्वज

Predeposit Parties पहले जमा करने वाले मांगकर्ता

Predetermined cost पूर्व निर्धारित लागत

Preface प्रस्तावना

Prefect प्रिफेक्ट राज्यपाल

Preferable वरीय —, **it would be** यह अधिक अच्छा होगा

Preference अधिमान/तरजीह —**to, give** को तरजीह/अधिमान देना

Pre-investment Survey of Forest Resources वन संसाधनों का निवेशपूर्व सर्वेक्षण

Prejudice (n.) 1. प्रतिकूल प्रभाव 2. पूर्वाग्रह **(vb.)** 1. प्रतिकूल प्रभाव डालना 2. पूर्वग्रह रखना —, **I have no** मुझे कोई पूर्वाग्रह नहीं है —, **without** बिना प्रतिकूल प्रभाव डाले **Prejudicial** प्रतिकूल/हानिकारक

Preliminary (adj.) प्रारंभिक/प्राथमिक **(n.)** प्रास्ताविक —**action** प्राथमिक कार्रवाई —**report** प्रारंभिक रिपोर्ट

Premature 1. समय पूर्व 2. अकाल **Premature cessation** समय पूर्व विरमन —**death** अकाल मृत्यु —**increment** समय पूर्व तरक्की

Premier प्रधान मंत्री

Premises, public लोक परिसर

Premium बीमा-किस्त/प्रीमियम —, **insurance** बीमा-किस्त/प्रीमियम

Prepage, from पिछले पृष्ठ से

Preparation तैयारी/उपक्रम

Preparatory to retirement निवृत्तिपूर्व/रिटायर होने से पहले

Pre-partition claims विभाजन से पहले के दावे **Pre-receipted bill** रसीद सहित बिल

Prerogative परमाधिकार; विशेषाधिकार —**mercy** दया का परमाधिकार

Prescribe विहित करना, निर्धारण करना **Prescribed** विहित/निर्धारित —**date** नियत तारीख —**form** विहित फार्म/निर्धारित फार्म —**Procedure** नियत प्रक्रिया **Scale of Pay** विहित वेतनमान

Presentation प्रस्तुतीकरण —**of bill** बिल पेश करना, बिल का प्रस्तुतीकरण

Preservation परिरक्षण —**of records** अभिलेख/रिकार्ड का परिरक्षण

Presided over the meeting बैठक/सभा की अध्यक्षता की

Presidency Magistrate प्रेसीडेंसी मजिस्ट्रेट —**Postmaster** प्रेजीडेंसी

पोस्टमास्टर

President 1. राष्ट्रपति 2. अध्यक्ष/सभापति **—Body-guard** राष्ट्रपति के अंगरक्षक **—Estate Officer** राष्ट्रपति-संपदा अधिकारी **—secretariat** राष्ट्रपति-सचिवालय **—vice** उपप्रधान, उपाध्यक्ष, उप-राष्ट्रपति **Presidential election** राष्ट्रपति का चुनाव

Presiding पीठासीन **—Officer** पीठासीन अधिकारी

Press 1. मुद्रणालय/प्रेस 2. समाचारपत्र/प्रेस **—, a claim** दावे पर जोर देना, दावे के लिए आग्रह करना **—Adviser** प्रेस सलाहकार **—censorship** प्रेस सेंसरी **—communique** प्रेस-विज्ञप्ति **—conference** पत्रकार सम्मेलन **—correspondent** संवाददाता **—Cutting Officer (Press Clipping Officer)** पत्र - कतरन अधिकारी **—Facilities Officer** प्रेस-सुविधा-अधिकारी **—gallery** पत्रकार दीर्घा/पत्रकार गैलरी **—hand-out** प्रेस-पत्रक **—Information Bureau** पत्र सूचना कार्यालय **—note** प्रेस-नोट **—Operator** प्रेस ऑपरेटर/मुद्रण-यंत्र प्रचालक **—party** पत्रकार दल **—printing** मुद्रणालय, छापाखाना, प्रेस **—reaction** अखबारी प्रतिक्रिया **—release** प्रेस-प्रकाशनी **—Reporter** समाचारदाता **—representative** पत्र प्रतिनिधि **—man** 1. प्रेसमैन/मुद्रण कर्मचारी 2. पत्रकार

Presumption is correct धारणा ठीक है **Presumptive pay** प्रकल्पित वेतन

Presupposed पूर्व-कल्पित **—reason** पूर्वकल्पित कारण

Prevail अभिभावी होना

Prevent रुकावट डालना **Prevention** निवारण/रोकथाम/निरोध **Preventive detention** निवारक निरोध **Preventive measure** निवारक उपाय

Previous and later references पिछले और बाद के हवाले **—service** पिछली सेवा **—Sanction** पूर्व मंजूरी

Price Control Officer मूल्य-नियंत्रण-अधिकारी **—list** कीमत सूची/दाम-सूची **—negotiation** कीमत संबंधी बातचीत **—Preference** मूल्य अभिधान **—variation** कीमत में उतार-चढ़ाव/कीमत परिवर्तन **—variation clause** मूल्य में उतार चढ़ाव सम्बन्धी घाटा

Prima facie प्रत्यक्षतः/प्रथम दृष्टि में **—case** प्रथम दृष्टि में प्रतीत

मामला —**evidence** प्रथम दृष्ट्या साक्ष्य

Primary प्राथमिक —**meeting** प्राथमिक बैठक —**receipt** मूल आवती —**rule** मुख्य नियम

Prime Minister प्रधान मंत्री —**Secretariat** प्रधान मंत्री सचिवालय

Principal (as in Principal Director) प्रधान —**(of College)** प्रधानाचार्य/प्रिंसिपल —**Information Officer** प्रधान सूचना-अधिकारी —**Postal Appraiser** प्रधान डाक मूल्य-निरूपक

Principle, in सिद्धान्त रूप में, सिद्धान्ततः

Print order छपाई आदेश, मुद्रण आदेश **Printer** मुद्रक **Printer and publisher** मुद्रक व प्रकाशक

Prior approval पूर्व मंजूरी, पूर्वानुमति **Priority** प्राथमिकता/अग्रता —**buyer** प्राप्त खरीददार/प्राप्त क्रेता —**grading** प्राथमिकता की कोटियां —**indent** प्राथमिकता मांग-पत्र/प्राथमिकता/इंडेंट —**indications** प्राथमिकता संकेत —**marking** प्राथमिकता अंकन/अग्रता अंकन

Prison कारागार —**sent to** कारागार भेज दिया गया **Prisoner** काराबन्दी

Private प्राइवेट/निजी/गैर-सरकारी —**Member** गैर-सरकारी सदस्य —**practice** प्राइवेट प्रैक्टिस/निजी प्रैक्टिस —**property** निजी-सम्पत्ति —**Secretary** निजी सचिव —**Sector** निजी क्षेत्र, खासगी क्षेत्र, असार्वजनिक क्षेत्र

Privilege, विशेषाधिकार —**Committee** विशेषाधिकार समिति —**ticket order** सुविधा-टिकट आदेश

Probable cause संभाव्य कारण **Probability** प्रायिकता

Probate Officer प्रोबेट अधिकारी

Probation परिवीक्षण/परख/आजमाइश **Probation officer** प्रोबेशन अधिकारी, परिवीक्षाधिकारी —**period** परिवीक्षाकाल/परिवीक्षाअ-वधि

Probationary service परिवीक्षाधीन सेवा —**Superintendent of Post Office** प्रशिक्षण-अधीन अधीक्षक, डाकघर **Probationer** परिवीक्षाधीन / परखाधीन / आजमाइश

Proceeds, sale बिक्री आय

Procedural rules क्रियाविधि नियमावली **Procedure** कार्यविधि/प्रक्रिया —**laid down** निर्धारित प्रक्रिया/क्रियाविधि **Proceedings** कार्यवाही —**be stayed** कार्यवाही

रोकी जाय

Process of law विधि प्रक्रम **Process Server** आदेशिका-वाहक

Pro-Chancellor (of University) सम-कुलाधिपति **Pro-Vice-Chancellor** सम-कुलपति

Proclamation उद्घोषणा —, **President's** राष्ट्रपति की उद्घोषणा **Proclaimed offender** उद्घोषित अपराधी

Proconsul प्रोकान्सुल

Proctor (of a University) कुलानुशासक/प्रॉक्टर

Procurement आसादन/प्रापण

Producer (Film) निर्माता — **(Radio)** प्रस्तुतकर्ता/प्रस्तुति अधिकारी

Production, agricultural कृषि उत्पादन —**Assistant** उत्पादन सहायक —**Commissioner** उत्पादन आयुक्त; उत्पादन कमिश्नर —**Engineer** उत्पादन अभियंता/उत्पादन इंजीनियर —**Manager** उत्पादन प्रबंधक —**Officer** उत्पादन-अधिकारी —**(Film)** निर्माण-अधिकारी **Productivity Centre** उत्पादन-केन्द्र

Profess मानना **Profession** वृत्ति; पेशा; व्यवसाय **Professor** आचार्य/प्रोफेसर

Proficiency प्रवीणता —**certificate** प्रवीणता (प्रमाण) पत्र —**test** प्रवीणता परीक्षण

Profit and loss account लाभ-हानि-लेखा

Proforma 1. प्रपत्र 2. निदर्शन-पत्र 3. फार्म —, **prescribed** विहित प्रपत्र/फार्म

Programme, annual वार्षिक कार्यक्रम/प्रोग्राम —**indent** कार्यबद्ध इंडेंट / कार्यक्रम-बद्ध मांगपत्र —**Supervisor** प्रोग्राम पर्यवेक्षक

Progress प्रगति —**chart** प्रगति चार्ट —**chaser** प्रगति अनुवीक्षक —**Gunner** प्रगति अनुवीक्षक गनर —**Inspector** प्रगति निरीक्षक —**Officer** प्रगति अधिकारी —**Recorder** प्रगति-रिकॉर्डर —**report** प्रगति रिपोर्ट/प्रगति विवरण —**Superintendent** प्रगति अधीक्षक —**Supervisor** प्रगति पर्यवेक्षक

Progressive development उत्तरोत्तर विकास —**total** आरोही योग/जोड़ **Progressman** प्रगति-वीक्षक

Prohibited निषिद्ध —**area** निषिद्ध/वर्जित क्षेत्र **Prohibition** 1. निषेध 2. नशाबंदी —**programme** नशाबन्दी कार्यक्रम —, **write of** प्रतिषेध-लेख **Prohibitory order** निषेधात्मक आदेश

Project परियोजना —**Co-ordination Division** परियोजना समन्वय प्रभाग —**Director** परियोजना निदेशक —**Evaluation Officer** परियोजना मूल्यांकन अधिकारी —**Officer** परियोजना-अधिकारी

Project report परियोजना सम्बन्धी रिपोर्ट **Projectionist** प्रक्षेपक —**cum-Mechanic** प्रक्षेपक-व-मेकैनिक

Promise वचन **Promised, as** वचन/वायदे के अनुसार **Promissory note** वचन-पत्र/रुक्का

Promote बढ़ावा; उन्नति करना; वृद्धि करना **Promotion** प्रोन्नति/पदोन्नति/तरक्की/वर्धन —,**accelerated** त्वरित पदोन्नति —,**acting** कार्यवाहक पदोन्नति —**Cadre** तरक्की संवर्ग —**Committee, Departmental** विभागीय पदोन्नति समिति —**department** विभागीय पदोन्नति —, **examination** तरक्की परीक्षा —**officiating** स्थानापन्न पदोन्नति —,**order of** पदोन्नति क्रम —**out of turn** क्रमोत्तर पदोन्नति —**post** प्रोन्नति —, **quasi-substantive** मूलवत् पदोन्नति —, **substantive** मूल पदोन्नति —, **suprsession in** पदोन्नति में अधिलंघन —, **temporary** अस्थायी पदोन्नति —,**timescale** समयमान पदोन्नति

Prompt तुरंत; शीघ्र; अचिर —**action** शीघ्र कार्रवाई

Promulgate प्रख्यापन करना **Promulgation** प्रख्यापन

Proof 1. प्रमाण 2. प्रूफ (प्रेस) —**Master** प्रूफ-मास्टर —**of despatch** प्रेषण का प्रमाण —**Officer** प्रूफ-अफसर —**Reader** प्रूफ-शोधक/प्रूफ-रीडर/प्रूफ वाचक

Proof, reliable विश्वसनीय प्रमाण

Propaganda प्रचार —**Assistant** प्रचार-सहायक —**Demonstrator** प्रचार-निदर्शक —**work** प्रचार-कार्य

Proper उचित —**form** उचित फार्म/रूप —**channel** विधिवत् —**guidance** उचित संदर्शन

Property सम्पत्ति; रिक्थ —**Inspector** संपत्ति-निरीक्षक —**return** सम्पत्ति-विवरण

Proportion अनुपात **Proportional representation** अनुपाती प्रतिनिधित्व **Proportionate amount** आनुपातिक राशि —**cost** आनुपातिक लागत/खर्च

Proposal प्रस्तावना / प्रस्ताव —, **implied** निहित प्रस्ताव

Proposed action प्रस्तावित कार्रवाई —, **as** यथा प्रस्तावित जैसा, प्रस्ताव किया गया —**estimate** प्रस्तावित प्राक्कलन —**staff** प्रस्तावित कर्मचारीवर्ग

Proposer प्रस्तावक; प्रज्ञापक **Proposition statement** प्रस्ताव विवरण **Proprietary stores** उसी छाप का माल

Propriety औचित्य —,**question of** औचित्य का प्रश्न

Proroque सत्रावसान

Pros and cons पक्ष-विपक्ष, आगा-पीछा

Prosecution witness अभियोग-गवाह

Prospectus विवरण-पत्रिका —, **of college** कालिज की विवरण-पत्रिका

Protection given to को दिया संरक्षण **Protector of Emigrants** उत्प्रवासी-संरक्षक

Protest note विरोध पत्र

Protocol, matter of नयाचार का मामला —**Officer** नयाचार-अधिकारी

Prototype production आदिप्ररूप उत्पादन —**Production and Training Centre** आदिप्ररूप उत्पादन तथा प्रशिक्षण

Prove सिद्ध करना; परखना **Proved** सिद्ध

Provident fund भविष्य निधि/निर्वाह निधि —**Account** भविष्य निधि लेखा —**Clerk** भविष्य-निधि लिपि

Provided शर्त यह है कि

Provincial Service प्रान्तीय सेवा

Provision 1. उपबंध/शर्त 2. व्यवस्था 3. रसद —, **budget** बजट व्यवस्था —**Depot** रसद डिपो —, **Special** विशेष उपबन्ध; विशेष व्यवस्था **Provisional** अनंतिम / अस्थायी / अन्तः कालीन —**agenda** अनन्तिम कार्य सूची —**figures** अस्थायी आँकड़े —**inspection** अन्तिम निरीक्षण —**list** अन्तिम सूची/अस्थायी सूची —**order** अस्थायी / अन्तःकालीन आदेश —**receipt** कच्ची रसीद **Provisions of the rule** नियम के उपबंध

Proviso परन्तुक/शर्त —**to this rule** इस नियम का परन्तुक

Provocation प्रकोपन —, **without** बिना उत्तेजना/प्रकोपन के

Provost Marshal प्रोवो मार्शल

Proxima आगामी मास का

Proxy प्रतिपत्र / प्रतिपत्री/परोक्षी —, **by** प्रतिपत्र/प्रतिपत्री/परोक्षी द्वारा

Psychologist मनोविज्ञानी

Psychiatrist मनश्चिकित्सक;

मनोरोगचिकित्सक **Psychological effect** मनोवैज्ञानिक प्रभाव

P.T.O. कृपया पृष्ठ उल्टें

Public (adj.) सार्वजनिक/आम/सरकारी, लोक **(n.)** जनता/पब्लिक **—Accounts Committee** लोक-लेखा समिति **Public auction** सार्वजनिक नीलाम **—address** सार्वजनिक भाषण **—Administration Institute** लोक-प्रशासन-संस्थान **—auction** सार्वजनिक नीलाम **· authority** लोक-प्राधिकरण **—bill** लोक-विधेयक **—body** सार्वजनिक निकाय **—call office** आम सार्वजनिक टेलीफोन-घर **—debt** राष्ट्र-ऋण **—Debt Officer** लोक - ऋण-अधिकारी **—demand** सार्वजनिक माँग **—employment** राज्याधीन नौकरी **—enquiry** सार्वजनिक जाँच **—expenditure** सार्वजनिक व्यय **—finance duty** लोक-वृत्त शुल्क **—fund** लोक-निधि **—health** लोक-स्वास्थ्य **—holiday** सार्वजनिक अवकाश छुट्टी **—interest** लोकहित **—notification** सार्वजनिक अधिसूचना **—nuisance** लोक न्यूसैंस/लोक उत्पात **—opinion** लोकमत/जनमत **—order** सार्वजनिक व्यवस्था **—property** लोक-संपत्ति **—Prosecntor** लोक-अभियोजक/सरकारी अभियोजक **—Relations Officer** जन - संपर्क - अधिकारी **revenue** लोक-राजस्व **—service** लोक-सेवा **—Service Commission** लोक-सेवा-आयोग **—Works Department** लोक-निर्माण-विभाग

Published data प्रकाशित आँकड़े **Published statistics** प्रकाशित आँकड़े

Punching machine वेधनी, पंच

Punctual, he is वह समय का पाबन्द है **Punctuality** समय-पालन, समय-पाबन्दी **—, sense of** समय-पालन की भावना

Punish दण्ड देना **Punishable with** से दण्डनीय

Punitive tax दण्डात्मक कर

Purchase local स्थानीय खरीद/क्रय

Pursuance अनुसरण **— of, in** के अनुसार, के अनुसरण में

Put up प्रस्तुत करना, पेश करना/करें/कीजिए **—for sale** विक्रय के लिये पुरोधृत

Putative marriage ख्याति विवाह, ख्यात विवाह

Quadruplicate 1. चतुर्गुण करना 2. चार प्रतियां **—, in** चार

प्रतियों में

Qualification अर्हता/योग्यता —**Pay** योग्यता वेतन **Qualifications, educational** शैक्षणिक/शिक्षा-सम्बन्धी योग्यताएँ —**,Essential** अनिवार्य योग्यता/अनिवार्य अर्हता —**,prescribed** निर्धारित योग्यताएं/अर्हताएँ

Qualified अर्हता प्राप्त/योग्य —**acceptance** सशर्त स्वीकृति —**candidate** योग्य उम्मीदवार —**report** साक्षेप रिपोर्ट

Qualify अर्हता प्राप्त करना **Qualifying examination** अर्हक परीक्षा —**marks** अर्हक अंक —**service** अर्हक सेवा

Qualitative distribution गुणात्मक वितरण **Qualities, he has several** उसमें अनेक गुण/विशेषताएँ हैं

Quality 1. गुण/विशेषता 2. गुणवत्ता/गुण 3. कोटि/प्रकार — **certificate** गुणता-पत्र/गुणता-प्रमाण-पत्र —**control** गुणता नियंत्रण —**Marking Officer** गुणता-अंकन-अधिकारी —**, of a different** अन्य प्रकार/किस्म/कोटि का

Quantity 1. मात्रा/परिमाण 2. राशि —**and quality checked by** ने मात्रा और गुणता की जांच की

Quantum क्वांटम/प्रमात्रा/मात्रा —**, of** की मात्रा/प्रमात्रा, का क्वांटम

Quarantine संगरोध/क्वारन्टाइन —**leave** संगरोध छुट्टी/क्वारंटाइन छुट्टी

Quarryman खदानकार

Quarter Master क्वार्टर मास्टर —**General** क्वार्टर मास्टर जनरल

Quarterly त्रैमासिक —**return** तिमाही/त्रैमासिक विवरण

Quasi वत्; कल्प —**judicial** न्यायिक कल्प —**Permanency** स्थायिवत्ता —**Permanent** स्थायिवत् —**Permanent Vacancy** स्थायिवत् रिक्त

Quay घाट; धक्का

Query प्रश्न, सवाल

Question प्रश्न —**Branch** प्रश्न-शाखा —**does not arise** प्रश्न नहीं उठता —**hour** प्रश्न-अवधि —**,in** प्रश्नास्पद, विवादास्पद —**of fact** तथ्य सम्बन्धी प्रश्न —**of law** विधि सम्बन्धी प्रश्न —**of priority** अग्रता-प्रश्न —**of propriety** औचित्य का प्रश्न

Questionnaire प्रश्नावली/प्रश्नमाला —**has been framed** प्रश्नावली/प्रश्नमाला बना ली गई है

Quid pro quo (benefit theory) तत्-प्रति तत्

Quinquennial report पंचवार्षिक प्रतिवेदन/रिपोर्ट

Quintuplicate, in पांच प्रतियां

Quit, notice to छोड़ने का नोटिस, खाली करने का नोटिस

Quod vide (p. v.) जो देखिए

Quorum कोरम **—, lack of** कोरम का अभाव

Quota कोटा

Quota certificate कोटा प्रमाणपत्र **—, pro-rata** यथानुपात कोटा

Quotation 1. भाव/दर 2. उद्धरण

Quoted उद्धृत **Quoted below** नीचे उद्धृत **Quotations from** से लिया उद्धरण **—received** प्राप्त हुए भाव/दर

Quotient भागफल; लब्धि

Race खानदान, जाति; जात **Racial** जातीय; जाति **—discrimination** जाति भेद **—tension** जातिगत तनाव

Radical मौलिक; मूल; मूलभूत

Rack यातना देना; कष्ट देना

Radio and Cable Board रेडियो और केबिन बोर्ड **—Mechanic** रेडियोमेकैनिक **—Operator** रेडियो प्रचालक **— Station** रेडियो स्टेशन **Radio stores depot** रेडियो सामग्री डिपो **Radiologist** विकिरण चिकित्सक/एक्स-किरण चिकित्सक

Radius of, within a के घेरे में, के क्षेत्र में, की परिधि में

Raid छापा, धावा

Railway रेल; रेलवे **Rail-Bus Driver** रेल-बस ड्राइवर/रेल-बस चालक **—Board** रेल बोर्ड **—Dak Sorter** रेल-डाक छँटाई-कार **—Hotel Manager** रेल-होटल मैनेजर **—Inspector** रेल-पथ निरीक्षक **- Mail Service** रेल-डाक सेवा **—material credit note** रेलवे सामग्री-जमा-पत्र **—Mistry** रेल-पथ मिस्त्री **—Protection Force** रेल-सुरक्षा दल **—receipt** बिल्टी, रेलवे रसीद **—reservation** रेलवे आरक्षण **—risk** रेलवे का दायित्व; रेलवे की जिम्मेदारी **—Sectional Officer** रेल अनुभागीय अधिकारी **—Tribunal** रेलवे अधिकरण

Raise ऊँचा करना **—objection** आपत्ति उठाना **Raised the plea** दलील पेश की **Raising of loans** उधार लेना

Raison d'etel (reason or justification for existence) अस्तित्व कारण

Random 1. यादृच्छिक 2. सांयोगिक 3. अनियमित **—check** स्थालीपुलाक जाँच

Range (Forest) रेंज/वन खंड **—(Defence)** चाँदमारी/मार **—(Distance)** परास **—Forest Officer** वन-खण्ड-अधिकारी

Ranger राजिक/रेंजर

Rank पद/ओहदा / श्रेणी/पंक्ति **—and file** जन साधारण **—front** आगे की पंक्ति **—, secured high** ऊँची श्रेणी प्राप्त की **Ranking officer, high** उच्चपदाधिकारी, ऊँचे ओहदे वाला अफसर

Rare विरल

Rate 1. दर/रेट 2. पोर-कर **—card** दर-पत्र / रेट कार्ड **—contract** रेट संविदा/रेट ठेका **—Inspector** दर निरीक्षक **—of, at the** की दर से **—of exchange** विनिमय दर **—payer** पौर-करदाता **—structure** दर रचना, दर संरचना **Rateable property** कर योग्य सम्पत्ति **Rates** महसूल **—and Freights Clerk** दर और भाड़ा-क्लर्क

Ratification अनुसमर्थन **—,partial** आंशिक अनुसमर्थन

Ratio chart अनुपात चित्र/चार्ट

Rational basis युक्तियुक्त आधार

Rationalization युक्तीकरण/औचित्य स्थापन **—of industries** उद्योगों का वैज्ञानिकरण

Ration allowance राशन-भत्ता

Rationing राशनव्यवस्था **—Officer** राशन-अधिकारी

Raw material कच्चा माल

Reaction प्रतिक्रिया **—,favourable** अनुकूल प्रतिक्रिया

Reader (University) उपाचार्य/रीडर **—(Courts)** पेशकार **—Postman** वाचक डाकिया

Reading, third तृतीय पठन

Ready-reckoner शीघ्र गणक **—reference** तत्काल निर्देश, सुलभ हवाला

Real intention असली मंशा/आशय

Realising Officer वसूली-अधिकारी **Realisation of bills** बिलों की उगाही/वसूली **Realization** वसूली/उगाही

Reappointment पुनर्नियुक्ति **— order** पुनर्नियुक्ति आदेश

Reappropriation पुनर्विनियोजन **— of funds** निधियों का पुनर्विनियोजन

Rear Admiral रियर ऐडमिरल

Rearrange the papers कागजों का पुनर्विन्यास कीजिए, कागजों को फिर से तरतीब से लगाइए

Reason of, by के कारण **— to believe** विश्वास करने का कारण **Reasons on which the order is based** वे कारण जिन पर आदेश आधारित है

Reasonable युक्तियुक्त **—expenses** उचित/यथोचित व्यय **— ground of suspicion** संदेह/संशय का युक्तिसंगत/यथोचित आधार **—notice/opportunity** यथोचित सूचना/अवसर **—wear and tear** उचित टूट-फूट

Reassessment पुनर्निर्धारण **—of value** मूल्य का पुनर्निर्धारण

Rebate घटौती/छूट **—Officer** छूट-अधिकारी **—on interest** ब्याज में घटौती

Recall प्रत्याह्वान/वापस बुलाना **—from leave** छुट्टी से वापस बुलाना

Recapitulation सार-कथन **—of facts** तथ्यों का सार कथन

Receipt 1. आय 2. आवती/प्राप्ति 3. रसीद **—and Issue Section** प्राप्ति और निर्गम अनुभाग **—book** रसीद बही **—certificate** प्राप्ति प्रमाण-पत्र **—Clerk** आवती लिपिक/आवती क्लर्क **—in acknowledgement** पावती रसीद **—register** आवती रजिस्टर **—voucher** प्राप्ति वाउचर **Receipted challan** रसीदी चालान **—, pre** पहले से रसीद लिखा हुआ **Receipts and disbursements** आय और संवितरण

Receive प्राप्त करना; प्राप्त होना; पाना **Receiver** 1. पानेवाला/प्राप्तकर्ता 2. रिसीवर/आदाता **—has been appointed** आदाता/रिसीवर नियुक्त किया गया **—of Wreck** नष्टपोत-आदाता **Receiving centre** आदान/ग्रहण केन्द्र

Recent decision हाल का निर्णय

Reception Room स्वागत कक्ष

Receptionist स्वागती

Recess अवकाश / विश्रांति **—, summer** ग्रीष्म अवकाश

Recipient पाने वाला/आदाता **—of benefits** लाभ पाने वाला

Reciprocal अन्योन्य/पारस्परिक/परस्पर **—demand** परस्पर माँग

Reciprocate परस्पर आदान-प्रदान करना **Reciprocity** अन्योन्यता/परस्परता

Reckon संगणना करना

Reckonable service संगणनीय सेवा **Reckoned as, may be** के रूप में संगणना/शुमार कर ली जाय

Reclamation उद्धार/उद्धारण/भूमि उद्धार **—of land** भूमि उद्धार

Recognised 1. मान्य/मान्यता-प्राप्त 2. अभिज्ञात **—body** मान्यता प्राप्त संस्था **Recognition** 1. मान्यता 2. पहचान/अभिज्ञान **—already granted will be withdrawn** पहले दी गई मान्यता वापस ले ली जाएगी

Recommend सिफारिश करना, अभिशंसा करना, संस्तुति करना **Recommendation** सिफारिश/अभिशंसा/संस्तुति **—made by the committee** समिति द्वारा की गई सिफारिशें **Recommendatory certificate** सिफारिशी प्रमाण-पत्र **Recommended** 1. संस्तुत 2. सिफारिश की जाती है

Reconcile 1. समाधान करना/मेल-मिलाप करना 2. समाधान कराना मेल-मिलाप करना **Reconciliation** समाधान/मेल-मिलाप **— of accounts** लेखा-समाधान **—Parliament** पुनर्मेल संसद **—register** समाधान रजिस्टर **—statement** समाधान-विवरण

Reconsideration पुनर्विचार **—,on** पुनर्विचार करने पर

Reconstituted committee पुनर्गठित समिति **Reconstitution** पुनर्गठन

Reconstruction पुनर्निर्माण **—of building** इमारत का पुनर्निर्माण

Record (n.) अभिलेख/रिकार्ड **(vb.)** दर्ज करना/अंकित करना **—Arranger** अभिलेख-विन्यासक **—book** रिकार्ड पंजी, अभिलेख पुस्तक **—Clerk** अभिलेख-क्लर्क **—Division** अभिलेख प्रभाग **—Keeper** अभिलेखपाल **—Lifter** अभिलेख-दफ्तरी/अभिलेख उद्वाहक **—of service** सेवा-वृत्त/सेवा-रिकार्ड **—room** अभिलेख-कक्ष **—Officer** अभिलेख-कक्ष अधिकारी **—sheet** अभिलेख पत्रक; वृत्त पत्रक **—Sorter** अभिलेख छँटाई-कार **—Supplier** अभिलेखदाता/अभिलेख प्रदायक **Recorded, as** जैसे दर्ज/अंकित/रिकार्ड किया गया है **—statement has been** बयान लिख लिया गया है **Recorder** अभिलेखक/रिकार्डर **Recording** अभिलेखबद्ध करना/रिकार्ड करना **—of files** फाइलों को अभिलेखबद्ध/रिकार्ड करना, फाइलों की रिकार्ड-बन्दी **Records of rights** अधिकार-अभिलेख

Recovery वसूली **—of dues** देय की वसूली **—of loss** नुकसान की वसूली **—Officer** वसूली अधिकारी

Recreation मनोविनोद **—Officer** मनोविनोद-अधिकारी **—room** मनोरंजन कक्ष

Recruit (n.) रंगरूट **(vb.)** भर्ती करना **—, Direct** सीधी भर्ती **—Officer** भर्ती-अधिकारी

Rectify परिशोधन करना/सुधार करना **Rectification** परिशोधन/सुधार **—the mistake** गलती ठीक करना, गलती सुधारना

Rector (of a University) रेक्टर, कुलदेशिक

Recurring आवर्ती / आवर्तक

—charge आवर्ती प्रभार

—expenditure आवर्ती व्यय

—grant आवर्ती अनुदान

Redeem छुड़ाना/मोचन करना

Redemption मोचन/छुड़ाना/प्रतिदान **—charge** विमोचन भार **—fund** विमोचन निधि

Red hot priority demand अति अग्रता मांग/अति प्राथमिकता मांग

—tapism लाल फीताशाही, काम लटकाए रखना

Redress (n.) निवारण **(vb.)** निवारण करना/दूर करना **—of grievance** व्यथा निवारण/दूर करना

Reduce घटाना/कम करना **—in rank** पद घटाना, पद कम करना **—to writing** लेखबद्ध करना **Reduction** कमी **—of staff** अमले में कमी करना

Redundant अनावश्यक/अतिरिक्त **staff** अनावश्यक/अतिरिक्त स्टाफ

Re-election पुनर्निर्वाचन **Re-employed officer** पुनर्नियुक्त/पुनर्नियोजित अधिकारी **Re-employment** पुनर्नियुक्ति/पुनर्नियोजन **Re-examination** पुनः परीक्षा

Refer 1. (विचारार्थ) भेजना 2. हवाला देना/उल्लेख करना 3. निर्देश करना

Refer to को (विचारार्थ) भेजना, हवाला देना, का उल्लेख करना

Referee निर्देशी/रेफरी **Referee, appointed as** निर्देशी/रेफरी के रूप में नियुक्त हुआ

Reference संदर्भ/निर्देश/हवाला **—, Back** पिछला संदर्भ/पिछला हवाला **—book** संदर्भ-पुस्तक **—Clerk** निर्देश-क्लर्क **— , Cross** प्रति निर्देश **—is invited to...** ...को देखिए, को देखने का कष्ट करें **—, Later** उत्तर संदर्भ/उत्तर निर्देश/बाद का हवाला **—, Previous** पूर्व संदर्भ/पूर्व निर्देश/पिछला हवाला **—register** हवाला रजिस्टर

—to, hawing के बारे में **—to, in** के प्रति निर्देश से; के बारे में **to with** के प्रति निर्देश से **Referencing** संदर्भ देना/हवाला देना

Referred to above उपरिनिर्दिष्ट **to as**··· ···के नाम से निर्दिष्ट

Refinery Attendant परिष्करण-परिचर

Refixation of pay वेतन का पुननियतन, वेतन का पुनः तय/स्थिर किया जाना

Reform सुधार; सुधार करना **Reformation of criminals** अपराधियों का सुधार **—Officer** सुधार-अधिकारी **Reformatory** सुधारालय

Refresher course पुनश्चर्या **Refreshment** जलपान/उपाहार **—room** जलपानगृह, उपाहारगृह **—Room Manager** उपाहार कक्ष प्रबंधक

Refugee Officer शरणार्थी-अधिकारी

Refund (n.) (धन) वापसी (vb.) धन लौटाना/धन फेरना **—and Compensation Claim Section** धन-वापसी और प्रतिकर-दावा अनुभाग **—of advance** अग्रिम-धन/पेशगी वापसी/प्रतिदाय **—of deposit** जमा की वापसी **—of excess amount** अतिरिक्त रकम को वापस करना **—order** वापसी का आदेश/धन वापसी का आदेश **Refundable** लौटाया जाने वाला

Refuse अस्वीकार करना/इनकार करना **—to accept** मानने से इनकार करना **Refused leave** अस्वीकृत/मना की गई छुट्टी

Refutation खंडन **—of charges** आरोपो का खण्डन **Refute** खंडन करना

Regard shall be had ध्यान रखा जाएगा **Regard to having** को ध्यान में रखते हुए **Regarding** के बारे में **Regards, as** के विषय में

Regiment Commander रेजिमेंट कमांडर **—Punjab** पंजाब रेजीमेंट

Region क्षेत्र/प्रदेश **Regional Cashier** क्षेत्रीय खजांची **—Commissioner** प्रादेशिक आयुक्त; प्रादेशिक कमिश्नर **—Council** क्षेत्रीय परिषद् **—Director (Food)** क्षेत्रीय निदेशक (खाद्य) **—fund** प्रादेशिक निधि **—Engineer** क्षेत्रीय अभियंता/क्षेत्रीय इंजीनियर **—Evaluation Officer** क्षेत्रीय मूल्यांकन अधिकारी **—Organisation** प्रादेशिक संगठन **—Passport Officer** क्षेत्रीय पारपत्र-अधिकारी/क्षेत्रीय पासपोर्ट अधिकारी **—Research Laboratory** क्षेत्रीय अनुसंधान-प्रयोगशाला

Register a case मामला दर्ज कीजिए **—Keeper** पंजीपाल/रजिस्टरपाल **Registered** पंजीकृत/पंजीबद्ध/रजिस्ट्री हुआ **—acknowledgement** रजिस्ट्री रसीदी डाक **—and insured articles** रजिस्ट्री और बीमा की गई वस्तुएं **—letter** रजिस्ट्री हुआ पत्र **—refugee** रजिस्टर्ड शरणार्थी **Registering Authority** पंजीयन प्राधिकारी/रजिस्ट्री प्राधिकारी

Registrar पंजीयक/पंजीकार/रजिस्ट्रार **—of Births and Deaths** जन्म-मृत्यु रजिस्ट्रार **—of Co-operative Societies** सहकारी समितियों का रजिस्ट्रार **—of Firms** फर्म-रजिस्ट्रार **—of Insolvency** दिवाला-रजिस्ट्रार **—of Joint Stock Company** संयुक्तपूंजी-कंपनी-रजिस्ट्रार **—of Marriages** विवाह-रजिस्ट्रार **—of Money Lenders** साहूकार-रजिस्ट्रार **—of Newspapers** समाचार पत्रों का पंजीयक/रजिस्ट्रार **—of Non-trading Corporation** व्यापारेतर - निगम - रजिस्ट्रार **Partnership Firm** साझेदारी-फर्म-रजिस्ट्रार **—of Trade** व्यापार-रजिस्ट्रार **—of Trade Unions** रजिस्ट्रार, मजदूर-संघ **—General and Census Commissioner** महा पंजीयक और जनगणना आयुक्त **— of India** भारत का महापंजीयक **(of University)** कुल-सचिव

Registration पंजीकरण/रजिस्ट्री **—, card** पंजी-पत्र, पंजी कार्ड **Export Clerk (P. & T.)** निर्गम रजिस्ट्री क्लर्क **—Import Clerk (P &T.)** आगम रजिस्ट्री क्लर्क **—Officer (Registering Officer)** पंजीयन अधिकारी/रजिस्ट्री अफसर

Regret (n.) खेद **(vb)** खेद प्रकट करना **Regrettable** खेद का विषय **—, it is** खेद का विषय है **Regretted, it is** खेद है

Regular service नियमित सेवा **Regularisation of** का नियमानुकूलन, को नियमित करना **Regulated** विनियमित **—market** नियंत्रित मण्डी **Regulating Officer** नियमन-अधिकारी **Regulation Officer** विनियमन-अधिकारी **Regulations** विनियम **—, as per** विनियमों के अनुसार **—framed thereunder** उसके अधीन बनाए गए विनियम

Rehabilitation पुनर्वास **—of displaced persons** विस्थापित व्यक्तियों का पुनर्वास

Rehearsal पूर्वाभ्यास **—, of** का पूर्वाभ्यास

Rcimbursement प्रतिपूर्ति **—of medical charges** चिकित्सा व्यय की प्रतिपूर्ति

Reinstate पुनःस्थापित करना/बहाल करना **Reinstated in service** नौकरी बहाल की गई **Reinstatement** बहाली

Reiterate दुहराना/फिर कहना **Reiterated it is** यह फिर से कहा जाता है. यह दुहराया जाता है

Reject अस्वीकार करना **Rejected**

अस्वीकृत —**bid** अस्वीकृत बोली **Rejection memo** अस्वीकृति पत्र —**slip** अस्वीकृति पर्ची

Rejoinder प्रत्युत्तर —, **has sent** प्रत्युत्तर भेज दिया है **Rejoined his duties** फिर कार्य ग्रहण कर लिया है, फिर काम पर आ गया है

Relates to से सम्बद्ध है **Relating to** से सम्बन्धित **Relative change/fact** सापेक्ष परिवर्तन/तथ्य

Relax छुट देना **Relaxable** छूट देने योग्य **Relaxation** 1. छूट/रियायत/ढील 2. श्रांति 3. शिथिलन—**of rules** नियम-शिथिलन, नियम ढीले करना, नियम में छूट/रियायत

Release 1. मुक्ति/रिहाई/छुटकारा/छूट निर्मुक्ति 2. (धन) दे देना 3. रिहा करना/मुक्त करना/छुटकारा देना —**date** निर्मोचन-तिथि —**date (of press note)** बंटन तिथि —**General** आम निर्मोचन —,**Press** प्रेस-प्रकाशनी **Released, grant has been** अनुदान राशि दी जा रही है —**on appeal** अपील करने पर मुक्त किया गया/छोड़ा गया —**on bail** जमानत पर छोड़ा गया, जमानत पर रिहा किया गया

Relevant संगत/सुसंगत —**extract** संगत उद्धरण, सम्बन्ध उद्धरण —**papers** संगत/सुसंगत/सम्बन्धित कागज **Relevant Provision** संबद्ध उपबंध, संबद्ध व्यवस्था

Reliable विश्वसनीय / पक्का —**person** विश्वसनीय व्यक्ति

Relic पुरावशेष

Relief 1. सहायता/राहत 2. बदल 3. अनुतोष —**and rehabilitation** सहायता और पुनर्वास —**Commissioner** सहायता-आयुक्त —**list** बदल/एवजी सूची —**train** सहायता/इमदादी गाड़ी —**work** राहत कार्य

Relieve (नौकरी से) छुट्टी देना/छुट्टी पाना/छुट्टी मिलना/भारमुक्त करना **Relieved on** को भार मुक्त किया गया —**officer** भार मुक्त अफसर / अधिकारी **Relieving Clerk** एवजी क्लर्क/एवजी लिपिक —**Officer** भारमोचन अधिकारी —**staff** एवजी कर्मचारी वर्ग —**Train Supervisor** एवजी गाड़ी पर्यवेक्षक —**Transhipment Assistant** एवजी यानांतरण सहायक

Religious endowment धर्मस्व

Relinquishment 1. त्याग 2. स्वत्वत्याग —**of charge** भारत्याग, कार्यभार छोड़ना —**of claim** दावा त्यागना

Reluctant to do करने को अनि-

च्छुक

Remain in force लागू/प्रभावी रहना, प्रवृत्त रहना

Remark (n.) विचार/अभ्युक्ति **(vb.)** विचार प्रकट करना **Remarkable fact** विलक्षण तथ्य, असाधारण बात **—,it is** यह उल्लेखनीय है **Remarks column** अभ्युक्ति/कैफियत का खाना **—of adverse nature** प्रतिमूल अभ्युक्तियां/कथन/टिप्पणी **—, offer** विचार प्रकट करना

Remedial measures उपचारी उपाय

Reminder स्मरणपत्र/अनुस्मारक **—diary** तकाजा डायरी; अनुस्मारक दैनिकी **—may be sent** अनुस्मारक/स्मरणपत्र भेजा जाए

Remission परिहार/माफी/छूट **—of rent** किराए/लगान की माफी/छूट **—of revenue** राजस्व की छूट/राजस्व की माफी

Remit 1. प्रेषण करना/भेजना 2. साफ करना/छोड़ना **Remittance** 1. प्रेषण/भेजना 2. प्रेषणा धन/भेजी गई रकम **—Cashier** धन प्रेषण खजांची **—Clerk** धन-प्रेषण-लिपिक **—received** भेजी हुई रकम प्राप्त, प्रेषित धन प्राप्त **—register** प्रेषण रजिस्टर **Remittee** प्रेषिती / पानेवाला **Remitter** प्रेषक/भेजने वाला

Removal 1. निष्कासन/हटाया जाना 2. अपनयन **from office** पद से हटाया जाना **—from service** नौकरी से हटाया जाना

Remunerate पारिश्रमिक देना; मेहनताना देना **Remuneration** पारिश्रमिक/मेहनताना **—, reasonable** उचित पारिश्रमिक/मेहनताना

Render an account लेखा/हिसाब देना **—the defaulter liable for punishment, will** गलती करने वाले को दण्ड का भागी बना देगा **Rendered service** की हुई सेवा **Rendition of accounts** हिसाब/लेखा देना

Renewal नवीकरण **—and repairs** नवीकरण तथा मरम्मत **—of demand** मांग का नवीकरण, मांग दुहराना **Renewed efforts** दुबारा प्रयास, नए सिरे से कोशिश

Rent 1. भाटक, किराया/भाड़ा 2. लगान **—, additional** अतिरिक्त किराया **—, annual** सलाना किराया **—Controller** भाटक-नियंत्रक **—due** देय लगान/किराया **—, standard** मानक किराया/भाटक **Rented space** भाड़े पर लिया स्थान

Reorganisation पुनः संगठन/पुनर्गठन **—of office** कार्यालय का पुनर्गठन

Repair and maintenance मरम्मत और अनुरक्षण

Repatriate देश-प्रत्यावर्तन/देश को लौटाना/देश वापस भेजना **Repatriation** देश-प्रत्यावर्तन/प्रत्यावासन **—, of** का देश प्रत्यावर्तन, को देश वापस भेजना

Repay 1. शोधन करना 2. चुकाना 3. लौटाना / वापस करना **Repayable** 1. शोध्य, 2. प्रतिदेय **Repayment** प्रतिदान **—of loans** ऋणों की अदायगी

Repeal (n.) निरसन **(vb)** निरसन करना **Repealed, Act has been** अधिनियम निरसित कर दिया गया है

Repeat order पुनरादेश **Repeated, this mistake should not be** यह गलती फिर न दुहराई जाए **Repeatedly told, he has been** उसे बार-बार बताया गया है

Replace बदलना **Replacement of rejected stores** अस्वीकृत माल/स्टोर की बदल

Reply to, in के उत्तर में

Report (n.) प्रतिवेदन/विवरण/रिपोर्ट **(vb.)** रिपोर्ट करना/रिपोर्ट देना/प्रतिवेदन देना/प्रतिवेदित करना **—, fortnightly/weekly** पाक्षिक साप्ताहिक रिपोर्ट / प्रतिवेदन **—submitted to···** ···को रिपोर्ट भेजी, ···के समक्ष रिपोर्ट रखी गई **Reporter** प्रतिवेदक / रिपोर्टर **—, press** पत्र संवाददाता **Reporting Authority** रिपोर्ट करने वाला प्राधिकारी **—officer** रिपोर्ट अधिकारी

Repository निधान/संग्रह

Represent 1. प्रतिनिधित्व करना 2. अभिवेदन देना **Representation** 1. प्रतिनिधित्व 2. अभ्यावेदन/अभिवेदन **—, Identical** समान अभिवेदन **Representation in writing** लिखित अभिवेदन **—, Majority** बहुमत प्रतिनिधित्व/बहुसंख्यक प्रतिनिधित्व **—, Minority** अल्पमत प्रतिनिधित्व/अल्पसंख्यक प्रतिनिधित्व **—, Proportional** आनुपातिक प्रतिनिधित्व **—received from** से प्राप्त अभिवेदन **Representative** प्रतिनिधि **Representative capacity, in** प्रतिनिधि के रूप में

Reprieve प्रविलंबन

Repugnance विरोध; जुगुप्सा

Reprimand (n.) फटकार/भर्त्सना **(vb.)** फटकारना / भर्त्सना करना **Reprimand for indifference** लापरवाही के लिए फटकार/भर्त्सना

Reproduction 1. पुनरुत्पादन

2. उद्धरण 3. प्रतिलिपि/प्रतिकृति 4. प्रजनन —, **correct** सही प्रतिलिपि/प्रतिकृति **Reproductive debt**/पुनरुत्पादी ऋण —**capacity** प्रजनन क्षमता/शक्ति

Repugnant प्रतिकूल/विरुद्ध —**to the context** प्रसंग के विरुद्ध/प्रतिकूल

Repurchase पुनः क्रय/फिर से खरीद

Request, as per अनुरोध के अनुसार **Requested, it is** अनुरोध है, निवेदन है

Required information may please be furnished/supplied without delay आवश्यक/अपेक्षित जानकारी कृपया अविलम्ब दी/भेजी जाए **Requirement** अपेक्षा/आवश्यकता —, **monthly** महीने भर की आवश्यकता —**of the rules** नियमों के अनुसार अपेक्षा **Requiring no proof** प्रमाण-अनपेक्ष सबूत की जरूरत नहीं

Requisite (adj.) आवश्यक/अपेक्षित —**information** अपेक्षित जानकारी/सूचना —**time for obtaining copy of the judgment** निर्णय की प्रतिलिपि प्राप्त करने के लिए आवश्यक समय **Requisites (n.)** अपेक्षित गुण/आवश्यक गुण अपेक्षित वस्तुएँ/आवश्यक वस्तुएँ

Requisition 1. माँग 2. अधिग्रहण —**form** मांग फार्म, मांगणी फार्म —, **land** भूमि का अधिग्रहण —**Officer** अधिग्रहण अधिकारी —**slip** माँग पर्ची/मांगणी पर्ची

Resale notice पुनः विक्रय की सूचना

Rescind विखंडन करना **Rescue, came to** रक्षा/मदद की —**Home** उद्धार-गृह **Rescued from drowning** डूबने से बचाया

Research गवेषणा/अनुसंधान —**and Development Assistant** अनुसंधान और विकास सहायक —**and Development Inspector** अनुसंधान और विकास निरीक्षक —**and Development Officer** अनुसंधान और विकास अधिकारी —**and Reference Division** अनुसंधान और संदर्भ प्रभाग —**Assistant** अनुसंधान-सहायक —**Fellow** अध्येता —**Unit** अनुसंधान एकक —**Associate** अनुसंधान सहकारी —**Officer** अनुसंधान अधिकारी —**work** अनुसंधान कार्य

Resents correction, he उसे भूल सुधारना अच्छा नहीं लगता **Reservation** आरक्षण/रक्षण —**Clerk** आरक्षण-लिपिक आरक्षण क्लर्क

Reservation of posts पदों का आरक्षण —**of seat** स्थान-आरक्षण, जगह रिजर्व करना

Reserve police रिजर्व पुलिस —**Police Inspector** रिजर्व पुलिस निरीक्षक —**price** आरक्षित मूल्य/कीमत **Reserve Service** प्रारक्षित सेवा, रिजर्व नौकरी —**stock** आरक्षित माल/स्टाक —**Supervisor** आरक्षण पर्यवेक्षक/आरक्षण सुपरवाइजर **Reserved accommodation** आरक्षित/रिजर्व हुआ स्थान **Reservist's Pay** प्रारक्षित सैनिक का वेतन **Reservoir Division** जलाशय-प्रभाग **Reserved right** प्रारक्षित अधिकार

Resettlement पुन; स्थापन/पुनर्व्यवस्थापन —**Officer** पुनर्व्यवस्थापन-अधिकारी

Residence निवास/आवास —**allotment of** निवास/ आवास का आबंटन **Resident** निवासी; स्थानिक; रेजिडेंट —**audit officer** स्थानिक लेखा परीक्षा अधिकारी —**Clerk** निवासी क्लर्क —**engineer** स्थानिक इंजीनियर —**Fisheries Development Adviser** निवासी मीन-उद्योग विकास सलाहकार —**Officer** निवासी अधिकारी **Residential** निवास/आवास —**quarters** आवास-गृह/निवास-क्वार्टर

Residuary power अवशिष्ट अधिकार

Residue अवशेष

Resign त्यागपत्र देना/इस्तीफा देना **Resignation** त्यागपत्र/इस्तीफा **Resignation of post** पद-त्याग पद से इस्तीफा/त्यागपत्र

Resolution संकल्प —**published in the gazette** राजपत्र मे प्रकाशित संकल्प

Resources 1. संसाधन / स्रोत 2. संपदा —**Natural** प्राकृतिक संपदा/प्राकृतिक संसाधन

Respect आदर; सम्मान —**,of in** के सम्बन्ध में **Respectfully** सादर — **I beg to say** सादर निवेदन है **Respective** अपनी-अपनी **Respectively** क्रमानुसार/क्रमशः —**and** क्रमानुसार/क्रमशः तथा **Respective places** अपनी अपनी जगह

Respite विराम

Respondent प्रत्यर्थी/प्रतिवादी —**in the case** वाद में प्रत्यर्थी/प्रतिवादी

Responsibility उत्तरदायित्व/दायित्व/जिम्मेदारी —**fixation of** उत्तरदायित्व/जिम्मेदारी नियत/निर्धारित करना

Rest House विश्राम-गृह **—Attendant** विश्राम गृह-परिचर

Restaurant भोजनालय

Restitution 1. प्रत्यानयन 2. प्रत्यवस्थान

Restore पुन: स्थापना/फिर से चालू करना **Restoration** पुन; स्थापना/फिर से चालू करना **Restoration of train services** गाड़ियां फिर से चालू करना

Restraint 1. अवरोध/नियंत्रण 2. निग्रह/संयम **Restraining order** अवरोधक आदेश **—acted with** संयम से काम लिया

Restricted प्रतिबंधित/सीमित **—distribution** सीमित वितरण **—interpretation** संकुचित निर्वचन/अर्थ निर्णय **—leave** प्रतिवन्धित छुट्टी **Restriction** प्रतिबंध/रोक के

Restriction, without any बिना किसी प्रतिबन्ध/रोक के

Resume (n) सार-वृत्त **(vb.)** पुन: आरंभ करना/पुन: शुरू करना **—duties** काम फिर संभाल लें

Resubmitted with previous papers पूर्व पत्रों/कागजों के साथ पुन: प्रस्तुत/पेश **Resulting from** से उत्पन्न **—of the case** मामले का सार वृत्त **—proceedings** कार्यवाही पुन: आरंभ कीजिए

Resumption पुनरारंभ **—of charge** भार पुन: ग्रहण करना, भार फिर से लेना, कार्य-भार पुन: संभाल लेना **—of talks** वार्ता फिर आरंभ करना, वार्ता का पुनरारम्भ

Retain lien लियन/पुनर्ग्रहणाधिकार बनाए रखना

Retire निवृत्त होना/रिटायर होना **Retired** निवृत्त **—officer** निवृत्त अधिकारी, रिटायर हुआ अधिकारी **Retirement** निवृत्ति **—benefit** निवृत्ति लाभ **—compulsory** अनिवार्य निवृत्ति **—from service** सेवा निवृत्ति **—optional** वैकल्पिक निवृत्ति **—voluntary** स्वैच्छिक निवृत्ति **Retiring pension** निवृत्ति पेंशन

Retoucher अनुशोधक **Retrenched staff** छंटनी किये गये कर्मचारी **Retrenchment** छंटनी **— Officer** छंटनी-अधिकारी **—order** छंटनी आदेश

Retrospective पूर्वव्यापी/भूतलक्षी **— effect, with** पूर्वव्यापी/भूतलक्षी प्रभाव के साथ, पीछे/पहले से लागू प्रभावी; पूर्वव्याप्ति सहित **—effect cannot be given to this sanction** इस मंजूरी को पूर्वव्यापी/भूतलक्षी प्रभाव नहीं दिया जा सकता, इस मंजूरी को

पीछे से प्रभावी नहीं माना जा सकता

Return (n.) 1. विवरणी, 2. प्रतिलाभ, 3 वापसी 4. उत्तर **(vb.)** 1. वापस करना/लौटाना 2. निर्वाचित करना/निर्वाचित होना **—Checker** विवरणी पड़ताल कर्ता **—Delivery Clerk** विवरणी सुपुर्दगी लिपिक **—journey** वापसी यात्रा **—of post, by** लौटती डाक से **—on investment** लगी पूंजी पर प्रतिलाभ **— periodical** नियत कालिक विवरणी **Returned for further consideration** और विचार के लिये लौटाया गया **—letter office** पुनः प्रेषण केन्द्र **Returning officer** निर्वाचन अधिकारी **Return** विवरणी/नियत विवरण

Revalidation पुनर्मूल्यन **—of licence** लाइसेंस का पुनर्वैधीकरण

Revaluation पुनर्मूल्यन **—of assets** परिसम्पत्ति का पुनर्मूल्यन

Revenue राजस्व **—commissioner** राजस्व कमिश्नर; माल आयुक्त; माल कमिश्नर **—division** राजस्व-प्रभाग; माल प्रभाग **—duty** राजस्व शुल्क **— minister** राजस्व-मंत्री; माल-मंत्री **—officer** राजस्व अधिकारी; माल-अधिकारी

Reverse उत्क्रम/प्रतिलोम/विपर्यास/उल्टा **—direction, in** उल्टी दिशा में **—please see on the** कृपया पीछे की ओर देखिए **Reversion** परावर्तन **—to a lower post** निचले पद पर परावर्तन

Reverted प्रत्यावर्तित **— to substantive post** मूल पद पर प्रत्यावर्तित

Review (n.) 1. समीक्षा, 2. पुनरीक्षण **(vb.)** 1. समीक्षा करना 2. पुनरीक्षण करना **—board** पुनरीक्षण-मण्डल **—book** पुस्तक समीक्षा **— the year under** आलोच्य वर्ष **Reviewed, position is being** स्थिति की समीक्षा की जा रही है **Reviewer** 1. समीक्षाकार/समीक्षक 2. पुनरीक्षक **Reviewing Officer** पुनरीक्षण-अधिकारी

Revise परिशोधित करना/दोहराना **Revised** संशोधित; दोहराया **— agenda** परिशोधिन कायसूची **—Budget Estimate** परिशोधित बजट प्राक्कलन **—decision has been** निर्णय उलट दिया गया है **—pension rules** पुनरीक्षित पेंशन नियम **—tender** परिशोधित टेंडर/परिशोधित निविदा **—estimate** दोहराया तखमीना **—tender** परिशोधित टेंडर **Revising Officer** पुनरीक्षण

अधिकारी **Revision** पुनरीक्षण/दोहराना/परिशोधन **—of pay scale** वेतनमान का पुनरीक्षण

Revival पुनरुज्जीवन/पुन: प्रवर्तन **Revive the case** मामले को फिर से उठाना/पुनर्जीवित करना

Revocation प्रतिसंहरण/निरसन **—of guarantee** गारण्टी का प्रतिसंहरण, गारण्टी को रद्द करना **Revoke** प्रतिसंहरण

Reward 1. पारितोषिक/पुरस्कार 2. प्रतिफल – **for service** सेवाओं का पारितोषिक/पुरस्कार

Reweighment Inspector पुन: तुलाई निरीक्षक

Rifleman बंदूकची/राईफलमैन

Rigger सज्जक/रिगर

Right उचित; सत् **—as of** साधिकार, अधिकारपूर्वक **—birth** जन्मसिद्ध-अधिकार **—civil** नागरिक अधिकार **—decision** ठीक विनिश्चय **—in rem** सर्वबंधी अधिकार **—moral** नैतिक अधिकार **—natural** प्राकृतिक अधिकार **—of appeal** अपील का अधिकार **—of assembly** सम्मेलन अधिकार **—of audience** सुनवाई का अधिकार **—of property** संपत्ति-अधिकार **—of vote** मताधिकार; राय देने का हक **—legal** कानूनी अधिकार, विधि-सम्मत अधिकार **—to a job** नौकरी पर अधिकार **—to live** जीवन का अधिकार **—to vote** मतदान का अधिकार

Rigid अनम्य; कठोर; दृढ़

Rigman रिगमैन

Rinderpest Officer रिंडरपेस्ट-अधिकारी

Ripe, the case is not yet मामला अभी परिपक्व नहीं है

Risaldar रिसालदार **—Major** रिसालदार मेजर

Rise and fall उत्थान-पतन, चढ़ाव-उतारघट-बढ़ **—in price** भाव बढ़ना, मूल्य-वृद्धि, मंहगाई

Risk, personal व्यक्तिगत जोखिम **—purchase** जोखिम-खरीद/जोखिम-क्रय **—sale** जोखिम बिक्री/जोखिम विक्रय

River Investigation Division नदी-अनुसंधान-प्रभाग **—Valley Project** नदी घाटी-परियोजना

Rivet Boy रिवेट बॉय **Rivetor** रिवेटकार

Road Inspector सड़क-निरीक्षक **—under repairs** सड़क की मरम्मत हो रही है **—van Inspector** रोडवैन निरीक्षक **—ways** सड़क मार्ग/रोडवेज

Roll (n) पंजी/नामावली/फर्द **(vb.)** लपेटना **—, Character** आचरण

पंजी **Roll, electoral** मतदाता सूची **Roller Caster** रोलर ढलाईकार

Roster रोस्टर **—Clerk** रोस्टर क्लर्क/रोस्टर लिपिक **Roster duty** ड्यूटी रोस्टर, ड्यूटी-क्रम

Rotary copying चक्रनकल, चक्र नकल उतारना

Rough copy कच्ची नकल **—draft** कच्चा मसौदा **—weather** खराब मौसम **Roughly speaking** मोटे तौर से, स्थूल रूप से **Round the clock** चौबीस घण्टे, दिन रात

Routine नेमी/दस्तूरी **—Clerk** नेमी-कार्य क्लर्क **Routine, in a** नेमी रूप में **—note** नेमीनोट/दस्तूरी नोट (तेलुगु) **—test** नेमी परीक्षण

Royalty रॉयल्टी **Royalty, amount of** रॉयल्टी की राशि

Rubber stamp रबड़ की मोहर

Rule नियम **—rough and ready** काम चलाऊ नियम, निर्वाह नियम **Ruled paper** लाइनदार कागज **Rules and regulations** नियम-विनियम **—entitlement** हकदारी-नियमावली **—framed under section...** धारा...के अधीन बनाए गए नियम **—liberalised leave** उदारीकृत छुट्टी नियमावली **—military leave** सैन्य-छुट्टी-नियमावली **—of business** कार्य संचालन नियमावली **—of procedure** प्रक्रिया-नियम, कार्य-विधि के नियम **—revised leave** —संशोधित छुट्टी नियमावली **—special leave** विशेष छुट्टी नियमावली

Ruling विनिर्णय **– court** अदालत का विनिर्णय **—party** शासक दल

Rummaging Inspector तलाशी-निरीक्षक

Runner हरकारा **Running contract** चालू संविदा/चालू ठेका **—repairs** छोटी मरम्मत, चालू मरम्मत **—Room Inspector** चालक-वर्ग कमरा निरीक्षक **—staff** परिचालक-वर्ग **—summary** क्रमिक सार **—Shed Supervisor** इंजन शेड पर्यवेक्षक **—Summary of facts** तथ्यों का क्रमिक सार

Rural ग्राम/ग्रामीण **—broadcast** देहाती प्रोग्राम, देहाती कार्यक्रम **— community** ग्राम-समुदाय **—Development** ग्राम विकास **— Officer** ग्राम-विकास-अधिकारी **—planning** ग्राम-आयोजना **—population** ग्रामीण जन-संख्या, देहाती आबादी **—uplift** ग्रामोद्धार; ग्राम सुधार

Sabotage तोड़फोड़/अन्तर्ध्वंस **—, act of** तोड़-फोड़ का कार्य

Sacrifice बलि; यज्ञ, त्याग

Safe सुरक्षित/निरापद/भय रहित/अभय **—conduct** 1. यात्रा-सुरक्षण, 2. अभय-पत्र 3. सुरक्षित रूप से जाया जाना **—custody** निरापद/सुरक्षित अभिरक्षा, संभाल के रखना, अभि-रक्षण **—working condition, in a** काम करने की निरापद दशा में

Safeguard सुरक्षण **—as a** सुरक्षण के रूप में **Safeguarding** रक्षात्मक/सुरक्षात्मक **—the interest of** के हितों की रक्षा

Safety सुरक्षा / संरक्षा /क्षेम **—device** संरक्षा साधन, सुरक्षा साधन **—Inspector** सुरक्षा निरीक्षक **—Officer** सुरक्षा-अधिकारी

Said, ru.e उक्त नियम

Salient मुख्य उभार **—points** प्रमुख बातें

Sail Maker सिलमाकुर **—Master** पाल कप्तान **Sailing date** चलने की तिथि, छूटने की तिथि **Sailor** नाविक/नौसैनिक

Sailors' Board नाविक बोर्ड

Salaried वैतनिक **—class** वेतन भोगी वर्ग **—office** सवेतन/वैतनिक पद

Salary वेतन/संबलम् **—, leave** छुट्टी वेतन

Sale account विक्रय-लेखा/बिक्री-लेखा **—deed** बैनामा **—letter** विक्रय-पत्र **—proceeds** विक्रयागम **—value** विक्रय-मूल्य/बिक्री-मूल्य

Sales, cash नकद-बिक्री **—in-charge** विक्रय प्रभारी **—man** विक्रेता **—tax** विक्रयकर/बिक्रीकर **Tribunal** विक्रयकर-अधिकरण

Saloon Attendant Incharge सैलून परिचर प्रभारी

Salutary effect स्वस्थ प्रभाव

Saluting base सलामी मंच

Salvage कबाड़/उबार/उबारना/भ्रंश उद्धार/उद्धारण **—and scrap** कबाड़ और रद्दी

Same manner, in the उसी प्रकार/तरह से

Sample नमूना/प्रतिदर्श/सैम्पल **—Collector** नमूना संग्राहक **—free** मुफ्त नमूना **—room** नमूनों का कमरा **—survey** प्रतिदर्श/नमूना सर्वेक्षण **—Taker** प्रतिदर्श गृहीता / नमूना गृहीता

Sanction 1. मंजूरी 2. अनुशास्ति **— , special** विशेष मंजूरी, विशिष्ट मंजूरी **—, Valid** सबल मंजूरी **Sanctioned as proposed** प्रस्ताव के अनुसार

मंजूरी दी गई —**budget** मंजूर हुआ बजट —**Budget Estimate** मंजूर बजट प्राक्कलन —**order** मंजूरी आदेश —**pay** मंजूर वेतन —**scale of Pay** मंजूर वेतन-मान —**work** मंजूर काम **Sanctioning authority** मंजूरी-दाता प्राधिकारी

Sand Testing Chargeman रेत परीक्षण चार्जमैन/रेत परीक्षण कार्येक्षक

Sanitary सफाई/स्वास्थ्यकर —**Inspector** सफाई-निरीक्षक/स्वच्छता निरीक्षक **Sanitation** सफाई/स्वच्छता/स्वास्थ्य-रक्षा

Satisfaction संतोष/संतुष्टि/तुष्टि/समाधान **Satisfactory** संतोषप्रद/संतोषजनक/समाधानप्रद

Save सिवाय; अन्यथा —**as otherwise Prescribed** यथा अन्यथा विहित को छोड़कर **Saving** बचत **Savingram** सेविंग्राम/बचत-तार **Savings** व्यावृत्ति

Saw Doctor आरा मरम्मतकार

Scaffolder पाड़ बांधने वाला

Scale माप/मान / मापक्रम / पैमाना मापनी/अनुमाप —**of Consumption** उपभोग-मान —**of Emoluments** परिलब्धिमान —**of pay** वेतनमान

Scarcity न्यूनता/कमी

Scenarist दृश्य लेखक

Schedule अनुसूची —**, Programme** कार्यक्रम-अनुसूची —**, Time** समय अनुसूची —**to tender** टेंडर अनुसूची, निविदा अनुसूची **Scheduled area** अनुसूचित क्षेत्र —**tribe** अनुसूचित जनजाति —**caste** अनुसूचित जाति —**caste and tribes** अनुसूचित जातियां और जनजातियाँ —**rate** अनुसूचित दर

Scheme योजना

Scherzer Bridge Operator सेजर पुल प्रचालक

Scholarship Division छात्रवृत्ति-प्रभाग

School of Artillery तोपखाना-स्कूल —**of Dental and Oral Surgery** दंत और मुख-सर्जरी स्कूल —**of Foreign Languages** विदेशी-भाषा-विद्यालय

Scientific and Technical Terminology, Commission for वैज्ञानिक तथा तकनीकी शब्दावली आयोग —**Officer** वैज्ञानिक अधिकारी —**research committee** वैज्ञानिक अनुसंधान समिति

Scope विषय क्षेत्र/कार्य क्षेत्र/परिधि/विस्तार

Scorer गणक
Scroll वर्ति-लेख
Scout बालचर / स्काउट
—**(Defence)** स्काउट —**Master** स्काउट मास्टर
Scrap value रद्दी का मूल्य
Script Writer वस्तु-लेखक
Scrutiny संवीक्षा/छानबीन **Scrutinizer** संवीक्षक
Sculptor मूर्तिकार
Seal 1. **(n.)** मुद्रा/मोहर 2. **(vb.)** मोहर लगाना —**pattern** मोहर बंद प्रतिरूप/मोहर बंद पैटर्न —**tender** मोहरबंद टेंडर/मोहरबंद निविदा **Sealer** मुद्रांकक
Seaman नाविक/सीमैन
Search खोज; तलाशी
Secession 1. पार्थक्य 2. पृथक् होना
Second Class Magistrate द्वितीय श्रेणी का मजिस्ट्रेट —**Engineer** द्वितीय इंजीनियर —**Lieutenant** सेकिण्ड लैफ्टीनेंट
Secondary 1. गौण 2. माध्यमिक —**Education Board** माध्यमिक शिक्षा बोर्ड —**Division** माध्यमिक शिक्षा प्रभाग
Secrecy गोपनीयता **Secret** गुप्त/गुप्त बात **Secret ballot** गुप्त मतदान —**cover** गुप्त लिफाफा/गुप्त आवरण —**instruction** गुप्त अनुदेश —**letter** गुप्त पत्र —, **Most** अति गुप्त —, **Top** परम गुप्त
Secretarial Assistant सचिवालयिक सहायक **Secretariate** सचिवालय —**and 'included' offices** सचिवालय और समाविष्ट कार्यालय **Secretary** सचिव —, **Additional** अपर सचिव —**and Accountant** सचिव और लेखापाल —, **Assistant** सहायक सचिव —, **Deputy** उप सचिव —**general** महासचिव —, **Joint** संयुक्त सचिव —, **Military** सैनिक सचिव —, **Parliamentary** संसदीय सचिव —, **Principal** प्रधान सचिव —, **Private** निजी सचिव —, **Railway Service Commission** सचिव, रेल सेवा आयोग —, **Special** विशेष सचिव —, **Under** अवर सचिव/अनुसचिव —**to General Manager** महाप्रबंधक का सचिव —**to the President** राष्ट्रपति के सचिव
Section 1. अनुभाग 2. धारा —, **Sub** उप-धारा —**Clerk** अनुभाग क्लर्क, अनुभाग लिपिक —**Commander** सेक्शन कमांडर —**Controller** अनुभाग नियंत्रक, सेक्शन नियंत्रण —**diary** अनुभाग

डायरी —**Head** अनुभाग प्रधान —**mark** अनुभाग-चिह्न **Officer** अनुभाग-अधिकारी —**wise** अनुभागवार **Sectional Assistant** अनुभागीय सहायक **note book** अनुभागीय नोट-बुक

Sector सेक्टर —, **Private** निजी क्षेत्र/प्राइवेट क्षेत्र —**Public** सार्वजनिक क्षेत्र/पब्लिक सेक्टर —**Commander** सेक्टर कमांडर

Secular लौकिक; ऐहिक धर्म-निरपेक्ष, लोकपरक

Security 1. प्रतिभूति, 2. सुरक्षा —**arrangement** सुरक्षा-प्रबंध —**bond** प्रतिभूति-पत्र —, **cash** नकद प्रतिभूति; नकद जमानत —**Clerk** सुरक्षा क्लर्क/सुरक्षा लिपिक —**deposit** प्रतिभूति जमा/जमानत जमा —**guard** सुरक्षा गारद —**instruction** सुरक्षा अनुदेश —**interest bearing** सब्याज प्रतिभूति —**measures** सुरक्षा उपाय —**Officer** सुरक्षा-अधिकारी —**Personal** वैयक्तिक प्रतिभूति, वैयक्तिक जमानत —, **Railway Protection Police (Armed wing)** सुरक्षा अधिकारी, रेल सुरक्षा पुलिस (सशस्त्र स्कंध)

Sedimentationist अवसादनविद्

Sedition राजद्रोह

Seed Multiplication Officer बीज-वर्धन-अधिकारी **Seedling House Attendant** नवोद्भिद् शाला परिचर

Seismologist भूकंप-विज्ञानी

Seizure अभिग्रहण

Select Committee प्रवर समिति

Selection 1. प्रवरण/सैलेक्शन 2. चयन —**Committee** प्रवरण-समिति —**grade** प्रवरण-कोटि/सैलेक्शन ग्रेड —**Clerk** प्रवरण कोटि लिपिक/सैलेक्शन ग्रेड क्लर्क —**post** प्रवरण-पद

Self contained स्वतः पूर्ण —**Contained Summary** स्वयं-पूर्ण सारांश —**defence** आत्मरक्षा —**explanatory** स्वतः स्पष्ट —**Printing Machine** स्वतः मुद्रण मशीन **Mechanic** मेकैनिक

Seminar विचार-गोष्ठी/संगोष्ठी

Semi Official अर्ध-सरकारी **Semi-skilled** अर्ध-कुशल —**Technical Clerk** अर्ध-तकनीकी लिपिक/अर्ध तकनीकी क्लर्क

Senate सीनेट/वरिष्ठ-सभा **Senator** सीनेटर

Sender प्रेषक

Senior ज्येष्ठ/वरिष्ठ —**Accountant** वरिष्ठ लेखापाल —**Accounts Officer (Construction)** वरिष्ठ

लेखा अधिकारी (निर्माण) —(finance) वरिष्ठ लेखा अधिकारी (वित्त) —(Store) वरिष्ठ लेखा अधिकारी (भंडार) —(Traffic Book) वरिष्ठ लेखा अधिकारी (यातायात पुस्तक) —Accounts Officer (Vigilance) वरिष्ठ लेखा अधिकारी (सतर्कता) —Advertising Assistant वरिष्ठ विज्ञापन सहायक —Assistant Planner and Estimator वरिष्ठ सहायक योजनाकार और प्राक्कलक —Chargeman वरिष्ठ चार्जमैन —Clerk वरिष्ठ क्लर्क/वरिष्ठ लिपिक —Commercial Officer (Catering) वरिष्ठ वाणिज्य अधिकारी (खान-पान) —(General) वरिष्ठ वाणिज्य अधिकारी (सामान्य) —Deputy General Manager वरिष्ठ उप-महाप्रबंधक —Design Assistant वरिष्ठ अभिकल्प सहायक —Draftsman वरिष्ठ प्रारूपकार —Electrical Engineer (Construction) वरिष्ठ बिजली इंजीनियर (निर्माण) —(Maintenance) वरिष्ठ बिजली इंजीनियर (अनुरक्षण) —(Power) वरिष्ठ बिजली इंजीनियर (इंजन) —(Training) वरिष्ठ बिजली इंजीनियर (प्रशिक्षण) —Estimator वरिष्ठ प्राक्कलक —grade वरिष्ठ श्रेणी —Grains Inspector वरिष्ठ खाद्यान्न निरीक्षक — Grain Shop Manager वरिष्ठ खाद्यान्न दुकान प्रबंधक —Head Message Checker वरिष्ठ प्रधान संदश पड़तालकर्ता —Inspector of Station Account वरिष्ठ स्टेशन लेखा निरीक्षक —Jig and Tool Designer वरिष्ठ जिग-औजार अभिकल्पक —Junior Commissioned Officer (Senior J.C.O.) वरिष्ठ जे० सी० ओ०/सीनियर जे० सी० ओ० —Law Assistant वरिष्ठ विधि सहायक —Lecturer वरिष्ठ प्राध्यापक — Luggage Clerk वरिष्ठ सामान लिपिक/वरिष्ठ सामान क्लर्क—Machinery Maintenance Inspector वरिष्ठ मशीन अनुरक्षण निरीक्षक —Maintenance Engineer वरिष्ठ अनुरक्षण इंजीनियर —Malaria Inspector वरिष्ठ मलेरिया निरीक्षक —Mechanic वरिष्ठ मेकैनिक —Mechanical Engineer (Diesel) वरिष्ठ यांत्रिक इंजीनियर (डीजल) —(Fuel) वरिष्ठ यांत्रिक इंजीनियर (ईंधन) — (Maintenance) वरिष्ठ यांत्रिक इंजीनियर (अनुरक्षण) —(Opera-

ting) वरिष्ठ यांत्रिक इंजीनियर (परिचालन) **—(Planning)** वरिष्ठ यांत्रिक इंजीनियर (योजना) **—(Production and Purchase)** वरिष्ठ यांत्रिक इंजीनियर (उत्पादन और खरीद) **—Mistry** वरिष्ठ मिस्त्री **—most** वरिष्ठतम **—Non-Commissioned Officer (Senior N. C. O.)** सीनियर ओहदेदार (सीनियर एन०सी०ओ०) **Senior Officer** ज्येष्ठ आफिसर; ज्येष्ठ अधिकारी **—Parcel Clerk** वरिष्ठ पार्सल क्लर्क/वरिष्ठ पार्सल लिपिक **—Pay Clerk** वरिष्ठ वेतन लिपिक/वरिष्ठ वेतन क्लर्क **—Personnel Officer** वरिष्ठ कार्मिक अधिकारी **—(Reservation)** वरिष्ठ कार्मिक अधिकारी (आरक्षण) **—(Special)** वरिष्ठ कार्मिक अधिकारी (विशेष) **—(Welfare)** वरिष्ठ कार्मिक अधिकारी (कल्याण) **—Photographer** वरिष्ठ फोटोग्राफर **—Physiotherapist** वरिष्ठ भौतिक चिकित्साविद् **—Publicity Assistant** वरिष्ठ प्रचार सहायक **—Recorder** वरिष्ठ अभिलेखक **—Research and Development Assistant** वरिष्ठ अनुसंधान और विकास सहायक **—Inspector** वरिष्ठ अनुसंधान और विकास निरीक्षक **—Scale** प्रवर वेतनमान; वरीय वेतनमान **—Salesman** वरिष्ठ विक्रेता **—Signal and Telecommunication Engineer** वरिष्ठ सिगनल और दूरसंचार इंजीनियर **Senior Signal and Telecommunication Engineer (construction)** वरिष्ठ सिगनल और दूरसंचार इंजीनियर (निर्माण) **—(Planning)** वरिष्ठ सिगनल और दूरसंचार इंजीनियर (योजना) **—(Telecommunication)** वरिष्ठ सिगनल और दूरसंचार इंजीनियर (दूरसंचार) **—(Works)** वरिष्ठ सिगनल और दूरसंचार इंजीनियर (संकर्म) **—Signaller** वरिष्ठ सिगनलर **—Special Inspector** वरिष्ठ विशेष निरीक्षक **—Statistical Inspector** वरिष्ठ सांख्यिकी निरीक्षक **—Stores Chaser** वरिष्ठ भंडार अनुवीक्षक **—Technical Inspector** वरिष्ठ तकनीकी निरीक्षक **—Officer** वरिष्ठ तकनीकी अधिकारी **—Telegraph Overseer** वरिष्ठ तार ओवरसियर **—Telephone Operator** वरिष्ठ टेलीफोन प्रचालक **—Teleprinter Operator** वरिष्ठ दुरमुद्रक संचालक **—Ticket Collector** वरिष्ठ टिकट कलक्टर/वरिष्ठ टिकट संग्रा-

हक —**Time-Scale** वरिष्ठ कालमान **Trade Inspector** वरिष्ठ व्यवसाय निरीक्षक —**Train Examiner** वरिष्ठ गाड़ी परीक्षक —**Transhipment Clerk** वरिष्ठ यानांतरण क्लर्क/वरिष्ठ यानांतरण लिपिक —**Transit Clerk** वरिष्ठ परिवहन क्लर्क/वरिष्ठ परिवहन लिपिक —**Translator** वरिष्ठ अनुवादक —**Transportation Officer (Coaching)** वरिष्ठ परिवहन अधिकारी (कोचिंग) —**(Goods)** वरिष्ठ परिवहन अधिकारी (माल) —**Travelling Ticket Examiner** वरिष्ठ चलटिकट परीक्षक —**Van Loading Inspector** वरिष्ठ यान लदान निरीक्षक —**Water and Drainage Inspector** वरिष्ठ जल और जलनिकासी निरीक्षक —**Welfare Inspector (Sports)** वरिष्ठ कल्याण निरीक्षक (खेल-कूद) —**X-Ray Technician** वरिष्ठ एक्सरे तकनीशियन/वरिष्ठ एक्स-रे प्रविधिज्ञ

Seniority ज्येष्ठता / वरिष्ठता —**of rank** पदस्थिति की प्रवरता

Sentence दंडादेश

Sentry संतरी

Separate पृथक् **Separate inquiry** पृथक् जांच

Sepoy सिपाही

Sequence अनुक्रम

Serjeant सरजेंट

Serial list क्रमसूची —**number** क्रमांक/क्रम संख्या

Sericulture Inspector रेशम-उत्पादन-निरीक्षक

Series आवलि

Serious गंभीर

Serologist सीरम-विज्ञानी

Servant सेवक/भृत्य/नौकर

Service 1. सेवा/नौकरी 2. व्यवस्था 3. सेवाई 4. तामील 5. सर्विस (विधि) —**book** सेवा-पंजी/सेवा-पुस्तिका —**Assistant** सेवापंजी-सहायक —**Contract** सेवा-संविदा —**division** सेवा प्रभाग —**element** सेवा तत्त्व —**fund** सेवा-निधि —**in the reserve** आरक्षित सैन्य सेवा —**, Indian Administrative** भारतीय प्रशासन सेवा —**, Indian Agricultural** भारतीय कृषि-सेवा —**, Indian Education** भारतीय शिक्षा-सेवा —**, Indian Foreign** भारतीय विदेश-सेवा **Service instruction** विभाग-अनुदेश, विभागीय अनुदेश/हिदायत —**of summons** समन तामील करना —**,personnel** फौजी कार्मिक —**,postage stamp** सरकारी डाक टिकट —**roll** सेवा-वृत्त —**sheet** सेवा-पत्र —**, Subordinate** अधीनस्थ सेवाएं

—,superior उच्च सेवा —telegram सरकारी/शासकीय तार —verification सेवा सत्यापन Services, essential अनिवार्य सेवाएं

Session 1. सत्र 2. अधिवेशन —of Parliament संसद सत्र —, Plenary पूर्ण अधिवेशन —, School शिक्षा सत्र/विद्यालय सत्र **Sessions Judge** सत्र-न्यायाधीश

Set 1. विन्यस्त 2. समुच्चय —apart पृथक् करना; अलग रखना —aside अपास्त करना —back धक्का, हानि —, complete पूरा सैट —forth में वर्णित, दिए गए —forth in Schedule अनुसूची में दिया गया —up (n.) व्यवस्था/ढाँचा (vb.) स्थापित करना —up, new नया ढाँचा

Setter सेटर

Settle बस जाना **Settlement** 1. बंदोबस्त 2. निपटारा/समझौता/व्यवस्थापन **Settlement, amicable** मैत्रीपूर्ण समझौता / निपटारा —Commissioner बंदोबस्त आयुक्त —Officer बंदोबस्त-अधिकारी, व्यवस्थापन अधिकारी

Several departments in अनेक विभागों में **Severally, jointly and** संयुक्त रूप से और पृथक्-पृथक् **Severe action** कठोर कार्रवाई **Severe cold** भयंकर/अतिठंड

Severence पृथक्करण / सम्बन्ध-विच्छेद/विभाजन **Severence of relations** सम्बन्ध-विच्छेद, सम्बन्ध तोड़ना

Sex लिंग/काम

Shall be aggregated संकलित कर लिया जाएगा —binding upon पर आबद्धकर होगा —carried into effect कार्यान्वित किया जाएगा **Shall be deemed to be included** शामिल/अंग समझा जाएगा —deemed to have vacated his office यह समझा जाएगा कि उसने अपना पद रिक्त कर दिया है। —determined by lot लाट द्वारा अवधारण किया जाएगा —forfeited to the Governor सरकार को समपहृत हो जाएगा —forwarded अग्रेषित किया जाएगा —free from से मुक्त रहेगा —guided by principles सिद्धांतों से मार्गदर्शित होगा —inserted जोड़ दिया जाएगा —laid on the table of Parliament संसद के पटल पर रखा जाएगा —liable to pay देना पड़ेगा —made available

उपलब्ध किया जाएगा —omitted निकाल दिया जाएगा —treated as confidential गोपनीय माना जाएगा —void लागू न होगा, प्रवृत्तिहीन होगा **Shall cease to have effect** समाप्त हो जायगा —to hold office पद धारण करना समाप्त हो जायगा **Shall continue to be such** वैसा बना/चलता रहेगा **Shall have effect** प्रभावी/लागू होगा —regard to का ध्यान रखेगा —the same effect का वही प्रभाव होगा **Shall not be called in question on any ground** किसी आधार पर आपत्ति नहीं की जाएगी —liable to be contested का प्रतिवाद नहीं किया जा सकेगा **Shall retire in every second year** हर दूसरे वर्ष के अवसान पर निवृत्त हो जाएँगे

Shaper आकृतिकार

Share (n.) 1. अंश/शेयर 2. भाग 1. भागी होना 2. साझी होना 3. भाग पाना

Share capital हिस्सा/शेयर पूंजी **Shares divided into** अंशों/हिस्सों में विभाजित —Turnes खरादी

Shed, clerk शेड क्लर्क **Turner** शेड खरादी **Shed, loco** लोको शेड

Shift पारी —, Day दिन पारी —Engineer पारी-इंजीनियर —, Night रात पारी —system **Shifting charge** स्थान बदलने का प्रभार/हटाने का प्रभार/खर्चा

Ship Wright Artificer पोतकार परिशिल्पी/शिपराइट आर्टीफिसर **Ship yard** पोत-प्रांगण **Shipping** जहाजरानी/पोत परिवहन **Shipping charge** पोत-परिवहन-प्रभार, जहाज से ढुलाई का खर्च/प्रभार **Shipping, coastal** तटीय जहाजरानी —Co-ordination Officer पोत परिवहन समन्वय अधिकारी **Development Fund Committee** पोत परिवहन विकास निधि समिति —Inspector पोत परिवहन निरीक्षक

Shops Inspector दुकान-निरीक्षक

Shore Serang तट सेरांग

Short landing कम उतरान **Shortage** कमी —written off बट्टे खाते में डाली गई घटती **Short-fall** कमी —Shorthand Instructor आशुलिपि-शिक्षक —Shorthand training आशुलिपि प्रशिक्षण —notice अल्प सूचना —term course अल्पकालीन पाठ्यक्रम **Shortest route** सबसे छोटा मार्ग

Show cause कारण बताइए —notice हेतुक दर्शित करने के लिए सूचना/कारण निदर्शन नोटिस/

कारण बताओ नोटिस —**why serious action should not be taken** कारण बताइये कड़ी कार्रवाई क्यों न की जाए

Shunter शंटर/शंटकर्ता —**(Diesel)** शंटकर्ता (डीजल) —**(Electric)** शंटकर्ता (बिजली) —**(Steam)** शंटकर्ता (भाप) **Shunting Jamadar** शंटिंग जमादार/शंटन जमादार —**Master** शंटिंग मास्टर/शंटन मास्टर

Sick बीमार

Side by side साथ-साथ

Sign 1. चिह्न/संकेत 2. हस्ताक्षर करना **Sign writer** पट्टिका-लेखक

Signal संकेत/सिगनल —**and Tele-Communication** संकेत और दूरसंचार —**Fitter** सिगनल फिटर —**Foreman** सिगनल फोरमैन —**Inspector** सिगनल निरीक्षक —, **railway** रेल का सिगनल —**Room Clerk** संकेत-कक्ष क्लर्क **Signaller** 1. सिगनलर/संकेतक/सिगनल वाला 2. तार-बाबू **Signalman** संकेतकार/सिगनल-मैन/सिगनल वाला

Signature हस्ताक्षर —**Officer** हस्ताक्षर-अधिकारी —**pad** हस्ताक्षर-पैड

Signed, sealed and delivered हस्ताक्षर करके और मुहरबंद करके दिया गया

Significance, of great बहुत महत्व का, अति महत्वपूर्ण

Silt Analyst गाद-विश्लेषक —**and Sediment Sampler** गाद और तलछट पारखी

Silviculturist वन-वृक्ष-वैज्ञानिक/वन संवर्धनिक

Similar सदृश/ऐसी ही/वैसे ही/समरूप **Similar case** वैसा ही/सदृश मामला

Simple interest साधारण ब्याज

Simplification of rules नियमों का सरलीकरण

Simultaneous 1. युगपत्/समक्षणिक, 2. एक साथ/एक ही समय पर **Simultaneous action** एक साथ/एक ही समय कार्रवाई

Since then तब से

Sincerely yours आपका

Sine die अनिश्चित काल के लिए, अनियत तिथि तक **Sine qua non** अनिवार्य शर्त/अपिहार्य शर्त

Single entry system एक प्रविष्टि-पद्धति —**journey ticket** इकतरफी यात्रा टिकट —**member Constituency** एक सदस्यीय निर्वाचन क्षेत्र —**tender** अकेला टेंडर —**transferable vote** एकल संक्रमणीय मत

Sinking fund शोधन निधि

Sir श्रीमन्/महोदय **—Dear** प्रिय महोदय **—the file is with Secretary** श्रीमन्, फाइल सचिव महोदय के पास है **Sister-in-charge** प्रभारी सिस्टर

Site स्थल/घटना स्थल/स्थान **—, at** स्थल पर, मौके पर, घटनास्थल पर **—plan** स्थल-नक्शा

Sitting member वर्तमान सदस्य/आसीन सदस्य **—over the papers** कागज दवा कर बैठना

Situation, critical नाजुक स्थिति

Six monthly छमाही

Sketch रेखाचित्र **—rough** कच्चा रेखाचित्र

Skidman स्किडमैन **—Supervisor** स्किड पर्यवेक्षक/स्किड सुपरवाइजर

Skilled Carpenter कुशल काष्ठकार/कुशल बढ़ई **—labour** कुशल/दक्ष/प्रवीण श्रमिक

Skipper स्किपर

Slander अपमान वचन

Slaughter House Inspector बूचड़खाना निरीक्षक

Sleeping accommodation सोने का स्थान, सोने की जगह **Sleeper Control Office** स्लीपर नियंत्रण अधिकारी **—Inspector** स्लीपर निरीक्षक **—Measurer** स्लीपर मापक **—Passing Officer** स्लीपर पारण अधिकारी

Slightly affected किंचित्/थोड़ा सा प्रभावित

Slip पर्ची **Slip A** पर्ची 'क'

Sluice Keeper जलकपाटपाल/तूमपाल

Slum गंदी बस्ती **—area** गन्दी बस्ती क्षेत्र

Small cause court लघुवाद न्यायालय **—Cause Court Judge** लघुवाद न्यायाधीश **—Industries Services Institute** लघु उद्योग सेवा संस्थान **—saving scheme** अल्प बचत योजना **—Saving Officer** अल्पबचत-अधिकारी **—scale** छोटे पैमाने का, लघु **—scalei ndustries** लघु उद्योग

Smuggle चोरी से लाना/चोरी से ले जाना/तस्कर व्यापार करना **Smuggled goods** चोरी से लाया गया सामान, तस्कर सामान **Smuggler** चोरी से लाने वाला/चोरी से ले जाने वाला/तस्कर व्यापारी **Smuggling** तस्कर व्यापार/चौकी मारी/चोरी से माल लाना-ले जाना

So and so अमुक **—as to ensure** ताकि यह सुनिश्चत हो **—far as may be** यथासम्भव, जहां तक

हो सके —**far as possible** यथासम्भव —**far practicable** यथासाध्य —**help me God** भगवान मेरी सहायता करे —**long as** जब तक कि —**often as** जब जब, जब तक, तब तक

Social institution सामाजिक संस्था —**Security** सामाजिक सुरक्षा —**Studies and Handicrafts Unit** सामाजिक अध्ययन और हस्तशिल्प एकक —**Welfare** समाज-कल्याण —**and Rehabilitation Directorate** समाज कल्याण तथा पुनर्वास निदेशालय —**Department** समाज कल्याण विभाग —**Officer** समाज कल्याण अधिकारी **Socialistic Pattern (of Society)** (समाज का) समाजवादी रूप

Society 1. समाज 2. सोसाइटी —**,agricultural** कृषक समिति —**,co-operative** सहकारी समिति

Soft currency area सुलभ मुद्राक्षेत्र

Soil मृदा/मिट्टी/भूमि —**Chemist** भूमि रसायन विज्ञानी/मृदा रसायनज्ञ —**Conservation Officer** भूमि-संरक्षण अधिकारी —**Research, Demonstration and Training Centre** भूमि-संरक्षण, अनुसंधान, प्रदर्शन तथा प्रशिक्षण केन्द्र —**Testing Laboratory** मृदा-परीक्षण-प्रयोगशाला

Sojourn अवस्थान/बिराम

Sole Arbitrator एकमात्र मध्यस्थ

Solemn सत्यनिष्ठ/गंभीर —**affirmation** सत्यनिष्ठा से प्रतिज्ञान **Solemnity** गंभीरता/गांभीर्य **Solemnly** सत्यनिष्ठापूर्वक/सत्यनिष्ठा से

Solicitor सॉलिसीटर —**General** महा सॉलिसीटर —**General of India** भारत का महा सॉलिसिटर

Solid State Physics Laboratory घन अवस्था भौतिकी प्रयोगशाला

Solitary case अकेला मामला —**confinement** एकान्त कारावास तनहाई कैद

Solution 1. साधन 2. हल —**of problem** समस्या का हल

Sorter छंटाईकार/सार्टर —**Inspector** छंटाई निरीक्षक **Sorting** छंटाई —**Machine Operator** छंटाई मशीन प्रचालक —**office** छंटाई दफ्तर —**Postman** छंटाई डाकिया —**table** छंटाई मेज

Sound proposal ठोस/साधार प्रस्ताव

Source स्रोत/उद्गम —**of income** आय स्रोत/साधन —**, reliable** विश्वस्त सूत्र

Souvenir सूवनियर

Sovereign अधिराट्/प्रभु/प्रभुसत्ता संपन्न/सर्वसत्ताधारी **—democratic republic** सम्पूर्ण प्रभुत्व-सम्पन्न लोकतन्त्रात्मक गणराज्य **—State** प्रभुराज्य **Sovereignty** प्रभुसत्ता/प्रभुत्ता/सर्वोच्च सत्ता

Spacing अंतर छोड़ना **—, proper** ठीक तरह से अन्तर छोड़ना

Spade work प्रारम्भिक कार्य

Spare copy अतिरिक्त/फालतू प्रति **—parts** अतिरिक्त भाग/पुर्जे **— time** अतिरिक्त/खाली समय

Speak on phone टेलीफोन पर बात करिए **—please** कृपया बात कर जाइए/बात करें

Speaker अध्यक्ष **—, Lok Sabha** अध्यक्ष, लोक सभा **Speaker of State Legistative Assembly** राज्य विधानसभा का अध्यक्ष **Speaking, generally** आम तौर से **— tube** बतनाल

Special विशेष **Special accommodation** विशेष स्थान/बास **—additional pension** विशेष अतिरिक्त पेंशन **—administrative Question** विशेष प्रशासकीय प्रश्न **—bill** विशेष विधेयक **—care** विशेष सावधानी **—Cash Witness** विशेष रोकड़ साक्षी **—constituency** विशेष निर्वाचन-क्षेत्र **—duty, Officer on** विशेषाधिकारी **—form of Procedure** प्रक्रिया का विशेष रूप **—grant** विशेष अनुदान **—jurisdiction or Power** विशेष अधिकारिता या शक्ति **—meeting** विशेष अधिवेशन; विशेष बैठक **—Permission** विशेष अनुमति **—Provision** विशेष उपबन्ध **– resolution** विशेष संकल्प

Specialist विशेषज्ञ **— service** विशेषज्ञ सेवा

Specific विनिर्दिष्ट **—denial** स्पष्ट खण्डन **— reason** विशिष्ट कारण **—recommendation** निश्चित सिफारिश **Specifically appropriated** विशेष रूप से विनियोजित **Specification** विनिर्देश/विनिर्दिष्ट **— according to** विनिर्देश के अनुसार **Specified in the certificate** प्रमाण-पत्र में उल्लिखित **Specify** उल्लिखित करना

Specimen निदर्श/नमूना **— signature** नमूना हस्ताक्षर

Speculation 1. सट्टा 2. अनुमान/अटकल **—, according to** अनुमान/अटकल के अनुसार **– business** सट्टा व्यापार

Speech भाषण **—, deliver a** भाषण देना

Speed चाल/रफ्तार/गति **—limit**

गति/रफ्तार सीमा

Sphere 1. गोला 2. क्षेत्र **—of duty** कार्य-क्षेत्र

Spinning Master कताई मास्टर

Spirit of the rule नियम की भावना

Sponsor (n.) प्रयोजक **(vb.)** प्रायोजित करना

Spontaneous action स्वजात/स्वत: स्फूर्त कार्रवाई

Sport क्रीड़ा **Sports** खेलकूद **—, annual** वार्षिक खेलकूद **—Organiser** खेलकूद आयोजक

Spouse विवाहित स्त्री या पुरुष/ पति या पत्नी

Squad स्क्वाड/दस्ता **—, Flying** उड़न दस्ता **Squadron Leader** स्क्वाड्रन लीडर

Square metre/ft वर्ग मीटर/फुट

Staff कर्मचारी-बृन्द / स्टाफ **—acquittance roll** कर्मचारिक-वृन्द वेतन चिट्ठा **—Artist** विभागीय कलाकार **– Captain** स्टाफ कैप्टन **—Car Driver** स्टाफ कार ड्राइवर **—Clerk** स्टाफ क्लर्क **—, excess** फालतू अमला/कर्मचारी वर्ग **—instructions** कर्मचारी-वर्ग को हिदायतें **—Nurse** स्टाफ नर्स/स्टाफ-परिचारक / स्टाफ - परिचारिका **—Officer** स्टाफ अफसर

Stage 1. रंगमंच 2, अवस्था/ प्रक्रम **—, at this** इस अवस्था में **—Director** रंगमंच-निदेशक **—, on the** मंच पर, रंगमंच पर

Stalk Maker डंडीकार/डंडी लोहार

Stamp 1. टिकट/स्टांप 2. मोहर 3. मुद्रांक **—duty** स्टांप शुल्क/ मुद्रांक शुल्क **—Officer** टिकट अफसर **—pad** मोहर पैड **—,postage** डाक-टिकट **—paper** स्टाम्प कागज **—revenue** रसीदी टिकट **—rubber** रबड़ की मोहर **—Vendor** स्टांप-विक्रेता/टिकट-विक्रेता **Stamped envelope** टिकट लगा लिफाफा **Stamping** मोहर लगाना **--Mechanic** मोहर मेकैनिक

Stand for प्रतीक होना, समर्थन करना, के लिए

Standard मानक/स्तर/दंड **—heads** मानक शीर्ष **—, of a high** उच्च स्तर का **—of living** जीवन स्तर **—, rate** मानक दर **—Service Period** मानक सेवावधि **—Skeleton draft** सामान्य मसौदे का ढांचा **Standardization** मानकीकरण **—, Committee** मानकीकरण समिति

Standards Office मानक-कार्यालय **— Officer** मानक-अधिकारी

Standing स्थायी **—Commission**

स्थायी आयोग — **committee** स्थायी समिति **guard file** स्थायी निदेश मिसिल — **order** स्थायी आदेश —**Screening Committee Inspector** स्थायी छानबीन समिति निरीक्षक

Standpoint दृष्टिकोण

Standstill agreement यथास्थिति करार

Starred तारांकित —**question** तारांकित प्रश्न **Start with, to** आरम्भ में

State 1. राज्य 2. स्थिति/दशा / अवस्था / हालत —**aid** राज्य/सरकारी/राजकीय सहायता —**Government** राज्य सरकार —**funds** राज्यनिधि —**guest** राजकीय अतिथि, सरकारी मेहमान —,**I amdirected to** मुझे यह कहने का निदेश हुआ है —,**in good** अच्छी दशा/हालत में — **language** राज्य भाषा —**list** राज्य-सूची —**Policy** राज्य नीति —**Prison** राज्य-कारागार —**Providnt** राजबंदी —**Provident fund** राज्य भविष्य निधि —**revenue** राज्य-राजस्व —**telegram** सरकारी तार — **territory** राज्य क्षेत्र —**trading** राज्य व्यापार —**Trading Corporation** राज्य-व्यापार-निगम

Statement 1. कथन 2. बयान/वक्तव्य/विवरण —**given by the accused** अभियुक्त द्वारा दिया गया बयान —**issued to the press** समाचार पत्रों को दिया गया वक्तव्य —**of account** लेखा विवरण —**of case** मामले का विवरण —**of facts** तथ्य कथन

Statesman राजमर्मज्ञ

Station स्टेशन/केन्द्र —**Commander** स्टेशन कमांडर —**Director (A.I.R.)** केन्द्र-निदेशक —**Inspector** स्टेशन निरीक्षक —**Master** स्टेशन मास्टर —**Outstanding Inspector** स्टेशन बकाया निरीक्षक —, **railway** रेलवे स्टेशन —**Superintendent** स्टेशन अधीक्षक —**Wagon Driver** स्टेशन-वैगन-ड्राइवर

Stationary Plant Driver स्थायी संयंत्र प्रचालक —, **to remain** स्थिर रहना

Stationery लेखन सामग्री — **and Forms Inspector** लेखन सामग्री और प्रपत्र निरीक्षक —**and printing** लेखन सामग्री और मुद्रण —**Superintendent** लेखन सामग्री अधीक्षक

Statistical सांख्यिकीय/सांख्यिकी — **analysis** सांख्यिकीय विश्लेषण —**Assistant** सांख्यिकी-सहायक

—branch संख्यान-शाखा —Bulletin सांख्यिकीय बुलेटिन —data सांख्यिकीय सामग्री, दत्त आंकड़े —division संख्यान-प्रभाग —information सांख्यिकीय सूचना —Inspector सांख्यिकी निरीक्षक —Officer सांख्यिकीय अधिकारी / सांख्यिकी-अधिकारी —picture सांख्यिकीय स्थिति —Summary सांख्यिकीय सारांश —survey सांख्यिकीय सर्वेक्षण —year book सांख्यिकीय शब्दकोष

Statistics 1. सांख्यिकी 2. आंकड़े

Statistician सांख्यिक/सांख्यिकी-विद् —and Intelligence Branch सांख्यिकी और आसूचना शाखा —and Method Branch सांख्यिकी और पद्धति-शाखा —Investigator सांख्यिकी अन्वेषक —of births and deaths जन्म और मरण के आंकड़े

Status स्थिति/हैसियत/प्रतिष्ठा/मर्यादा —, diplomatic राजनयिक हैसियत —, high ऊंची हैसियत/स्थिति/प्रतिष्ठा —quo यथापूर्व स्थिति

Statute कानून/संविधि

Statutory कानूनी/विधिक/संविधिक —authority सांविधिक प्राधिकार —body कानूनी निकाय —declaration कानूनी घोषणा —deduction कानूनी कटौती —lien कानूनी धारणाधिकार —meeting कानूनी बैठक —orders कानूनी/विधिक/संविधिक/आदेश —power कानूनी शक्ति/प्राधिकार —report कानूनी रिपोर्ट —rule कानूनी नियम

Sterling equivalent of pay वेतन की स्टर्लिंग समराशि

Stay of proceedings कार्यवाही रोकना —Order रोकने का आदेश

Steam Driver भाप ड्राइवर/भाप चालक —Operator भाप प्रचालक

Steamer Clerk स्टीमर क्लर्क/स्टीमर लिपिक —Fire Engine Operator स्टीमर फायर इंजन ऑपरेटर —Fitter स्टीमर फिटर

Steel Controller इस्पात-नियंत्रक —Inspector इस्पात निरीक्षक

Steering Committee विषय-निर्वाचन समिति

Stencil स्टेंसिल

Steno स्टेनो/आशु लेखक —grapher आशुलिपिक/स्टेनोग्राफर —graphy test आशुलिपि परीक्षा —typist आशु-टंकण/स्टेनो-टाइपिस्ट

Step child सौतेला बच्चा/बालक

Steps, may take necessary

आवश्यक कदम/पग उठाएं जाए, आवश्यक उपाय किए जाएं

Stereo Maker स्टीरियो-निर्माता **—Typer** स्टीरियो टंकक/स्टीरियो टाइपर **—typed** रूढ़/रूढ़िबद्ध **—typed reply** रूढ़िबद्ध उत्तर

Stet (let it stand) तिष्ठतु (ति०)

Steward स्टूवर्ड

Stigma, unnecessary अनावश्यक लांछन

Stipend वृत्तिका / वजीफा **—, monthly** मासिक वृत्तिका/वजीफा **Stipendiary** वृत्तिका-ग्राही/वैतनिक **—magistrate** वैतनिक मजिस्ट्रेट

Stipulate अनुबंध करना **Stipulated, as** यथाकल्पित, जैसा सोचा गया था **—conditions** अनुबद्ध शर्तें **Stipulation** अनुबंध **—, according to** अनुबन्ध के अनुसार

Stock 1. सामान/माल/स्टाक, 2. शेष माल **—Assistant** स्टॉक-सहायक **—Clerk** स्टॉक क्लर्क/स्टाक लिपिक **— Committee** विषय निर्धारिणी समिति **—exchange** शेयर बाजार; क्रय विक्रय स्थल **—Holder** स्टॉक धारी **—inventory** स्टाक तालिका **—register** भण्डार/स्टाक रजिस्टर **—taking** माल की पड़ताल/स्टॉक-मिलान **—verifier** स्टॉक सत्यापक **Stocker** स्टोकर **Stockist** स्टॉकिस्ट

Stoppage at efficiency bar दक्षता राध पर विराम/रुकना

Storage संचयन/गोदाम में रखना/भण्डार में रखना **—and Inspection Directorate** संचयन और निरीक्षण निदेशालय **—charges** गोदाम भाड़ा **— Officer** संग्रह-अधिकारी/भण्डार अधिकारी **— space** माल रखने की जगह/स्थान

Store भण्डार/गोदाम **— account** भण्डार-लेखा **—and Tool Keeper** भण्डार और औजार रक्षक **—Delivery Sircar** भण्डार सुपुर्दगी सरकार **— Houseman** भण्डार वाला **—Inspector** भण्डार निरीक्षक **—Issuer** भण्डार जारीकर्ता **—Keeper** भण्डारी **—, Catering** भण्डारी, खानपान **Storeman** भण्डार कर्मी **—room** भण्डार/गोदाम **rules** भण्डार-नियमावली **—Van Clerk** भण्डार यान क्लर्क/भण्डार यान लिपिक **—Wright** स्टोर राइट **—Imprest Inspector** भण्डार अग्रदाय निरीक्षक **Stores** सामान/सामग्री/भण्डार **—Chaser** भण्डार-अनुवीक्षक **—directorate** भण्डार-

निदेशालय —**officer** भण्डार-अधिकारी —**Purchase Committee** स्टोर क्रय समिति; सामान क्रय समिति, —**received** प्राप्त हुआ सामान/सामग्री —**Representative** भण्डार प्रतिनिधि

Strained relations मनोमालिन्य, बिगड़े सम्बन्ध

Stretcher Bearer स्ट्रेचर वाहक

Strict discipline कड़ा अनुशासन —**interpretation** यथावत् निर्वचन **Strictly relevant** सर्वथा सुसंगत — **speaking** यथार्थ रूप से/में

Stricture अवक्षेप

Strike 1. हड़ताल/संप (मराठी); 2. आघात करना —**a blow** चोट पहुंचाना, आघात करना —**a total** योग निकालना, जोड़ लगाना —, **hunger** भूख हड़ताल —**off the name** नाम काट देना, नाम निकाल देना **Stringer** फुटकर संवाददाता **Strive one's best** भरसक प्रयत्न/प्रयास करना

Strong, financially आर्थिक दृष्टि से सुस्थिर/सुदृढ़ —**opposition** तीव्र/प्रबल विरोध —**position** मजबूत/अच्छी स्थिति —**room** कोष कक्ष

Structure संरचना **Structural changes** संरचनात्मक परिवर्तन, बनावट में परिवर्तन —**Engineer** संरचना-अभियंता / संरचना-इंजीनियर

Student विद्यार्थी/छात्र **Student's agitation** विद्यार्थियों/छात्रों का आन्दोलन

Studio Attendant स्टूडियो-परिचर

Study, deep गम्भीर अध्ययन

Stupefying जड़िमाकारी —**drug** जड़िमाकारी औषधि/जड़िमाकारी औषध

Stylographic pen स्टेंसिल कलम/स्टेंसिल लेखनी

Sub (Subordinate) नायब/छोटा/उप —**Area Commander** सब एरिया कमांडर —**Classification** उपवर्गीकरण —**clause** उप-खण्ड —**committee** उप-समिति — **contract** उप-ठेका/उप-संविदा — **Division (Territory)** 1. उप-मण्डल / सबडिवीजन 2. उपखण्ड —**divisional** उपप्रभागीय; उप-मण्डलीय —**Divisional Magistrate** उपमण्डल मजिस्ट्रेट/उपखण्ड मजिस्ट्रेट —**divisional office** उपमण्डल दफ्तर; उपमण्डल कार्यालय —**head of account** लेखा उपशीर्ष —**Fire Station Officer** नायब दमकल अधिकारी —**Inspector** नायब-निरीक्षक —**(Police)** दरोगा —**(Schools etc.)** नायब निरीक्षक —**Judge**

उपन्यायाधीश —let order उप-ठेका आदेश —Lieutenant सब लेफ्टिनेंट —Overseer Mistry नायब ओवरसियर मिस्त्री —paragraph उप-पैरा — rule उप-नियम —Store Keeper नायब भण्डारी —tenant अनु-भाटकी, शिकमी किरायेदार/काश्त-कार —Vigilance Inspector नायब सतर्कता निरीक्षक —Water Works Inspector नायब जलकल निरीक्षक —Subedar सूबेदार —Major सूबेदार मेजर

Subject 1. विषय 2. प्रजा —**in dispute** विवादग्रस्त विषय —**thereto** उसके अधीन —**to** . . .के अधीन, अधीन रहते हुए—**to approval** बशर्ते अनुमोदन प्राप्त हो —**to confirmatiion** पुष्टि होने पर — **to jurisdiction** क्षेत्राधिकार में — **to, Shall be** के अध्याधीन किया जायेगा —**to the condition that** इस शर्त पर कि — **to the observation of** के पालन करने पर —**to the provisions of** के उपबन्धों के अधीन —**to the terms thereof** उसमें दी शर्तों के अधीन —**to verification** सत्यापित हो जाने की शर्त पर

Submission 1. निवेदन 2. अधीनता स्वीकार करना 3. प्रस्तुतीकरण/पेशी 4. अधीनता 5. मान लेना/मानना —**, file is under** फाइल मिसिल अधिकारी के पास है —**of papers** कागजात पेश/प्रस्तुत करना —**, it is my** मेरा यह निवेदन है

Submitted for favour of sympathetic consideration सहानुभूतिपूर्ण विचार के लिए प्रस्तुत —**for approval/consideration / information /order/ perusal** अनुमोदन/विचार/सूचना/आदेश/अवलोकन के लिए प्रस्तुत —**for information** सूचनार्थ —**, it is respectfully** सादर निवेदन है —**with reference to Joint Secretary's order on prepage** संयुक्त सचिव द्वारा पूर्व पृष्ठ पर दिए गए आदेश के प्रसंग में प्रस्तुत

Subordinate अधीन/अधीनस्थ/मातहत — **Office** अधीनस्थ कार्यालय — **Service** अधीन सेवा — **Staff** अधीन कर्मचारी-वर्ग/अधीनस्थ स्टाफ

Subscribe to 1. चन्दा/शुल्क देना, ग्राहक बनना 2. का समर्थन करना, से सहमत होना **Subscription, yearly** वार्षिक चन्दा/शुल्क

Subsequent बाद का/उत्तरवर्ती/

अनुवर्ती / उत्तरभाव (विधि) —**action** बाद की कार्रवाई, उत्तरवर्ती/अनुवर्ती कार्रवाई

Subsidiary 1. गौण, 2. सहायक, 3. समनुषंगी —**Intelligence Bureau** सहायक खुफिया ब्यूरो —**mandate** सहायक अधिदेश —**register** सहायक रजिस्टर **Subsidise** सहायता देना **Subsidised** इमदादी/आर्थिक सहायताप्राप्त **Subsidy** सहायिकी/ इमदाद

Subsistence निर्वाह / वर्तिता —**allowance** निर्वाह-भत्ता —**grant** निर्वाह-अनुदान

Substance 1. द्रव्य 2. सार 3. पदार्थ **Substantial damage** भारी हानि/ क्षति **Substantially identical** व्यापक रूप में समान, काफी एकसा, बहुत मिलता-जुलता

Substantive मौलिक/मूल **Substantive appointment / post/scale** मूल/मौलिक नियुक्ति/पद/वेतनमान

Substitute 1. एवजी/प्रतिस्थानी 2. प्रतिस्थापित करना —**the following** निम्नलिखित के स्थान/ एवज/बदले में रखिए —**will be required** एवजी/प्रतिस्थानी की आवश्यकता होगी **Substituted rule** प्रतिस्थापित नियम

Subversive activities तोड़फोड़ की कार्रवाई, उच्छेदक चेष्टाएं

Succeeding अनुवर्ती / उत्तरवर्ती —**paragraph** अनुवर्ती पैरा, आगे का पैरा

Successful tenderer सफल टेंडर-दाता/सफल निविदा देने वाला

Succession उत्तराधिकार/उत्तरवर्तन —**tax** उत्तराधिकार कर **Successor** उत्तराधिकारी **Successive phases, in** क्रमिक/ उत्तरोत्तर चरणों में

Such action as may be deemed necessary ऐसी कार्रवाई को आवश्यक समझी जाए —**and such** अमुक अमुक —**as that** यथा, जैसे

Sue मुकदमा चलाना/वाद चलाना —**in the court** अदालत में मुकदमा चलाना

Sufficient पर्याप्त —**cause/ groundmeans** पर्याप्त कारण/ आधार/साधन

Suffrage मताधिकार —, **adult** मताधिकार

Sugar Controller शक्कर-नियंत्रक/ चीनी-नियंत्रक **Sugarcane Breeding Institute** गन्ना प्रजनन संस्थान

Suggestion book सुझाव पुस्तक

Sui-juris आत्माधीन, स्वाधीन

Suit दावा / मुकदमा /वाद —**for**

partition बंटवारे के लिए बाध/दावा/मुकदमा **Suitability** उपयुक्तता **Suitable action** उपयुक्त/उचित कार्रवाई

Sukani सुकानी

Summary (adj.) 1. संक्षिप्त/सरसरी **(n.)** 2. सारांश/संक्षेप **—of case** मामले का सारांश **—procedure** क्षिप्र / संक्षिप्त प्रक्रिया **—trial** संक्षिप्त विचारण **Summarily dealt with** संक्षेपतः निर्णीत

Summon आहूत करना **—,power to** आहूत करने का अधिकार, बुलाने की शक्ति **—,service of** सम्मन की तामील

Sum payable देय राशि

Sumptuary allowance सत्कार भत्ता/आतिथ्य भत्ता/समुचरी भत्ता

Sundry expenses विविध व्यय

Superannuate निर्वतन/निवृत्त होना **Superannuation** निवर्तन/अधिवर्षिता **—,age of** वार्द्धक्य/निवर्तन की आयु **—allowance** निवर्तन भत्ता

Superintendence अधीक्षण

Superintendent अधीक्षक **—,Delhi Zoological Park** अधीक्षक, दिल्ली चिड़ियाघर **—,Hindi Section** अधीक्षक, हिन्दी अनुभाग **—of Police** पुलिस अधीक्षक **—of Post Offices** डाकघर अधीक्षक **—, Parks and Gardens** उद्यान-अधीक्षक **—, Power** 1. शक्ति अधीक्षक 2. बिजली अधीक्षक **—,Printing and Stationery** अधीक्षक, मुद्रण और लेखन सामग्री **—,Reformatory** सुधारालय-अधीक्षक **—,Rescue Home** अधीक्षक, उद्धार-गृह **—,Statistics** सांख्यिकी अधीक्षक **—,Virus Vaccine** अधीक्षक, वाइरस वैक्सीन **Superintending Engineer** अधीक्षक-अभियंता/अधीक्षक इंजीनियर

Superior वरिष्ठ/उच्च **—establishment** उच्च सिब्बंदी **—service** वरिष्ठ सेवा **—to** से बढ़िया/उच्च

Supernumerary Assistant अधिसंख्य सहायक **—post** अधिसंख्य पद

Superscribe ऊपर लिखना

Superscription 1. उपरिलेख/सरनामा 2. पता

Supersede अतिक्रमण करना/अधिक्रमण करना

Supersession अधिक्रमण **—of, in** का अधिक्रमण करते हुए **Supersedeas** कार्यवाही रोक आदेश

Super-tax अधिकर

Supervision पर्यवेक्षण/देखरेख **Supervision Officer** पर्यवेक्षण-अधिकारी **—charges** पर्यवेक्षण व्यय **—, under his** उसके पर्यवेक्षण/देखरेख में

Supervisor पर्यवेक्षक/सुपरवाइजर **—, Operative Offices** पर्यवेक्षक, प्रचालक कार्यालय

Supplement (n.) 1. जोड़ बंध 2. अनुपूरक **(vb.)** 1. जोड़ना 2. अनुपूरण

Supplementary अनुपूरक **—budget** अनुपूरक बजट **—estimate** अनुपूरक प्रक्कलन, अनुपूरक अन्दाजा **—grant** अनुपूरक अनुदान **—question** अनुपूरक प्रश्न **—Officer** पूर्ति अधिकारी **—Programme indent** अनुपूरक कार्यक्रम इण्डेंट

Snpply (n) पूर्ति/प्रदाय **(vb.)** प्रदाय करना **—section** पूर्ति अनुभाग

Supplier संभारक, संभरक, दायक

Support of, in के समर्थन में

Supposed right कल्पित अधिकार

Suppression of civil liberties नागरिक स्वतन्त्रता का दमन

Supreme authority सर्वोच्च सत्ता; सर्वोच्च प्राधिकारी **—Command** सर्वोच्च समादेश **—Court** उच्चतम न्यायालय

Sur-charge अधिभार **—on fare** किराये पर अधिकर

Surety 1. प्रतिभू/जामिन 2. जमानत **—Bond** जमानत बंधपत्र **—, stand** जामिन बनना

Surface inspection ऊपरी निरीक्षण **—route, by** स्थल मार्ग से

Surgeon शल्य-चिकित्सक/सर्जन **—, Civil** सिविल सर्जन **Surgery** शल्य-चिकित्सा सर्जरी

Surmised, as अटकल/अनुमान के अनुसार

Surname कुलनाम

Surpius अधिशेष **—budget** लाभ का बजट **—report** अधिशेष रिपोर्ट **—staff** बशी/फालतू कर्मचारी **—stores** अधिशेष सामान

Surprise check आकस्मिक जांच **—inspection** आकस्मिक निरीक्षण **—visit** आकस्मिक निरीक्षण

Surrender अध्यर्पण **—one's share** अपना हिस्सा छोड़ देना

Surreptitious inspection चुपके से निरीक्षण, प्रच्छन्न निरीक्षण

Surveillance Controller निगरानी-नियंत्रक

Survey सर्वेक्षण **—report** सर्वेक्षण रिपोर्ट **—of India** भारतीय

सर्वेक्षण **—report** सर्वेक्षण-रिपोर्ट **—, Sample** नमूना सर्वेक्षण

Surviving 1. अवशिष्ट 2. उत्तर-जीवी **—children** उत्तरजीवी/जीवित बच्चे

Suspect, there is no reason to संदेह/संशय करने का कोई कारण नहीं

Suspend मुअत्तल करना/निलम्बित करना **Suspended** मुअत्तिल कर दिया गया; रोक दिया गया **—from service** नौकरी से मुअत्तल/निलम्बित किया गया

Suspense and reminder diary निलम्बित मामलों और अनुस्मारकों की डायरी **—account** उचंत/निलम्बित लेखा **—, to keep in** दुविधा/अनिश्चय की दशा में रखना **Suspension** मुअत्तली/निलम्बन **—form service** नौकरी से मुअत्तली **—of firms** फर्मों का निलम्बन

Swear शपथ लेना; शपथ दिलाना **Swearing in** शपथ ग्रहण

Syllabus, new नया पाठ्य विवरण

Symbol of unity एकता का प्रतीक

Sympathetic consideration, for सहानुभूतिपूर्ण विचार के लिए

Symposium on के विषय में परि-संवाद **—,poetic** कवि सम्मेलन

Synopsis of the case मामले का सार

System, Card board filing दफ्ती फाइल पद्धति **—, follow-up** क्रमिकलेखन पद्धति **—of keeping records** अभिलेख रखने की पद्धति/प्रणाली **—, Press-letter work** पुस्तक दाब पद्धति

Systematic work व्यवस्थित/क्रमबद्ध कार्य, बाकायदे काम **Systemalically** यथा-पद्धति; बाकायदा

Table 1. सारणी/तालिका 2. मेज **—of contents** विषय सूची **—Officer** पटल-अधिकारी **—of the House, on the** सभा पटल पर **—, time** समय सारणी

Tabulator सारणीकार/तालिकाकार **Tabulated statement (table)** सारणीबद्ध विवरण **Tabulating Machine Operator** सारणित्र संचालक **Tabulation** सारणीयन/सारणीकरण/सारणी बनाना **—of information received** प्राप्त सूचना की सारणी बनाना

Tacit acceptance मौन स्वीकृति

Tactics, delaying देर करने के हथकंडे, विलम्बकारी युक्तियां

Tag (n.) टैग **(vb.)** नत्थी करना **—these papers** कागजों में टैग

लगा दें, कागजों की नत्थी कर दें

Tailor (uniform maker) दर्जी (वर्दी बनाने वाला)

Take care ध्यान/सावधानी रखना **—care of** देखभाल करना **—effect** प्रभावी होना **—exception** आपत्ति उठाना **—for granted** मान लेना, मान कर चलना **—notice** ध्यान में रखना **—over** ले लेना, प्रभार लेना, कार्य-भार संभालना **—part in** में भाग लेना **—place** होना, घटित होता **—step** पग/कदम उठाना, अग्रसर होना **—stock of the situation** स्थिति को समझ लेना **—such measures** ऐसे उपाय करना **—the chair** सभापति बनना **—the salute** सलामी लेना **—up** हाथ में लेना, उठा लेना, ले लेना

Talkie Operator टॉकी ऑपरेटर/बोलपट-प्रचालक

Tally card मिलान कार्ड **—Clerk** मिलान क्लर्क/मिलानलिपिक

Tamper with a document दस्तावेज बिगाड़ना

Tangible result मूर्त फल/परिणाम

Tank Wagon Inspector टंकी डिब्बा निरीक्षक

Tanner चर्मशोधक

Tare खाली गाड़ी का भार/टेयर

Target लक्ष्य **—of production** उत्पादन लक्ष्य

Tariff 1. टैरिफ 2. दर सूची **—Board** टैरिफ बोर्ड **—Revision Committee** टैरिफ परिशोधन समिति

Task Force कृतिक-बल **—Commander** कृतिक-बल कमांडर **—work allowance** उजरती भत्ता **—Work Messenger** उजरती संदेशवाहक

Taungya Teacher टौंगिया शिक्षक

Tax कर **—assessment of** कर-निर्धारण **—Assessor** कर-निर्धारक **—Callings** आजीविका-कर **—Capitition** प्रति व्यक्ति कर **—Collector** कर-समाहर्ता/कर-कलक्टर. **—, export** निर्यात-कर **—evasion** कर-वंचन, कर छिपाना **—free** करमुक्त **—, income** आय-कर **—payer** करदाता **—, sales** विक्रय-कर **—terminal** सीमा-कर

Taxable कर-योग्य **—income** कर-योग्य आय/आमदनी **Taxation** कर लगाना/कराधान/करारोपण **—Inspector** कराधान-निरीक्षक **—inter-state** अन्तर्राज्य कराधान **—Officer** कराधान-अधिकारी

Teacher शिक्षक/अध्यापक

Technical तकनीकी / प्राविधिक/

शिल्पक **advice/qualification** तकनीकी सलाह / योग्यता **—Adviser** तकनीकी सलाहकार **—Assistant** तकनीकी सहायक **—, Electrical Department** तकनीकी सहायक, बिजली विधान **—, Workshop** तकनीकी सहायक, कर्मशाला **— data** तकनीकी आधार-सामग्री **—Development Section** तकनीकी विकास अनुभाग **Education Division** तकनीकी शिक्षा प्रभाग **— error** प्राविधिक भूल **Examiner** तकनीकी परीक्षक **expression** पारिभाषिक पदावली **—Group Instructor** तकनीकी वर्ग शिक्षक **—Inspector** तकनीकी निरीक्षक **— officer** तकनीकी अधिकारी **—Organiser** तकनीकी आयोजक **—qualification** तकनीकी योग्यता **—terminology** पारिभाषिक शब्दावली **— training** तकनीकी प्रशिक्षण **Technician** तकनीकविद्/प्रविधिज्ञ/ तकनीशियन **Technique** तकनीक **—, modern** आधुनिक तकनीक **Technologist** शिल्पविज्ञानी **Technology** 1. प्रौद्योगिकी 2. उद्योग-विद्या

Telecommunication Engineer दूर-संचार अभियंता/दूर-संचार इंजीनियर **—Inspector** दूरसंचार निरीक्षक **—Mechanic** दूरसंचार मेकैनिक

Telegram तार **— code** कोड तार **—, Cypher** बीज-लेख तार **—, Enclair** शब्दबद्ध तार **√en clair** शब्द बद्ध तार

Telegraph Inspector तार निरीक्षक **(Maintenance)** तार निरीक्षक (अनुरक्षण) **—Master** तार मास्टर **—Mechanic** तार मेकेनिक **—Overseer** तार ओवरसियर **—Signaller** तार सिगनलर/ तार बाबू **—Superintendent** तार अधीक्षक **Telegraphic address** तार का पता, तार-पता **Telegraphist** तार संकेतक **—Instructor** तार संकेतक शिक्षक

Telephone Attendant टेलीफोन परिचर **—call** टेलीफोन कॉल **—Clerk** टेलीफोन क्लर्क **— exchange** टेलीफोन केन्द्र **—Mechanic** टेलीफोन मेकैनिक **—Monitor** टेलीफोन मॉनीटर/ टेलीफोन अनश्रोता **— Operator** टेलीफोन प्रचालक **Telephonist and Radio Telephone Operator** टेलीफोन और रेडियो टेलीफोन प्रचालक/टेलीफोन और रेडियो टेलीफोन ऑपरेटर

Teleprinter message दूरमुद्रक संदेश, टेलीप्रिंटर संदेश **—Operator** दूरमुद्रक-प्रचालक/

टेलीप्रिंटर ऑपरेटर —**Supervisor** दूरमुद्रक-पर्यवेक्षक/टेलीप्रिंटर-पर्यवेक्षक **Teletypewriter Operator** दूर-टंकणयंत्र प्रचालक/टेलीटाइपराइटर ऑपरेटर

Temperately worded संयत शब्दों में

Template and ferro Incharge टैमलेट और फेरो प्रभारी/आकार-पट्ट लोह प्रभारी

Temporal 1. कालिक 2. ऐहिक (विधि)

Temporary अस्थायी **Temporarily settled areas** अस्थायी रूप से बसे हुए क्षेत्र —**appointment** अस्थायी नियुक्ति —**purely** बिल्कुल अस्थायी —**Service** अस्थायी सेवा; कच्ची नौकरी

Tendency, general सामान्य प्रवृत्ति/रवैया

Tender (n.) 1. टेंडर/निविदा **(vb.)** 2. टेंडर देना 3. देना/प्रस्यावित करना **(adj.)** —**box** टेंडर पेटी/निविदा पेटी **Clerk** निविदा लिपिक/टेंडर क्लर्क —**fee** टेंडर-फीस; निविदा शुल्क —**money** टेंडर की रकम —**notice** टेंडर-नोटिस/निविदा-सूचना —**samples** टेंडर के नमूने **Tendered resignation** इस्तीफा/त्याग-पत्र दिया —**rates** निविदा/टेंडर भाव/दर **Tenderer** टेंडरदाता

Tensile test तनाव-परीक्षण

Tenet (कार्मिक) सिद्धान्त/नियम **Tentative** अस्थायी/परीक्षात्मक —**scheme** अस्थायी/परीक्षात्मक योजना

Tenure 1. अवधि/कार्यालय 2. पट्टा/भूधृति —**of appointment** नियुक्ति अवधि —**of duty** ड्यूटी कार्यकाल —**of land** पट्टेदारी/भूधृति —**of office** पदावधि, कार्यकाल —**post** सावधिक पद —**of work** ठेका-अवधि —**post** सावधिक पद

Term 1. अवधि/मियाद/शर्त/निबंधन 2. शब्द —**of office** पदावधि **short** अल्पकाल, अल्पकालिक —**technical** पारिभाषिक/तकनीकी शब्द

Term of office पदावधि —**of reference** विचारार्थ विषय —, **short** अल्पकाल, अल्पकालिक —, **technical** पारिभाषिक/तकनीकी शब्द **Terms and conditions** शर्तें —**of delivery** परिदान की शर्तें, (माल) देने की शर्तें

Terminable समापनीय/समाप्य

Terminable at one month's notice एक महीने के नोटिस पर समापनीय —**lease** समापनीय पट्टा

Terminal advantages पर्यंत-लाभ **Terminal (reports etc.)** आवधिक **—charges** चुंगी **—leave** छुट्टी **—tax** सीमा कर **—tax Inspector** सीमाकर-निरीक्षक/चुंगी-निरीक्षक **—Toll Tax Inspector** सीमांत पथ-कर निरीक्षक

Termination (of services) समाप्ति **—notice** समाप्ति सूचना/नोटिस **—of post** पदावसान, पद की समाप्ति

Territorial Army प्रादेशिक सेना **—integrity** प्रादेशिक अखंडता **Jurisdiction** प्रादेशिक क्षेत्राधिकार **—waters** क्षेत्रिक सागर, भूभागी जल, समुद्री सीमा **Territory, neighbouring** पड़ौसी राज्य क्षेत्र

Test परीक्षण/परख/जांच **—certificate** परीक्षण प्रमाणपत्र **—charge** परीक्षण-खर्च **—check** जांच परीक्षण **—Checker** परीक्षण पड़तालकर्ता **—Clerk** परीक्षण क्लर्क **—house** परीक्षणालय **—, personality** व्यक्तित्व परीक्षण **—report** जांच रिपोर्ट **Tester** परीक्षक

Testamentary वसीयती **—succession** वसीयती उत्तराधिकार

Testing officer परीक्षण अधिकारी **—Telegraphist** परीक्षण-तार संकेतक

Testimonial शंसा-पत्र **Testimonials, copies of** शंसा-पत्रों की नकल

Text (of a letter) कलेवर/मजमून **—book** पाठ्य पुस्तक **—Book Committee** पाठ्य-पुस्तक-समिति **—of the correspondence** पत्र-व्यवहार का मूलपाठ/मजमून

Textile Commissioner वस्त्र-आयुक्त **—Enquiry Committee** कपड़ा-जांच-समिति

That is (i.e) अर्थात् **—to say** अर्थात्

Then and there वहीं का वहीं, तत्काल **—existing** उस समय विद्यमान/वर्तमान

Theoretical problem सैद्धान्तिक समस्या **Theory and practice of** के सिद्धान्त और व्यवहार

Therapeutist चिकित्सा-विज्ञानी

Thereabout वहीं कहीं, लगभग, आसपास **—after** तदनन्तर **—, mentioned** उसमें उल्लिखित **—, in respect** उसके सम्बन्ध में **—to fore** उसके पूर्व, तत्पूर्व **—upon** ऐसा होने पर, तिस पर **—with** उसके साथ, तत्सह

Think fit, as he may जैसा वह उपयुक्त समझे **Thinking,**

constructive रचनात्मक चिंतन

Third party तृतीय पक्ष, अन्य पक्ष

This case relates to यह मामला से सम्बन्ध रखता है —**is to certify** यह प्रमाणित किया जाता है —**is to inform that** सूचना दी जाती है कि —**office has no information** इस कार्यालय को कोई सूचना नहीं है

Thoroughfare, No सार्वजनिक/आम रास्ता नहीं है **Thorughly satisfied** पूर्णतया संतुष्ट **Through journey** धुर/सीधी यात्रा —**out** सर्वत्र, सब ओर, साद्यन्त —**over-sight** नजर चूक जाने से, भूल से —**proper channel** उचित माध्यम से, उचित सरणि द्वारा, विधिवत्

Thought, after giving serious गम्भीरता से विचार करने के पश्चात्

Threatened by floods बाढ़ से पैदा हुआ डर/खतरा **Threats, repeated** बार-बार की धमकियां

Throw light upon पर प्रकाश डालना बताना, समझाना —**open** खोलना

Thumb impression अंगूठा-निशानी

Tiket Collector टिकट संग्राहक/टिकट-कलक्टर —**Counter** टिकट गणक —**Cutting Machine Operator** टिकट कर्तनित्र प्रचालक —**Inspector** टिकट निरीक्षक —**, monthly** मासिक टिकट —**Printer** टिकट मुद्रक

Till further orders अगले/अन्य आदेश होने तक

Timber Examiner इमारती लकड़ी-परीक्षक

Time barred कालातीत —**Keeper** समयपाल/टाइम कीपर —**limit** कालावधि —**Office** समय कार्यालय/दफ्तर —**schedule** समय अनुसूची —**scale** समय-मान, काल-मान —**stamp** समय-मोहर —**table** समय-सारणी —**Clerk** समय-सारणी-लिपिक **Timed programme** नियत कालिक कार्यक्रम **Timely action** समय पर कार्रवाई —**compliance** समय के अन्दर पूर्ति, समय से पूरा करना

Tin and Copper Smith टीन-ताम्रकार **Tinsmith** टीनकार **Tindal** टिंडल

Title 1. शीर्षक 2. खिताब/पदवी 3. हक **by purchase** क्रय से प्राप्त हक —**of a book** पुस्तक का नाम —**of an act** अधिनियम का शीर्षक —**of honour** मानोपाधि, खिताब —**of goods** वस्तुओं/माल पर हक —**page**

मुख-पृष्ट

To : Shri··· सेवा में : श्री··· **—let** किराये पर देना है, किराये के लिए खाली है **—the best of ability** पूरी योग्यता से **—the best of my knowledge** जहां तक मुझे पता है **—the contrary** इसके विपरीत/प्रतिकूल **—the exclusion of** को छोड़कर/निकाल कर **—the extent of** की मात्रा/सीमा तक **—the following effect** नीचे दिए अभिप्राय का, निम्नलिखित अभिप्राय का **—the point** विषयानुकूल, सुसंगत, प्रासंगिक

Together with के साथ

Token 1. सांकेतिक 2. टोकन **Token, bank** बैंक टोकन **—cut/grant** सांकेतिक कटौती/अनुदान

Toll collector पथ-कर संग्राहक, चुंगी/महसूल लेने वाला **—house** टोल-घर

Tool Checker औजार पड़ताल-कर्त्ता **—Fitter** औजार-फिटर **—Keeper** औजार रक्षक **—Maker** औजार बनाने वाला **Tool room** औजार कक्ष

Top priority परम अग्रता/परम पूर्णता **—secret** परम गुप्त

Topass टोपस

Topic प्रकरण/विषय/प्रसंग

Topman टॉपमैन

Total brought forward अग्रेनीत/आगे लाया गया जोड़ **—destruction** पूर्ण विनाश, पूरी बरबादी **income** कुल आय **—Service** कुल सेवा

Tour दौरा **—diary** दौरा-डायरी **programme** दौरा कार्यक्रम **Publicity Officer** पर्यटन-प्रचार-अधिकारी **—Report** दौरा-रिपोर्ट **Tourism** पर्यटन **Tourist, foreign** विदेशी पर्यटक **—Guide** पर्यटक परिदर्शक **—Officer** पर्यटन-अधिकारी **Town (city)** नगर/शहर **—and Village Planner** नगर और ग्राम-योजनाकार **—Planner** नगर-योजनाकार **—area** नगर क्षेत्र

Toxicologist विष-विज्ञानी

Trace out the previous papers and put up पहले के कागजों का पता लगाइए और प्रस्तुत कीजिए **Traceable, the file is not readily** मिसिल तत्काल नहीं मिल रही है **Tracer** अनुरेखक/खोजकर्त्ता

Track Supply Depot Superintendent रेलपथ पूर्ति डिपो अधीक्षक **—Officer** रेलपथ पूर्ति अधिकारी/पथ पूर्ति अधिकारी

Traction Inspector(Sub station) कर्षण निरीक्षक (उप स्टेशन)

—**Power and Traction Controller** कर्षणशक्ति तथा कर्षण नियंत्रक —**Power Controller** कर्षण शक्ति नियंत्रक —**Superintendent** कर्षण अधीक्षक —**Train Examiner** कर्षण ग.ड़ी परीक्षक

Tractor Driver ट्रैक्टर-चालक/ट्रैक्टर ड्राइवर

Trade Agency व्यापार-अभिकरण/व्यापार-एजेंसी —**Agent** व्यापार-अभिकर्ता/व्यापार-एजेंट —**book** व्यापार-पंजी —**Commissioner** व्यापार आयुक्त; व्यापार कमिश्नर —**group** व्यापार-ग्रुप/व्यापार-वर्ग —**mark** ट्रेड मार्क/व्यापार चिह्न —**mark of, with the** छाप/मार्का सहित —**union** श्रमिक संघ, ट्रेड यूनियन **Tradesman** दस्तकार/कारीगर

Traditional practice पारम्परिक/परम्परागत व्यवहार/रिवाज

Traffic यातायात —**Accounts Officer** यातायात लेखा अधिकारी **Inspector** यातायात निरीक्षक; परियात निरीक्षक —**Manager** यातायात-प्रबंधक —**Police** —**rules** यातायात-पुलिस – **rules** यातायात नियम —**Signaller** यातायात सिगनलर/यातायात तार बाबू

Trailel Pump Driver अनुयान पम्प ड्राइवर/अनुयान पम्प चालक —**Operator** अनुयान पम्प प्रचालक

Train Clerk गाड़ी क्लर्क —**Controller** गाड़ी नियंत्रक —**Despatcher** गाड़ी प्रेषक —**Engine Examiner** गाड़ी इंजन परीक्षक —**Examiner** गाड़ी परीक्षक —**Indicator Recorder** गाड़ी संकेतक अभिलेखक —**Inspector** गाड़ी निरीक्षक —**Lighting Inspector** गाड़ी प्रकाशक निरीक्षक —**Recorder** गाड़ी अभिलेखक —**Starter** गाड़ी प्रवर्तक **Train, through** सीधी गाड़ी

Trainer प्रशिक्षक **Training** प्रशिक्षण/ट्रेनिंग —**Commander** प्रशिक्षण-कमांडर —**Division** प्रशिक्षण प्रभाग —**Officer** प्रशिक्षण-अधिकारी —**period** प्रशिक्षण काल —**within Industry Centre** उद्योगांतर्गत प्रशिक्षण केन्द्र/अंत: उद्योग प्रशिक्षण केन्द्र

Tranquility प्रशान्ति

Transact business, to कार्य-संपादन, कार्य करना **Tranaction** संचालन —**of bnsiness** 1. कार्य करना 2. कारोबार का संचालन

Transcriber लिप्यंतरकार/प्रतिलेखक

Transcription प्रतिलेखन/नकल/लिप्यंतरण

Transfer (n.) बदली/अंतरण/स्थानांतरण/हस्तांतरण **(vb.)** बदली होना/बदली करना/अंतरित करना/अंतरण करना **—allowance** बदली भत्ता **— entry** अंतरण प्रविष्टि **— memorandum** स्थानांतरण आदेश **— order** स्थानांतरण/बदली आदेश, तबादले का आदेश **—of property** सम्पत्ति का हस्तांतरण/अंतरण

Trans-frontier trade सीमापार व्यापार

Tranship Clerk यानांतरण क्लर्क **— ment** यानांतरण **— Clerk** यानांतरण क्लर्क/यानांतरण लिपिक **—Inspector** यानांतरण निरीक्षक

Transit 1. संक्रमण 2 अभिवहन **— Clerk** पारवहन क्लर्क/पारबहन लिपिक **—duty** संक्रमण शुल्क **—, goods in** मार्गस्थ माल, माल मार्ग में, माल रास्ते में **—office** पारगमन कार्यालय **—pass** पारगमन पास **Transit depot** पारगम डिपो

Transition samples संक्रम-नमूना **Transitional** संक्रमणकालीन **—period** संक्रमण काल, संक्रमण-कालीन अवधि

Translation अनुवाद **— Section** अनुवाद अनुभाग **Translator** अनुवादक

Transliteration लिप्यंतरण

Transliterated into Devanagari देवनागरी में लिप्यंतरण किया

Transmission Officer प्रसार-अधिकारी

Transhipment, process of यानान्तरण की प्रक्रिया

Transmitting Station प्रसारण-केन्द्र

Transport परिवहन **— and Petroleum Division** परिवहन और पेट्रोलियम प्रभाग **—charges** परिवहन प्रभार, ढुलाई खर्च **— Commissioner** परिवहन आयुक्त/परिवहन कमिश्नर **—Inspector** परिवहन निरीक्षक **—pass** पारगमन पास **—Service** परिवहन व्यवस्था **Supervisor** परिवहन पर्यवेक्षक **Transportation Apprentice** परिवहन शिशु **—for life** आजीवन निर्वासन **— Inspector (Transport Inspector)** परिवहन निरीक्षक **— Officer** परिवहन अधिकारी **Superintendent (Safety)** परिवहन अधीक्षक (संरक्षा)

Transposition उलटना

Travelling allowance यात्रा भत्ता **—bill** यात्रा भत्ता बिल

—**concession** यात्रा सम्बन्धी रियायत **Parcel Clerk** चलपार्सल क्लर्क/चल पार्सल लिपिक

Tray ट्रे

Treasure Sircar कोष सरकार —**trove** निखात निधि **Treasurer** कोषपाल **Treasury** कोष/खजाना —**benches** मंत्री-कक्ष —**Deposit Receipt (T. D. R)** खजाना जमा रसीद —**Officer** कोषाधिकारी/खजाना अधिकारी —**receipt** खजाना रसीद

Treatment of a subject विषय का प्रतिपादन —**of disease** रोग का उपचार/चिकित्सा/इलाज

Treaty obligation संधि-बंधन

Trend, general आम/सामान्य रुख

Trial जांच/परख —**Driver** परीक्षण चालक —**Engine Driver** परीक्षण इंजन चालक/परीक्षण इंजन ड्राइवर —**period** परख काल, परीक्षण अवधि

Tribal area आदिवासी क्षेत्र —**Welfare** आदिवासी कल्याण

Tribunal अधिकरण —, **labour** श्रम अधिकरण

Triennial त्रैवार्षिक **Triennial report** त्रैवार्षिक रिपोर्ट

Trifling amendment तुच्छ संशोधन

Tripartite agreement त्रिपक्षीय/त्रिदलीय करार

Triplicate (adj.) तिहरा/तीसरी प्रति **(n.)** तृतीयक —**of a bill** बिल की तृतीयक, बिल की तीसरी प्रति

Trolly Driver ट्रॉली ड्राइवर —**man** ट्राली वाला

Troubled, need not be को कष्ट देने की आवश्यकता नहीं

Truce अवहार/युद्ध विराम संधि

True accounts सच्चा लेखा —**copy** पक्की नकल/सही प्रतिलिपि —**statement** सत्यकथन —**value** ठीक मूल्य, सही मूल्य

Truly, yours आपका

Trust 1. न्यास/ट्रस्ट 2. विश्वास —, **I** मुझे विश्वास है —**money** न्यास-धन —**property** न्यास-सम्पत्ति —**worthy hand** विश्वसनीय व्यक्ति **Trustees, Board of** न्यासी-मण्डल

Tube-well नल-कूप —**Operator** नलकूप प्रचालक

Tuition fee शिक्षा शुल्क

Turbine Operator टरबाइन ऑपरेटर

Turner खरादी/टर्नर —**welders** खरादी वेल्डर; खरादी झलाईगर

Turning point मोड़, परिवर्तन

Tuteloge संरक्षण

Two-fold action दुहरी कार्रवाई

Type **(n.)** टाइप/छापा/मुद्रलेख **(vb.)** टंकित करना/टाइप करना **—, Redistribution of** टाइप पुर्नवितरण **—script** टाइप प्रति **—subject** टाइप-विषय (वर्ग) **Typed note** टाइप किया नोट, टंकित नोट **Types, of various** विभिन्न वर्गों/टाइप/प्रकार का **Typewriter** टाइपराइटर **—Hindi** हिन्दी टाइपराइटर **Typewriting** टाइपकारी/टाइप करना/टंकण **Typing** टाइपिंग **Typist** टंकक/टाइपिस्ट/टाइपकार **Typographical error** मुद्रण/छपाई/टाइप की भूल

Uberous उर्वर; फलदार

Uberrima fides परम सद्भाव; चरम विश्वास

Ulterior परतर **—motive** अंतरस्थ हेतु

Ultimate अंतिम/चरम **—analysis** अन्तिम विश्लेषण **—consignee** अंतिम माल पाने वाला/अंतिम परेषिती **—cost** अंतिम लागत **—destination** अन्तिम गन्तव्य स्थान/स्थल **—goal** अंतिम लक्ष्य **—objective** अंतिम उद्देश्य **Ultimately this has to be done** अन्ततः यह करना ही होगा

Ultimatum अंतिमेत्थम; अंतिम प्रस्ताव; अंतिम चेतावनी

Ultimo गतमास का **—fifth** गत मास की पांच तारीख

Ultra vires शक्ति बाह्य, अधिकार के बाहर

Umpire निर्णेता/अम्पायर/मंच/अधिनिर्णायक

Unacceptable to me मुझे अस्वीकार्य

Unaffected, will remain अप्रभावित रहेगा

Unaided असहायता प्राप्त

Unalterable decision अपरिवर्त्य निर्णय, न बदला जाने वाला फैसला

Unanimity एकमत/ऐकमत्य/मतैक्य/सर्वसम्मति **—, absolute** पूर्ण एकमत **—qualified** सीमित एकमत

Unanimous एकमत/सर्वसम्मत **—decision** एकमत/सर्वसम्मत निर्णय **Unattested** अनुप्रमाणित **Unauthorised** अनधिकृत/अप्राधिकृत **—action** अप्राधिकृत कार्रवाई अनधिकृत कार्य

Unavoidable अनिवार्य/अपरिहार्य **—circumstances** अपरिहार्य परिस्थितियां

Unbalanced views असन्तुलित विचार

Unbias निष्पक्ष करना **—opinion** निष्पक्ष राय, पक्षपात रहित सम्मति

Unbroken chain अटूट श्रृंखला

Uncalled for अनाहूत, अयाचित, अनुचित

Uncashed बिना भुनाया **—cheque** बिना भुनाया चैक

Unceasing efforts अविरामी प्रयत्न

Uncertainty, state of अनिश्चितता की अवस्था

Unclaimed baggage अ-दावी/लावारसी सामान

Unclassified posts अवर्गीकृत पद

Unconditional बिना शर्त/उपबंध रहित **—undertaking** बिना शर्त वचन

Unconfirmed अपुष्ट **—report** अपुष्ट समाचार/रिपोर्ट

Unconscious state चेतना-शून्य/अचेतन अवस्था, मूर्छा, बेहोशी

Unconstitutional असांविधानिक

Uncontested निर्विरोध/अविरोध **—election** निर्विरोध चुनाव

Unco-operative attitude असहयोगी रवैया

Uncovered demand अपूरित मांग

Undated cheque अदिनांक चैक, बेतारीख चैक

Undeliverable article अपरिदेय/वस्तु, न बट सकने वाली वस्तु

Under 1. अधीन/अवर, 2. कम/न्यून **—age** कम उम्र, अल्प वय **—bid** कम बोली बोलना/लगाना **—certificate of posting** डाक प्रमाणित **—charge** न्यूनप्रभार, कम शुल्क/किराया/दाम लेना **—consideration** विचाराधीन **—developed countries** अल्पविकसित देश **—estimate** अवप्राक्कलन, कम कूतना, कम अनुमान **—fire, the bill was** विधेयक की कड़ी आलोचना की गई **—go a change** परिवर्तन होना **—go a sentence of imprisonment** कारादंड भोगना, कैद की सजा भुगतना **—ground Inspector** अंतर्भोम-निरीक्षक **— ground railway** भूमिगत रेल **—hand** गुप्त; प्रच्छन्न **—his hand and seal** अपने हस्ताक्षर और मुद्रा सहित **—influence** प्रभाव में; प्रभावान्वित **—intimation to this office** इस कार्यालय को सूचना देते हुए **—lying idea** अन्तर्हित विचार **—mentioned** निम्नलिखित **—mine the administration** प्रशासन को दुर्बल करना **—my authority** मेरे प्राधिकार से **—my hand** मेरे हस्ताक्षर सहित **—one's hand**

अपने हस्ताक्षर सहित —**orders of transfer** बदली के आदेश हो चुके —**production** न्यून/कम उत्पादन —**protest** सापत्ति, आपत्ति के साथ —**reference** प्रसंगाधीन, प्रसंग गत, चर्चाधीन, निर्देशाधीन —**review** समीक्षाधीन —**Secretary** अवर सचिव/अनुसचिव —**standing** 1. समझौता/समझ 2. समझदारी 3. बोध/प्रतिपत्ति —**take** 1. लेना 2. वचन/देना/वचनबद्ध होना —**taking** 1. उपक्रम 2. वचन / वचनबंध/जिम्मा लेना/भार अपने ऊपर लेना —**taking given** दिया वचन —**taking, industrial** औद्योगिक उपक्रम —**valuation** अल्पमूल्यांकन —**valuation of property** सम्पत्ति का अल्प-मूल्यांकन

Undesirable अवांछनीय —**action** अवांछनीय कार्य/कार्रवाई

Undetcrmined value अनिर्धारित मूल्य

Undignified अशोभन / अभद्र / मर्यादाहीन —**behaviour** अभद्र व्यवहार **Undischarged** अनुमुक्त

Undivided अविभाजित/अविभक्त —**family** अविभाजित/अविभक्त/सम्मिलित कुटुम्ब

Undue अनुचित/असम्यक् —**delay** अनावश्यक देरी —**influence** अनुचित प्रभाव

Uneconomic cultivation अलाभकर कृषि, घाटे की खेती

Unemployment बेकारी/बेरोजगारी —**problem** बेकारी/बेरोजगारी की समस्या

Unencumbered estate अ-भारग्रस्त सम्पदा

Unexpected delay अप्रत्याशित विलंब

Unexpired असमाप्त/अनवसित

Unfavourable प्रतिकूल/अनुकूल —**balance** प्रतिकूल संतुलन

Unfit for human consumption मानव उपभोग के अयोग्य

Unforeseen अदृष्ट/अनवेक्षित —**charges** अदृष्ट प्रभार —**circumstances** अनपेक्ष/अप्रत्याशित परिस्थिति

Unfunded debt अ-निधिबद्ध ऋण

Ungentlemanly behaviour अभद्र आचरण/बर्ताव

Unhampered action अबाधित कार्रवाई

Unicameral एकसदनी —**legislature** एकसदन विधान मण्डल/एकसदनी विधान मण्डल

Unified scale एकीकृत/एक वेतनमान —**Scale of pay** एकीकृत वेतनमान

Uniform 1. एकरूप 2. वर्दी

Uniformity एकरूपता **—in procedure** प्रक्रिया में एकरूपता

Unifying factor एकता का साधक

Unilateral एकपक्षीय **—action** एकपक्षीय/इकतरफा कार्रवाई

Uninterrupted use निर्विघ्न/अबाध उपभोग

Union संघ **—list** संघीय सूची **—of India** भारत का संघ **—Praliament** संसद **—Public Service Commission** संघ लोक सेवा आयोग **—Territories** संघ-राज्य क्षेत्र

Unit 1. एकक 2. मात्रक 3. इकाई/यूनिट **—, Hindi** हिन्दी एकक

United Nations Technical Assistance Board संयुक्त राष्ट्र सहायता बोर्ड **—Nations Organistion** संयुक्त राष्ट्र संघ

Unity एक; एकता

Universal demand विश्वव्यापी/सर्वव्यापी मांग

University Court विश्वविद्यालय कोर्ट **—degree** विश्वविद्यालय की डिग्री **—Grants Commission** विश्वविद्यालय - अनुदान-आयोग

Unlawful purpose अवैध प्रयोजन

Unless the context otherwise requires जब तक प्रसंग से दूसरी बात अपेक्षित न हो **—there be something repugnant in the subject or context** जब तक विषय या प्रसंग में कोई बात प्रतिकूल न हो

Unline विजातीय; प्रतिकूल; विषम

Unlimited number असंख्य **—power** असीम शक्ति/अधिकार

Unnatural death अस्वाभाविक मृत्यु

Unofficial अशासनिक/अशासकीय/अनौपचारिक / गैर - सरकारी **—letter** अशासकीय/गैर-सरकारी पत्र **—note** अशासनिक नोट

Unparliamentary असंसदीय **—word** असंसदीय शब्द

Unproductive labour अनुत्पादी श्रम

Unprotected land अरक्षित भूमि

Unqualified 1. अप्रतिबद्ध 2. अयोग्य **—apology** बिना शर्त क्षमा-याचना

Unquestionable right प्रश्नातीत/पूर्ण अधिकार

Unrealisable sum अप्राप्य/डूबी राशि

Unregistered article अ-रजिस्ट्रीकृत वस्तु **—company** अ-पंजीकृत/अरजिस्ट्रीकृत कम्पनी **—firm** अपंजीकृत फर्म/अरजिस्टरित फर्म

Unrestricted interpretation अनियन्त्रित निर्वचन

Unserviceable article बेकार वस्तु

Unskilled labour अकुशल/अदक्ष श्रमिक, सामान्य मजदूर

Unsoundness of mind चित्त विकृति

Unstable administration अस्थिर प्रशासन

Unstarred अतारांकित

Unsuited to our requirement हमारी आवश्यकता के अनुकूल नहीं

Untenable (Argument) असमर्थ-नीय/अपुष्ट

Until further order दूसरा आदेश मिलने तक/अगले आदेश तक **—otherwise provided for** जब तक अन्य उपबन्ध या व्यवस्था न हो **—the contrary is shown** जब तक इसके विपरीत सिद्ध न किया जाए

Unusual matter असामान्य मामला

Unwieldy दुर्वह

Unwritten agreement अलिखित करार

Upgrade ग्रेड बढ़ाना/कोटि उच्च करना **Upgrading** उन्नयन **—of posts** पदों की क्रमोन्नति, पदों का ग्रेड बढ़ाना, पदों को उच्चकोटि के करना, पदोन्नयन

Uphold 1. पुष्ट करना 2. मर्यादा बनाए रखना **—the dignity of** की मर्यादा बनाए रखना **—the lower authority's decision** नीचे के प्राधिकारी के निर्णय की पुष्टि करना

Upholsterer पोशिशसाज

Upkeep of building इमारत की देखभाल

Upper age limit ऊपरी आयु सीमा/ऊपरी उम्र सीमा **—division clerk** उच्च श्रेणी लिपिक **—subordinate service** उच्च अवर सेवा; उच्चतर मातहत श्रेणी

Upto and including तक तथा समेत/सहित **—to-date** आज तक का, अद्यतन, नवीनतम, ताजा

Upward limit ऊपरी सीमा

Urban नगरीय/शहरी **—areas** नगर क्षेत्र, शहरी इलाके

Urdu Munshi उर्दू मुंशी

Urgent अविलम्ब / अर्जेंट **—application** अतिआवश्यक आवेदन; अर्जेण्ट आवेदन **—call** तुरत कॉल, अर्जेन्ट कॉल **—, most** अति, तुरंत/आवश्यक **—slip** 'तुरंत' पर्ची/'अति आवश्यक' पर्ची

Urgently required अविलम्ब अपेक्षित, तुरन्त चाहिए

Usage, according to रूढ़ि/अभ्यास/प्रयोग के अनुसार

Useful hint काम की बातें, लाभ-कारी संकेत

Use of force बल प्रयोग

Usual सामान्य/प्रायिक **– action**

सामान्य/प्रायिक कार्रवाई **Usually this is done** प्रायः यह किया जाता है

Utilise उपयोग होना; उपयोग करना **Utilisation of funds** निधि का उपयोग

Utmost care अधिकतम/अत्यन्त सावधानी **—endeavour, shall use his** अपना अधिकतम प्रयास करेगा **—exertion** भरसक प्रयास

Utter ignorance घोर अज्ञान **Utteror of coin** सिक्का चलाने-वाला

Vacancy रिक्त/रिक्तता **Vacancies** रिक्तियां **—, filling up of** रिक्तियों का भरना, खाली जगहों का **—, leave** छुट्टी-रिक्ति **—in office** पद खाली होना; पद में रिक्ति **Vacant (Post)** रिक्त (पद)

Vacate खाली करना **Vacated, house has been** मकान खाली कर दिया गया है **Vacation** अवकाश/विश्रामावकाश **—department** अवकाश विभाग **—In-charge** अवकाश-प्रभारी **—of office** पदरिक्ति **—of Seats** स्थानों का रिक्त होना **—pay** अवकाश वेतन

Vaccination टीका **Vaccinator** टीका लगाने वाला

Vagrancy आहिंडन; आवारागर्दी

Vague अस्पष्ट/अनिश्चित **—idea** अस्पष्ट विचार

Valedictory address विदाई भाषण

Valid विधिमान्य **—, action taken is** की गई कार्रवाई विधि-मान्य है **—argument** मान्य दलील **—votes polled** प्राप्त विधिमान्य मत **Validation of papers** प्रलेखों का वैधीकरण **Validity** विधिमान्यता **—date** मान्यता तिथि/तारीख **—of an act** अधिनियम की विधि मान्यता

Valuation, periodical आवधिक मूल्यन **—Officer** मूल्यांकन-अधिकारी **—statement** मूल्यांकन विवरण

Value, above par अधिमूल्य **—, below par** अवमूल्य

Van Loading Inspector यान लदान निरीक्षक

Variation विभिन्नता/परिवर्तन **—in figures** अंकों में विभिन्नता

Various posts विभिन्न पद

Vegetable Oil Products Controller नियंत्रक, वनस्पति-तेल-उत्पादन

Vehicle वाहन

Vendor बेचने वाला

Venereologist रतिजरोग-विज्ञानी

Venue स्थान/स्थल **—of meeting** बैठक का स्थान/स्थल

Verbal मौखिक; शाब्दिक **—alteration** शाब्दिक परिवर्तन **—order** मौखिक/जबानी आदेश **—or written promise** मौखिक या लिखित वचन **—statement** मौखिक कथन, जबानी बयान **Verbatim report** शब्दशः रिपोर्ट

Verification सत्यापन **—certificate** जाँच-पत्र **—of accounts** लेखा सत्यापन **—of age** आयु का सत्यापन करना **—of antecedents** पूर्ववृत्त की पड़ताल **—of stores** माल का सत्यापन **—Officer** सत्यापन-अधिकारी **—sheet** सत्यापन पत्र **Verified and found correct** पड़ताल की और ठीक पाया **—copy** सत्यापित प्रति **Verify** सत्यापन करना; जांचना **—the accuracy** शुद्धता को सत्यापित करना **Verifying Machine Operator** सत्यापित मशीन प्रचालक

Version 1. अनुवाद 2. रूप/पाठ 3. कथन **—, English** अंग्रेजी अनुवाद **—, Hindi** हिन्दी अनुवाद **—, original** मूल पाठ **—, other side's** दूसरे पक्ष का कथन

Versus, State सरकार बनाम···

Vessel जलयान/पोत

Vested interest निहित स्वार्थ

Veterinary पशु-चिकित्सा **—Doctor** पशु-चिकित्सक **—hospital** पशु चिकित्सालय **—Inspector** पशुनिरीक्षक **—Practitioner** पशु चिकित्सक; सलोत्तरी **—Surgeon** पशु चिकित्सक; सलोत्तरी

Veto वीटो/निषेधाधिकार **—power** विषेधाधिकार

Via media मध्यम मार्ग, बीच का रास्ता

Vice उप **—Chairman** उप-सभापति, उपाध्यक्ष **—Chancellor** उप-कुलपति **—President** 1. उपराष्ट्रपति 2. उपाध्यक्ष/उप सभापति **—President of India** भारत का उपराष्ट्रपति **vice versa** प्रतिलोमतः, विपरीत क्रम से, इसका उल्टा

Vicious circle दुष्चक्र

Vide letter number... पत्र संख्या ···देखिए

View of, in को देखते हुए, की दृष्टि से **—, point of** दृष्टिकोण **—to, with a** की दृष्टि से

Vigilance सतर्कता/चौकसी **—Inspector** सतर्कता निरीक्षक **—Officer** सतर्कता अधिकारी **—Section** सतर्कता अनुभाग/चौकसी अनुभाग **Vigilant**

control सतर्क नियन्त्रण

Village area देहाती क्षेत्र, गांव का क्षेत्र **—council** ग्राम-परिषद् **—defence society** ग्राम रक्षा समिति **—headman** मुखिया; लम्बरदार **—Level Worker** ग्राम-सेवक **—Postman** देहाती डाकिया **—records** ग्राम अभिलेख

Visible representation दृश्य निरूपण

Violation अतिक्रमण/उल्लंघन **—of frontiers** सीमा का अतिक्रमण **—of law** कानून का उल्लंघन

Virologist वायरस-विज्ञानी

Virtue of, by के आधार पर, के कारण

Virus Entomologist वाइरस कीट-विज्ञानी

Visa वीजा/प्रवेश पत्र **vis-a-vis** के सामने/—की तुलना में/बनाम

Visible card index प्रकट कार्ड बाक्स

Visit (n.) 1. आगमन 2. वीक्षण/निरीक्षण 3. भेंट/मुलाकात **(vb)** 1. आना-जाना 2. निरीक्षण करना 3. भेंट करना/मुलाकात करना **—, Director's** निदेशक का आगमन, **—, periodical** आवधिक निरीक्षण आना-जाना **—remark** मुआइना कैफियत

Visiting Artist अतिथि कलाकार **—hours** मिलने/मुलाकात का समय **—party** निरीक्षण दल **—professor** अतिथि प्राध्यापक

Visitor आगंतुक/दर्शक/मुलाकाती **(of a University)** कुलाध्यक्ष

Visitor's book आगंतुक पंजी **—gallery** दर्शक बीथी

Visual Inspection दृष्टिक निरीक्षण **Visualised, it could be** इसकी कल्पना/की जा सकती थी

Vital question मार्मिक/महत्वपूर्ण प्रश्न **—statistics** जीवन-संबंधी आंकड़े / जन्म - मृत्युसांख्यिकी **—Clerk** जन्म-मृत्यु-सांख्यिकी-क्लर्क **—Section** जन्म-मृत्यु सांख्यिकी अनुभाग

Vitiate the proceedings कार्रवाई प्रदूषित/निष्फल करना

Viva-voce मौखिक परीक्षा

Vivid account विशद/सजीव विवरण/वृत्तांत

Vocalist गायक

Vocation व्यवसाय **—Guidance Officer** व्यवसाय-निर्देशन अधिकारी **Vocational training** व्यावसायिक प्रशिक्षण

Void शून्य **—, ab initio** आरम्भत: शून्य **—contract** शून्य/प्रवृत्तिहीन संविदा/ठेका

Volume 1. आयतन 2. मात्रा/

परिमाण 3. जिल्द/खण्ड —of work काम की मात्रा/परिमाण —One of...Rules ···नियमावली की जिल्द एक

Voluntary स्वैच्छिक —**effort** स्वैच्छिक प्रयत्न, अपनी इच्छा से किया प्रयास —**statement** स्वैच्छिक बयान

Votable मतदेय —**expenditure** मतदेय व्यय

Vote (n) मत/वोट **(vb.)** मत देना/वोट देना —**by ballot** गुप्त मतदान; पर्ची-वोट —**casting** निर्णायक मत —**of censure** निन्दा-प्रस्ताव —**of confidence** विश्वास प्रस्ताव —**of credit** प्रत्ययानुदान —**on account** लेखानुदान —**of no-confidence** अविश्वास प्रस्ताव —**, secret** गुप्त मतदान **Voted** दत्तमत **Voter** मतदाता —**list** मतदाताओं की सूची **Votes, counting of** मतगणना **Voting by postal ballot** डाक मतपत्र द्वारा मतदान —**by proxy** परोक्षों द्वारा मतदान —**Paper** मत पत्र —**Power** मतदान शक्ति

Voucher वाउचर —**, receipt** प्राप्ति वाउचर

Voyage समुद्र-यात्रा

V. P. Parcel वी० पी० (मूल्यदेय) पार्सल —**Clerk** वी० पी० (मूल्यदेय) पार्सल क्लर्क

Vulnerable points आक्राम्य स्थान, भेद्य स्थान, दुर्बल स्थल/अंश

Wage मजदूरी/मजूरी —**, fair** उचित मजदूरी/मजूरी —**Inspector** मजदूरी निरीक्षक —**, living** निर्वाह मजदूरी **Wages, time** अमानी

Wagon Chaser माल डिब्बा अनुवीक्षक —**Chasing Inspector** माल डिब्बा अनुवीक्षण निरीक्षक —**Checker** माल डिब्बा पड़तालकर्ता —**Controller** माल डिब्बा नियंत्रक —**Inspector** माल डिब्बा निरीक्षक —**Movement Inspector** माल डिब्बा संचालन निरीक्षक —**Tracer** माल डिब्बा खोजकर्ता/माल अनुरेखक **Wagons, allotment of** माल डिब्बों का आबंटन

Waiting list प्रतीक्षा-सूची

Waive recovery न लेना, वसूली छोड़ देना —**restriction** निबंधन/पाबंदिया हटाना **Waived his rights** अपने अधिकार छोड़ दिए **Waiving** छूट —**of audit objection** लेखा-परीक्षा का एतराज छोड़ देना —**of depart-**

mental charges विभागीय शुल्क का अधित्याग; विभागीय शुल्क की छूट —of ground rent जमीन के किराये की छूट —of lower age limit निचली आयु सीमा की छूट —of recovery वसूली छोड़ देना —of upper age limit ऊपरी आयु सीमा की छूट

Want of confidence विश्वास का अभाव **Wants me, he** वह मुझे बुला रहे हैं

War risk insurance युद्ध जोखिम बीमा —**Service** युद्ध सेवा —**Service benifit** युद्ध सेवा लाभ —**time surplus** युद्ध कालीन अधिशेष

Ward वार्ड —**, female** महिला वार्ड —**Keeper** वार्ड-रक्षक —**Master** वार्ड मास्टर **Warden** वार्डन – **(of student's hostel)** छात्रपाल/वार्डन **Warder** वार्डर

Warehouse गोदाम/भांडागार —**keeper** भंडारी **Warehousing charges** गोदाम प्रभार

Warning चेतावनी

Warrant वारण्ट/अधिपत्र —**of arrest** गिरफ्तारी का वारण्ट/अधिपत्र —**of precedence** पूर्वता अधिपत्र

Washing allowance धुलाई भत्ता

Wastage छीजन/बरबादी —**,avoid** बरबादी बचाइए —**, normal** सामान्य छीजन **Wasteful expenditure** अपचय-कारक व्यय

Waste Land परती-भूमि —**paper basket** रद्दी की टोकरी

Watch and Clock Repairer घड़ीसाज —**and ward** पहरा-निगरानी **Watcher** प्रहरी/चौकीदार **Watchman** प्रहरी/चौकीदार **Watching of delivery** (माल) देने की देख-रेख/परिदान की देख-रेख —**of progress** प्रगति की देख-रेख

Water and Drainage Inspector जल और जल निकासी निरीक्षक —**Carrier** जलवाहक —**rates** जल कर —**Softening Chargeman** जल मृदुकरण कार्यवेक्षक —**Supply and Primary Health Centre** जलपूर्ति और प्राथमिक स्वास्थ्य केन्द्र —**Treatment Supervisor** जल उपचार पर्यवेक्षक —**Works** जलकल विभाग —**man** पानी वाला —**ways Construction Division** जलपथ-निर्माण-प्रभाग

Way bill मार्ग पत्रक/रवन्ना —**of Penalty by** शास्तिस्वरूप —**usual** प्रायिक रीति **Ways and means** अर्थोपाय, उपाय और

साधन —**Committee** अर्थोपाय समिति

We are not concerned with this इसका हमसे सम्बन्ध नहीं है

Wear and tear टूट-फूट

Weaving Master बुनाई मास्टर

Weeding (of records) (अभिलेखों की) छंटाई —**out** छंटाई

Week सप्ताह —**days** हफ्ते के दिन, काम के दिन **Weekly** साप्ताहिक —**arrear statement** बचे हुए कामों का साप्ताहिक विवरण —**holiday** साप्ताहिक छुट्टी —**progress** साप्ताहिक प्रगति —**return** साप्ताहिक अंकपत्र

Weighbridge Clerk तुलाचौकी क्लर्क/तुलाचौकी लिपिक —**Inspector** तुलाचौकी निरीक्षक **Mistry** तुलाचौकी मिस्त्री **Weighing clerk** तुलाई क्लर्क —**Machine Malutainer** तुलाई मशीन अनुरक्षक **Weighman** तोलकार/तुलाईकार **Weighment charges** तोल-खर्च —**inspector** तोल निरीक्षक

Weighted average भारित औसत **Weight, net** निवल भार/वजन **Weights and measures** बाट और माप

Welcome (n.) स्वागत **(vb.)** स्वागत करना **Welcome, address of** अभिनन्दन पत्र

Welcomed, proposal was प्रस्ताव का स्वागत किया गया

Welder वेल्डर

Welfare कल्याण; हित —**adviser** कल्याण सलाहकार —**Commissioner; Mica Mines Welfare Fund** कल्याण आयुक्त, अभ्रक खान कल्याण-निधि —**Inspector** कल्याणनिरीक्षक —**Officer** कल्याण-अधिकारी —**state** कल्याणकारी राज्य —**Superintendent** कल्याण-अधीक्षक

Well-known person विख्यात व्यक्ति —**to-do person** सम्पन्न

Wharf घाट —**Supervisor** घाट-पर्यवेक्षक **Wharfage** घाट-भाड़ा

Whatever may be the circumstances जो भी परिस्थिति हो

When called upon अपेक्षित किये जाने पर —**it is found necessary** जब कभी यह जरूरी समझा जाए

Whereas it is expedient यत: यह समीचीन है —**it was his duty to attend** जब कि उपस्थित होना उनका कर्तव्य था **Wherever found** जहां कहीं मिले **Whether of law or fact** चाहे विधि सम्बन्धी हो अथवा तथ्य सम्बन्धी

Whichever is earlier जो भी

पहले हो या पहले पड़ता हो या पहले घटित हो —will have the effect जिसका प्रभाव होगा

Whip सचेतक —, chief मुख्य सचेतक

White paper श्वेत-पत्र

Whoever does it जो कोई यह करे

Whole, as a कुल मिलाकर

Wholesale price थोक मूल्य/भाव —time पूर्णकालिक —empoyee पूर्णकालिक कर्मचारी —service पूर्णकालिक निदेशक —work पूर्णकालीन काम, पूरे समय का रोजगार

Wholly or partly पूर्णतः अथवा अंशतः

Wild Life Inspector वन-जंतु-निरीक्षक/जंगली-जीव निरीक्षक

Wilful negligence जान बूझकर प्रमाद/उपेक्षा

Will be dealt with severely कठोरता से काम लिया जाएगा —you please state कृपया बताइए

Wind up the office कार्यालय का समापन

Wing स्कंध/खण्ड —Commander विंग कमांडर —Havildar Major विंग हवलदार मेजर —Officer विंग अफसर —Publications प्रकाशन स्कंध/खण्ड

Wireless Adviser बेतार सलाहकार —Instructor बेतार शिक्षक —License Inspector बेतारलाइसेंस-निरीक्षक —Mechanic बेतार मेकैनिक —message बेतार सन्देश —Officer बेतार-अधिकारी —Operator बेतार-प्रचालक —Planning Coordination wing बेतार योजना और समन्वय स्कंध —Signal clerk बेतार सिगनल क्लर्क —Supervisor बेतार-पर्यवेक्षक —Telegraph Inspector बेतार-प्रेषण-निरीक्षक —Telegraphic Operator बेतार-प्रेषण-प्रचालक/बेतार प्रेषण ऑपरेटर —Traffic Inspector बेतार यातायात निरीक्षक —Supervisor बेतार यातायात पर्यवेक्षक

Wireman तार-मिस्त्री/वायरमैन

With a view of इस दृष्टि से कि —a view to की दृष्टि से —care and diligence सतर्कता और तत्परता के साथ With due deligence सम्यक् तत्परता के साथ —due regard to का सम्यक् ध्यान रखते हुए —due regard to seniority ज्येष्ठता का सम्यक् ध्यान रखते हुए —effect from से, से प्रभावी —full particulars पूरे ब्यौरे

सहित, पूरे विवरण के साथ **—great risk of life** बड़ी जोखिम में जान डालकर हथेली पर प्राण रखकर **—his own hand** स्वयं अपने हाथ से **—immediate effect** इसी समय से, तत्काल **—intent to annoy** तंग करने के अभिप्राय से **—one another** एक दूसरे से **— or without** सहित या रहित **—permission to affix and suffix** आदि और अन्त में जोड़ने की अनुज्ञा दी **—reference to** के सम्बन्ध में को निर्दिष्ट करके, के प्रसंग **—regard to** के बारे में, के सम्बन्ध में **— regards/respects** सादर **—respect to** के सम्बन्ध में **—retrospective effect** पूर्व व्याप्ति सहित, पहले से **—strong hand** शक्ति पूर्वक, कठोरता से **—the compliments of** साभिवादन, द्वारा सादर **— the concurrence of** की सहमति से **—the meaning of** के अर्थ के अन्तर्गत **— the result that** जिसके फलस्वरूप/परिणामस्वरूप, फल यह हुआ कि

Withdraw रुपया निकालना **Withdrawal** वापसी **—form** वापसी/निकासी फार्म **—of Candidature** उम्मीदवारी वापस लेना **—of complaint** परिवाद का प्रत्याहरण **—of motion** प्रस्ताव वापस लेना, प्रस्ताव की वापसी

Withheld रोका हुआ **Withholding of increment** वेतन वृद्धि/तरक्की रोक लेना

Within a radius of के घेरे में, के क्षेत्र में **—one month** एक मास के भीतर **—the local limits** स्थानीय सीमाओं में **— the mischief of law/act/tax** कानून/अधिनियम/कर की परिधि/पकड़ में

Without any further reference बिना और किसी निर्देश के **— fail** बिना चूके, अवश्य **—let or hinderance** बेरोक टोक **— prejudice** बिना प्रतिकूल प्रभाव डाले

Witness साक्षी/गवाह **— produced** पेश किए गए गवाह/साक्षी

Woman Searcher तलाशी-महिला **—Police** महिला-पुलिस

Wood Caulker लकड़ी संदबंदगर/वुंड कॉकर **—Engraving Teacher** काष्ठ तक्षण-शिक्षक **—Polisher** लकड़ी - पालिशगर **—Turner** लकड़ी-खरादी

Work agent एजेंट/कारिंदा **—contre** उद्यम घर**—certificate** कार्यप्रमाण पत्र **— charged Post** निर्माण प्रभारित पद **—day (working day)** कार्य दिवस, काम

का दिन —**load** कार्य भार —**order** कार्यादेश —**Order Clerk** कार्य आदेश क्लर्क —**sheet** कार्य पत्रक

Worker कामगार

Working (adj.) 1. कार्यकारी 2. श्रमजीवी 3. व्यावहारिक/काम-चलाऊ 4. सक्रिय/चालू 5. कार्य-चालन **(n.)** —**arrangement** काम चलाऊ प्रबन्ध —**committee** कार्यसमिति, कार्यकारिणी समिति —**days** कार्य दिवस/काम के दिन —**hours** काम के घंटे, कार्य-समय —**journalists** श्रमजीवी पत्रकार —**knowledge** व्यावहारिक ज्ञान —**order, in** चालू हालत में

Workman's compensation कामगार मुआवजा —**Compensation Commissioner** कर्मकार-मुआवजा आयुक्त/कर्मकार प्रतिकर-आयुक्त

Workmanship कर्म-कौशल —**,fine** बढ़िया कर्म-कौशल

Works 1. संकर्म 2. कर्मशाला 3. निर्माण —**Accountant** संकर्म लेखापाल —**Electrical Engineer** कर्मशाला बिजली इंजीनियर —**Foreman** कर्मशाला फोरमैन —**, major** प्रधान कार्य/कर्म —**Manager** कर्मशाला-प्रबंधक/कारखाना प्रबंधक —**, minor** लघु कार्य/कर्म —**Mistry** संकर्म मिस्त्री —**of Irrigation** सिंचन संकर्म —**, petty** अतिलघु कर्म/कार्य —**Planning Section** निर्माण आयोजना अनुभाग

Workshop 1. वर्कशाप/कर्मशाला 2. कार्यगोष्ठी —**Medical Officer** कर्मशाला चिकित्सा अधिकारी —**rules** कर्मशाला/कार्यशाला/वर्कशाप के नियम —**Supervisor** कर्मशाला-पर्यवेक्षक

Wound Pension क्षत पेंशन/घायल पेंशन **Wounded in action** लड़ाई में घायल

Writ रिट

Write off बट्टे खाते डालना **written acknowledgment** लिखित अभिस्वीकृति —**authority** लिखित प्राधिकार —**instruction** लिखित अनुदेश —**order** लिखित आदेश

Wrongfully discharged सदोष सेवोन्मुक्त **wrongly detcrmined** गलत अवधारित किया गया

X-Ray Assistant एक्सरे-सहायक —**Teahnician** एक्सरे प्रविधिज्ञ/एक्सरे तकनीशियन

Yard Boy यार्ड-बॉय —**Foreman** यार्ड-फोरमैन —**Gunner** यार्ड गनर —**Inspector (Production**

Department) यार्ड निरीक्षक (उत्पादन विभाग) —**Inspector (Yard Shop)** यार्ड निरीक्षक (यार्ड दुकान) —, **railway** रेलवे यार्ड

Yarn Inspector सूत-निरीक्षक

Year वर्ष —**book** शब्द कोश —, **calender** संवत्/पंचांग वर्ष —, **financial** वित्तीय वर्ष, वित्त-वर्ष —**to year** वर्षानुवर्ष **Yearly** वार्षिक

Yeoman of signals सिगनल-योमन

Yield उपज; उत्पाद; पैदावार —, **annual** वार्षिक उपज —**table** उपज सारणी

You are called upon to show cause आप कारण बताइए कि —**suspended from duty** आप ड्यूटी/कार्य से निलम्बित किए गये

Your Lordship श्रीमान; हुजूर —**presumption is correct** आपकी धारणा ठीक है —**request cannot be acceded to** आपकी प्रार्थना स्वीकार नहीं की जा सकती **Yours faithfully** भवदीय **Yours sincerely/truly** आपका

Young soldier नौजवान सैनिक

Youth यौवन —**conference** युवक सम्मेलन **Youthful** युवा; किशोर

Y-Services 'य' शाखा

Zamindari abolition जमींदारी उन्मूलन —**Committee** जमींदारी उन्मूलन समिति

Zanana जनानखाना

Zeal उत्साह;

Zonal 1. मंडलीय/कटिबंधीय 2. आंचलिक —**Council** आंचलिक परिषद् —**Office** आंचलिक कार्यालय, जोन दफ्तर

Zone अंचल/जोन

Zoological Survey of India भारतीय प्राणि-सर्वेक्षण-विभाग

Appendix I

Some comments, expressions and phrases commonly used in administration

A chronological summary of the case is placed below.

इस मामले का तारीखवार सारांश नीचे रखा है ।

A copy of abovementioned report is circulated among all Sections . . , for their information and necessary action. Sections may keep extracts of relevant portions. After circulation the copy may be retained by...Section.

ऊपर उल्लिखित रिपोर्ट की एक प्रति ··· प्रभाग के सभी अनुभागों में उनकी सूचना और आवश्यक कार्रवाई के लिए घुमाई जा रही है । ...अनुभाग को छोड़कर सभी अनुभाग, संगत अंशों के उद्धरण अपने पास रख लें । सभी अनुभागों में घुमाने के बाद प्रति···अनुभाग में रख ली जाए ।

A copy of p.u.c. has been sent to Chief Engineer of General Section. He will no doubt furnish the requisite information...If the information is not received by the prescribed date, a reminder will be put up. At present the p.u.c. is for information only.

सामान्य अनुभाग द्वारा विचाराधीन पत्र की मुख्य इंजीनियर को एक प्रतिलिपि भेज दी गई है ।···वह निःसन्देह ··· अपेक्षित सूचना भेज देंगे । यदि विहित तारीख तक सूचना न मिली तो अनुस्मारक प्रस्तुत कर दिया जाएगा । इस समय विचाराधीन पत्र केवल सूचना के लिए है ।

A copy of the Ministry of . . . O.M. No...dated is placed on the file.

···मंत्रालय के दिनांक ··· के ज्ञापन सं० ··· की प्रतिलिपि फाइल में रख दी गई ।

A copy of the undermentioned papers is forwarded to...for information/for information and guidance/for necessary action/ for favour of a reply/for early compliance.

नीचे लिखे कागजों की एक प्रतिलिपि सूचना/सूचना और संदर्शन/ आवश्यक कार्रवाई/उत्तर/शीघ्र अनुपालन के लिए...को भेजी जा रही है ।

A draft sanction letter is put up for approval. Ministry. . . may please see for concurrence.

मंजूरी-पत्र का मसौदा अनुमोदन के लिए प्रस्तुत है ।...मन्त्रालय कृपया सहमति के लिए देख लें ।

A list of cases disposed of . . . during week ending...is placed below . . . Section may please remove it.

...को समाप्त होने वाले सप्ताह में जिन मामलों का निपटारा...उनकी पूरी सूची नीचे रखी है ।...अनुभाग कृपया निकाल लें ।

A revised draft memorandum is put up as desired by......

...को इच्छानुसार ज्ञापन का परिशोधित मसौदा प्रस्तुत है ।

A short history of the case under consideration is given on pp . . . ante.

विचाराधीन मामले का संक्षिप्त वृत्त पीछे पृष्ठ...पर दिया गया है ।

A statement showing the latest position of sanctioned temporary and permanent posts in the......Deptt. is placed on the file as directed.

जैसा निदेश दिया गया था,...विभाग के मंजूर हुए अस्थायी और स्थायी पदों की अद्यतन स्थिति बताने वाला एक विवरण फाइल पर रख दिया गया है ।

A substitute may be appointed against the leave vacancy as an interim arrangement.

अन्तरिम व्यवस्था के रूप में छुट्टी के कारण रिक्त हुई जगह पर एवजी नियुक्त कर लिया जाए ।

Action may be taken as proposed.

यथाप्रस्तावित कार्रवाई की जाए ।

Administrative approval may be obtained.

प्रशासनिक अनुमोदन प्राप्त किया जाए ।

After issue of the draft the file may be sent to...for comments on the points raised by us on pp . . . ante.

मसौदे को भेजने के बाद हमारे द्वारा पीछे पृष्ठ ··· पर उठाई गई बातों पर टिप्पणी देने के लिए फाइल को···के पास भेज दिया जाये ।

All concerned should note carefully.

सभी सम्बन्धित व्यक्ति इसे ध्यान से नोट कर लें ।

An electric call bell may kindly be got installed in Room No . . .

कमरा नं०···में कृपया एक बिजली की घंटी लगवा दी जाये ।

Application forms for allotment of residential accommodation from the following persons are placed below for onward transmission to the Directorate of Estates.

निवास स्थान के आबंटन के लिये निम्नलिखित व्यक्तियों के आवेदन-पत्र नीचे रखे हैं । इन्हें सम्पदा निदेशालय को भेज दिया जाये ।

Application may be rejected.

आवेदन अस्वीकार कर दिया जाये ।

As the Ministry of...is concerned in the matter, the p.u.c. may be transferred to them for consideration.

चूंकि इस विषय का सम्बन्ध ··· मन्त्रालय से है, इसलिये विचाराधीन कागज उनके पास विचारार्थ भेज दिया जाये ।

As the Ministry of...is not in favour of the proposal we may not press the matter further.

···मन्त्रालय इस प्रस्ताव के पक्ष में नहीं है, अतः हम इस मामले पर और आग्रह न करें ।

Await further report.

आगे और विवरण की प्रतीक्षा कीजिये ।

Await reply.

उत्तर की प्रतीक्षा करें ।

Before offering our comment we would like to see the papers leading to the decision referred to at 'A' on p...c.

अपनी टिप्पणी देने से पहले हम पृष्ठ···/पत्राचार में 'क' पर उल्लिखित निर्णय के साधक कागजों को देखना चाहेंगे ।

Before we consider their proposal, we would like to see the papers leading to the issue of letter No...dt...referred to at 'B' on p...c.

इस प्रस्ताव पर विचार करने से पहले हम उन कागजों को देखना चाहते हैं जिनके आधार पृष्ठ···/पत्राचार में 'ख' पर बताया गया दिनांक··· का पत्र सं०···भेजा गया था ।

Before we examine the proposal, we would request the Ministry of...to add the papers in which the concessions were originally sanctioned.

प्रस्ताव पर विचार करने से पूर्व हम···मन्त्रालय से उन कागजों को साथ लगा देने का अनुरोध करते हैं जिनमें ये रियायतें मंजूर की गई थीं ।

Bill No...dated...for Rs...mentioned above has been accepted and passed for payment.

···रु० की राशि का दिनांक···का उपर्युक्त बिल संख्या···स्वीकार कर लिया गया है और भुगतान के लिये पारित कर दिया गया है ।

Casual leave applied for may be granted.

मांगी गई/आवेदित आकस्मिक छुट्टी दे दी जाये ।

Certified that amount of the bill has been disbursed to the proper persons.

यह प्रमाणित किया जाता है कि बिल की रकम सही व्यक्तियों को चुकाई गई है ।

Certified that the purchases have been made at the lowest market rate.

यह प्रमाणित किया जाता है कि खरीद बाजार के न्यूनतम भाव पर की गई है ।

Chappals were issued to Shri...last year. This will be taken into account at the time of issuing the winter uniform.

श्री···की चप्पलें पिछले वर्ष दी गई थीं । जाड़े की (गरम) वर्दी देते समय इस बात का ध्यान रखा जायेगा ।

Character and antecedants of the candidate have been verified and found to be satisfactory.

उम्मीदवार के चाल-चलन और पूर्ववृत्त का सत्यापन कर लिया गया है और उसे सन्तोषजनक पाया गया है ।

Copy forwarded for information/necessary action to :—

प्रतिलिपि/नकल सूचना/आवश्यक कार्रवाई के लिये निम्नलिखित को भेजी जा रही है :—

Copy may also be sent to.........Fair endorsement is put up for signature.

प्रतिलिपि···को भी भेज दी जाये। स्वच्छ पृष्ठांकन हस्ताक्षर के लिये प्रस्तुत है।

Delay in returning the file is regretted.

फाइल को लौटाने में हुई देरी के लिये खेद है।

Delay in the submission of the case is regretted.

मामले की प्रस्तुत करने में हुई देरी के लिये खेद है।

......Deptt. may kindly see for interim information and return the papers urgently so that case may be pursued further with the Ministry of...

···विभाग अन्तरिम सूचना के लिये देख ले और कागजों को शीघ्र लौटा दे ताकि यह मामला आगे···मन्त्रालय से चलाया जाये।

Draft approved as amended.

मसौदा संशोधित रूप में अनुमोदित किया जाता है।

Draft as directed by...is submitted for approval.

···के निदेशानुसार मसौदा अनुमोदन के लिये प्रस्तुत है।

Draft has been amended accordingly.

मसौदा तदनुसार संशोधित कर दिया गया है।

Draft is concurred in.

प्रारूप पर सहमति दी जा रही है।

Draft may now be issued.

प्रारूप अब जारी कर दिया जाए।

Draft reply is put up for approval,

उत्तर का मसौदा अनुमोदन के लिए प्रस्तुत है।

Draft reply on the lines suggested above may be put up.

ऊपर के सुझावों के आधार पर उत्तर का मसौदा तैयार कीजिए।

Draft will be put up if the suggestions made in paras 1 and 3 above are approved.

यदि ऊपर पैरा 1 और 3 में दिए गए सुझावों को अनुमोदित कर दिया गया, तो मसौदा प्रस्तुत कर दिया जाएगा ।

Enquiry may be completed and its report submitted at an early date.

जांच पूरी की जाए और रिपोर्ट जल्दी प्रस्तुत की जाए ।

Explanation may be called for.

स्पष्टीकरण मांगा जाए ।

Extracts from these notes will be kept on our file on return.

वापसी पर इन टिप्पणियों के उद्धरण अपनी मिसिल में रख लिए जाएंगे ।

For information only.

केवल सूचना के लिए ।

For such action as deemed fit.

ऐसी कार्रवाई के लिए जो उचित समझी जाय ।

For the reason now explained I concur in the proposal.

अब जो कारण बताए गए हैं उनको दृष्टि में रखते हुए मैं इस प्रस्ताव पर अपनी सहमति देता हूँ ।

Formal approval is necessary. The same may be obtained.

औपचारिक अनुमोदन आवश्यक है उसे प्राप्त कर लिया जाए ।

F. R. is for information for the present. Final reply may be awaited for another month.

नई आवती अभी सूचना के लिए है । अन्तिम उत्तर की एक मास तक और प्रतीक्षा कर ली जाए ।

Further communication will follow on receipt of the information from...

...से सूचना आने पर आगे और पत्र भेजा जाएगा ।

Further report from the Director...may be awaited.

...निदेशक से और रिपोर्ट की प्रतीक्षा कर ली जाए ।

...Has seen.

...ने देख लिया ।

Having regard to the facts stated above (facts of the case) the orders passed by...are set aside.

ऊपर जिन तथ्यों का उल्लेख किया गया है उनको (मामले के तथ्यों को) देखते हुए···द्वारा दिए गए आदेशों को रद्द किया जाता है।

Having regard to the merits of the case the order passed by the...is in order. I do not see any reason to intervene.

···ने जो आदेश दिया है वह मामले के गुण-दोषों को देखते हुए उचित ही है। मुझे हस्तक्षेप करने का कोई कारण दिखाई नहीं देता।

He may be advised to get his name registered in the nearest Employment Exchange if not already done.

उसे सूचित कर दिया जाए कि यदि उसने अपना नाम अभी तक अपने पास के किसी रोजगार कार्यालय में दर्ज न कराया हो तो अब दर्ज करा ले।

Head of account has not been given on the final bill.

इस अन्तिम बिल पर लेखा शीर्ष नहीं लिखा गया है।

I agree.

मैं सहमत हूं।

I fully agree with the office note. Orders may be issued.

कार्यालय की टिप्पणी से मैं पूरी तरह सहमत हूँ। आदेश जारी कर दिए जाएं।

If adequate precautions had been taken to safeguard Govt. interests, this infructuous expenditure would have been avoided.

यदि सरकार के हितों की रक्षा के लिए यथेष्ट सावधानी बरती जाती, तो यह व्यर्थ खर्च न हुआ होता।

Immediate disposal of the life is requested.

इस फाइल का निपटारा शीघ्र करने का अनुरोध किया जाता है।

In consultation with the Ministry of...it has been decided that...

···मन्त्रालय से परामर्श करके यह निश्चय किया गया है कि···

In his present representation Shri...has reiterated the same points as were mentioned in his earlier representation and which have already been considered. There appears to be no justification to alter our earlier decision. This representation may, therefore, be rejected and Shri ... be informed that in future no further representation on this subject will be entertained.

श्री···ने अपने वर्तमान अभिवेदन में वे ही बातें दोहराई हैं जो उनके पहले अभिवेदन में कही जा चुकी हैं और जिन पर पहले ही विचार किया जा चुका है। अपना पूर्व निर्णय बदलने का कोई औचित्य नहीं दिखाई पड़ता। अतः इस अभिवेदन को अस्वीकार कर दिया जाए तथा श्री···को कह दिया जाए कि भविष्य में इस विषय पर और कोई अभिवेदन नहीं लिया जाएगा।

In the circumstances we may issue a revised notification in supersession of the one at page.../c.

ऐसी स्थिति में हम पृष्ठ···पत्राचार पर के पत्र का अधिक्रमण करते हुए एक परिशोधित अधिसूचना जारी कर दें।

In the recovery statement attached to the final bill, certain credit has been allowed for the material returned but no transfer entry order has been prepared.

अन्तिम बिल के साथ जो वसूली विवरण लगा है उसमें वापस की गई सामग्री के लिए कुछ राशि जमा खाते में दिखाई गई है। परन्तु उसके लिए अन्तरण टीप-आदेश तैयार नहीं किया है।

In this connection attention is invited to the noting at pp... or file No...

इस सम्बन्ध में फाइल संख्या के पृष्ठ···की ओर ध्यान आकर्षित किया जाता है।

In view of the circumstances explained in the p. u. c. we may permit air travel.

विचाराधीन कागज में स्पष्ट की गई परिस्थिति को ध्यान में रखते हुए हम हवाई यात्रा की अनुमति दे दें।

In view of the circumstances stated above, we may agree to the suggestion.

ऊपर बताई गई परिस्थितियों में हम सुझाव मान लें।

In view of the circumstances stated above, we may support the proposal.

ऊपर स्पष्ट की गई स्थिति को देखते हुए हम इस प्रस्ताव का समर्थन कर दें।

In view of the need for utmost economy we may request the...not to press for the proposal.

अधिक से अधिक किफायत करने की आवश्यकता को ध्यान में रखते हुए हम•••से अनुरोध करें कि वे इस प्रस्ताव पर जोर न दें।

Inspite of a thorough search the relevant file is not traceable.

भली भांति खोज करने पर भी सम्बन्धित मिसिल मिल नहीं रही है।

Issue as amended.

यथा संशोधित भेज दीजिए।

Issue reminder urgently.

तुरन्त अनुस्मारक भेजिए।

Issue today.

आज ही भेज दिया जाए/भेजिए।

It has been verified from the old records that no payment has been made so far in respect of bill No . . . . dated......

पुराने रिकार्ड से पड़ताल करली गई है कि दिनांक···के बिल नम्बर ···का अभी तक भुगतान नहीं किया गया है।

It is felt that further reference to the Ministry of...is now not necessary.

ऐसा समझ में आता है कि अब इसे···मंत्रालय को भेजने की जरूरत नहीं है।

It is obvious that the family is in dire distress due to the premature death of the earning member. His son Shri... may be appointed as a Clerk in relaxation of the prescribed procedure regarding recruitment through Employment Exchange.

यह स्पष्ट है कि अर्जक सदस्य की अकाल मृत्यु के कारण उसका परिवार बहुत संकट में है। रोजगार कार्यालय की मार्फत ही भर्ती करने के निर्धारित तरीके में कुछ ढील बरतते हुए उसके पुत्र श्री ···को क्लर्क की जगह नियुक्त कर लिया जाए।

It will be necessary to obtain the following particulars before agreeing to the proposal.

प्रस्ताव पर सहमत होने से पहले नीचे लिखे ब्यौरे मंगाना जरूरी होगा।

It would be against public interest to give the permission. The request may be rejected.

अनुमति देना लोकहित के प्रतिकूल होगा । प्रार्थना अस्वीकृत कर दी जाए ।

It would be necessary to fix the responsibility before the amount is written off.

इस राशि को बट्टे खाते में डालने से पहले जिम्मेदारी निर्धारित करना जरूरी होगा ।

Its issue is authorised.

इसे प्राधिकार से जारी किया जा रहा है ।

Kindly acknowledge.

कृपया पावती भेजिए ।

...may be informed accordingly.

...को तदनुसार सूचित कर दिया जाए ।

May be recorded for five years.

पांच साल के लिए रिकार्ड कर दिया जाए ।

...may kindly see the Ministry of ... note at p ... ante and clarify the position.

...कृपया...मन्त्रालय की पिछले पृष्ठ...पर लिखी टिप्पणी देखें और स्थिति स्पष्ट करें ।

...may note it carefully.

...इसे सावधानी से नोट कर लें ।

...may please see for approval.

...कृपया अनुमोदन के लिए देखें ।

...may please see for concurrence.

...कृपया सहमति के लिए देख लें ।

Ministry of...have not yet returned our file. We may send a D. O. reminder under advice to the...

मंत्रालय ने हमारी मिसिल अब तक नहीं लौटाई है । हम एक अर्ध-सरकारी पत्र अनुस्मारक के रूप में...को सूचित करते हुए भेज दें ।

...Ministry (Deptt.) may see the preceding note with reference to their query at prepage.

...मन्त्रालय (विभाग) पिछले पृष्ठ पर की गई पूछताछ के सम्बन्ध में इससे पहले की टिप्पणी देख ले ।

Ministry of...may be consulted.

...मंत्रालय से परामर्श किया जाए ।

Ministry of...may be requested kindly to reconsider.

...मन्त्रालय से कृपया दुबारा विचार करने के लिए अनुरोध किया जाए ।

Ministry of ... may consider the desirability of issuing general orders on the subject.

...मन्त्रालय इस मामले में सामान्य आदेश निकालने की आवश्यकता पर विचार करे ।

Ministry (Deptt,) of...may kindly see for remarks in the first instance.

पहले...मंत्रालय (विभाग) इसे देखकर कृपया अपने विचार प्रकट करे ।

Ministry of...may kindly see with reference to the telephonic conversation with Shri . . . on the

श्री...से...को टेलीफोन पर हुई बातचीत के संदर्भ में...मंत्रालय कृपया इसे देख ले ।

Ministry of . . . may please see and remove their file.

मंत्रालय कृपया देखे और अपनी फाइल निकाल ले ।

. . . need not be bothered.

...महोदय को कष्ट देने की जरूरत नहीं ।

Needful has been done.

जरूरी कार्रवाई कर दी गई है ।

. . . needs a bookshelf for keeping reference books. It may either be purchased or got made on order.

...को संदर्भ पुस्तकें रखने के लिए किताबों की अलमारी की आवश्यकता है । इसे या तो खरीद लिया जाए या आर्डर देकर बनवा लिया जाए ।

No action on our part seems to be called for. If approved the papers may be recorded.

इस पर हमारी ओर से किसी कार्रवाई की जरूरत नहीं दीखती । यदि अनुमति हो तो कागजों को रिकार्ड कर दिया जाए ।

No action seems to be called for on our part.
हमारी ओर से इस पर कोई कार्रवाई जरूरी नही मालूम पड़ती।

No assurance in the matter can be given at this stage.
इस मामले में इस समय कोई आश्वासन नहीं दिया जा सकता।

No communication has yet been received from the . . . He may be reminded as per fair memo put up for signature.

…अभी कोई उत्तर नहीं मिला है। हस्ताक्षर के लिए प्रस्तुत किए गए स्वच्छ अनुस्मारक के द्वारा उन्हें याद दिला दी जाए।

No decision has so far been taken in the matter.
इस मामले पर अभी तक कोई निर्णय नहीं हुआ है।

No further action is called for.
आगे कोई कार्रवाई अपेक्षित नहीं है।

Notes and orders at pages . . . may be seen in this connection.

इस सम्बन्ध में पृष्ठ…पर दिए गए आदेश और टिप्पणियां देख ली जाएं।

Noting at pp...ante may please be glanced through.
पीछे पृष्ठ…के टिप्पणी पर कृपया निगाह डाल ली जाए।

Noting on p....ante recalls the case.
पिछले पृष्ठ…की टिप्पणी इस मामले का स्मरण कराती है।

Our call bell is not in working order. Please get it repaired soon.
हमारी घण्टी काम नहीं कर रही है। कृपया इसे शीघ्र ठीक करा दें।

Papers have been amalgamated.

कागज-पत्र मिला दिए गए हैं।

Payment is to be made quarterly at the rates given in this estimate.
भुगतान इस अनुमान में दी गई दरों से त्रैमासिक करना है।

Please discuss.
आकर चर्चा कर लें। (कृपया चर्चा कर जाइए)।

Please circulate and file.
कृपया सभी को दिखाकर फाइल कर दीजिए।

Please inform...accordingly.
कृपया···को तदनुसार सूचित कर दीजिए ।

Please make a special note of this decision.
कृपया इस निर्णय को विशेष रूप से नोट करें ।

Pleasc prepare a precis of the case.
कृपया मामले की संक्षेपिका तैयार कीजिए ।

Please put up a self-contained note (summary).
कृपया स्वतः पूर्ण टिप्पणी (सारांश) प्रस्तुत कीजिए ।

Please see the preceding notes.
कृपया पिछली टिप्पणियां देख लें ।

Please speak.
बात कर जाइये ।

President is pleased to direct.
राष्ट्रपति निर्देश देते हैं ।

President is pleased to sanction.
राष्ट्रपति कृपापूर्वक···की मंजूरी देते हैं ।

Provision exists in the budget for incurring the expenditure during the current financial year.
इस व्यय के लिए चालू वित्तीय वर्ष के बजट में व्यवस्था है ।

Reference notes on prepage. This Section has got no such information to furnish.
पिछले पृष्ठ पर टिप्पणी के संदर्भ में । इस अनुभाग के पास इस प्रकार की कोई सूचना देने के लिए नहीं है ।

Relevant orders are flagged.
संगत आदेशों पर पर्चियां लगा दी गई हैं ।

Requisite files are placed below.
अपेक्षित मिसिलें (फाइलें) नीचे रखी हैं ।

Retrospective effect cannot be given to this order.
इस आदेश को पीछे की तारीख से लागू नहीं किया जा सकता ।

Return of the file (papers) may kindly be expedited.
मिसिल (कागज-पत्र) कृपया शीघ्र वापिस कीजिए ।

Return of the main file may be awaited.
मुख्य मिसिल के वापस आने की प्रतीक्षा की जाए ।

Returned in original with the remarks that the requisite information has already been sent in this office letter No. . . dated...

इसे मूल रूप में ही इस टिप्पणी के साथ लौटाया जाता है कि अपेक्षित सूचना इस कार्यालय के दिनांक···के पत्र सं०···द्वारा पहले ही भेजी जा चुकी है ।

Ruling from. . . should be obtained.

···से व्यवस्था प्राप्त की जाए ।

...Section has no comments to offer.

···अनुभाग को इस पर कोई टिप्पणी नहीं करनी है ।

...Section has nothing to suggest for inclusion in the fortnightly statement to be submitted for the information of Deputy Minister/Minister for...in respect of the fortnight ending...

मंत्री/उपमंत्री के सूचनार्थ···को समाप्त होने वाले पखवाड़े के बारे में भेजे जाने वाले पाक्षिक विवरण में शामिल किए जाने के लिए···अनुभाग को कोई सुझाव देना है ।

. . . Section has reported that both the typewriters in that section are not in working order. They have requested for early arrangements to get the typewriters repaired. M/s......may be asked to furnish an estimate for the repairs.

···अनुभाग ने रिपोर्ट भेजी है कि उनके अनुभाग के दोनों टाइपराइटर काम नहीं कर रहे हैं। उन्होंने इन टाइपराइटरों की मरम्मत की शीघ्र व्यवस्था करने का अनुरोध किया है । सर्वश्री···को . मरम्मत व्यय का अनुमान भेजने के लिए कहा जाए ।

...Section may please see.

···अनुभाग कृपया देख ले ।

...Section may please see with reference to their note overleaf.

···अनुभाग अपने पिछले पृष्ठ की टिप्पणी के सन्दर्भ में इसे देख ले ।

Seen and passed on to...for necessary action.

देख लिया । इसे···को आवश्यक कार्यवाई के लिए भेजा जा रहा है ।

Seen and returned.
देखकर वापिस किया जाता है।

Seen and returned with thanks.
देखकर सधन्यवाद वापिस किया जाता है।

Seen in...Section.
...अनुभाग ने देख लिया है।

Seen in the Ministry (Deptt) of...
...मंत्रालय (...विभाग) में देख लिया गया।

Seen, thanks.
देख लिया, धन्यवाद।

Service from...to...verified from the office copies of the pay bills.

दिनांक...से...तक की सेवा का, वेतन बिलों की कार्यालय प्रतियों के आधार पर, सत्यापन कर लिया गया है।

Shri...has applied for two months earned leave which is at the credit. No substitute has been asked for. The leave may, therefore, be sanctioned. Draft office order is put up for approval.

श्री...ने दो मास की अर्जित छुट्टी मांगी है, जो उनके हिसाब में जमा है। उनकी जगह किसी एवजी की मांग भी नहीं की गई है। अतः छुट्टी मंजूर कर दी जाए। कार्यालय आदेश का मसौदा अनुमोदन के लिए प्रस्तुत है।

Shri...has been transferred here from the office of... We may ascertain from that office for our records and future guidance the details of uniform issued to Shri...

श्री...का तबादला (स्थानान्तरण)...के कार्यालय से यहां को हुआ है। उस कार्यालय से हम अपने रिकार्ड तथा आगे संदर्शन के लिए श्री...को दी गई वर्दी का ब्यौरा मालूम कर लें।

Shri...has joined this office today. We may ask the Security Officer to issue him a temporary pass for a month.

श्री...ने इस कार्यालय में आज कार्यभार सम्भाला है। हम सुरक्षा अधिकारी को कहें कि उनको एक महीने के लिए अस्थायी पास जारी कर दें।

Shri…has returned from leave and has resumed his duties on…His charge report may be sent to the Accounts Officer.

श्री…छुट्टी से वापिस आ गए हैं और उन्होंने…को अपने पद का कार्य-भार संभाल लिया है। उनकी कार्य-भार रिपोर्ट लेखा अधिकारी को भेज दी जाए।

Shri…in this Ministry has been allotted quarter No… by the Directorate of Estates. In this connection he may please see the attached Memo No… dated…from the Directorate and state whether the allotment offered to him by the Dirctorate of Estates is acceptable to him.

इस मन्त्रालय के श्री…को सम्पदा निदेशालय द्वारा क्वार्टर संख्या…का आबंटन किया गया है। इस सिलसिले में वह कृपया उस निदेशालय के तारीख…के संलग्न ज्ञापन संख्या…को देखें और यह बताएं कि क्या उन्हें सम्पदा निदेशालय द्वारा किया गया आबंटन स्वीकार है।

Shri…was sanctioned leave with effect from… Report of relinquishment of charge has been received. Leave may be notified in the Gazette.

श्री…की…से छुट्टी मंजूर हुई थी। उनके कार्य-भार छोड़ने की रिपोर्ट मिल गई है। छुट्टी को राजपत्र (गजट) में अधिसूचित कर दिया जाए।

Shri…who was granted earned leave from…to…vide this Ministry's memorandum of even number dated…, resumed duty on…

श्री…जिनको इस मन्त्रालय के समसंख्यक दिनांक के…ज्ञापन में ता०… से ता०…तक अर्जित छुट्टी मंजूर की गई थी, अपने काम पर ता०…को हाजिर हो गए हैं।

Submitted for information.
सूचना (जानकारी) के लिए प्रस्तुत है।

Submitted for orders.
आदेश के लिए प्रस्तुत है।

Submitted with reference to…note above.
…की ऊपर की टिप्पणी के प्रसंग में प्रस्तुत है।

The…is pressing hard for a reply.
उत्तर के लिए…बहुत अधिक जोर दे रहे हैं।

The acceptance of this proposal will set up an embarrassing precedent and we will not be in a position to resist similar requests from other...

इस प्रस्ताव को मान लेने से यह एक उलझनकारी उदाहरण बन जाएगा और हम इस स्थिति में नहीं होंगे कि दूसरे···के इसी प्रकार के अनुरोध को टाल सकें।

The application seems to be in order. We may have no objection to accord necessary permission as in the draft sanction put up.

आवेदन-पत्र ठीक लगता है। मंजूरी के मसौदे के अनुसार आवश्यक अनुज्ञा देने में हमें कोई आपत्ति नहीं होनी चाहिए।

The bill has been verified. This is in order. May be passed for payment.

बिल का सत्यापन कर लिया गया है। यह ठीक है। भुगतान के लिए पारित (पास) किया जाए।

The bill is returned herewith with the following objections.

बिल निम्नलिखित आपत्तियों के साथ वापिस किया जाता है।

The case is fully explained in the note at pp... ante/page... et seq.

इस मामले को पीछे पृष्ठ···पृष्ठ···और उससे आगे की टिप्पणियों में भली भांति स्पष्ट किया गया है।

The case is hanging for a long time.

यह मामला बहुत समय से लटका हुआ है।

The case is resubmitted as directed on prepage.

पिछले पृष्ठ पर दिए गए निदेश के अनुसार मामला फिर से प्रस्तुत किया जाता है।

The case may be shown to...on return.

यह मामला···को उनको वापसी पर दिखा दिया जाए।

The cash in chest has been counted by me and found to be Rs...

तिजोरी की रोकड़ मैंने गिन ली है, वह···रुपए है।

The. . . ccmpany may be requested to send their mechanic to examine the defects in the typewriter.

···कम्पनी से अनुरोध किया जाए कि वे टाइपराइटर के दोषों की जांच करने के लिए अपना मैकेनिक (मिस्त्री) भेज दें।

The draft need not be issued.
प्रारूप को जारी करने की आवश्यकता नहीं है।

The expenditure involved is chargeable/debitable to head...
इसमें जो खर्च होगा वह···शीर्ष पर प्रभार्य है।

The explanation furnished by Shri......is not at all satisfactory. We may convey the displeasure of the Government as per draft put up for approval.

श्री···द्वारा दिया गया स्पष्टीकरण बिल्कुल सन्तोषजनक नहीं है। हम अनुमोदन के लिए प्रस्तुत किए मसौदे के अनुसार सरकार की अप्रसन्नता व्यक्त कर दें।

The favour of an early reply will be highly appreciated.
शीघ्र उत्तर भेज दें तो बड़ी कृपा होगी।

The file has not yet been received back from the......inspite of repeated reminders......may like to speak to the......on the phone.

बार-बार याद दिलाने पर भी मिसिल···विभाग से अभी तक वापस नहीं आई है।···कदाचित् इस बारे में···से फोन पर बातचीत करना चाहें।

The file in question is placed below.
सम्बन्धित मिसिल (फाइल) नीचे रखी है।

The file is not readily traceable. Efforts are being made to trace it.

मिसिल तत्काल मिल नहीं रही है। उसे खोजने की कोशिश की जा रही है।

The file may be referred to the...for comments.
यह मिसिल टिप्पणी के लिए···को भेज दी जाए।

The file may kindly be returned early after keeping extracts.
उद्धरण रखने के पश्चात् कृपया इस मिसिल को शीघ्र लौटा दिया जाए।

The final bill is not on the prescribed form.
अन्तिम बिल निर्धारित प्रपत्र (फार्म) पर नहीं है।

The F. R. may please be seen for information.
नई आवती सूचना के लिए देख लें।

The furniture required by...is not in stock at present. We may call for quotations for their purchase from firms...of repute.

...द्वारा मंगाया गया फर्नीचर इस समय भण्डार में नहीं है। हम इसको खरीदने के लिए...प्रख्यात फर्मों से भाव मंगा लें।

The G. P. Fund Account of Shri... for the last year has not yet been received from the... We may issue a routine reminder as per fair letter put up for signature.

श्री...के सामान्य भविष्य निधि का पिछले साल का हिसाब अभी तक ...से नहीं आया है। हम हस्ताक्षर के लिए प्रस्तुत स्वच्छ पत्र के अनुसार नेमी अनुस्मारक भेज दें।

The information we had called for on this subject from our...offices has so far been furnished by only...of them. The remaining offices may be asked to send the requisite information by the...

इस विषय में हमने...कार्यालयों से जो सूचना मांगी थी, वह अब तक उनमें से केवल...ने भेजी है। शेष (बाकी) कार्यालयों से अपेक्षित सूचना... तक भेज देने को कहा जाए।

The matter has been referred to the... We may send an interim reply to F. R. as per draft placed below.

मामला...को भेजा गया है। हम नई आवती का अन्तरिम उत्तर प्रस्तुत किए गए मसौदे के अनुसार भेज दें।

The matter is still under consideration of the...
मामला अभी भी...के विचाराधीन है।

The orders on the subject are not quite clear. We may seek clarification from the...of...

इस विषय पर आदेश पूरी तरह स्पष्ट नहीं है। हम...से उनको स्पष्ट करा लें।

The p. u. c. has not been acknowledged.
विचाराधीन पत्र की प्राप्ति सूचना नहीं भेजी गई है।

The papers asked for by the...have been added to this file. These may be returned when done with.

...ने जो कागज मांगे हैं वे इस फाइल के साथ दिए गए हैं। काम हो जाने पर इन्हें वापस लौटा दिया जाए।

The papers are sent herewith.

कागज-पत्र इसके साथ भेजे जा रहे हैं।

The point for consideration on this file is whether there is adequate justification for deviation from normal rules.

इस मिसिल पर विचारार्थ बात यह है कि क्या सामान्य नियमों से विचलित होने के लिए पर्याप्त औचित्य है।

The point is not free from doubt. We may ask...of...to clarify.

यह बात सन्देहरहित नहीं है...से हम इसे स्पष्ट करने के लिए कहें।

The present position of the case may please be intimated to this office.

कृपया इस कार्यालय को मामले की वर्तमान स्थिति की सूचना दी जाय (से अवगत कराया जाय)।

The previous papers on the subject have been transferred to...Section who may kindly see for further action.

इस विषय के पहले कागज पत्र...अनुभाग को दिए गए हैं। वह अनुभाग कृपया इस बारे में आगे की कार्रवाई के लिए देख ले।

The proposals contained in the p. u. c. are reasonable. We may have no objection to their acceptance. Ministry of . . . may also kindly see for concurrence.

विचाराधीन कागज में जो प्रस्ताव रखे गए हैं वे उचित हैं। हमें उनके स्वीकार करने में कोई आपत्ति नहीं हो सकती। ...भी कृपया सहमति के लिए देख लें।

The proposal for the creation of . . . post of . . . sent by the . . . of . . . does not have adequate justification. We may regret our inability to agree to it.

...द्वारा...का एक.. पद बनाने के विषय में जो प्रस्ताव भेजा गया है उसमें काफी औचित्य नहीं है। उसे मानने में हम सखेद अपनी असमर्थता प्रकट कर दें।

The proposal is quite in order.
यह प्रस्ताव बिल्कुल नियमानुकूल (ठीक) है ।

The proposal is self-explanatory.
प्रस्ताव अपने आप में स्पष्ट है ।

The proposal is self explanatory. It may be accepted.
प्रस्ताव अपने आप में स्पष्ट है । इसे मान लिया जाए ।

The quarterly progress report in respect of translation of English forms in Hindi for the period ending . . . may be sent to the Ministry of . . . Draft is put up.

अंग्रेजी फार्मों के हिन्दी अनुवाद की त्रैमासिक प्रगति की रिपोर्ट···को समाप्त हुई अवधि के लिए···को भेज दी जाए । मसौदा (प्रारूप) प्रस्तुत है ।

The receipt of the letter has been acknowledged.
पत्र मिलने की सूचना भेज दी है (पावती भेज दी गई है) ।

The representation has not been received through proper channel. We need not take any action on it.
अभिवेदन उचित माध्यम से नहीं मिला है । हमें इस पर कोई कार्रवाई करने की आवश्यकता नहीं ।

The representationist has not raised any fresh points. His request may be rejected again and he may be informed that no further representation on the subject will be entertained in future.

अभिवेदनकर्ता ने कोई नई बात नहीं उठाई है । उसकी प्रार्थना को फिर अस्वीकार कर दिया जाए और उसे सूचित कर दिया जाए कि भविष्य में उसका इस विषय पर कोई अभिवेदन ग्रहण नहीं किया (नहीं लिया) जाएगा ।

The required information has been called for from . . . and will be furnished as soon as the same is received.
वांछित सूचना···से मंगाई गई है, वहां से प्राप्त होते ही भेज दी जाएगी ।

The required information is being obtained from . . . and will be furnished on receipt.
अपेक्षित जानकारी···से मंगाई जा रही है और प्राप्त होने पर भेज दी जाएगी ।

The required papers are placed below.

अपेक्षित कागज-पत्र नीचे रखे हैं ।

The requisite information is given in the statement enclosed in duplicate/triplicate in so far as.........Section/the marginally noted organisation is/are concerned.

जहां तक···अनुभाग/हाशिए में दिए गए संगठनों का सम्बन्ध है, अपेक्षित जानकारी साथ में लगे विवरण में दो/तीन प्रतियों में भेजी जा रही है ।

The requisite information is not available in this...We may ask the...to furnish the same.

अपेक्षित जानकारी इस···में उपलब्ध नही है । हम···से यह भेज देने के लिए कहें ।

The report of the week ending...on the above subject in so far as . . . Section is concerned, may be treated as 'nil'.

जहां तक···अनुभाग का सम्बन्ध है, उक्त विषय पर···को समाप्त होने वाले सप्ताह की रिपोर्ट 'कुछ नहीं' (या 'शून्य') समझी जाए ।

The same procedure may be followed in the present case also.

इस मामले में भी वही तरीका/कार्यविधि अपनाया/अपनाई जाए ।

The source of getting the rates has been shown against each item.

प्रत्येक मद के सामने यह दिखा दिया गया है कि उसकी दर कहां से ली गई है ।

The statements showing cases which could not be finally disposed of within one month are placed below.

ऐसे मामलों के विवरण, जिनका निपटारा एक महीने के भीतर पूरी तरह से नहीं हुआ नीचे है ।

The suggestion has been considered on several occasions in the past but it has not been agreed to on account of the reasons stated in the note at p . . . /n of file No...

पीछे कई बार इस सुझाव पर विचार किया जा चुका है परन्तु फाइल संख्या···के पृष्ठ···टिप्पण पर दिए कारणों से इस पर सहमति नहीं दी गई (इसे नहीं माना गया) ।

Will the undermentioned Section(s) kindly refer to this Section's circular of even number dated the......on the subject noted above and furnish the requisite information without any further delay ?

क्या नीचे लिखे अनुभाग कृपया उक्त विषय पर इस अनुभाग के इसी संख्या तारीख के परिपत्र को देखेंगे और अपेक्षित जानकारी बिना और विलम्ब किए भिजवा देंगे ?

We may issue necessary notification as per draft placed below for approval.

अनुमोदन के लिए नीचे लिखे मसौदे के अनुसार हम आवश्यक अधिसूचना निकाल दें।

We may keep the matter in abeyance until a decision on the general question of...has been taken.

जब तक · · · के सामान्य प्रश्न पर निर्णय न हो जाए, हम इसे स्थगित रखें।

We may now obtain the comments of the . . .

अब हम · · · की राय प्राप्त कर लें।

We may remind the...after a month.

हम · · · को एक महीने बाद याद दिलाएं।

We would also be interested to know the decision taken in this case.

हम भी इस मामले पर हुए निर्णय को जानना चाहते हैं।

Weekly arrears statement for the week ending...is submitted for perusal.

· · · को समाप्त होने वाले सप्ताह की बकाया का साप्ताहिक विवरण अवलोकन के लिए प्रस्तुत है।

Will all concerned Sections of the...send to... Section material for the...immediately and latest by...? The material should be very brief and not exceed...pages.

क्या · · · के सभी सम्बन्धित अनुभाग · · · के लिए सामग्री तत्काल या अधिक-से-अधिक · · · तक · · · अनुभाग को भेज देंगे ? यह सामग्री बहुत ही संक्षिप्त होनी चाहिए और किसी भी हालत में · · · पृष्ठों से अधिक नहीं होनी चाहिए।

Will...kindly arrange to supply per bearer the undermentioned paper(s) for use in this...

क्या · · · कृपया नीचे लिखे कागज-पत्र इस · · · में उपयोग के लिए ग्राहक के हाथ भेजने की व्यवस्था करेंगे ?

Appendix II

Sentences commonly used in administration

Attention is invited to the Ministry of Finance office memorandum of even number dated...

आपका ध्यान तारीख · · · के वित्त मंत्रालय के इसी संख्या (सम संख्या) के कार्यालय ज्ञापन की ओर आकर्षित किया जाता है ।

I am directed to acknowledge the receipt of your letter.

मुझे आपके पत्र की पावती भेजने का निर्देश हुआ है ।

I am directed to forward the accompanying letter.

मुझे संलग्न पत्र आपके पास भेजने का निर्देश हुआ है ।

I have been directed to inform you/request you/ask you...

मुझे निर्देश हुआ है कि मैं आपको सूचित करूं/आपसे निवेदन करूं/आपसे पता करूं · · · ।

I have the honour to refer to...
मुझे · · · का हवाला देने का सम्मान मिला ।

In compliance with the request contained in your letter No...dated...

आपने तारीख · · · के अपने पत्र संख्या · · · में जो अनुरोध किया था, उसके अनुपालन में/उसको मानते हुए · · · ।

In confirmation of my letter No...dated...

दिनांक/तारीख · · · के पत्र संख्या · · · की पुष्टि में · · · ।

In continuation of my letter (or this Ministry's letter) No... dated...

दिनांक/तारीख · · · के अपने पत्र (अथवा इस मंत्रालय के पत्र) संख्या · · · का प्रसंग जारी रखते हुए · · · ।

In reply to your letter No...dated...

आपके तारीख · · · के पत्र संख्या · · · के उत्तर में · · · ।

In this connection I have to state...

इस सम्बन्ध में मुझे कहना है कि···।

It may further be added...

इसके बारे में यह और लिखना है कि · · ·

Kindly refer to my d. o. letter No....dated...

कृपया दिनांक · · · का मेरा अर्ध सरकारी पत्र संख्या · · · देखिए ।

Please refer to my endorsement No...dated...

कृपया तारीख · · · के मेरे पृष्ठांकन संख्या · · · की ओर ध्यान दीजिए ।

Please refer to your letter No...dated...

कृपया अपने तारीख · · · के पत्र संख्या · · · की ओर ध्यान दीजिए ।

Please treat this as strictly confidential.

कृपया इसे पूरी तरह गोपनीय समझिए ।

Reference is invited to...

· · · की ओर ध्यान दें ।

This is to acknowledge the receipt of your letter No... dated . . .

आपका तारीख · · · का पत्र संख्या · · · मिला है ।

Under intimation to this office.

इस कार्यालय को सूचना देते हुए ।

Will you please refer to your D. O. letter...dated... regarding.

कृपया · · · के बारे में लिखें तारीख · · · के अपने अर्ध-सरकारी पत्र संख्या · · · की ओर ध्यान दें ।

With reference to the correspondence resting with (or ending with) your/this Ministry's letter No...dated...

आपके इस मंत्रालय के पत्र संख्या · · · तारीख · · · के रुके हुए (या समाप्त होने वाले) पत्र-व्यवहार का हवाला देते हुए · · · ।

With reference to your application/representation dated...
आपके तारीख · · · के आवेदन/अभिवेदन के प्रसंग में · · · /

With reference to your letter No. . . . dated...
आपके तारीख · · · के पत्र के प्रसंग में · · · ।

With reference to your memo cited above, I beg to state...

ऊपर आपके जिस ज्ञापन का उल्लेख किया गया है, उसके सम्बन्ध में निवेदन है कि · · ·

Appendix III

Degrees, Diplomas and Certificates

BACHELOR'S DEGREES

Bachelor of Arts (B. A.) कला-स्नातक (क० स्ना०)

Bachelor of Commerce (B. Com.) वाणिज्य-स्नातक (वा० स्ना०)

Bachelor of Education (B. Ed.) शिक्षा-स्नातक (शि० स्ना०)

Bachelor of Teaching (B. T.) अध्यापन-स्नातक (अध्या० स्ना०)

Bachelor of Oriental Learning (B. O. L.) प्राच्यविद्या-स्नातक (प्रा० स्ना०)

Bachelor of Literature (B. Litt.) साहित्य-स्नातक (सा० स्ना०)

Bachelor of Law of Laws (B. L.) (LL. B.) विधि-स्नातक (विधि स्ना०)

Bachelor of Civil Law (B.C.L.) सिविल-विधि स्नातक (सि० विधि स्ना०)

Bachelor of Science (B. Sc.) विज्ञान-स्नातक (वि० स्ना०)

Bachelor of Music (B. Mus.) संगीत-स्नातक (सं० स्ना०)

Bachelor of Technology (B. Tech.) प्रौद्योगिकी-स्नातक (प्रौ० स्ना०)

Bachelor of Textiles (B. Tex.) वस्त्र विज्ञान-स्नातक (व० वि० स्ना०)

Bachelor of Architecture (B. Arch.) वास्तुविद्या-स्नातक (वास्तु०-स्ना०)

Bachelor of Agriculture (B. Agri.) कृषि-स्नातक (कृ० स्ना०)

Bachelor of Mechanical Engineering (B. M. E.) यांत्रिक-इंजीनियरी-स्नातक (यां० इंजी० स्ना०) यांत्रिक अभियांत्रिकी-स्नातक (यां० अभि० स्ना०)

Bachelor of Electrical Engineering (B. E. E.) वैद्युत-इंजीनियरी-स्नातक (वै० इंजी० स्ना०), वैद्युत-अभियांत्रिकी स्नातक (वै० अभि० स्ना०)

Bachelor of Chemical Engineering (B. Ch. E.) रसायन-इंजीनियरी-स्नातक (र० इंजी० स्ना०)/रसायन-अभियांत्रिकी स्नातक (र०अभि० स्ना०)

Bachelor of Tele-Communication Engineering (B. Tel. E.) दूर-संचार इंजीनियरी-स्नातक (दू० सं० इंजी० स्ना०)/दूर-संचार अभियांत्रिकी-स्नातक (दू० अभि० स्ना०)

Bachelor of Civil Engineering (B. C. E.) सिविल-इंजीनियरी-स्नातक (सि० इंजी० स्ना०)/सिविल-अभियांत्रिकी स्नातक (सि० अभि० स्ना०)

Bachelor of Engineering (B.E.) इंजीनियरी-स्नातक (इंजी० स्ना०)/अभियांत्रिकी-स्नातक (अभि० स्ना०)

Bachelor of Chemical Technology (B. Chem. Tech.) रसायन-प्रौद्योगिकी-स्नातक (र० प्रौ० स्ना०)

Bachelor of Veterinary Science (B. V. Sc.) पशुचिकित्सा-विज्ञान-स्नातक (पशु चि० स्ना०)

Bachelor of Veterinary Science and Animal Husbandry (B. V. Sc. & A. H.) पशुचिकित्सा तथा पशुपालन-विज्ञान स्नातक (पशुचि० व पशुपा० स्ना०)

Bachelor of Dental Surgery (B. D. S.) दन्त-शल्य-चिकित्सा-स्नातक (दन्त श० स्ना०)

Bachelor of Nursing (B. Nur.) परिचर्या-स्नातक (परि० स्ना०)

Bachelor of Medicine and Bachelor of Surgery (B. M. B. S. or M. B. B. S.) आयुर्विज्ञान तथा शल्यविज्ञान-स्नातक (आ० श० स्ना०)

Bachelor of Pharmacy (B. Pharm.) भेषजी-स्नातक (भे० स्ना०)

Ayurvedacharya, Bachelor of Medicine and Surgery (A. M. B. S.) आयुर्वेदाचार्य, कायचिकित्सा तथा शल्य-चिकित्सा-स्नातक (आ० का० श० स्ना०)

Bachelor of Ayurvedic Medicine (B. A. M.) आयुर्वेद-स्नातक (आ० स्ना०)

Bachelor of Ayurvedic Medicine and Surgery (B.A.M. & S.) आयुर्वेद कायचिकित्सा तथा शल्यचिकित्सा-स्नातक (आ० का० व श० स्ना०)

Bachelor of Unani Medicine and Surgery (B. U. M. S.) यूनानी कायचिकित्सा तथा शल्य-

चिकित्सा-स्नातक (यू० का० श० स्ना०)

Bachelor of Sanitary Science (B. S. Sc.) स्वच्छता विज्ञान-स्नातक (स्व० वि० स्ना०)

Bachelor of Indian Medicine (B. I. M.) भारतीय आयुर्विज्ञान-स्नातक (भा० आ० स्ना०)

Bachelor of Physical Education (B. P. E.) शारीरिक-शिक्षा-स्नातक (शा० शि० स्ना०)

MASTER'S DEGREES

Master निष्णात (नि०)

Master of Arts (M. A.) कला-निष्णात (क० नि०)

Master of Commerce (M. Com.) वाणिज्य-निष्णात (वा० नि०)

Master of Education (M. Ed.) शिक्षा-निष्णात (शि० नि०)

Master of Oriental Learning (M. O. L.) प्राच्यविद्या-निष्णात (प्रा० नि०)

Master of Law or Laws (M.L./LL. M.) विधि-निष्णात (विधि० नि०)

Master of Letters or Master of Literature (M. Litt.) साहित्य-निष्णात (सा० नि०)

Master of Philosophy (M. Phil.) दर्शन-निष्णात (द० नि०)

Master of Indology (M. Ind.) भारतीय विद्या-निष्णात (भा० नि०)

Master of Social Work (M.S.W.) समाज-कार्य निष्णात (स० का० नि०)

Master of Business Administration (M. B. A.) व्यवसाय-प्रबंध-निष्णात (व्य० प्र० नि०)

Master of Music (M. Mus.) संगीत-निष्णात (सं० नि०)

Master of Library Science M. Lib. Sc.) पुस्तकालय-विज्ञान-निष्णात (पु० वि० नि०)

Master of Science (M. Sc.) विज्ञान-निष्णात (वि० नि०)

Master of Technology (M. Tech.) प्रौद्योगिकी-निष्णात (प्रौ० नि०)

Master of Engineering (M. E.) इंजीनियरी-निष्णात (इंजी० नि०) अभियांत्रिकी-निष्णात (अभि० नि०)

Master of Electrical Engineering (M E. E.) वैद्युत-इंजीनियरी-निष्णात (वै० इंजी० नि०)/ वैद्युत-अभियांत्रिकी-निष्णात (वै० अभि० नि०)

Master of Mechanical Engineering (M. M. E.) यांत्रिक-इंजीनियरी-निष्णात (यां० इंजी० नि०) यांत्रिक-अभियांत्रिकी-निष्णात (यां० अभि० नि०)

Master of Chemical Engineering (M. Ch. E.) रसायन-इंजीनियरी-निष्णात (र० इंजी० नि०)/ रसायन-अभियांत्रिकी-निष्णात (र० अभि० नि०)

Master of Textile (M. Tex.) वस्त्र विज्ञान-निष्णात (व० वि० नि०)

Master of Veterinary Science (M.V. Sc.) पशुचिकित्सा विज्ञान-निष्णात (पशु चि० नि०)

Master of Planning (M. Plan.) योजना-निष्णात (यो० नि०)

Master of Architecture (M. Arch.) वास्तुविद्या-निष्णात (वा० नि०)

Master of Surgery (M. S.) शल्यविज्ञान.निष्णात (श० नि०)

Master of Pharmacy (M. Pharm.) भेषजी-निष्णात (भे०नि०)

Master of Obstetrics (M. O.) or Master of Obstetrics and Gynaecology (M. O. & G.) प्रसूतितंत्र-निष्णात अथवा प्रसूतितंत्र तथा स्त्री रोग विज्ञान-निष्णात (प्र० नि०) या (प्र० व० स्त्री०नि०)

Master of Statistics (M. S.) सांख्यिकी-निष्णात (सां० नि०)

Master of Chirugial (M. Ch.) शल्यविज्ञान-निष्णात (श० नि०)

Master of Physical Education (M P. E.) शारीरिक-शिक्षा-निष्णात (शा० शि० नि०)

DOCTORAL DEGREES

Doctorate of Letters or Doctor of Literature (D. Litt. or Litt. D.) साहित्य-वारिधि (सा० वारि०)

Doctor of Philosophy (Ph. D. or D. Phil.) विद्या-वाचस्पति (विद्या० वाच०)

Doctor of Oriental Learning (D. O. L.) प्राच्य-विद्या-वाचस्पति (प्रा० वि० वाच०)

Doctor of Laws (LL D.) विधि-वारिधि (विधि वारि०)

Doctor of Law (D. L.) विधि-वारिधि (विधि वारि०)

Doctor of Science (D. Sc. or Sc. D.) विज्ञान-वारिधि(वि०वारि०)

Doctor of Medicine (M. D.)

आयुर्विज्ञान-वाचस्पति (आ० वाच०)

Doctor of Hygiene (D. Hy.) स्वास्थ्य विज्ञान-वाचस्पति (स्वा० वाच०)

Doctor of Music (D. Mus.) संगीत-वाचस्पति (सं० वाच०)

Doctor of Education (D. Edu.) शिक्षा-वाचस्पति (शि० वाच०)

Doctor of Engineering (D. Eng.) इंजीनियरी-वाचस्पति/(इंजी० वाच०), अभियांत्रिकी-वाचस्पति (अभि० वाच०)

CERTIFICATES and DIPLOMAS

Certificate प्रमाण-पत्र

Diploma उपाधिपत्र/सनद (उपा०)/(स०)

Diploma in Painting चित्रकला-उपाधिपत्र (चि० उपा०)

Diploma in Teaching अध्यापन-उपाधिपत्र (अध्या० उपा०)

Diploma in Engineering (D. E.) इंजीनियरी उपाधिपत्र (इंजी० उपा०), अभियांत्रिकी उपाधि पत्र (अभि० उपा०)

Diploma in Music संगीत उपाधिपत्र (सं० उपा०)

Diploma in Dance नृत्य उपाधि-पत्र (नृत्य उपा०)

Diploma in Gynaecology and Obstetrics (D G. O.) प्रसूति-तंत्र तथा स्त्री-रोग विज्ञान उपाधि-पत्र (प्र० स्त्री० उपा०)

Diploma in Dramatics नाट्य उपाधिपत्र (ना० उपा०)

Diploma in Physical Education (Dip. P. E.) शारीरिक शिक्षा उपाधिपत्र (शा० शि० उपा०)

Diploma in Medical Radiology and Electrotherapy (D.M. R. E.) चिकित्सा एक्सकिरण तथा विद्युतचिकित्सा उपाधिपत्र (चि० ए० वि० उपा०)